BECOMING HUMAN

SEXUAL CULTURES
General Editors: Ann Pellegrini, Tavia Nyong'o, and Joshua Chambers-Letson
Founding Editors: José Esteban Muñoz and Ann Pellegrini

Titles in the series include:

Becoming Human

*Matter and Meaning in
an Antiblack World*

Zakiyyah Iman Jackson

NEW YORK UNIVERSITY PRESS

New York

NEW YORK UNIVERSITY PRESS
New York
www.nyupress.org

© 2020 by New York University
All rights reserved

ISBN: 978-1-4798-9004-0 (hardback)
ISBN: 978-1-4798-3037-4 (paperback)

For Library of Congress Cataloging-in-Publication data, please contact the Library of Congress.

New York University Press books are printed on acid-free paper, and their binding materials are chosen for strength and durability. We strive to use environmentally responsible suppliers and materials to the greatest extent possible in publishing our books.

Manufactured in the United States of America

10 9 8 7 6 5 4 3 2 1

Also available as an ebook

For Derrick, my cosmic love

CONTENTS

Color insert appears after page 118

On Becoming Human

An Introduction

Becoming Human: Matter and Meaning in an Antiblack World argues that key texts of twentieth-century African diasporic literature and visual culture generate unruly conceptions of being and materiality that creatively disrupt the human–animal distinction and its persistent raciality. There has historically been a persistent question regarding the quality of black(ened) people's humanity. African diasporic literature and cultural production have often been interpreted as a reaction to this racialization—a plea for human recognition. *Becoming Human* takes a different approach, investigating key African American, African, and Caribbean literary and visual texts that critique and depose prevailing conceptions of "the human" found in Western science and philosophy. These texts move beyond a critique of bestialization to generate new possibilities for rethinking ontology: our being, fleshy materiality, and the nature of what exists and what we can claim to know about existence. The literary and visual culture studied in *Becoming Human* neither rely on animal abjection to define being (human) nor reestablish "human recognition" within liberal humanism as an antidote to racialization. Consequently, they displace the very terms of black(ened) animality as abjection.

Becoming Human argues that African diasporic cultural production does not coalesce into a unified tradition that merely seeks inclusion into liberal humanist conceptions of "the human" but, rather, frequently alters the meaning and significance of being (human) and engages in imaginative practices of worlding from the perspective of a history of blackness's bestialization and thingification: the process of imagining black people as an empty vessel, a nonbeing, a nothing, an ontological zero, coupled with the violent imposition of colonial myths and racial hierarchy.[1] Toni Morrison's *Beloved*, Nalo Hopkinson's *Brown Girl in the Ring*, Audre Lorde's *The Cancer Journals*, Wangechi Mutu's *Histology of the Different Classes of Uterine Tumors*, Octavia Butler's "Bloodchild," Ezrom Legae's *Chicken Series*, and key speeches of Frederick Douglass both critique and displace the racializing assumptive logic that has grounded Western science's and philosophy's debates on how to distinguish human identity from that of the animal, the object, and the nonhuman more generally. In complementary but highly distinct ways, these literary and visual texts articulate being (human) in a manner that neither relies on animal abjection nor reestablishes liberal humanism as the authority on being (human). Instead, they creatively respond to the animalization of black(ened) being by generating a critical praxis of being, paradigms of relationality, and epistemologies that alternately expose, alter, or reject not only the racialization of the human–animal distinction found in Western science and philosophy but also challenge the epistemic and material terms under which the specter of animal life acquires its authority. What emerges from this questioning is an unruly sense of being/knowing/feeling existence, one that necessarily disrupts the foundations of the current hegemonic mode of "the human."

While we often isolate African diasporic literary studies from the fields of science and philosophy, I contend that African diasporic literature and visual culture introduce dissidence into philosophical and scientific frameworks that dominate definitions of the human: evolution, rights, property, and legal personhood. By reading Western philosophy and science through the lens of African diasporic literature and visual culture, we can situate and often problematize authoritative (even if troubling) conceptualizations of being and material existence, demonstrating that literary and visual cultural studies have an important role to play in the histories of science and philosophy. Using literature and visual art, my study identifies conceptions of being that do not rely on the animal's negation, as repudiation of "the animal" has historically been essential to producing classes of abject humans. *Becoming Human* reveals that science and philosophy share many characteristics with literature and visual art despite the espoused objectivity and procedural integrity of scientific and philosophical discourses. In debates concerning the specificity of human identity with respect to "the animal," science and philosophy both possess foundational and recursive investments in figurative, and arguably literary, narratives that conceptualize blackness as trope, metaphor, symbol, and a kind of fiction. Instead of thinking of philosophy and science as separate and unrelated sites of knowledge production, my study reveals their historical entanglement and shared assumptive logic with regard to blackness. As conceived by evolutionary theory and Western Enlightenment philosophy, extending into legalistic conceptions of personhood, property, and rights, antiblackness has sought to justify its defacing logics and arithmetic by suggesting that black people are most representative of the abject animalistic dimensions of humanity, or the beast.

While many scholars have critiqued the conflation of black humans with animals found in Enlightenment discourses, I argue that prior scholarship has fundamentally misrecognized the logic behind the confluence of animality and racialization. I reinterpret Enlightenment thought not as black "exclusion" or "denied humanity" but rather as the violent imposition and appropriation—inclusion and recognition—of black(ened) humanity in the interest of plasticizing that very humanity, whereby "the animal" is one but not the only form blackness is thought to encompass. Plasticity is a mode of transmogrification whereby the fleshy being of blackness is experimented with as if it were infinitely malleable lexical and biological matter, such that blackness is produced as sub/super/human at once, a form where form shall not hold: potentially "everything and nothing" at the register of ontology.[2] It is perhaps prior scholarship's interpretation of this tradition as "denied humanity" that has facilitated a call for greater inclusion, as a corrective to what it deems is a historical exclusion of blackness. One consequence of this orientation is that many scholars have essentially ignored alternative conceptions of being and the nonhuman that have been produced by blackened people.

This project examines how African diasporic literary and visual texts generate conceptions of being that defy the disparagement of the nonhuman and "the animal." The terms of African diasporic art and literature's canonization have suggested that African diasporic cultural production does little more than refute racism and petition for assimilation into the very definition of humanity that produces racial hierarchy or, as Henry Louis Gates Jr. would put it in *The Signifying Monkey: A Theory of African-American Literary Criticism*: "[T]he texts of the slave could only be read as testimony of defilement: the slave's representation and reversal of the master's attempt to transform a human being into a commodity, and the slave's simultaneous verbal witness of the possession of a humanity shared in common with Europeans" (Gates 140).[3] Rather than seek an assimilationist transubstantiation via the "Talking Book," the texts in my study are better understood as providing unruly yet generative conceptions of being—generative because they are unruly. Yet, they are not always framed as an explicit critique of the dominant—thereby refusing the terms of liberal multicultural recognition, which require either the evocation of animalized depictions of blackness in order to point out the suffering these images cause or the reversal of stereotype in a bid for "inclusion." Instead, they often just get on with upending and inventing at the edge of legibility. The chapters in this book explore the critique and innovative thought that emerge from within the contradictions of competing conceptions of modernity's crucible—the human. I argue that the cultural production examined in the following pages reveals a contrapuntal potential in black thought and expressive cultures with regard to the human–animal distinction.

In order to facilitate a fuller appreciation of the conceptions of ontology identified in *Becoming Human*, I pose three arguments that fundamentally reframe the animalization of blackness. First, I argue that philosophers' and historians' emphasis on antiblack formulations of African reason and history have overlooked the centrality of gender, sexuality, and maternity in the animalization of blackness.[4] Namely, I argue that black female flesh persistently functions as the limit case of "the human" and is its matrix-figure. This is largely explained by the fact that, historically, the delineation between species has fundamentally hinged on the question of reproduction; in other words, the limit of the human has been determined by how the means and scene of birth are interpreted. Second, I demonstrate that Eurocentric humanism needs blackness as a prop in order to erect whiteness: to define its own limits and to designate humanity as an achievement as well as to give form to the category of "the animal." Third, I look beyond recognition as human as the solution to the bestialization of blackness, by drawing out the dissident ontological and materialist thinking in black expressive culture, lingering on modes of being/knowing/feeling that gesture toward the overturning of Man.

In debates concerning the specificity of human identity with respect to "the animal," science and philosophy foundationally and recursively construct black femaleness, maternity, and sexuality as an essential index of abject human animality. Furthermore, gender, maternity, and sexuality are central to the autopoesis of racialized animalization that philosophers, theoreticians, and historians of race hope to displace. While black feminist and queer theories of race have underlined the intersectional nature of gender, race, and sexuality, few studies have ventured to identify the autopoetic operations of these very intersections (Maturana and Varela 78). Therefore, any study that attempts to provide an account of how racialization operates must offer an explanation of the intransigent, recursive, self-referential, and (re)animating power of abject constructs of black gender and sexuality. Contributing to studies of the *longue durée* of antiblackness and "afterlife of slavery," I offer a materialist theory of both blackness's ontologized plasticization and the temporality of antiblackness whereby I extend and revise Sylvia Wynter's theories of sociogeny and the autopoesis of racialization, in other words, antiblackness's auto-institution and stable replication as a system and its consequences for our being both bios and mythos.[5]

Much has been written about the roles of Reason and History in the production of "dehumanization." This discourse is most commonly represented by Georg Wilhelm Friedrich Hegel's claim that "the African," never attaining immanent differentiation or the clarity of self-knowledge, is imprisoned by immediacy and is, in other words, ahistorical. However, in the chapters that follow, I am most interested in the roles of gender and sexuality in the production of blackness as "animal man." Negating discourses on African "history" and "reason" are not the only—and perhaps not even the most frequently deployed— concepts through which "the African" is posited as *animal*. Gender and sexuality feature prominently in animalizing discourse, as a measure of both the quality of the mind and an index of spirit.

Gendered and sexual discourses on "the African" are inextricable from those pertaining to reason, historicity, and civilization, as purported observations of gender and sexuality were frequently used to provide "evidence" of the inherent abject quality of black people's human animality from the earliest days of the invention of "the human." Christian Europe had already privileged gender and sexuality as indicators of "civilization," and visual observation, namely culturally situated perspective, had not emerged as an epistemological problem for thought (Haraway, "Situated Knowledges"). During the so-called "Age of Discovery," observation and the visual, imagined as transparent and in opposition to the opaque, could overcome the practical problem of differences in worldings. Thus, observation of gender and sex was deployed in the interest of producing race as a visualizable fact. The body was believed to provide presence—a supplement to the immateriality of reason and historicity.

The black body's fleshiness was aligned with that of animals and set in opposition to European spirit and mind. As Winthrop Jordan documents in *White over Black: American Attitudes toward the Negro, 1550–1812*, Africans and apes were linked through physiognomic comparison and sexuality. Englishmen had only encountered nonhuman primates vicariously through travel writing and gossip. They were unfamiliar with anthropoid primates, such as gorillas, chimpanzees, and orangutans. Encounters with sub-Saharan Africans occurred adjacent to these encounters, leading to unbridled speculations linking primates and Africans (Jordan 29, 229). These speculations were an outgrowth of an epistemological foundation that had already been circulating tales of mythical human-animal hybrids and humanoid animals based on ancient reports and medieval morality (Jordan 29). Africa was seen as a land of new monsters. Though Africans were rarely perceived as a kind of ape, it was more commonly suggested that Africans and apes shared libidinous sexual characteristics or were sexually linked (Jordan 32, 227, 230–32, 237). For the English, sex was barbaric, as the body was host to sin; and when they did not perceive Africans as observing the same Christian worldview, they evaluated them negatively. According to Jordan, Africans were linked with sins of the body, and their blackness was believed to testify to their unlawful and ungodly nature (Jordan 17–20, 36, 41). The purported carnality of the African female was thought to be exemplary of African sexuality more generally, as the female sex was the measure of a race's civility (Jordan 35).

While the discussion here notes Jordan's comments on the role of sexuality in the antiblack production of the discourse of African animality, one could reasonably suggest that at times this now-classic text naturalizes racial difference as a visualizable fact of the body with immediate, unitary aesthetic effects for Europeans. In Kathleen Brown's reinterpretation of Jordan's early modern sources, she notes that divisions of household labor between the sexes, manners and customs, and mores were as, if not more, central to West Africans' function as foils to the emergent concept of Europeanness as skin color and hair texture (Brown, "Native Americans" 82). Despite what one might expect from reading Jordan's conclusions, skin color was not the essence of racial difference in the pre-1650 sources: writers of the period devoted considerable space to descriptions of indigenous peoples' adornments of their bodies, "the consequences of which were no less startling to English observers than differences which allegedly originated in nature" (K. Brown 90). The common criteria for bestial otherness were measures of degrees of civility in Iberian and English sources rather than complexion. One of the most common refrains in early European accounts of people living near the so-called torrid zones was "the people goeth all naked" (K. Brown 88). The appearance of allegedly naked bodies had contradictory evocations: on the one hand, nakedness conjured images of the garden of Eden and a prelapsarian state of mind, arrested development, and innocence; on the other hand, "Nudity also communicated sexual promiscuity and the absence of civility to Europeans, which they sometimes described as 'beastly' living" (K. Brown 88). Rather than simply, or decisively, a matter of color, projected sexual mores and virility were crucial determinants for measuring the being of Africans.

As Jennifer Morgan has shown, the imagined proof of the enslaved's incivility and degraded humanity was frequently located in African females' purported childbearing and child-rearing practices, whereby the breast of the enslaved took on mythic proportions. In this context, the breast took on an emblematic status: "European writers turned to black women as evidence of a cultural inferiority that ultimately became encoded as racial difference. Monstrous bodies became enmeshed with savage behavior as the icon of women's breasts became evidence of tangible barbarism" (191). African female breasts were depicted as exaggeratedly long, even as bestial additional limbs. As Morgan asserts, what this history demonstrates is not that "gender operated as a more profound category of difference than race," but rather that "racialist discourse was deeply imbued with ideas about gender and sexual difference that, indeed, became manifest only in contact with each other" (169). What observers and commentators did not question was their own universality, their grid of intelligibility, and how it conditioned not just what they saw, or even how they observed, but how they *knew* what they saw. This is an issue of perception that exceeds the question of what was *actually* observed and what was "made up" or "imagined"; instead of debating the facticity of a story, it is imperative to interrogate how we would go about evaluating any empirical truth claim. This calls into question how we "know what we know," not only about a world "out there" but also how we "know ourselves." Epistemology is a problem not of the past but one that is constituent with our being.

By the nineteenth century, the Chain of Being's physical anthropology, using human and animal physical measurements, sealed the connection between Africans and apes as scientific fact. One must only recall the manner in which Sara Baartman, the so-called Hottentot Venus, was displayed for the British and French public as both pornographic spectacle and scientific specimen (Gilman 88). Her physiognomic characteristics—posterior and genitals—were presumed to signal a difference in sexuality that was pronounced enough to further divide the categories of "female" and "woman": an idealized white femininity became paradigmatic of "woman" through the abjection of the perceived African "female" (Gilman 83–85). Female, rather than woman, African femaleness is paradoxically placed under the sign of absence, lack, and pathology in order to present an idealized western European bourgeois femininity as the normative embodiment of womanhood (Gilman 85–108).

In this context, the potential recognition of womanhood in blackness, and especially black femininity, is placed in tension with the discourses on black female sexuality. Hortense Spillers put it this way: "In the universe of unreality and exaggeration, the black female is, if anything, a creature of sex, but sexuality touches her nowhere . . . the female has so much sexual potential that she has none at all that anybody is ready to recognize at the *level of culture*" (*Black, White, and in Color* 155, emphasis in original). The perpetual specter of black female lack in the realm of culturally and historically produced femininity, at the register of both performativity and morphology, produces "the African female" as paradigmatically indeterminate in terms of gender and paradigmatically the human's limit case.

The spectacularization of the posterior has perhaps blinded our critical attention to the manner with which ontologizing racial characterization not only divides and stratifies gender but also calls into question the very meaning of sexual difference. Shifting critical attention from the posterior to the breast, I demonstrate that racism not only posits cleavages in womanhood such that black womanhood is imagined to be a gender apart (an "other" gender) but also an "other" sex. Additionally, antiblackness itself is sexuating, whereby so-called biological sex is modulated by "culture." In other words, at the registers of both sign and matter, antiblackness produces differential biocultural effects of both gender and sex. Such a frame raises the stakes of recent feminist materialism's inquiry into both the inter(intra)actional relations of discursivity and materiality as well as the gendered politics of hylomorphism, or the form–matter distinction. Thus, antiblack formulations of gender and sexuality are actually essential rather than subsidiary to the metaphysical figuration of matter, objects, and animals that recent critical theory hopes to dislodge. I argue the plasticization of black(ened) people at the register of sign and materiality is central to the prevailing logics and praxis of the human and sex/gender.

Recent scholarship in black queer theory suggests we can no longer presume that gender is a metonym for "woman" and sexuality a metonym for "queer." The wanton manipulation of gendered and sexual codes is essential to the production of antiblackness generally, irrespective of self-identification.[6] Queer theory scholars have argued that the masculine–feminine dynamic is on the register of the symbolic, rather than the biological, even though it masquerades as if the borders dividing masculine from feminine map neatly onto the "natural" polarity of sex.[7] What feminism has not sufficiently interrogated is the manner in which the masculine–feminine dichotomy is racialized. We have neither adequately identified that racialization is intrinsic to the legibility of its codes and grammar, namely that antiblackness constitutes and disrupts sex/gender constructs, nor determined the consequence this has for the matter of the sexed body.

Such a predicament creates conditions of gendered and sexual anxiety and instability. As Spillers states, "[I]n the historic outline of dominance, the respective subject-positions of 'female' and 'male' adhere to no symbolic integrity," as their meaning can be stripped or appropriated arbitrarily by power, as black females' claim to "womanhood and femininity still tends to rest too solidly on the subtle and shifting calibrations of a liberal ideology" ("Mama's" 204, 223). Thus, while codes of gender are cultural rather than prediscursive, one must also attend to the matter of the body, as the body's materiality is thought to provide the observable "fact" of animality.

The African's "failure" to achieve humanity has historically been thought to be rooted in "the body," in an insatiable appetite that made it impossible for the African to rise above "the body," "the organ," in order to come back to itself in self-reflection, never achieving the distance required in order to contemplate the self (Mbembe 190). Gender, and especially sexuality, was leveraged against counterclaims acknowledging black reason and civility. For thinkers such as Thomas Jefferson, black gender and black kinship stood as an impediment to black progress. So, while it seems that the human must be reconsidered, a critical engagement with the discourses of gender and sexuality must be coincident to our interrogation of both dominant and emergent *praxes* of being.

At this time, most feminist scholars can agree that an "intersectional" approach to the question of subjectivity is required, but scholars have not clarified how the different elements of subjectivity braid together historically and culturally. In the chapters that follow, I hope to provide more precise thinking in this area. Our task would be to take seriously the particularization of gender and sexuality in black(ened) people in the context of a humanism that in its desire to universalize, ritualistically posits black(female)ness as opacity, inversion, and limit. In such a context, the black body is characterized by a plasticity, whereby raciality arbitrarily remaps black(ened) gender and sexuality, nonteleologically and nonbinaristically, with fleeting adherence to normativized heteropatriarchal codes. In such a context of paradoxical (un)gendering, and by gendering I mean humanization, power only takes direction from its own shifting exigencies—a predicament that might be described as chaos. This chaos by design is used to marginalize black(ened) genders and sexualities as the border of the sociological: a condition I refer to as ontologized plasticity.

Plasticity in *Becoming Human* describes what Stephanie Smallwood, in her study of the Middle Passage and slavery, identifies as "an enduring project of the modern Western world": the use of black(ened) flesh for "probing the limits up to which it is possible to discipline the body without extinguishing the life within" (36). "Plasticity" has been, as concept and thematic, taken up by a range of thinkers including Hegel, Lévi-Strauss, Darwin, and most notably Catherine Malabou. I distinguish my concept from these alternatives in chapter 1. Here I would like to distinguish my usage from Kyla Schuller's more recent use of a similar term: impressibility. Recently Schuller, in *The Biopolitics of Feeling*, (re)interprets nineteenth-century US biopolitics, arguing that in Lamarckian sentimental discourse and its theories of evolutionary optimization, the conception of life's plasticity was grounded in the notion of mutable inheritance rather than determinism, and that somatic potential was qualified by purported degrees of binary sex differentiation, cast as the crowning achievement of the "civilized." By comparison, black(ened) people appeared to be inert and undifferentiated—in other words, excessive to the domain of sexual difference.[8]

In contrast, the concept of plasticity in *Becoming Human* indexes a mode of domination that conditions the discourse and practices of optimization at the center of nineteenth-century sentimentality and accompanying theories of evolution, by suggesting that racial slavery fleshed out its imagination and provided the experimental means for exploring the possibilities and boundaries of the kind of optimization Schuller elucidates.[9] Plasticity's telos, I argue, is not the optimization of life per se but the fluidification of "life" and fleshly existence. Plasticity is certainly an antiblack mode of the human concerned with apportioning vitality and pathologization, but it is more than that. Plasticity is a praxis that seeks to define the essence of a black(ened) thing as infinitely mutable, in antiblack, often paradoxical, sexuating terms as a means of hierarchically delineating sex/gender, reproduction, and states of being more generally.

My suggestion is that slavery, as an experimental mode, sought to define and explore the possibilities and limits of sex, gender, and reproduction on the plantation and beyond in a manner distinct from but relational to the assumed proper subject of "civilization," and, in fact, enabled hegemonic notions of sex/gender and reproduction such as "woman," "mother," and "female body."[10] I demonstrate that racial slavery as well as early modern proto-racializing conceptions of "monstrous" races and births are integral to ideas of sex/gender, reproduction, and indeed what it means to possess a body such that receding and emergent idea(l)s of mutability and optimization provide cover for historical and ongoing discursive-material modes of domination that precede and surround its idealized and retroactively constructed white(ened) subject and from which historical and current biomedical and philosophical discourses of plasticity seek to distance and obscure. Because antiblack modes of sex/gender and reproduction are generated by means and in terms different from the dominant, it is commonly assumed that such "excess" lay beyond the boundaries of the productions of sex/gender; *Becoming Human* suggests, instead, that the long arc of modern raciality reveals that the production of the "civilized" subject of sex/gender and reproduction is a retroactive construction and dependent on modes of generating sex/gender and reproduction imagined as excessive to its proper domain or otherwise invisibilized.

Liberal humanism's basic unit of analysis, "Man," produces an untenable dichotomy—"the human" versus "the animal," whereby the black(ened) female is posited as the abyss dividing organic life into "human" or "animal" based on wholly unsound metaphysical premises. Thus, as a result of being abjectly animalized, those marginalized have had to bear the burden of a failed metaphysics. *Becoming Human* furthers black studies' interrogation of humanism by identifying our shared being with the nonhuman without suggesting that some members of humanity bear the burden of "the animal."

My second intervention is to demonstrate that exigencies of racialization, have, commonly, prefigured discourses on animals and the nonhuman, more generally and that the categories of "race" and "species" have coevolved and are actually *mutually reinforcing* terms. Current scholarship in posthumanism, animal studies, new materialism, and theories of biopolitics has begun a broad inquiry into the repercussions of defining "the human" in opposition to "the animal." Much of the recent scholarship suggests that race is a by-product of prior negation of nonhuman animals. These fields, particularly animal studies, are slowly advancing the thesis that human–animal binarism is the original and foundational paradigm upon which discourses of human difference, including, or even especially, racialization was erected. The chapters that follow will take an alternative approach.

Far from being an inevitable feature of our thought, this dualism has been traced to none other than René Descartes. In "The Eight Animals in Shakespeare; or, Before the Human," Laurie Shannon argues that historical attention to lexicons reveals that the "human–animal divide" descends from "Enlightenment modes of science and philosophy that have been largely qualified in contexts like subjectivity, rationality, and liberalism . . . To put it in the broadest terms: before the cogito, there was no such thing as 'the animal'" (474). To illustrate the recentness of "the animal" as an impounding preoccupation, Shannon makes a striking observation: "While references to the creatures now gathered as animals defy inventory, the collective English word *animal* appears a mere eight times across the entire verbal expanse of Shakespeare's work. His practice on this point of nomenclature tilts overwhelmingly against the word" (Shannon 474). Two of the eight uses of the word, Shannon notes, "involve persons failing a (gender-vexed and class-inflected) human standard": "lack of self-government," "unchastity," quoting *Much Ado* "savage sensuality," and in *Love's Labor's Lost* animality is evoked as intellectual inferiority.

Philosophers of race and Caribbeanist literary scholars have also detected the incipience of modern racialization in the work of Shakespeare.[11] This scholarship notes that in *The Tempest*, Caliban, too, is placed under the sign of "the animal," namely irrational and sexual intemperance. My argument is not simply that Caliban is animalized but rather that figures like Caliban are constitutive to "the animal" as a general term. Arguably more a personified idea than a traditional character, Caliban emerged in the context of publicity surrounding European voyages to the coast of Africa and the Caribbean.[12] The black body, held captive as a "resource for metaphor," has been discussed in the work of Frantz Fanon, in which he contends that black men's bodies, like Caliban, are projection screens for white anxiety about sexuality (Spillers, "Mama's" 205). But, instead of recognizing their projections as just that, projection, white anxiety imposes an image of black(ened) men as a bestial sexual threat: a powerful sexual menace, initiator of sexual activity unrestricted by morality or prohibition, or one who monopolizes gendered sexual pleasure. The result is envy, punishment, or masochistic pleasure; for the black is not *the symbol* of sexual threat but *is* sexual threat—the penis becomes the synecdoche of black manhood (Fanon 170, 177). My suggestion is that these subjects—"animal" as a generic term and the racialized masculine figure of Caliban—are intertwined and that their interrelation is ordered in relation to the absent presence of the material metaphor of the black female as matrix-figure.[13] By uncovering the centrality of racialized gender and sexuality in the very human–animal binarism that scholars are looking to problematize or displace, I demonstrate the necessity of the abjection and bestialization of black gender and sexuality for both the normative construction of "the human" as rational, self-directed, and autonomous and as the reproduction of the scientific matrix of classification.

In addition to providing a crucial reexamination of African diasporic literature and visual culture's philosophical defiance of Western scientific and philosophic definitions of "the human," *Becoming Human* clarifies the terms of the relationship between what Cary Wolfe calls the "discourse of species" and racial discourse by demonstrating that racialized gender and sexuality serve as an essential horizon of possibility for the production of "the animal" as a preoccupation of Modern discourse (*Animal Rites* 2). Reading the existential predicament of modern racial blackness through and against the human–animal distinction in Western philosophy and science not only reveals the mutual imbrication of "race" and "species" in Western thought but also invites a reconsideration of the extent to which exigencies of racialization have preconditioned and prefigured modern discourses governing the nonhuman. As I demonstrate, at times antiblackness prefigures and colors nonhuman animal abjection. I argue that anxieties about conquest, slavery, and colonial expansionism provided the historical context for both the emergence of a developmental model of "universal humanity" and a newly consolidated generic "animal" that would be defined in nonhuman *and* human terms. In this context, discourses on "the animal" and "the black" were conjoined and are now mutually reinforcing narratives in the traveling racializations of the globalizing West. I demonstrate that both science's and philosophy's foundational authority articulate black female abjection as a prerequisite of "the human," and this abjection helps give credence to the linear taxonomical (ontological) thinking present scholarship is trying to displace. Thus, racialized formations of gender and sexuality are actually central rather than subsidiary to the very human–animal binarism recent scholarship hopes to dislodge.

Becoming Human emphasizes cultural production that philosophically challenges the abjection of animality and highlights alternative modes of being. The cultural production examined here does not figure the challenge of transforming ways of relating to animality as separate from the urgent need to reimagine (human)being because the semio-material burden of living as black virtually forecloses the "on behalf of" structure that characterizes so much of animal studies and, especially, its antecedents—animal ethics and animal rights philosophy. As I have established thus far, Western humanism has not produced African diasporic subjectivity in a manner that would permit black people to decisively remove themselves from being subjected to violence against "the animal." For the Enlightenment humanists mentioned above, *"the African"* does not symbolize *"the animal"*; *"the African" is "the animal."* The black philosophical dissidence highlighted in this book speaks to the biopolitical entanglement of discourses on animals, environment, and African diasporic peoples. Thus, critical black studies must challenge animalization on at least two fronts: animalizing discourse that is directed primarily at people of African descent, and animalizing discourse that reproduces the abject abstraction of "the animal" more generally because such an abstraction is not an empirical reality but a metaphysical technology of bio/necropolitics applied to life arbitrarily.

Additionally, this project is not limited to a critique of anthropocentricism. As I have suggested here and will elaborate in the pages that follow, antiblackness's arbitrary uses of power do not comply with the hierarchies presumed by critics of anthropocentricism. Furthermore, viruses, bacteria, parasites, and insects all commonly exercise dominance over human populations. Thus, critics such as Jacques Derrida and Cary Wolfe have foregrounded a need for a critical and accountable humanism rather than seeking ever-vigilant forms of anti-anthropocentricisms.[14] However, it is crucial to critically engage with what it means to *be* in a biopolitical context that is characterized by entanglements of humans both historically recent and distant, nonhumans both big and small, and environments both near and far. *This criticality would interrogate the epistemology of "the human," as an idea, and that would guide its ethico-political practices rather than reify the presumptuous conceit of a received notion of the humane.*

A critique of anthropocentricism is not necessarily a critique of liberal humanism. Critics have advocated "on behalf of" animals without questioning the epistemic and material project of liberal humanism. Many critics of anthropocentricism have mistakenly perceived that the problem of our time is anthropocentricism rather than a failed praxis of being. Such critics of anthropocentricism often proceed by humanizing animals in the form of rights, welfare, and protections without questioning how advocates are constructing themselves in the process. In other words, they do not subject the very humanity they want to decenter and/or expand to sufficient interrogation.[15] As a result, they authorize the violence of the state, one that protects, criminalizes, enforces, and prosecutes differentially based on race, class, gender, sexuality, national origin, religion, ability, and immigration status. For example, advocacy projects that seek greater legal protection for the Great Apes and more strenuous criminal prosecution for those who transgress protective laws find themselves at odds with impoverished people in African nations that have been burdened by IMF and World Bank policies. Such nations may not be able to provide even limited protections for their human citizens and even fewer economic opportunities for the people who would be prosecuted under international animal protection legislation. An impoverished person may participate in capturing animals for pay, given that the illegal wildlife trade is the world's second largest transnational trading industry, estimated to be worth $20 billion annually, second only to drugs. Yet, impoverished people do not gain the majority of the monetary value derived from the trade; the captured animals and the wealth generated from their labor spiral upward to the West—*but not the criminal prosecution.*[16] In this context, it is not difficult to glean how such international (read: universalist) legislation drafted by exponents from more powerful and stable nations (because they continue to be imperialist) places strain on already fragile postcolonial state resources (because they continue to be colonized). One really does have to wonder what we mean by justice and rights when states and their citizens are put in such untenable positions.

At present, animal studies scholarship tends to presume a humanity that is secure within the logic of liberal humanism rather than engage with a humanity that is often cast as debatable or contingent.[17] To render one's humanity provisional, where the specter of nullification looms large, is precisely the work that racism does. Yet when the authors of this field speak of a human, they most commonly speak of one whose ontological integrity is assumed and idealized rather than plasticized, even when the goal of posthumanism and animal studies is ultimately to interrogate or undermine that certainty. For these fields to do accurate, fully theorized, and principled work, they must show how the question of the animal bears on the question of hierarchies of humanity. In the pages that follow, I investigate blackness's relation to animality rather than presuppose black(ened) people's relative power and privilege *as human*, vis-à-vis nonhuman animals. Thus, my work focuses on humans whose humanity is a subject of controversy, debate, and dissension in order to reveal the broader political stakes of "the animal" as a problem for contemplation.

In what follows, I hope to demonstrate that the African diaspora does indeed have a stake in overturning the production of "the animal." However, the economies of value presumed in posthumanism and animal studies need to be historicized and transformed, namely, the presumption that all humans are privileged over all animals by virtue of being *included* in humanity, or that racism is a matter of suggesting that black people are like animals based on a prior and therefore precedential form of violence rooted in speciesism. The chapters that follow are an attempt to clarify, historicize, and more precisely situate black(ened) humanity vis-à-vis animality. I engage contemporary critical theory in the fields of biopolitics, posthumanism, new materialism, and animal studies. However, my intent is to critically build on these fields' insights, *not* to replicate them.

What you will find in the subsequent chapters is less a systematic critical engagement with preexisting arguments in posthumanism, the new materialisms, and animal studies and more an establishment of a different conversation on ontology with different entry points because *Becoming Human* is more interested in redefining terms than entering into preestablished ones. *Becoming Human* contends that the aforementioned fields, in the main, position blackness in the space of the unthought, and therefore are not *sufficient* grounds for theorizing blackness. This is not to suggest, however, that their insights hold no purchase for black studies. Departing from such a reactionary position, *Becoming Human* is instead learned and deliberative—borrowing freely from and extending these fields' insights when and where it is useful to do so. To the extent to which *Becoming Human* does engage the fundaments of these fields, its primary aim is to clarify how blackness conditions a given discourse. *Becoming Human* observes some crucial distinctions: there is a difference between identifying how (anti)blackness is a condition of possibility for hegemonic thought and assuming the hegemonic terms of a given discourse. Moreover, not all engagements with a given discourse are a ceding of ground but might very well be the generative unsettling of it. By placing scholarly and creative work on blackness in dialogue with posthumanism and related fields, I am able to more fully theorize the binaristic and hierarchical logics that structure relations among humans and between animals and humans. I not only show that antiblackness is actually central to the very construction of "the animal" that recent scholarship wants to interrogate and move beyond but also that (anti)blackness upends these fields' frameworks of analysis and evaluative judgments.

Becoming Human's third argument is a decisive break with a commonly held position in the study of race. I do not propose the extension of human recognition as a solution to the bestialization of blackness. Recognition of personhood and humanity does not annul the animalization of blackness. Rather, it reconfigures discourses that have historically bestialized blackness. In the chapters that follow, forms of human recognition—inclusion in biological conceptions of the human species and the transition from native to universal human subject in law and society—are not at odds with animalization. Thus, animalization is not incompatible with humanization: what is commonly deemed dehumanization is, in the main, more accurately interpreted as the violence of humanization or the burden of inclusion into a racially hierarchized universal humanity.

The inquiry into being and matter here does not justify itself by reproducing the specter of the flesh, of the bestial, of the passions, of nature in need of human domination. The black cultural producers in this study have chosen representational strategies that redirect modern technologies (the magazine, ink-and-paper drawing, photography, painting, the short story, and the novel) by disrupting the foundational racialized epistemological presuppositions and material histories embedded in the archive of these forms. These are technologies that have not only reflected abject animalized depictions of blackness but invented them as well. Rather than solely rehearse debates about the ideological potential or pitfalls of genres and technology, the cultural production in my study mobilizes these technologies differently, producing not only disruptive conceptions of blackness but also of ontology and epistemology more generally. African diasporic cultural production intervenes productively in reconsidering the role of "the animal" or the "animalistic" in the construction of "the human" by producing nonbinaristic models of human–animal relations, advancing theories of trans-species interdependency, observing trans-species precarity, and hypothesizing cross-species relationality in a manner that preserves alterity while undermining the nonhuman and animality's abjection, an abjection that constantly rebounds on marginalized humans. I suggest that only by questioning rather than presupposing the virtuousness of human recognition will we be able to develop a praxis of being that is not only an alternative to the necropolitical but opposes it (Derrida, *The Animal* xi).

Ultimately, I suggest that the normative subject of liberal humanism is predicated on the abjection of blackness, which is not based on figurations of blackness as "animal-like" but rather casts black people as ontologically plastic. Therefore, the task before us is realizing being in a manner that does not privilege the very normativity cohered by notions of abject animality and the discursive-material plasticity of black(ened) flesh. This requires that scholars of race extend the radical questioning of "the human" established by African diasporic critics of Western humanism in a direction potentially unanticipated by prior scholarship, by interrogating the very construction of the animal beyond a condemnation of its racialized application and scope. Both critics who seek more equitable inclusion in liberal humanism and those who pursue a radical transformation of the normative category of "the human" have commonly overlooked the centrality of the animal question for black existential matters. *Becoming Human* extends the insights of African diasporic critics of "the human" by demonstrating that key texts in black cultural production move beyond a demand for recognition and inclusion in the very normative humanity that theorists such as Frantz Fanon, Lewis Gordon, Saidiya Hartman, Hortense Spillers, Fred Moten, Aimé Césaire, Sylvia Wynter, Frank Wilderson III, Katherine McKittrick, Christina Sharpe, Denise Ferreira da Silva, Achille Mbembe, and Alex Weheliye have shown is fundamentally antiblack, while also calling into question the presumptive logic undergirding the specter of animalization.[18]

The cultural production examined here spans three continents and three centuries because antiblackness has been central to establishing national borders and readily crosses them. Antiblackness has also been diasporically challenged and refused, making it central to what comprises the very notion of the African diaspora and of blackness. It is precisely *through* rather than *against* historically demarcated regional, national, linguistic, and state preoccupations that this discourse cyclically reorganizes itself. Antiblackness's pliability is essential to the intransigent, complementary, and universalizing impetus of antiblack paradigms. Irrespective of the innumerable and ever-transient definitions of black identity across the diaspora, which by definition are ephemerally produced, all black(ened) people must contend with the burden of the antiblack animalization of the global paradigm of blackness, which will infringe on all articulations and political maneuverings that seek redress for present and historical violence.

Within the structure of much thought on race there is an implicit assumption that the recognition of one as a human being will protect one from (or acts as an insurance policy against) ontologizing violence. Departing from a melancholic attachment to such an ideal, I argue that the violence and terror scholars describe is endemic to the recognition of humanity itself—when that humanity is cast as black. A recognition of black humanity, demonstrated across these pages, is not denied or excluded but weaponized by a conception of "the human" foundationally organized by the idea of a racial telos. For Wynter, the Negro is not so much excluded from the category Man and its overrepresentation of humanity but foundational to it as its antipodal figure, as the nadir of Man.[19] I argue that the recognition of humanity and its suspension act as alibis for each other's terror, such that the pursuit of human recognition or a compact with "the human" would only plunge one headlong into further terror and domination. Is the black a human being? The answer is hegemonically yes. However, this, in actuality, may be the wrong question as an affirmative offers no assurances. A better question may be: If being recognized as human offers no reprieve from ontologizing dominance and violence, then what might we gain from the rupture of "the human"?

Animalization is a privileged method of biopolitical expression of antiblackness; however, historians' and theoreticians' response to the centrality of animalization has been inadequate, as scholars have misrecognized the complexity of its operations. Binaristic frameworks such as "humanization versus dehumanization" and "human versus animal" are insufficient to understand a biopolitical regime that develops technologies of humanization in order to refigure blackness as abject human animality and extends human recognition in an effort to demean blackness as "the animal within the human" form. This is not to say that expressions and practices of antiblackness never radically exclude black people from the category of "the human"; rather, the point is that inclusion does not provide a reliable solution because, in the main, black people have been included in (one might even say dominated by) "universal humanity"— but as the incarnation of abject dimensions of humanity for which "the human" is foundationally and seemingly eternally at war. Thus, black people are without shelter, whether invited into or locked out of "the human."

I seek to investigate black revisionist and counter-discursive practices in the context of liberal humanism's *selective and circumscribed recognition* of humanity in black people. While black people cannot *simply* opt out of humanism, as liberal humanism is the primary mode of recognition in the global historical present, nevertheless, I argue that the severe limitations of liberal humanism and notions of "the human," the conscripting humanity imputed to black people, has led to a radical questioning of "the human," and in particular the status assigned to animality, in key works of black cultural expression. This questioning is suggestive of a desire for, perhaps, a different "genre of the human" or may even signal, as I propose, an urgent demand for the dissolution of "human" but, in either case, is not simply a desire for fuller recognition within liberal humanism's terms (Wynter and Scott 196–197).[20]

Making Humans: Animalization as Humanization

Everything happens as if, in our culture, life were what cannot be defined, yet, precisely for this reason, must be ceaselessly articulated and divided.
—Giorgio Agamben, *The Open*

No, they were not inhuman. Well, you know, that was the worst of it—this suspicion of their not being inhuman. It would come slowly to one. They howled and leaped, and spun, and made horrid faces; but what thrilled you was just the thought of their humanity—like yours—the thought of your remote kinship with this wild and passionate uproar.
—Joseph Conrad, *Heart of Darkness*

The uncompromising nature of the Western self and its active negation of anything not itself had the counter-effect of reducing African discourse to a simple polemical reaffirmation of black humanity. However, both the asserted denial and the *reaffirmation* of that humanity now look like two sterile sides of the same coin.
—Achille Mbembe, *On the Postcolony* (emphasis in original)

As Achille Mbembe in *On the Postcolony* observes, discourse on Africa "is almost always deployed in the framework (or on the fringes) of a meta-text about the animal—to be exact, about the beast: its experience, its world, and its spectacle" (2). During the eighteenth and nineteenth centuries Western philosophy's architects, figures such as Hume, Hegel, Jefferson, and Kant, constructed a theory of blackness's inherent animality based on either "the African's" purported physical or mental likeness to nonhuman animals, or as a result of the underdeveloped condition of African humanity. The former relied on the establishment of "laws of nature" whereby Africans and animals found on the African continent developed similar deficiencies based largely on geographical determinants. In such a model, privileging human–animal comparison, the environment itself is black(ened), and its inferiority in turn stymies African humanity. Thus, African peoples qualify as human but only tentatively so, given their purported physical or mental similarity to nonhuman animals and vice versa. In the latter case, a developmental model, humanity is marked as an achievement and teleology. Here "the African," while also human, is nevertheless defined by their animality. Rather than being animal-like, black people are animals occupying the human form. The two positions have different routes but the same destination: in short, black(ened) people are the living border dividing forms of life such that "the animal" is a category that may apply to animals and some humans. Thus, the category of "the animal" develops in a manner that crosses lines of species. Furthermore, in either case, in the process of animalizing "the African," *blackness would be defined as the emblematic state of animal man, as the nadir of the human.* By virtue of racialization, the category of "the animal" could even potentially racialize animals in addition to animalizing blackness. The debate over whether blackness is a subspecies of the human or another type of being altogether haunted scientific debates concerning "monogenesis versus polygenesis." However, the line between these two approaches is only partially maintained in the thinkers discussed across this book's pages. It is not always clear, not only on what side of the border "the African" is placed, but also the total number of borders posited at any given point in this debate. *What is certain, though, is that monogenesis or racially inclusive constructions of "the human" complemented rather than detracted from animalized depictions of blackness.* Such debates were instrumental in codifying and institutionalizing both popular and scientific perceptions of race. There are too many examples to enumerate them all—but in the following, I have chosen what I believe are the most cited cases.

ON BECOMING HUMAN | 23

Much of this history is known; it is commonly referred to in critiques of humanism that advance a conception of "dehumanization," in which dehumanization is treated as sufficient shorthand for humanist thought (especially Enlightenment thought) concerning blackness. Enlightenment is a multivocality with contradiction and moving parts, and thus not reducible to its more infamous ideas. However, this section reinterprets a powerful and ever-present strand of racist Enlightenment thought.[21] After careful investigation, I have come to some new conclusions that inform the chapters that follow: First, I replace the notion of "denied humanity" and "exclusion" with bestialized humanization, because *the African's humanity is not denied but appropriated, inverted, and ultimately plasticized in the methodology of abjecting animality.* Universal humanity, a specific "genre of the human," is produced by the constitutive abjection of black humanity; nevertheless, the very constitutive function of this inverted recognition reveals that this black abjection is transposing recognition, and an inclusion that masks itself as an exclusion. Second, blackness is not so much derived *from* a discourse on nonhuman animals—rather the discourse on "the animal" is formed through enslavement and the colonial encounter encompassing *both human and nonhuman* forms of life. Discourses on nonhuman animals and animalized humans are forged through each other; they reflect and refract each other for the purposes of producing an idealized and teleological conception of "the human." Furthermore, antiblack animalization is not merely a symptom of speciesism; it is a relatively distinctive modality of semio-material violence that can be leveraged against humans or animals (Singer 6, 18, 83). Similarly, speciesism can be mobilized to produce racial difference. Thus, the animalizations of humans and animals have contiguous and intersecting histories rather than encompassing a single narrative on "animality." This is a crucial point, as it allows us to appreciate the irreducibility of both antiblackness *and* species as well as investigate the respective semio-material trajectories of black(ened) bodies and nonhuman animal bodies take in their historical and cultural specificity.

Hume extrapolated from his understanding of the natural environment that "inferior" climates produce "inferior nations." He believed that if plants and "irrational" animals were influenced by degree of heat and cold, then the character of humans must also be influenced by air and climate. These environmental factors rendered minds "incapable of all the higher attainments of the human mind," which prompted him to "suspect negroes and in general all other species of men to be naturally inferior to the whites . . . No ingenious manufactures amongst them, no arts, no sciences" (Hume 125n). He went as far as to infamously declare, "In Jamaica, indeed, they talk of one negroe as a man of parts and learning; but it is likely he is admired for slender accomplishments, like a parrot who speaks a few words plainly" (Hume 213). Hume, like most Enlightenment thinkers mentioned here, accepted the Aristotelian conception of the human as an animal, but what marked human's uniqueness, according to Aristotle, was rationality.[22] The human was a "rational animal." Thus, humanity was not defined in strict opposition to "the animal," but one's humanity was determined by the nature of one's rationality. For Hume, in the case of African rationality, it was either deficient or negligible. Therefore, the humanity of the Negro "species of men" was acknowledged, but in a hierarchical and taxonomical frame.

Kant, like Hume, looked to "the animal kingdom" as an analogue for humanity, but what is astonishing is the manner in which his articulations of "species" and "race" are interdependent and concentric epistemological constructions. Whether in the work of Carl Von Linne, Georges-Louis LeClerc, Comte de Buffon,[23] or in the following statement by Kant, animal and human "race" are co-articulations:

> Among the deviations—i.e., the hereditary differences of animals belonging to a single stock—those which, when transplanted (displaced to other areas), maintain themselves over protracted generation, and which also generate hybrid young whenever they interbreed with other deviations of the same stock, are called races. . . . In this way Negroes and Whites are not different species of humans (for they belong presumably to one stock), but they are different *races*, for each perpetuates itself in every area, and they generate between them children that are necessarily hybrid, or blendlings (mulattoes). (17)

In such formulations, there is much anxiety about maternity and sexual difference. It is difficult to maintain that either the logic of raciality or the animalization of blackness is merely symptomatic of attempts to domesticate "nature" or "animals" under an ordering system. Rather, the demand for taxonomical and hierarchical races is foundational to the project of assimilating newly "discovered" plants and nonhuman animals into a system, as the vastness of nature would overwhelm and exceed the limits of the time and location's reigning epistemological frame (but not its appetite for mastery).[24] Race can only be subsidiary to the desire to animalize nonhuman animals or make "nature" knowable if one abstracts this desire from its historical context: "The Age of Discovery," which is to say the age of slavery and conquest.[25]

If, as Foucault maintains in *The Order of Things*, our current hegemonic, "universalist" conception of "man" is a mutation of prior metaphysical conceptions of being, then I would qualify this insight by insisting that this mutation was and remains an effect of slavery, conquest, and colonialism. The metaphysical question of "the human," as one of *species* in particular, arose through the organizational logics of racialized sexuation and the secularizing imperatives (largely economic, but not exclusively so) of an imperial paradigm that sought dominion over life, writ large. At the meeting point of natural philosophy and the so-called Age of Discovery, natural science instituted its representational logics of somatic difference in ever-increasingly secularized ontological terms.

Hegel represents perhaps the most extreme articulation of "the African's" animality, one in which animality is thought not only to be a feature, but *the essence* of African life. At times, from reading Hegel's (and arguably Kant's) geographical theories, one could conclude that his theory of nature and animals is animated by a desire to fix race as teleological hierarchy: to make race knowable and predictable. For Hegel declares:

> Even the animals show the same inferiority as the human beings. The fauna of America includes lions, tigers, and crocodiles. But although they are otherwise similar to their equivalents in the Old World, they are in every respect smaller, weaker, and less powerful. (163)

In this case, it is not the native's likeness to animals that defines human animality; instead animals' likeness to American Indians defines animals in their animality. The quality of American Indian being becomes the term through which "nature" is defined. This is not to say that his thoughts on nonhuman animals are merely a justification for his theories of race, but rather it does demonstrate that we cannot assume that racism does not animate conceptions of some of our most foundational theories of nature and nonhuman animality. Most of the humanist thought discussed here was developed during the eighteenth and nineteenth centuries when the slave trade was increasingly under scrutiny by abolitionists. Contestation had risen to unprecedented levels, and as a result, slavery increasingly required justification (Jordan 27, 231–232). These justifications relied heavily on the African's purported animality. Even Georges Leopold Cuvier's classification of humanity into three distinct varieties—Caucasian, Mongolian, and Ethiopian—emphasized the superiority of the Caucasian and is elaborated in his book titled *Animal Kingdom* (Cuvier 50).

In *Notes on a State of Virginia*, Thomas Jefferson attempts to qualify the essence of black people's humanity. What is crucial is that Jefferson defines black people as "animal" not based on a direct correlation to nonhuman animals but on the specificity of black people's humanity, particularly with regard to black embodiment, sexuality, intelligence, and emotions: aesthetically displeasing form, bestial sexuality, and minor intelligence and feeling. Regarding the heart and mind, he states:

> They are more ardent after their female; but love seems with them to be more an eager desire, than a tender delicate mixture of sentiment and sensation. Their griefs are transient. Those numberless afflictions, which render it doubtful whether heaven has given life to us in mercy or in wrath are less felt, and sooner forgotten with them. (Jefferson 46)

Jefferson's arguments recognize black humanity, but the question is what kind of humanity is imputed to black(ened) people? As he states, "It is not against experience to suppose, that different species of the same genus, or varieties of the same species, may possess different qualifications" (Jefferson 151).

Following Aristotle, humanity and animality are not mutually exclusive terms in much Eurocentric humanistic thought—however, there is an important qualification: the logic of conquest, slavery, and colonialism produced a linear and relational conception of human animality. Whereas Europeans are moral/rational/political animals, the recognition of black people's humanity did not unambiguously and unidirectionally elevate black people's ontologized status vis-à-vis nonhuman animals. "Being human" instead provided a vehicle for reinforcing a striated conception of human species. Thus, the extension and recognition of shared humanity across racial lines is neither "denied" nor mutual, reciprocal human recognition; rather, it is more accurately deemed bestializing humanization and inverted recognition. Instead of denying humanity, black people are humanized, but this humanity is burdened with the specter of abject animality. In fact, all of the thinkers above identify black people as human (however attenuated and qualified); thus, assimilation into the category of "universal humanity" should not be equated with black freedom. Assimilation into "universal humanity" is precisely this tradition's modus operandi. But what are the methods? And what are the costs?

Too often, our conception of antiblackness is defined by the specter of "denied humanity" or "exclusion." Yet as Saidiya Hartman has identified in *Scenes of Subjection: Terror, Slavery, and Self-Making in Nineteenth-Century America*, the process of making the slave relied on the abjection and criminalization of slave humanity, rather than the denial of it. Hartman asks:

> suppose that the recognition of humanity held out the promise not of liberating the flesh or redeeming one's suffering but rather of intensifying it? Or what if this acknowledgment was little more than a pretext for punishment, dissimulation of the violence of chattel slavery and the sanction given it by the law and the state, and an instantiation of racial hierarchy? What if the endowments of man—conscience, sentiment, and reason—rather than assuring liberty or negating slavery acted to yoke slavery and freedom? Or what if the heart, the soul, and the mind were simply the inroads of discipline rather than that which confirmed the crime of slavery. (5)

Hartman contends that the recognition of the enslaved's humanity did not redress slavery's abuses nor the arbitrariness of the master's power since in most instances the acknowledgment of the humanity of the enslaved was a "complement" to the arrangement of chattel property rather than its "remedy"(6). She demonstrates that recognition of the enslaved's humanity served as a pretext for punishment, dissimulation of chattel slavery's violence, and the sanction given it by the law and the state (Hartman 5). What's more, rather than fostering "equality," this acknowledgment often served as an instantiation of racial hierarchy, as the slave is "recognized" but only as a lesser human in (pre)evolutionist discourse or criminalized by state discourses. In other words, objecthood and humanization were two sides of the same coin, as ties of affection could be manipulated and will was criminalized.

The enslaved bifurcated existence as both an object of property and legal person endowed with limited rights, protections, and criminal culpability produced a context where consent, reform, and protection extended the slave's animalized status rather than ameliorated objectification. From this perspective, emancipation is less of a decisive event than a reorganization of a structure of violence, an ambivalent legacy, with gains and losses, where inclusion could arguably function as an intensification of racial subjection. Echoing Hartman, I would argue for reframing black subjection not as a matter of imperfect policy nor as evidence for a spurious commitment to black rights (which is undeniably the case) but rather as necessitating a questioning of the universal liberal human project. "The human" and "the universal" subject of rights and entitlements assumed a highly particularized subject that is held as paradigmatic, subjugating all other conceptions of being and justice. Furthermore, if the following assertion by Achille Mbembe is correct, "the obsession with *hierarchy* . . . provides the constant impetus to count, judge, classify, and eliminate, both persons and things" in the name of "humanizing" the colonized, I ask, how can we confidently distinguish humanization from animalization (Mbembe 192)? What we have at hand is more complicated than a simple opposition such as "exclusion versus inclusion," "the human" versus "the animal," and "humanization versus dehumanization." Consequently, a new epistemology and transformative approach to *being* is needed rather than the extension of human recognition under the state's normative conception.

As long as "the animal" remains an intrinsic but abject feature of "the human," black freedom will remain elusive and black lives in peril, as "the animal" and "the black" are not only interdependent representations but also entangled concepts. While there are particular Euroanthropocentric discourses about specific animals, just as there are particular forms of antiblack racialization based on ethnicity, gender, sexuality, and national origin, for instance, these particularizing discourses are in relation to the organizing abstraction of "the animal" as "the black." To disaggregate "humanity" from the production of "black humanity," the one imposed on black(ened) people, assumes one could neutralize blackness and maintain the human's coherence. But the neutralization of blackness requires the dissolution of discourses on "the animal" and vice versa, but that is, to say the least, unlikely because "the animal" is a mode of being for which Man is at war. What is more plausible is that attempts to neutralize blackness and "the animal" will continue to be in practice, if not word, a means of discipline and eradication.

When humanization is thought to be synonymous with black freedom, or even a means to freedom, one risks inadvertently minimizing or extending the violence of "universal humanity." The "universal" is a site of imperial imposition and constant contestation rather than simply an ideal. The ongoing process of universalization is purchased precisely through the abjection and ontologizing plasticization of "the African." As Hegel argued, Africans are barred from universal humanity or spirit because they are not aware of themselves as conscious historical beings, a consequence of two intrinsic qualities. First, Africans worship themselves or nature rather than God. Second, Africans kill their king, which is a failure to recognize the superiority of a higher authority than themselves, whether that of God or law.

The African character, according to Hegel, springs from a geographical climate hostile to the achievement of spirit. Hegel builds on earlier theories that suggest that climate is not simply fertile ground for the cultivation of nature but is also the root of a teleological human character. He believed the "torrid" and "frigid" zones, "where nature is too powerful," do not provide the sufficient conditions for the dialectic of becoming, or the attainment of "freedom by means of internal reflection," whereby humanity is achieved in opposition to nature (Hegel 154). One achieves spirit by rising above nature, distinguishing oneself from one's natural surroundings. Only by passing through this stage is one able to recognize the presence of God as separate from the self and above Nature. Thus, God "exists in and for itself as a completely objective and absolute being of higher power" determining the course of everything in nature and humanity (Hegel 178). Hegel declares, "The Negro is an example of animal man in all his savagery and lawlessness" and the African's "primitive state of nature is in fact a state of animality" (177, 178).

The practice whereby Africans "worship the moon, the sun, and the rivers," animating these natural forms "in their imagination, at the same time treating them as completely independent agents," Hegel believes, ultimately makes the mistake of identifying nature's power without identifying that nature has an eternal law or providence behind it, providing universal and permanent natural order (Hegel 178). The African's "arbitrariness" triumphs over permanent natural order. Thus, the African is not capable of the rational universality embedded in the concepts of law, ethics, and morality. As free rational laws are, for Hegel, the bases of freedom, Hegel formulates most systematically a conception of "the African" that is both *of* humanity but not *in* humanity. Thus, humanity is not strictly a biological imperative but a cultural achievement in Hegelian thought.

Hegel pronounces "the African" an animal precisely through the rejection of African political and spiritual rationality, even while denying the existence of African rational capability all together. One must ask, how can one deny the presence of African rationality through a method that acknowledges its existence? And, to what extent is black humanity "excluded" when it is central to the construction of European humanity as an achievement? Infamous pronouncements aside, Hegel's conclusion is circular: his logic collapses against the weight of his precepts and method. This circuitous logic is one we inherit when a *difference* in Reason is interpreted as *absence or chaos.*[26]

As Mbembe notes in *On the Postcolony*, the problem of universal humanity shapes current conditions of ethics and justice:

> Each time it came to peoples different in race, language, and culture, the idea that we have, concretely and typically, the same flesh, or that in Husserl's word, "My flesh already has the meaning of being a flesh typical in general for us all," became problematic. The theoretical and practical recognition of the body of "the stranger" as flesh and body just like mine, the *idea of a common human nature, a humanity shared with others*, long posed, and still poses, a problem for Western consciousness. (2)

Hegel's theory of "universal humanity" has influenced the culture of rights and law, including human rights law, but at the cost of erasing competing conceptions of being and justice that *are not* rooted in the opposition between Man and Nature.

A conception of humanity that Hegel dismissed as "nature-worship" animates the work of famed South African artist Ezrom Legae, in particular his *Chicken Series* (Hegel 133). Legae created artworks in ink and pencil as well as totemic bronze sculptures (Figure P.1). In 1977, Legae expressed his feelings about the gunned-down child protesters during the Soweto uprising and the murder of Bantu antiapartheid leader Steve Biko at the hands of the police through chiaroscuro, a set of pencil and ink drawings. In *Biko's Ghost*, Shannen Hill asserts that the *Chicken Series* remains among two of the best known of all works that explore Steve Biko's death (116). A medium that mobilizes the polarity of black:white, by mixing light and substance, according to Richard Dyer, chiaroscuro can become a key feature of the representation of white humanity as translucence: privileging the "radiant white face" and obscuring "the opaque black one," "which is at the very least consonant with the perceptual/moral/racial slippages of western dualism" (115–116). Channeling Anne Hollander, Dyer argues that chiaroscuro is a technique used to "discipline, organize and fix the image, suggesting the exercise of spirit over subject matter" (Dyer 115). If, as Dyer suggests, chiaroscuro "allows the spiritual to be manifest in the material" because it selectively lets light through, Legae's subversion, his chiaroscuro's representation of spirit, bends the semiotics of the Christian West and black South Africa in a direction that calls for the overthrow of (state) hierarchies of race and "the human" rooted in polarities of the enlightened and benighted.[27] In the drawings, there are fragile domestic fowls and human–bird hybrids: broken bones, battered, impaled, crucified, fragmented, and swollen. Tortured bodies are alongside eggs, figures of renewal. The drawings collectively speak to the torture, sacrifice, and regeneration of South Africa's Black Consciousness movement.

As John Peffer notes, in terms of its manifest content, the image is that of Christian martyrdom: a crucified chicken. However, the animal aspect is not simply a metaphor for the pained existence of human life under the rule of apartheid; it also illustrates the animal potential of the human. This felt conception of humanity's animal potential is rooted in a cosmological system, a philosophy where the potency of animals may be shared with humans. Humans, especially those who are spiritually powerful, such as community leaders or healers, harness the spiritual and even physical characteristics of animals. For South Africans such as Legae, those depicted in his work are no longer simply human, as they are transformed by the taking on of the physical and psychical potential of animals. Thus, they are not merely metaphorically animals, but are altered in a physical and psychical sense. His work is a challenge to Manichean distinctions between the physical and the spiritual as well as "human versus the animal" (Peffer 58–59).

When the prevailing notion of (human) being becomes synonymous with "universal humanity" or "the human" in discourses of law and popular consciousness, this is an outcome of power, whereby one worldview is able to supplant another onto-epistemological system with a different set of ethical possibilities. The more "the human" declares itself "universal," the more it imposes itself and attempts to crowd out correspondence across the fabric of being and competing conceptions of being. The insistence on the universality of "the human" allows for the multiplication and proliferation of this abstraction's aggression. To overcome a competing model, Western humanism has historically harnessed the force of the state; not only does this take the form of direct state violence, but it is also accomplished by epistemic erasure. Attacks on indigenous forms of knowledge are essential to the process of normalizing a colonial episteme. In bids for recognition and legibility of suffering, within national and global judicial bodies, one's legal identity and injury must speak the language of a particular philosophy of the human. This is so despite the fact that universal humanity, as defined by Hegel and taken up in liberal humanist judicial bodies, is rooted in an anti-African epistemology.

However, under the circumstances, Legae's protest did benefit, *to an extent*, from its opacity and incommensurability with respect to the state's conception of the human, as its critique was obscured from the state. Its cosmological codes, its animating conception of humanity, were rendered illegible by the same force of law that sparked his outrage and grief. *However, what was opaque to the state was immediately identifiable to South Africans like himself.* The current conception of universal humanity does not move beyond a Western, secularized cultural mode and thus misrecognizes and occludes African subjectivity. Thus, we cannot take universal humanity at its word that it is indeed "universal." Hegel's conception of universal humanity aggressively negates Legae's conception of being and world. Namely, Hegel's humanism disregards the rationality, reflexivity, and abstract reasoning and idiom of representation that constitute Legae's vitalizing mode of insubordination. According to Hegel, such a considered act could never spring from "nature-worship" cosmological worldviews (133).

Ironically, the manner in which "the human" announces its universality provides the occasion for Legae's protest to slip under the radar of the apartheid South African government and elude censorship. Evoking the latent animal potential of those brutalized by the state's violence, an alternative mode of being (human) and attendant to spirit, the *Chicken Series* bypasses the problem of the representationalism and its historical reification of the traumatized black body. Thus, Legae could provide powerful witness to events barred from public discourse by an apartheid government, challenging apartheid state terror overtly (opaque). His conception of being, or ontology, defends indigenous African life from the encroachment of a humanism that universalizes itself through torture and intimidation, yes, but also via imperial epistemology, ontology, and ethics.[28] Considering that much of the world does not adhere to a worldview guided by human–animal binarism nor is legible within these terms, I wonder what other modes of relating, epistemologies of being, and ethical possibilities exist beyond the horizon of "the human" and "the animal"?

Some believe, like Lewis Gordon, that black people must be humanists for the "obvious" reason, that the dominant group can "give up" humanism for the simple fact that their humanity is presumed, while other communities have struggled too long for the "humanistic prize" (Gordon 39–46). But what if the enslaved and colonized "no longer accept concepts as gift, nor merely purify and polish them, but first make and create them, present them and make them convincing?" (Nietzsche 409). The elusive "humanist prize"—the formal, symmetrical extension of European humanism—makes *achieving* its conception of "the human" a prerequisite of equitable recognition, yet its conception of humanity already includes the African, but as abject, as plastic. Thus, in order to *become* human without qualification, you must already *be* Man in its idealized form, yet Man, understood simultaneously as an achievement and bio-ontology, implies whiteness and specifically nonblackness.

We misdiagnose the problems of Western globalizing humanism when we take universalism at its word, seeing its failures as simply a problem of implementation or procedure. This results in a further misdiagnosis of the causes and outcomes of freedom and unfreedom. Freedom itself is an evolving practice rather than a normative ideal (D. Roberts, *Killing* 183). As an ideal, freedom is shielded from critique by alternative conceptions rooted in another order of being/knowing/feeling. That said, I also believe that we have misrecognized the refractory desires of black culture, which are commonly not to assimilate but to transform.

After Man

In the Enlightenment thought mentioned above, "the African" is a discourse that develops out of the specific historical context of slavery and expansionism beyond the so-called temperate zones, an expansion into what came to be called Africa and the Caribbean. The discourses that developed to narrate Africa as a land of abject bestial humanity spiraled out and sought to take possession of all African diasporic peoples beyond the geo/ethno/linguistic specificities of "the African" and "the Hottentot." As Mbembe puts it, "What we have said about the slave also holds for the *native*. From the point of view of African history, the notion of the native belongs to the grammar of animality" (236). Thus, while the black thinkers in *Becoming Human* were born in different nations—South Africa, Cuba, Kenya, the United States, among others— all must define themselves in a globalizing antiblack order that raises "the animal question" as ultimately an existential one.

In this project, I am interested in how African diasporic writers and artists not only critique animalization but also exceed critique by over-turning received ontology and epistemic regimes of species that seek to define blackness through the prism of abject animality. By doing so, they present possibilities that point our attention to the potential of modes of worlding that are more advantageous to life writ large. I home in on the epistemic locations of science and philosophy not only because these are the sites that have continued to be privileged in a contest over meaning and truth but also because the questions pursued in *Becoming Human* are biocultural, or more precisely sociogenic: they concern the ways that we are Homo Narrans, both bios and mythos.[29] Instead of aiming for a comprehensive approach to African diasporic perspectives on the so-called animal question, this study does not claim to be all-inclusive, but it does claim that the strategies examined here offer a set of cases that enlarge the field of being's possibility beyond antiblack ontological plasticity. They initiate what appears impossible and create that which is to come.

In *Habeas Viscus*, Alexander Weheliye maintains, "The greatest contribution to critical thinking of black studies—and critical ethnic studies more generally—is the transformation of the human into a heuristic model and not an ontological fait accompli" (8). *Becoming Human's* contribution to this effort is its concept of plasticity, which maintains that black(ened) people are not so much as dehumanized as nonhumans or cast as liminal humans nor are black(ened) people framed as animal-like or machine-like but are cast as sub, supra, and human *simultaneously* and in a manner that puts being in peril because the operations of simultaneously being everything and nothing for an order—human, animal, machine, for instance—constructs black(ened) humanity as the privation and exorbitance of form. Thus the demand placed on black(ened) being is not that of serialized states nor that of the in-between nor partial states but a statelessness that collapses a distinction between the virtual and the actual, abstract potential and situated possibility, whereby the abstraction of blackness is enfleshed via an ongoing process of wresting form from matter such that raciality's materialization is that of a dematerializing virtuality.

What sets *Becoming Human* apart is the manner in which it takes seriously that black literary and visual culture theorizes and philosophizes. While certainly highlighting historical and contemporary individual black philosophical thinkers, this project is equally interested in the philosophical thought that occurs in/as expressive culture. Given that, historically, black people have, in the main, been excluded from the more recognized domains of politics, religion, and philosophy, I maintain that black arts and letters has often been a key site for philosophy, theology, and political theory. *Becoming Human* acknowledges the historical and ongoing exclusions of black people from the domain of the "properly" theoretical and philosophical, but in what follows, you will not find an effort justifying or trying to convince anyone that black thought has something to say about European Continental thought and it is valuable to do so; it just gets on with the work of reading black arts and letters philosophically. Such a reading is not content with reading a novel or poem or work of visual art as mere example of the ideas of an individual "great" thinker; rather, in reading literature and visual art for theory, the approach is that of placing the theories of/as literary and visual art in conversation with more recognizable means and forms of philosophy. It is not an attempt to be exhaustive or comprehensive rather it takes aim at assumptive logics by disrupting and reconstellating the frame through which we have come to question blackness's relation to Man, particularly as it pertains to "the animal" and "species." Thus, the aim is to establish new entry points into the conversation about the nature of the problem and point to other horizons rather than purport to exhaust the monumental question of race and "the human." Subscribing to the view all is present, when it comes to modern blackness, *Becoming Human*—while historically situating and contextualizing "theory"—has the principal intention of depth in its critical aims rather than producing the effects of the historian.

The modes of being examined in *Becoming Human* do not advocate a politics based on rights and entitlements under the law, precisely because their forms are undergirded by demands that are either criminalized, pathologized, or simply rendered illegible by law and the normative mode of "the human"; these demands emerge from a different way of being/knowing/feeling existence than the ones legible and codified in law and the dialectics of Man. Their contestation invests in speculation and expressive culture as a site of critique and creativity. They put forth transient and fleeting expressions of potentiality in the context of the incongruity between substantial freedom and legal emancipation as well as that of colonialism and decolonization. These gestures of potentiality are often incomplete but point to a desire and world-upending claim that is not currently recognized in the social orders that gave rise to them. Each chapter of *Becoming Human* engages a different aspect of what it is to problematize the category of Man from that space that has been foreclosed in order for the category to exist.[30]

The arc of *Becoming Human* starts with the grounding reference of slavery. It puts forward the theory of ontologized plasticity based on reading across Frederick Douglass's 1845 *Narrative* and 1873 speech on "Kindness to Animals" and Toni Morrison's *Beloved* for their respective elaboration and philosophical interventions into the idea of the Chain of Being and its racialization of the human–animal distinction. Next, it examines the concept of "the world," by reading Nalo Hopkinson's genre-defying and literary philosophical *Brown Girl in the Ring* for its upending of Heideggerian metaphysics, in particular Heidegger's highly influential tripartite system of human, animal, and stone, through the text's allegorical examination of the matter of black women's being in the world. *Becoming Human* then turns to a reading of Octavia Butler's "Bloodchild," a text that deconstructs the racialized gendered and sexual imaginary of body and self, accompanying scientific debates about the origin of life itself and symbiosis, a theory of cross-species evolutionary association. Finally, *Becoming Human* concludes with Wangechi Mutu's *Histology of the Different Classes of Uterine Tumors* and Audre Lorde's *The Cancer Journals*; Mutu's visual art and Lorde's journals bring to the forefront the problem of antiblackness, in the mode of a discourse of species, and its role in reproductive health disparity. *Becoming Human* closes with a coda that initiates a black feminist theory of the necropolitical. The last two chapters and coda concern the pertinence of the biopolitics of antiblackness to historically recent and contemporary theories of biological discourse and species. However, all of the texts in my study underscore the recursive trajectory of discourses on black animality.

Chapter 1, "Losing Manhood: Plasticity, Animality, and Opacity in the (Neo)Slave Narrative," is introduced by Frederick Douglass's provocation from his 1845 *Narrative*, "You have seen how a man was made a slave; you shall see how a slave was made a man" (389). Slavery, in particular the slave narrative, established the terms through which we commonly understand the bestialization of blackness. Douglass's 1845 *Narrative* has been central to interpretations that read African American literature through the framework of a petition for human recognition. Douglass, himself, arguably the nineteenth century's most iconic slave, grounds his critique of slavery in natural law. However, Douglass's later speeches problematize his commitment to the natural rights tradition found in his 1845 *Narrative*, by disrupting its racially hierarchical conception of being and challenging the animal abjection that is foundational to its ontology.

Beloved recalls rhetorical strategies, such as appeals to sentimentality and the sovereign "I" employed by Frederick Douglass, that diagnose racialization and animalization as mutually constitutive modalities of domination under slavery. Chapter 1 examines how we might read Morrison as productively problematizing sentimentality as well as gendered appeals to discourses of the Self rooted in religio-scientific hierarchy, specifically the *scala naturae* or Chain of Being, as both discourses have historically recognized black humanity and included black people in their conceptualization of "the human," but in the dissimulating terms of an imperial racial hierarchy. *Beloved* extends Douglass's intervention by subjecting animality's abjection to further interrogation by foregrounding nonhuman animal perspective, destabilizing the epistemological authority of enslaving modernity, including its gendered and sexual logics. By doing so, *Beloved* destabilizes the very binaristic and teleological epistemic presumptions that authorize the black body as border concept. Re-constellating the slave narrative genre, Morrison opens up a new way to interpret the genre, not as one that exposes slavery's dehumanization but rather as one that meditates on the violence of liberal humanism's attempts at humanization. Unsettling calcified interpretations of history and literary slave narratives, *Beloved* identifies the violation of slavery not in an unnatural ordering of man and beast but in its transmogrification of human form and personality as an experiment in plasticity and its limits therein, while also exploring what potential opacity holds for a generative disordering of being.

Chapter 2, "Sense of Things: Empiricism and World in Nalo Hopkinson's *Brown Girl in the Ring*," is a reading of Nalo Hopkinson's 1999 Locus Award–winning near-future novel *Brown Girl in the Ring*. *Becoming Human* avers that gendered antiblack metaphysics continues to subtend scales of world among humans, animals, and objects in Heidegger's still highly influential thought despite being imagined as a corrective to previous scales, such as the *scala naturae* or the Chain of Being examined in chapter 1. It explores what other sense of world becomes available in spaces of abjection and the unthought. Martin Heidegger once wrote regarding the relation between thought and being: "[1.] the stone (material object) is *worldless* [weltlos]; [2.] the animal is *poor in world* [weltarm]; [3.] man is *world-forming* [weltbildend]" (*Fundamental* 177). Chapter 2 argues that the absent presence of the black female figure functions as an interposition that subtends and therefore paradoxically holds the potential to topple the logic of this schema and investigates how, as a consequence of this system's imperialist worldmaking and monopolization of sense, the matter of the black female body is vertiginously affected. An inquiry into onto-epistemology, this chapter explores the reciprocal production of aesthesis and empiricism, both the seemingly scientific and the perceptual knowledge that signify otherwise under conditions of imperial Western humanism.

I argue that as an enabling condition of an imperial Western humanist conception of *the* world *as such*, the black *mater*(nal) marks the discursive-material trace effects and foreclosures of the dialectics of hegemonic common sense and that the anxieties stimulated by related signifiers, such as the black(ened) maternal image, voice, and lifeworld, allude to the latent symbolic-material capacities of black *mater*, as mater, as matter, to destabilize or even rupture the reigning order of representation that grounds the thought–world relation. In other words, the specter of black mater—that is, nonrepresentability—haunts the terms and operations tasked with adjudicating the thought–world correlate or the proper perception of *the* world *as such*, including hierarchical distinctions between reality and illusion, Reason and its absence, subject and object, science and fiction, speculation and realism, which turn on attendant aporias pertaining to immanence and transcendence. Exploring the mind-body-social nexus in Hopkinson's fiction, I contend that in *Brown Girl in the Ring*, vertigo is evoked as both a symptom and a metaphor of inhabiting a reality discredited (a blackened reality) that is at once the experience of the carceral and the apprehension of a radically redistributed sensorium. I argue that black mater holds the potential to transform the terms of reality and feeling, therefore rewriting the conditions of possibility of the empirical.

While remaining attentive to the role of the scientific in the philosophical and the philosophical in scientific throughout, the second half of *Becoming Human* turns, more centrally, to the question of "species" in scientific discourse. Having established the plastic function of blackness in the still active metaphysics of The Great Chain and the conditioning absent presence of black mater for Heideggerian scales of being, *Becoming Human* moves from an investigation of the philosophical production of "the animal" to the scientific production of "species." I demonstrate that in scientific discourse, antiblackness functions there, too, as an essential means of arranging human–animal and human–nonhuman distinctions. Chapter 3, the penultimate chapter, "'Not Our Own': Sex, Genre, and the Insect Poetics of Octavia Butler's 'Bloodchild,'" begins an inquiry into the constitutive role of antiblackness for the logics of scientific taxonomical species hierarchies. The chapter identifies the agentic capaciousness of embodied somatic processes and investigates how matter's efficacies register social inscription. Chapter 3 provides a reading of risk, sex, and embodiment in Butler's "Bloodchild," a text that affirms the continued importance of risk for establishing new modes of life and worlding, despite historical violence and embodied vulnerability. "Bloodchild" is instructive for situating the racial, gendered-sexual politics of the idea of evolutionary association, or symbiogenesis, in the historical discourses of evolutionary and cell biology, as well as deposing a cross-racially hegemonic conception of the autonomous, bounded body that underwrites phantasies of possessive individualism, self-ownership, and self-determination. Perhaps surprisingly, one organism in particular—lichen—has played no minor role in the idea of evolutionary association. As a material actor, lichen has been a source of imagination for troubling the idea of the human individual.

In 1868, when Swiss botanist Simon Schwendener put forth his theory that lichen were actually an association of a fungus or algae—modified fungi, rather than one or the other—he employed vexed social imagery (Schwendener). He argued that lichens represented a master–slave relation: the master was a fungus of the order Ascomycetes, "a parasite which is accustomed to live upon the work of others; its slaves are green algals, which it has sought out or indeed caught hold of, and forced into its service" (Schwendener 4). As Jan Sapp describes, his theory was met with "bitter opposition," considered a threat to taxonomical classification and disciplinary boundaries (4). One commentator described the theory as "the unnatural union between a captive Algal damsel and tyrant Fungal master" (4). This theory would eventually be known as symbiosis. Similarly, the term "colonialism," Eric C. Brown explains in *Insect Poetics*, "replays one of the most visible ways in which humans and insects have been compared: insect colonies take their name from the Latin verb *colere*, meaning 'to cultivate,' especially agriculturally" (xiv). This poetic Latinization of the zoological world extends the bygone Roman Empire into the realms of contemporary biological science and political theory.

If, as Donna Haraway states in *How Like a Leaf*, "science fiction is political theory," the penultimate chapter demonstrates that in Butler's narratives, interspecies relations between humans and insects, parasites, viruses, protoctists, fungi, and bacteria open up the question of what it means to be (human) rather than neatly map onto intrahuman relations and histories (120). This chapter aims to critically examine the stakes, possibilities, and problems of trans-species metaphors at the interface of Butler's fiction and its criticism by examining how racial slavery and colonial ideas about gender, sexuality, and "nature," more generally, have informed *evolutionary discourses on the origin of life itself* and our ideas of cellular biology by looking at the racialized history of the theory of symbiosis in relation to "Bloodchild," Butler's 1984 Hugo and Nebula Award–winning short story that creatively and philosophically reimagines symbiosis as well as what it means to be (human) and to have a body. Departing from the substitutional logic Sapp and Brown identify, chapter 3 explores how Butler's fiction overturns commonly held conceptions of "the human's" relation to the nonhuman not by analogy but by dislodging established presumptions regarding the fundaments of human subjectivity and the materiality of the body. With "Bloodchild," Butler offers a reorientation to the subject and its related associated notions of subjectivity and subjectivation. Butler challenges conventions of literary genre and those genres of the human predicated on racial slavery and colonial narratives of possessive individualism, sovereignty, and self-determination through a literary meditation on sexuality beyond heteronormativity, sexuation beyond dimorphism, and reproduction beyond the man–woman dyad.

The fourth and final chapter, in an alternate reading of Audre Lorde's *The Cancer Journals* and Wangechi Mutu's cyborg figures in *Histology of the Different Classes of Uterine Tumors*, identifies the manner in which the nullification of black mater as *mater*, as matter, continues to underwrite contemporary species hierarchies, including that of race, as race is a "discourse of species." This chapter, "Organs of War: Measurement and Ecologies of De*mater*ialization in the Works of Wangechi Mutu and Audre Lorde," identifies the contemporary reorganization of racially sexuating bio-economies by examining biotechnology, tissue economies, and epigenetic discourse as well as furthers an investigation into the stakes of the manner in which the agencies of the organismic body shape and are shaped by an antiblack world. "Racism," Sylvia Wynter argues, "is an *effect* of the biocentric conception of the human" ("Biocentric" 364, emphasis added). Biocentrism, as defined by Wynter, is a peculiar yet hegemonic logic of species; it espouses the belief that we are "biological beings who then create culture" (361). In other words, according to a biocentric logic, human cultural practices are linearly determined by groups' respective bio-ontological composition, which are vertically arranged by nature itself. Wynter contrasts this belief system's reductive investment in DNA as substratum and mechanistic causation with an alternative she terms *sociogeny*: "My proposal is that we are bio-evolutionarily prepared by means of language to inscript and autoinstitute ourselves in this or that modality of the human, always in adaptive response to the ecological as well as to the geopolitical circumstances in which we find ourselves" ("Biocentric" 361). With sociogeny, Wynter joins other critics of nature–culture binarism, perhaps most notably Haraway's natureculture, which has been recently extended by eco-feminist and feminist materialist conceptions such as Samantha Frost's "bioculture," Staci Alaimo's "trans-corporeality," and Karen Barad's "entanglement" and "intra-action."[31] But Wynter raises the stakes of these critiques by arguing that affect and desire are determinant of both nature and culture as their coproduction (matter and meaning) is given dynamic expression by biocentrism's raciality, which is to say our studied critiques of nature–culture oppositions and the phenomenon itself are inside of the economies of affect and desire generated by raciality.

Departing from an *exclusive* focus on structure, whether it be that of the double-helix or scaled up to the symbolic order, I argue that black female sex(uality) and reproduction are better understood via a framework of emergence and within the context of iterative, intra-active multiscalar systems—biological, psychological, environmental, and cultural. Mutu's *Histology of the Different Classes of Uterine Tumors* crucially reveals the stakes of this intra-activity as it pertains to the semio-material history of "the black female body," reproductive function, and sex(uality) as linchpin and opposable limit of "the human" in scientific taxonomies and medical science, particularly that of Linnaeus's *Systema Naturae* and Ernst Haeckel's highly aesthetic approach to evolutionary theory.[32] Mutu's art is notable for its constructive reorientation of the theorization of race via a reflexive methodological practice of collage, one that reframes

the spectatorial encounter from that of a determinate Kantian linear teleological drama of subjects and objects to that of intra-active processes
and indeterminate feedback loops. Thus, this is not a study of a reified
object but of an intra-actional field that includes material objects but is
not limited to them.

While chapter 4 is principally concerned with the work of Mutu, I
maintain that Lorde offers insights that are generative for a fuller appreciation of Mutu's critical artistic engagement with the racialization
of biological reproductive systems and its somatic effects. Lorde's *The
Cancer Journals* was one of the first critical analyses of female reproductive cancers to put forth an understanding of the body as an emergent
and co-productive intra-actional system and to emphasize that semio-
affective-psychic relations are crucial determinants of physiological processes. Lorde contends in *The Cancer Journals* that carcinogenesis is a
feedback loop encompassing biological, psychological, environmental,
and cultural agencies and, therefore, neither a matter of individualized
disease nor inferior biology but rather a somaticization of politics, and,
by politics, I mean war.

The coda closes *Becoming Human* with a consideration of recent
developments in the biological sciences and biotechnology that have
turned their attention to narrating the problem of "racial health disparity" in reproductive health. I suggest that work on the epigenome, mostly
housed in the regulatory sciences—epidemiology and public health—
possesses contradictory potential and thus uncertain possibilities with
respect to (dis)articulating the antiblack logics that have conditioned
the symbiosis of teleological determinism and evolutionary thought
(whereby a developmental conception of "the human" is only one of its
most obvious instantiations). Bringing the epigenome in conversation
with my theory of ontologized plasticity, I argue that Mutu's aesthetic
strategies, along with those of Legae, Douglass, Morrison, Hopkinson,
and Lorde, featured in *Becoming Human* reveal a potential (with neither
guarantee nor a manifest horizon of possibility—but a potential, nonetheless) for mutation beyond a mode of thought and representation that
continually adheres to predefined rules and narratives that legitimate
antiblack ordering and premature death.

I do not suggest consensus across the texts in this study, rather I am
highlighting evidence of a disturbance within "the human's" epistemolo-

gies and horizon of meaning. This disturbance is suggestive of how we might theorize anew the paradoxes of regimes of knowledge and being that gave rise to the ongoing exigencies of enslavement and colonial modernity. Furthermore, they are highly innovative, creatively offering contrary and often counterintuitive approaches for how we might see humans and animals differently. I am less interested in finding a universal posture toward humanism in the form of a prescription on how we should be (human) or treat animals. That would run the risk of simply inverting the paradigmatic universal subject, obscuring the particular situatedness of my subject(s) by reproducing the normative logic of imperial humanism, one that equates an idealized Western subjectivity with universal law and universal law with justice. And, as we have seen, law may obscure ethics and justice because laws always point to a specific lived, historical, and embodied subjectivity—one that is not universally shared. I approach what follows without investing in any foundational authority, whether in philosophy, law, or science, because I do not believe it is necessary for ethical action; instead, this study takes as its central task the unsettling of foundational authority. It is precisely the condition of the absence of foundational authority that has commonly grounded black ethics.

Historically, foundational authority has either been hostile to or denied the possibility of black intellectualism and disqualified black people from ethical consideration. The seeds planted in the pages that follow spring from the embattled epistemology of peoples living at the vanishing point between direct domination and hegemony but who nevertheless generate a centrifugal and dissident way of being, feeling, and knowing existence.

1

Losing Manhood

Plasticity, Animality, and Opacity in the (Neo)Slave Narrative

The very essence of the male animal, from the bantam rooster to the four-star general, is to strut.
—Daniel Patrick Moynihan, *The Negro Family: A Case for National Action*

You have seen how a man was made a slave; you shall see how a slave was made a man.
—Frederick Douglass, *Narrative of the Life of Frederick Douglass*

Slavery and colonialism not only catalyzed the conscription of black people into hegemonically imperialist and racialized conceptions of "modernity" and "universal humanity" but also inaugurated Western modernity's condition of possibility, initiating a chain of events that have given rise to a transnational, capitalist order.[1] In light of this history, it stands to reason that we should critically remember New World slavery as epochal rupture.[2] Slavery's archival footprint is a ledger system that placed black humans, horses, cattle, and household items all on the same bill of purchase. This ledger's biopolitical arithmetic—its calculation of humanity—dislocated, depersonalized, and collapsed difference, except in the area of market value. In "Mathematics Black Life," Katherine McKittrick states that "this is where historic blackness comes from: the list, the breathless numbers, the absolutely economic, the mathematics of the unliving" (17). The ledger's life promised the social death of those enslaved.[3]

"Slave humanity" is an aporia with which we have yet to reckon. It may well mark the limit of the reckonable. Rather than view the paradoxical predicament of enslaved humanity through the lens of dehumanization, I contend that the concept of humanity itself is fractured and relational. In place of assuming the virtuousness of human recognition or humanization, I interrogate the methods upon which an imperialist and racialized conception of "universal humanity" attempted to "humanize" blackness. In the case of slavery, humanization and captivity go hand in hand. Too often, our conception of antiblackness is defined by the specter of "denied humanity," "dehumanization," or "exclusion," yet, as Saidiya Hartman has identified in her path-breaking study *Scenes of Subjection: Terror, Slavery, and Self-Making in Nineteenth-Century America*, the process of making the slave relied on the abjection and criminalization of the enslaved's humanity rather than merely on the denial of it.[4] Thus, humanization is not an antidote to slavery's violence; rather, slavery is a technology for producing a *kind* of human.

Following Hartman, my interest is in drawing attention not only to the manner in which black people have been excluded from the "life and liberty" of universal rights and entitlements but also to the conditions under which black people have been *selectively incorporated* into the liberal humanist project. Blackness has been central to, rather than excluded from, liberal humanism: the black body is an essential index for the calculation of degree of humanity and the measure of human progress. From the aporetic space of this inclusion that nevertheless masks itself as exclusion, I query how Toni Morrison's *Beloved* might disarticulate Eurocentric humanism while negotiating blackness's status as interposition in the ever-shifting biopolitical terms and stakes of "the human versus the animal." *Beloved*'s questioning of liberal humanism's selective recognition of black humanity is suggestive of a desire for a different mode of being/knowing/feeling and not simply a desire for fuller recognition within liberal humanism's terms.[5]

Toni Morrison's 1988 Pulitzer Prize–winning novel, *Beloved* (1987), is a neo-slave narrative that departs from and transforms the slave narrative convention of juxtaposing the degradation of slaves with that of animals in order to draw our attention not to the violence of dehumanization but rather to the violence of humanization.[6] More specifically, *Beloved* suggests that animalization and humanization of the slave's personhood are not mutually exclusive but mutually constitutive. In other words, the slave's humanity (the heart, the mind, the soul, and the body) is not denied or excluded but manipulated and prefigured as animal whereby black(ened) humanity is understood, paradigmatically, as a state of abject *human* animality.

Morrison's text recalls rhetorical strategies employed by Frederick Douglass that diagnose racialization and animalization as mutually constitutive modalities of domination under slavery. Douglass has become an icon of nineteenth-century slavery, perhaps due to his dexterous navigation of competing liberal humanist rhetorical modes and affective registers, in particular sentimentality and religio-scientific hierarchy. Douglass calls into question the biopolitical logics and practices of slavery with respect to both humans and animals. However, he does so in a manner that reveals the seemingly near-inescapable paradoxes of liberal humanist recognition to the extent that one is conscripted by its terms—appeals to discourses of sentiment and Self.

Both sentiment and the sovereign "I" return us to racialized, gendered master narratives of identity and feeling, which the rooster's gaze in *Beloved* productively destabilizes.[7] Mister's gaze, or the exchange of glances between Mister and Paul D, offers a much-needed critical alternative to sentimental ethics—sympathy, compassion, protection, stewardship, care, and the humane—which has historically been conceived within the terms of a racialized, heteropatriarchal economy of sensibility. In what follows, I examine how we might read Morrison as productively problematizing sentimentality as well as gendered appeals to discourses of the Self rooted in religio-scientific hierarchy considering both discourses have historically recognized black humanity and included black people in their conceptualization of "the human" but in the dissimulating terms of an imperial racial hierarchy.

Re-constellating the slave narrative genre, Morrison opens up a new way to interpret the genre, not as one that exposes slavery's dehumanization but rather as one that meditates on the terror of liberal humanism's attempts at humanization. Unsettling calcified interpretations of history and literary slave narratives, *Beloved* identifies the violation of slavery not in an unnatural ordering of man and beast but in its transmogrification of human form and personality, as an experiment in plasticity and its limits therein. To put it differently, New World slavery established a field of demand that tyrannically presumed, as if by will alone, that the enslaved, in their humanity, could function as infinitely malleable lexical and biological matter, at once sub/super/human. What appear as alter-

nating, or serialized, discrete modes of (mis)recognition—sub/super/
humanization, animalization/humanization, privation/superfluity—are
in fact varying dimensions of a racializing demand that the slave be all
dimensions at once, a simultaneous actualization of the discontinuous
and incompatible: everything and nothing at the register of ontology
such that form shall not hold. Blackness, in this case, functions not simply as negative relation but as a plastic fleshly being that stabilizes and
gives form to human and animal as categories.

"How a Slave Was Made a Man": Racialized Animality and the Paradoxes of Recognition

Canonized among literary studies of blackness, Douglass's 1845 *Narrative*
has served as many critics and readers' introduction to the routine bestialization experienced by those enslaved in the southern United States.
The text relies heavily on bestializing images and juxtapositions of slave
and animal degradation, a strategy that sought to provoke moral persua-
sion and/or Christian outrage over a system of "unnatural" ordering that
was discordant with God's law. For instance, Douglass describes how,
upon the death of a master, the enslaved were divided and appraised:

> We were all ranked together at the valuation. Men and women, old and
> young, married and single, were ranked with horses, sheep, and swine.
> There were horses and men, cattle and women, pigs and children, all
> holding the same rank in the scale of being. . . . After the valuation, then
> came the division. . . . We had no more voice in that decision than the
> brutes among whom we were ranked. (*Narrative* 271, 282)

As Jennifer Mason has observed, the "scale of being" to which Douglass
refers is the *scala naturae*, or the Chain of Being, predicated on the commonplace view that all living beings could be placed on the rungs of a
linear, hierarchical, and continuous ladder that extended from Earth to
Heaven. Each step of the ladder corresponded to a different measure of
perfection: God was at the top, humans were suspended between angels
and animals, and inanimate things occupied the lowest rung (Mason 124).[8]

Douglass published the 1845 *Narrative* while acting as an orator for
William Lloyd Garrison's Massachusetts Anti-Slavery Society. As Dou-

glass knew well, the philosophy of natural rights and its hierarchies of being—human superiority and uniqueness—were cornerstones of the rhetorical arsenal for abolitionists like Garrison. Yet, the adoption of the Chain of Being framework neither provides the slave standing nor authorizes the slave's testimony.

While the Chain of Being may have suggested that placing humans and animals on the same rank was discordant with God's law, it did not provide a stable place for black people to argue for symmetrical, liberal humanist recognition, much less redress, since the enslaved were merely a rung away from animals or possibly even conjoined with their animal neighbors as "animal humans" on what was a *continuous* scale. Once (human) being became coincident with animality, recognition of one's humanity as such would not guarantee a respite from violence based on race because humans were measured by their purported capacity to be more or less "animal."[9] As Winthrop Jordan has noted, the strategic use of the Great Chain was exceedingly tricky for abolitionists because

[o]n the one hand the existence of the Chain of Being was difficult to deny categorically without implying that Nature was not so highly ordered as it might be. Contrarily, to admit the possibility that Nature was hierarchically ordered was to open the door to inherent inferiority, no matter how strenuously the unity of the human species was objected. (496)[10]

As in this case, if black people were human but represented the lowest human rung of the ladder and, thus, embodied the specter of "the animal" within the human, then the extension of human recognition dissimulated rather than simply abated race's animalizing discourse.

As exemplified by the Chain of Being, modern racialized animalization stratified humanity, preemptively barring or excluding black participation in the symbolic order while also establishing or including black humanity as an object in the discursive-material institution of protoscientific Western humanism. Here, human recognition is extended, but only to serve further objectification. The recognition of the slave's humanity was cast in the terms of a globally expansive debate over what *kind* of human black(ened) people represented. To put it plainly, the discourse of race is a discourse of speciation and thus indissociable from the historical development of what Cary Wolfe has called the "discourse of species" and "the animal" as a fundamental site of onto-epistemo-ethical reflection.[11]

The Chain of Being and related frameworks provided a sense of order and stability at the dawn of an expanding imperial order, which was newly conceived in global terms. As noted by Jordan, the Great Chain and related systems developed in a manner that was responsive to global political and epistemological shifts that emerged in the wake of slavery including the French Revolution and the ascendancy of comparative anatomy in natural philosophy (485). The slave's disputed humanity would ground claims about what was proper to man by functioning as its plastic limit case. Therefore, I suggest that slave labor be principally understood not as forced, unwaged labor exploitation in the master's enclave but as an essential enabling condition of the modern grammar of the Subject, a peculiar grammar of kind or logic of species, one that approaches and articulates the planetary scale.[12] Yet as Jordan reminds us, while blackness might have functioned as a stabilizer, the logic of the Great Chain was always inherently tautological; the Great Chain lapsed into incoherence once specific cases came into view:

> To obtain criteria for ranking all creatures on a single scale was virtually impossible. . . . When natural philosophers tried to decide whether the ape, the parrot, or the elephant was next below man, for instance, the grand Chain began to look like an unprepossessing pile of ill-assorted links. . . . Any sharp increase in detailed knowledge of the multitude of species was bound to make hierarchical construction impossible even for the most masterful craftsman. How was one going to rank thousands of species of plants in exact order? (222)

It was for these precise reasons, I would argue, that the compulsive repositioning of blackness as limit case, in its abstraction, as type was not only necessary but also an essential stabilizer.

The Chain of Being framework was a compromise between the increasing authority of science and the powerful sway of Christianity. Christian abolitionists deployed the Chain of Being as a rhetorical strategy in the hope of rousing a largely white, northern, Christian readership to ethical action. Most white Christian denominations at the time sanctioned slavery based on a reactionary interpretation of scripture. Abolitionists countered by producing interpretations that repurposed biblical authority. But both pro- and antislavery factions, by appropriating an established discourse, necessarily obscured the singular nature of New World slavery's cataclysmic violence.[13] Rather than registering the seismic stakes of the enslaved's claim to being or attending to the contradiction inherent in *racializing* humanity, the twin strategies of moral suasion and Christian outrage joined the fray of contemporaneous debates concerning the potential consequences of slavery for the fate of the white soul and/or the future of the republic.[14]

Many scholars have underscored the exceptional originality of Douglass's 1845 *Narrative*. Deborah McDowell has even suggested that it might be best understood as "sui generis."[15] However, it is worth asking: how might the *Narrative*'s subversion of genre or innovation of both slave and abolitionist literature as noted by scholars *necessarily* exist alongside and even be enabled by the fraught rhetorical inheritance that occasioned Douglass's textual performance? In particular, I want to consider the ways in which abolitionist discourse and its conventions are constitutive of Douglass's textual performance of the "truth" of slavery and the veracity of experience. Those formerly enslaved, like Douglass, were pressured from within white-led abolitionist circles to trope one's personally nuanced experience of slavery to produce recognizable characters, plot devices, and rhetorical strategies because the slave narrative had become a genre, and like all genres, it had narrative strictures.

In a study that investigates "the discursive terrain" awaiting slave testimony, Dwight McBride observes the following:

> If the situation of the discursive terrain is that there is a language about slavery that preexists the slave's telling of his or her own experience of slavery, or an entire dialogue or series of debates that preexist the telling of the slave narrator's particular experience, how does one negotiate the terms of slavery in order to be able to tell one's own story? The importance of this idea is that the discursive terrain does not simply function to create a kind of overdetermined way of telling an experience; it creates the very codes through which those who would be readers of the slave narrative understand the experience of slavery.

. . . Even more radically, the discourse of slavery is what allowed the slave to speak in the first place. But to speak what? It allowed for speech on one's very experience as a slave. That is, it produced the occasion for bearing witness, but to an experience that had already been theorized and prophesied. . . . Before the slave ever speaks, we know the slave; we know what his or her experience is, and we know how to read that experience. Although we do not ourselves have that experience, we nevertheless know it and recognize it by its language.[16]

"To be heard at all," McBride argues, the witness writes to, if not for, an imagined reader, who is, in turn, discursively constructed out of a cacophonous debate concerning the controversy surrounding the being of the witness (2). This scenario arguably positions the witness as an object of discourse and/or noise—an actant rather than an interlocutor.[17] It is likely that the slave's actual perspective (rather than unmediated experience, which is ineligible for strict narration by the very nature of representation) was often only obliquely present in the text's inconsistencies, ellipses, and constrained speech. The writing of subsequent versions of Douglass's narrative reveals *the text's and the self's* opacity and instability as "origin."

Following McDowell, I want to inquire into rhetorical inheritance: In what ways does Douglass's corpus exist inside and outside of slavery's and abolitionism's textuality? Or more precisely, how does this polarity undermine our ability to identify and assess the enabling conditions of textuality? Moreover, as a number of scholars have observed, reading slave narratives as unmediated truth would not only reinforce the problematic conflation between black authors and their texts but also potentially undermine our ability to critically examine both their content and the historical context of their production, considering that they arose within a literary cultural industry and often under the duress of fugitivity's criminalization.[18]

The point here is not to criticize Douglass's strategic use of the Chain of Being framework or his adroit facility with sentimentality but to take stock of its constraints. Those untimely voices negated by the prevailing episteme of their age may never find the words to satisfactorily describe their experience, or their speech may be rendered illegible or inaudible by power. This is so even when their voices are, like Douglass's, bold

and eloquent. That said, the insistence that slavery's violation be articulated as a mistake of categorization (rendering humans as beasts) or
application undercuts our ability to subject racialization's justifications
to fuller critique. This approach undermines our capacity for a more
thorough assessment of the life-and-death stakes of slavery's equation
of black humanity with a state of animality. A fuller critique would risk
calling into question not only its application but also its epistemic foundations. Antiracism has too often limited our critique of "animalization"
to a critique of the term's scope instead of disrupting its authority in
the management of life. Power has legitimated itself by taking refuge in
the presumed necessity of managing, disciplining, criminalizing, and
extinguishing "the animal." The debate or controversy over black humanity is itself a form of necropolitics. I am interested in how we can
undermine the assumptive logic of the debate rather than reinforce its
starting places. What I am suggesting is that "freedom" is a practice of
onto-epistemology as well as of affect or feeling. "The animal" as symbol, as trope, as locus of possibility, must be *rethought and transformed*;
otherwise, it will continue to animate antiblack discourse and institute
itself biopolitically.

Here I want to suggest that although it is often taken to be the case,
Douglass's 1845 *Narrative* may not in fact be representative of how the
enslaved saw their place in relation to animals. Liberal humanist frameworks of "inclusion" and "recognition" have obscured and/or insufficiently
examined other possible modes, some authored by Douglass himself, of
relating to animals—forms of relating that problematize biopolitical arrangements engendered by slavery. While ultimately I will argue that Douglass problematizes rather than resolves the biopolitical arrangements he
scrutinizes, shifts in his rhetorical strategy confound his earlier position
in the 1845 *Narrative*—revealing that testimony, social structural position,
and political diagnosis must be understood as an improvised rather than
reified interrelation in the corpus of Douglass's thought.

In the years immediately following the formal end of slavery, Douglass produced speeches that have a noticeably more vexed and irresolute
relation to the 1845 *Narrative*'s philosophies of natural rights and the
Chain of Being, philosophies that are premised on concepts of human
superiority and uniqueness. For instance, on Friday, September 19, 1873,
the *Tennessean* published a speech that Douglass had delivered the day

before at Nashville's "Colored Fair Grounds." When discussing the topic of "Kindness to Animals," Douglass states the following:

> There is no denying that slavery had a direct and positive tendency to produce coarseness and brutality in the treatment and management of domestic animals, especially those most useful to the agricultural industry. Not only the slave, but the horse, the ox, and the mule shared the general feeling of indifference to the right naturally engendered by a state of slavery.... It should be the study of every farmer to make his horse his companion and friend, and to do this, there is but one rule, and that is, uniform sympathy and kindness.... All loud and boisterous commands, a brutal flogging should be banished from the field, and only words of cheer and encouragement should be tolerated. A horse is in many respects like a man. He has the five senses, and has memory, affection, and reason *to a limited degree*.[19]

Here, Douglass suggests that *slavery introduces brutality* into the lives of humans and animals such that brutality is understood as synonymous with the institution, and he advocates for human–animal cooperation in farming in place of rivalry or brutalization. More than that, while stopping short of foreclosing difference, his understanding of (human) being, presumably including his being, does not arise in binaristic opposition to, or in negation of, "the animal" as a "horse is in many respects like a man."[20] More importantly, for this discussion, Douglass's "many respects like" and the use to which these words are put confound the terms of his earlier testimony.

Nevertheless, what if the rhetoric of sentimentality and empathetic identification itself reintroduces hierarchies of feeling and capacity engendered by slavery rather than remedies them as his "to a limited degree" might suggest? The *Tennessean* reports that Douglass ends the section of his speech devoted to "Kindness to Animals" with the following:

> When young, untrained and untamed, he (a horse) has unbounded faith in his strength and fleetness. He runs, jumps, and plays in the pride of his perfections. But convince him that he is a creature of law as well as of freedom, by a judicious and kindly application of your superior power,

and he will conform his conduct to that law, far better than your most law-abiding citizen. (4)

While a horse is "perfect" rather than in a state of privation as the Chain of Being might suggest, according to Douglass the horse, like a citizen, must still defer to the "kindly application" of "superior power" and "law." Rather than read Douglass's sentimental animal ethics and deference to state power as either an unqualified reversal of the 1845 *Narrative* or prescriptively, I read both statements as critically wrestling with (but still very much conscripted by) slavery's hierarchies of being and feeling—even extending the institution's palliative logic of "humane" reform.[21]

The "humane" is an ideal that suggests humanity is gained by performing acts of kindness and attuning oneself to the suffering of those of inferior status and lesser capacity; as such, it does not posit humanity as simply an inherent or a priori aspect of being (human). As in John Locke's highly influential *Thoughts on Education* (1693), rather than forestall domination, "humane" discourse, in effect, made human identity contingent on hierarchical relationality—encounters between those with refined sensibilities and those presumably without, in particular children, animals, and slaves—as "humane" education in the United States concerned itself with the proper cultivation of sympathy and behavior conducive to the successful *reproduction of the established order.*[22] Saidiya Hartman has argued that "the humane in slave law was totally consonant with the domination of the enslaved" and, more specifically, that sentiment routinely regulated and preserved the institution rather than effected a reversal of its relations (*Scenes of Subjection* 93):

> On one hand, there was an increased liability for white violence committed against slaves; and on the other, the law continued to decriminalize the violence thought necessary to the preservation of the institution and the submission and obedience of the slave. If anything, the dual invocation of law [property and person] generated the prohibitions and interdictions designed to regulate the violent excesses of slavery and at the same time extended this violence in the garb of sentiment. . . . To be subject in this manner was no less brutalizing than being an object of property.

In the arena of affect, the body was no less vulnerable to the demands and the excesses of power. The bestowal that granted the slave a circumscribed and fragmented identity as a person in turn shrouded the violence of such a beneficent and humane gesture. (94)

While scholars of the US nineteenth century have put forth varying accounts of how racial slavery shaped white racial anxiety and the increasing prominence of sentimentality as a mode of civic engagement and pedagogy, a shared scholarly conviction that extends far beyond Hartman holds that sentimentality, perhaps the century's most privileged rhetorical mode, acted to safeguard existing power relations, even in its abolitionist deployment, by masking the reorganization of domination and violence in the emerging secularizing terms of empathetic identification on the one hand and hierarchical bonds of kindness, domesticity, and laws of nature on the other.[23] Regarding Douglass, Robert Fanuzzi notes, "Above all, Douglass knew what it meant to produce the position of the outsider as a kind of performance, through a political rhetoric that was also an art. His infamous mimicry of venerable orators, his reiteration of civic pedagogy, and his inversion of political symbolism all betrayed a formal mastery" of genres of masculine, republican elocution (206).

But what if this lesson in civic pedagogy addressed to the "colored citizens" of Tennessee in 1873—exemplary pedagogy of civic manhood— actually reinscribes (even as it appears to renounce) the terms of their continued subjugation, even in slavery's putative absence? I invoke Douglass's equivocations here to suggest we read the inchoate and incomplete nature of his intervention, its fugitivity, as a provocation and an effort to refuse modes of relating that were established under slavery. However, Douglass's hierarchized conception of feeling and capacity, even in its deployment as empathetic identification with animals, actually rehearses the assumptive logics of racial subjection. After all, the racialization of capacity and feeling preconditions and prefigures the occasion of Douglass's speech on at least two counts: the city's spatiotemporal arrangement—the "Colored Fair Grounds"—and the honorifics bestowed on Douglass—"the most distinguished of their race," "The Colored American's Chosen Moses," "distinguished gentleman, statesman, and lover of his race."[24] In addition to hypostatizing racial difference, the regularity of such plaudits throughout Douglass's career implies that while Douglass represents black people, he is not representative of blackness but exceptional not simply as an orator but as a black person. In fact, in Douglass's case, assessments of his skill as an orator is inseparable from his racialization: it is precisely his reported exceptional capacity as an orator that simultaneously marks his racial difference and purportedly sets him apart from other black people.

Douglass's acclaim as an orator began with his career as a lecturer in Garrison's Massachusetts Anti-Slavery Society and grew precipitously with the publication of his 1845 *Narrative*. At the time, some skeptics questioned whether a slave, a black, could have produced such an eloquent and moving piece of literature. The credibility of black authorship—in other words, the facticity of black capacity for reason and feeling—was so routinely questioned that slave narratives were commonly underwritten by white abolitionists. For instance, the 1845 *Narrative* was published under Garrison's imprimatur presumably because he was axiomatically credible by virtue of his whiteness.

However, Jacques Derrida has productively called into question how securely "the human," understood in its white Western imperial form, possesses the characteristics it claims for itself and denies to others (*The Animal* 135). In *The Animal That Therefore I Am*, the late French philosopher Jacques Derrida contends "the question" of "the animal" in philosophy refers "not to the animal but to the naive assurance of man." In critically approaching the "bestiary at the origin of philosophy," Derrida clarifies that it is less a matter of asking "whether one has the right to refuse the animal such and such a power . . . [than of] asking whether what calls itself human has the right rigorously to attribute to man, which means therefore to attribute to himself, what he refuses the animal, and whether he can ever possess the pure, rigorous, indivisible concept, as such, of that attribution" (*The Animal* 135). Moreover, what of the capacities that exceed human identification? What of those things and creatures with which it is not (yet) possible to confer identification or with which identification is denied? Sentimental ethics is an arbitrary order of perception and sense making that disqualifies from ethical consideration all those incalculable opacities and yet-to-be-recuperated differences with which it does not and, by design, cannot identify. Moreover, sentimentality is a relation, not a sensibility; conceived as a sensibility, sentimental feeling has historically functioned as a pretext for racial hierarchy in the forms of a pedagogy in white ideality and the pathologization and criminalization of blackness.[25] If, as I suggest, sentimental ethics typically proceeds without sufficiently interrogating the vexed terms of identification or even pausing to consider whether or not identification should organize ethics, is such an order of consideration ethical? And if so, by what measure?

These vexed terms of identification are precisely what are under investigation in *Beloved*, and in the process of investigation, a hasty, prescriptive, sentimental ethics is exchanged for an exploration of affectivity and its relational effects.[26] Eschewing both sentimentalism and naturalized hierarchy with *Beloved*, Morrison pulls apart and reconstellates the slave narrative form. In doing so, Morrison invites the reader to relinquish a reified understanding of "the truth of slavery" so that we might investigate New World slavery as an ever-present mode of violent ontologizing that includes but exceeds the animalization of the slave, as blackness was always subject to something more.

Ontological Plasticity in *Beloved*

I have always been struck by the speed with which "handsome young Negro" turns into "young colt" or "stallion."
—Frantz Fanon, *Black Skin, White Masks*

At the close of Derrida's highly influential essay, a number of interrelated questions at the center of what he calls the "philosophical bestiary" nevertheless remain. In particular, if sexual difference and its attendant Oedipal anxieties and oppositions structure the foundational violence of the Western philosophical tradition, a violence that is constitutive with and recalled by human–animal oppositions, how might a consideration of the mode by which the symbolic logics of both dualisms are cut and qualitatively intensified by antiblack racialization clarify the terms and stakes of his inquiry? I suggest that *Beloved* (1987) sheds light on a constitutive lacuna in Derrida's thought by thinking a being for whom normative symbolics of gender and personhood do not take hold due to a concerted attempt to apportion and delimit characteristics presumed to be proper to Man in a manner that accords with the paradoxical dictates of a racializing Law. Morrison's *Beloved* is suggestive for identifying how blackness constitutes and disrupts the historical and philosophical terms and assumptive logic of Derrida's meditation. However, the primary investment here is not a systematic critique of Derrida's essay but drawing out Morrison's philosophical meditation on antiblack slavery as a mode of ontologizing and identifying its implications for resetting our thinking on ontology. Namely, I argue that blackness is the missing term in Derrida's analysis of the antinomy of man and animal and that it is blackness in the mode of ontological plasticity that stabilizes and gives form to "human" and "animal" as terms.

The bestialization of blackness has been central, even essential, to reanimations of antiblack discourse from the early days of the American republic until today. Often when this occurs, the evocation of black animality is either unquestioningly reified or criticized for reinforcing antiblack racism and quickly dismissed. Toni Morrison avoids both approaches; instead, she problematizes these strategies by critically engaging the assumptive logic of racialized animality and redirecting antiblack animal imagery such as the bestializing compositions found in Douglass's 1845 *Narrative*. Morrison critically observes the fundaments of animalized representation up close rather than negating them at a distance. Instead of performing a straightforward rejection of racially oppressive imagery, her text exposes the complexity and contradictions that produce blackness and animality as proxies, not through the refutation of bestial imagery but rather through its magnification and deconstruction. It is Morrison's deconstructive approach that reveals the convolutedness of racialized animalization as an essential feature of the historical institution of liberal humanism, including its lexical and ethical possibilities.[27]

Beloved does not resolve the ethical blindness of liberal humanism through empathy between the reader and the narrative's characters, or between human and animal as general categories, but instead reopens the field of ethics by reminding readers of alterity's intractable insistence.[28] Instead of offering a dialectical solution or providing an answer or prescription on ethical action, the text uncompromisingly insists on the problem of ethics that accompanies asymmetrical relations, in this case between Paul D, a slave, and Mister, a rooster.[29]

Beloved identifies the site of a potential breach in the epistemological project of humanistic perspective: What is behind Mister's gaze? More accurately, *Beloved* intensifies "animal perspective," a disruption that is already there—latent and repressed—in liberal humanism's textuality. As a result, the novel facilitates reconsideration of perspective's consequence for ethics, given liberal humanism's stubborn refusal to authorize (or even avow) the perspective of the animalized (human and nonhuman) while also failing to attend to its own pernicious limitations.

This refusal is the result of at least three contiguous presuppositions: first, "the animal" lacks perspective; second, "the African" is animal in the form of a human and, thus, is devoid of the achievement of Reason or the full realization of perspective; and third, because "the animal"—human and nonhuman—is lacking, animality disqualifies one from ethical consideration. Mister's gaze calls into question the ethical authority of this formulation by countering the epistemological certainty upon which principled judgment is made and questioning, rather than presuming, the ontological distinctions upon which ethical judgments rest. *Beloved* rearticulates, rather than resolves, the problem of ethics in light of differential embodiment by questioning and destabilizing slavery's economy of sense and perceptual logic, that is to say, its religio-scientific taxonomies and foreclosures that rely on a white patriarchal authority alternately supported by naturalistic, divine, or positivistic pretense. *Beloved* invites a critical reopening of the orders of ethical authority and ontological distinction, thus rendering them not as the context of investigation but rather as the object to be critically reexamined. As the foreclosing of animal perspective reinforces the logic of enslavement, the novel prompts us to reconsider how animal perspective potentially undermines one of race's most formative epistemic presumptions.

With *Beloved*, Morrison provides a rich exploration of the seemingly contradictory construction that is black(ened) humanity, namely the entanglement of racialized, gendered, and sexual discourses with those concerning animality. Largely focusing on the animalization of black male gender, sexuality, and subjectivity under conditions of enslavement, I investigate how the captive's gender and sexuality were constructed in relationship to humanity *and* animality in the text.

Critics of *Beloved* have largely ignored the presence of Mister the rooster despite the text's insistent return to Mister's gaze in scenes that make and undo the significance of both humanity and manhood—where gendered, sexual, and ontological violence produce and mark the limits of manhood for Paul D. If one considers the rooster as both figurative actor *and material entity* in the novel rather than mere *projection of Paul D's trauma*, the gaze of Mister—the exchange of glances between Mister and Paul D—takes on the quality of a caesura, a disruption of the prevailing grammar of gender, knowledge, and being.

Taking up the narrative's insistence on Mister's gaze, in particular, I investigate the distinctive quality of Paul D and Mister's relationality and explore its implications for contemporary theorization of biopolitics and the onto-epistemo-ethical stakes of non/in/humanity designations. Problematizing literary conventions of form and interpretive method, *Beloved* performs narrative at the register of a structural analysis of the modern grammar of the Subject. Reaching to meet the fullness of Morrison's intervention into theory, mine is a literary criticism that explores how narrative texture performs and excites philosophical engagement. I will read Paul D's encounter with Mister the rooster as bringing into stark relief Paul D's gendered sexual alienation and existentially debilitating circumstances.

The practice of gender at Sweet Home, the fictional plantation that provides the setting for much of *Beloved*, would appear to depart from the generalized principles that characterized slavery as depicted in the text. At Sweet Home, male slaves are considered "men," breaking with the commonplace slaveholder logic, which typically withheld acknowledgment of manhood or even adulthood among those enslaved. It was believed that reciprocal recognition between white and black men would disrupt the natural order of plantation life. Normative modes of gender such as patriarchal authority and filial recognition are the entitlements of manhood in the Oedipal symbolic economies of the US South, but manhood and enslavement were commonly viewed as incommensurate by proponents of slavery. As one slaveholder put it, "Ain't no nigger men" (*Beloved* 13).[30] Yet, Mr. Garner would appear to break with this tradition by being "tough enough and smart enough to make and call his own niggers men" (*Beloved* 13). However, with Garner, Morrison explores dimensions of sovereign power that often go undetected and unremarked. Garner is emblematic not of sovereignty's power to expropriate and withhold recognition but of that aspect of sovereignty (self-)authorized to give and bestow, to create and legitimate.

So that he might "demonstrate . . . what a real Kentuckian was," Garner consolidated his manhood in the bestowal of abject manhood on the enslaved in the figure of the "Sweet Home man." The concept of "Sweet Home men" was initially introduced by Morrison's omniscient narrator in the following way: "There had been six of them who *belonged* to the farm" (*Beloved* 11, emphasis added). That they belonged to the farm, rather than the other way around, alerts readers to their nonnormative relation to property. Owning property is an emblem of white patriarchal masculinity; in contrast, Paul D belonged to property. The enslaved men's fungibility, or replaceability and interchangeability, was built into their names.[31] There are three Pauls at Sweet Home, with Garner's surname qualifying their proper name. His surname does not announce their entitlement to patrilineal wealth, as it would seem to suggest, but marks them, brands them, as belonging to the arrangements of the property relation. Another is named after a number, Sixo—the wild man. His name possibly references the "60 million or more" lost to the Middle Passage. And then there is Halle Suggs, Sethe's husband and the father of her children—only he disappears, going "wild eyed" after witnessing Sethe's mammary rape by Schoolteacher.

Paul D's encounter with Mister initiates wonder: When Garner refers to them as men, "was he naming what he saw or creating what he did not?" (*Beloved* 260). He is "allowed" or "encouraged" to correct Garner; defiance is even tolerated. He can invent ways of doing things and can "attack" problems without permission. He can buy a mother, choose a horse or a wife, handle guns, and "even learn reading" (*Beloved* 147). But even these forms of masculine prerogatives still leave him with the feeling that Sweet Home men are "trespassers among the human race" (*Beloved* 148). They are "watchdogs without teeth, steer bulls without horns; gelded workhorses whose neigh and whinny could not be translated into a language responsible humans spoke" (*Beloved* 148). "He did manly things," yet Paul D cannot come to a clear conclusion about whether that was Garner's gift, or his own will (*Beloved* 260). He wonders if his manhood rests entirely on the word of a white man, stirring within him a nascent question: Is his sense of manhood the product of a "wonderful lie" (*Beloved* 260)?

After his encounter with Mister, Paul D continues to wrestle with creeping unease concerning his own manhood. What becomes increasingly apparent is that Garner recognized Paul D's mutual humanity but then proceeded to manipulate and exploit it. What was commonly believed to distinguish human from animal, for Garner, are merely opportunities for manipulation; human capability—sentiment, sexuality, rationality, intention, and intelligence—were instrumentalized in order to plasticize Paul D's humanity rather than guarantee a just intersubjectivity. Again, Garner recognized Paul D's humanity but inverted it, in the interest of property and ego, rather than affirmatively recognizing their shared humanity as the grounds of a principled intersubjectivity. Garner transgresses behavioral polarities that normatively characterized the master–slave relation, not as recognition of the injustice of denied intersubjectivity but as a performance of his dominance. In other words, he invited the disruption of hierarchical coded behavior without sacrificing his dominance over the enslaved, precisely because he solicited the transgression. Thus, by inviting the slave to transgress slavery's limitations, he displays the arbitrariness of his power, and Garner's "superior" manhood rests on the arbitrariness of his power.

Paul D had no substantive authority over himself or the definition of manhood at Sweet Home, in Alfred, Georgia; Ohio; or Delaware. He could respond to Garner's definition, but he had no power to generate a definition to his liking: at least, not in a "language responsible people spoke" (*Beloved* 148). That Garner's slaveholding estate is named "Sweet Home" points to the manner in which language is used ironically in the text. Language, the deadly play of signification over terms like "manhood," is exactly what the narrative alerts us to, as Paul D qualifies of Sweet Home: "It wasn't sweet, and it sure wasn't home" (*Beloved* 16). Garner, as patriarch, was so powerful that the enslaved could hardly believe he could die. He is elevated even beyond death. The extent to which his life defined theirs is revealed in his death—when Schoolteacher arrives.

It is Schoolteacher and his necropolitical pedagogy—but especially Mister's gaze—which destabilizes the illusion Garner had worked so hard to create. Paul D desperately tries to cling to his genre of manhood by recalling his past demonstrations of corporeal masculinity:

> He, he. He who had eaten raw meat barely dead, who under plum trees bursting with blossoms had crushed through a dove's breast before its heart stopped beating. Because he was a man and a man could do what he would: be still for six hours in a dry well while night dropped; fight raccoon with his hands and win; watch another man, whom he loved better than his brothers, roast without a tear just so the roasters would know what a man was like. And it was he, *that* man, who had walked from Georgia to Delaware, who could not go or stay put where he wanted in 124—shame. (*Beloved* 148)

The stuttering "he" initiating the passage above testifies to both a stubborn pursuit and an uncertain arrival. Paul D wants to believe that he is a fully autonomous man, coherent, and whole. Ironically, the more Paul D clings to rugged expressions of masculinity—curtailed emotion, mastery over bodily sensation, and killing if need be—the more he is boxed into not simply animality but plasticity: he can be manipulated and poured into a mold designed by Garner, and later by Beloved—acting as an avatar for slavery. For Paul D, masculinity is a symbol of his *presence* as a human. However, his manhood is decidedly qualified at Sweet Home because he is not an architect of a language under the aegis of power, but rather, he is subjected to its mocking grammar.

The expressions of masculinity that he offers as evidence of his manhood are easily appropriated as evidence of his savagery and animality; yet these paradoxical symbols of manhood are the only aspects of masculinity available to him. Autonomy and a rugged code of masculinity have failed Paul D. Whereas they might provide white masculinity solace, for him, they only mock. Instead of a steadiness in the conviction of his manhood, he is flushed with shame and disquietude, the kind of shame that produces nausea and repulsion. Before his encounter with a rooster named Mister, Paul D affirmatively identified as a "Sweet Home man" as defined within the terms of Garner's racially qualified and hierarchical definition of manhood.

Yet, with the arrival of Schoolteacher and the subsequent encounter with Mister, Paul D begins to question the meaning of his manhood (*Beloved* 11). Schoolteacher "arrived to put things in order" (*Beloved* 11). A man who "always wore a collar, even in the fields," Schoolteacher was an emblem of both the epistemic powers and abuses of scientific and biblical authority under relations of domination (*Beloved* 44).[32] Through the use of free indirect discourse, Paul D's telegraphed subterranean thoughts oscillate between (self)assurance and worry: "He grew up thinking that, of all the Blacks in Kentucky, only the five of them were men. . . . Was that it? Is that where the manhood lay? In the naming done by a whiteman who was supposed to know?" (*Beloved* 147). He tries to reassure himself that, in fact, he has nothing to worry about, his identity secure, yet the stark and near total domination introduced under Schoolteacher's rule, culminating in his encounter with Mister, ushers in creeping doubt. He recounts:

[Mister] sat right there . . . looking at me. I swear he smiled. My head was full of what I'd seen of Halle a while back. I wasn't even thinking about the bit. Just Halle and before him Sixo, but when I saw Mister I knew it was me too. Not just them, me too. One crazy, one sold, one missing, one burnt and me licking iron with my hands crossed behind me. The last of the Sweet Home men. (*Beloved* 85–86)

As I will demonstrate, in this scene, the recurring phrase "*the last* of the Sweet Home men" (emphasis added), and Paul D's self-identification with it, takes on an ironic quality. It suggests incipient possibilities and the unsettling of identity rather than mere reification. Paul D might in fact be able to experience something the other Pauls had not—a life beyond the farm—that introduces discontinuity into the fetters of ownership and gendered identification. In its way, his growing envy of Mister in this scene is an acknowledgment of doubt, but Paul D initially refuses that knowledge due to his attachment to heteropatriarchy and its sovereign "I."

It is not until Paul D has an encounter with a rooster that destabilizes his sense of his own manhood that he begins to recognize that tyrannical power not only denies but also permits. This is a realization that ultimately leads him to question Sweet Home's fetters of obligation.

When Paul D comes face-to-face, eye to eye, male to male with Mister the rooster, he is compelled to confront what is in plain view: the state of his manhood is not one of coherence, unification, and integrity but is, rather, riven, circumscribed, and indefinite. In the eyes of Garner, Paul D is not decisively and symmetrically "man" but is, instead, an occasion for the theater of sovereign power and manipulated matter—a plastic. The encounter with Mister sets in motion the interrelated processes of relinquishing his identification as a "Sweet Home man" and redefining his gender and being in improvisational terms rather than in fidelity to those inherited from slavery. Crucially, Morrison desentimentalizes this loss of identity by framing loss as an invitation to invention, such that the loss of manhood, the relinquishment of what never properly belonged to him and compelled renegotiations of identity, becomes the arc of Paul D's development as a character. The scene with Mister sets Paul D in a direction away from liberal humanism's hierarchical ordering in an improvisational manner and, thus, initiates movement without predetermined terminus but nevertheless in an insistent direction. Similarly, Fred Moten describes improvisation as not "without foresight" but rather a "deviance of form" that always "operates as a kind of foreshadowing, if not prophetic, description" as well as a "trace of another organization" and "extemporaneous formation and reformation of rules, rather than the following of them" (46, 63).

Elliptically returning in the novel, Mister's gaze pushes Paul D to confront that doubt, turn toward it rather than away from it, and go deeper into it by stripping him of an identity that never belonged to him and revealing the depth of the violence that upholds it. Merging Paul D's voice with the narrator's, a tremble would register that he was not free of Mister even when Mister appeared far from Paul D's consciousness: "OUT OF SIGHT of Mister's sight, away, praise His name, from the smiling boss of roosters, Paul D began to tremble" (*Beloved* 125, small caps in original).

Morrison's insistence on Mister's gaze, via free indirect discourse, invites a reconsideration of ontological and gendered meaning: If an essential feature of your existence is that the norm is not able to take hold, what mode of being becomes available, and what mode might you invent? How might an injunction against an avowed commonality in being by an ontologized conception of racialized gender paradoxically provide access to an alternative mode of being/knowing/feeling—a realm of invention whereby an alternative operates or becomes manifest in the recesses of powers of interdiction?[33] How might the singular burden and (im)possibilities of blackness be reconceived in a manner other than as a melancholic attachment to the norm? What modes of correspondence between humanity and animality open up? Again, Morrison desentimentalizes this loss of identity by framing loss as invitation to invention such that the loss of manhood—the relinquishment of what never properly belonged to him—compels renegotiations of identity and becomes a caesura, or a space for something other than what Paul D has previously known and desired to occur.

Due to Sethe's resentment of her husband Halle's unexplained disappearance, Paul D feels compelled to recount not only the events that led to Halle's disappearance but also the events that indelibly shaped his own history. In conversation with Sethe, Paul D, despite himself, attempts to recount unspeakable events. He recalls how he found himself with a horse bit between his jaws: the bit immobilizing his tongue, tearing the corners of his mouth, forcing it open, plasticizing by pulling and ripping. Paul D's retelling prompts Sethe, in turn, to remember witnessing similar episodes, "Men, boys, little girls, women. The wildness that shot up into the eye the moment the lips were yanked back. Days after it was taken out, goose fat was rubbed on the corners of the mouth but nothing to soothe the tongue or take the wildness out of the eye." She said, "People I saw as a child . . . who'd had the bit always looked wild after that . . . it put a wildness where before there wasn't any" (*Beloved* 84). *Beloved* suggests that the forcing of a bit into a human mouth, the plasticization of the body, puts wildness into the eyes rather than reveals the wildness that is presumed to already characterize black people.

For Paul D, however, the bestializing bit is not the worst part—the em dash giving emphasis to this point. He recounts, "[I]t wasn't the bit—that wasn't it. . . . The roosters. . . . Walking past the roosters looking at them look at me. . . . Must have been five of them perched up there, and at least fifty hens" (*Beloved* 85). It is seeing himself being seen in the gaze of a rooster named Mister. Reflected in Mister's eyes, he sees for the first time the extent to which his being has been distorted by slavery. He is ashamed that Mister is witness to all of it.

More specifically, rather than an inability to hide his shame, it is *Unheimlich* identification that is "the worst part": what unmoors Paul D is that somehow Mister knows, that Mister has seen what Paul D cannot. Shame would give shape to recognition of his abjection and subjection to another. Paul D watches Mister walk from the fence post before ultimately choosing his favorite spot: "I hadn't took twenty steps before I seen him. He come down off the fence post there and sat on the tub . . . [l]ike a throne" (*Beloved* 85). Now perched on a tub, Mister is one of the five roosters and at least fifty hens Paul D believes are observing him. However, Paul D fixates on Mister, perhaps because Mister appears to possess aspects of masculinity that Paul D believes are his by entitlement or ought to be the rightful property of his manhood, but at the same time, as Freud might characterize it, Paul D is "dimly aware, in a remote corner of his own being," that they are not.[34] Despite Mister's "bad feet," "he whup(ed) everything in the yard" (*Beloved* 85). Unlike Mister, who can overcome his "bad feet" and triumph over every opponent in the yard to become a "Mister," Paul D cannot untie his hands. In contrast, Mister is described:

> Comb as big as my hand and some kind of red. He sat right there on the tub looking at me. I swear he smiled. My head was full of what I'd seen of Halle a while back. I wasn't even thinking about the bit. Just Halle and before him Sixo, but *when I saw Mister I knew it was me too. Not just them, me too.* One crazy, one sold, one missing, one burnt and me licking iron with my hands crossed behind me. The last of the Sweet Home men. (*Beloved* 85–86, emphasis added)

Staring at Paul D, evil-eyed, Mister, his uncanny double, his large red comb, Mister's phallus, smiles in the face of his torture, flaunting his sovereignty, or so Paul D believes.

Paul D, with his hands tied behind his back and hobbled, begins to envy Mister, who "looked so . . . free. Better than me. Stronger, tougher. Son of a bitch couldn't even get out of his shell by hisself but he was still king and *I was . . .*" (*Beloved* 86, emphasis added). Paul D sees Mister as "better" because he symbolizes masculinist aspects of a normative conception of "freedom" felt increasingly contingent at Sweet Home: autonomy over the body, over movement, over one's sexuality.[35] It would appear to Paul D that plantation slavery has somehow accorded Mister aspects of "life and liberty" as well as manhood withheld from him. Paul D can no longer be appeased by the relative freedoms afforded Sweet Home men, freedoms that are diminishing quickly under Schoolteacher's rule. To Paul D, Mister is "king" (*Beloved* 86). Paul D laments, "Mister was allowed to be and stay what he was. But I wasn't allowed to be and stay what I was" (*Beloved* 86). Here Paul D not only describes a scene of interspecies male rivalry characterized by a melancholic longing for the purported whole of the mythical phallus, but he also identifies an ontological aporia, one that is so foundational that it reverberates across the entire horizon of discourses governing the Subject. "I wasn't allowed to *be* and *stay* what I was," says Paul D (*Beloved* 86, emphasis added).

So, what is the *being* of blackness? Ultimately, (anti)blackness appears to be a matrix: a mold, a womb, a binding substance, a network of intersections, functioning as an encoder or decoder. It is an essential enabling condition for something of, but distinguishable from, its source—and therefore, it performs a kind of natality, performing a generative function rather than serving as an identity.

If (anti)blackness is a matrix, then the normative conception of "the human" and the entire set of arrangements Sweet Home allegorizes have their source in abject blackness. In the process of distinguishing itself from blackness, normative humanity nevertheless bears the shadowy traces of blackness's abject generativity. As "the defined" rather than the "definers," the enslaved's abjection places blackness under the sign of the feminine, the object, matter, and the animal regardless of sex. Paul D hints at the slave's abject generative function when recounting the fact that he was the one who enabled Mister's birth:

> Was me took him [Mister] out the shell, you know. He'd a died if it hadn't been for me. The hen had walked on off with all the hatched peeps trailing behind her. There was this one egg left. Looked like a blank, but then I saw it move so I tapped it open and here come Mister, bad feet and all. (*Beloved* 85)

In describing his presumably indispensable role in Mister's birth, Paul D both identifies with and abjects the hen. Realizing that he has thus far been blind to crucial aspects of slavery's gendered violence, his initial response is to displace those feelings onto Mister, as representative of a loss of the illusion of a proper gendered role. And it is this natality, this irreducible femininity, that Paul D resents as Mister reminds him of the plasticity of his manhood or, more precisely, that such plasticity represents the impossibility for unqualified manhood to take hold. Mister momentarily appears before Paul D as "a blank," yet with respect to Garner and the gendered, symbolic arrangements of slavery more generally, Paul D begins to fear that it is actually *he* who signifies as "a blank" or even that he fails to signify at all (*Beloved* 85). This unsettling encounter marks the beginning, not the completion, of Paul D's meditation on the violent nature of Sweet Home's ordered hierarchy in the renegotiated terms of an identity's un/becoming.

So, if blackness here is a natal function rather than an identity or experience, then what/who are black people? The slash conjoining who and what is not there to offend but to open up the question as widely as needed, which Morrison invites us to do, in order to identify whatever answer arises in the narrative. Paul D states, "Even if you cooked him [Mister] you'd be cooking a rooster named Mister. But wasn't no way I'd ever be Paul D again, living or dead" (*Beloved* 86). Paul D is irrevocably changed by the violent terms of his enslavement, but into what? The statement about the cooking of Mister recalls the cooking of Sixo—a Sweet Home man burned to death by Schoolteacher. However, Paul D is establishing something more specific, a condition or quality that differentiates these two modes of roasting an other, of meat production, to evoke Abdul JanMohamed.[36]

The enslaved are not only conscripted by hierarchical economies of commodification, property, and killing (which would position Paul D and Mister as proxies), but Paul D's heart, mind, soul, and flesh are also conscripted by and must contend with whatever the master effects. *The blackened embodied mind is, therefore, rendered plastic by a demand that includes and exceeds the authorized killing, consumption, and disposability of fleshly existence.* Paul D's body, hobbled with a bit in his mouth, is subject to be transmogrified according to purported registers of "animality" *and* "humanity." In this act of transmogrification—the changing of something into a different form or appearance (especially a fantastic or grotesque one)—the coordinates of the human body are forcefully altered into a different shape or form—bizarre and fantastic: human personality is made "wild" under the weight of blackness's production as seemingly pure potentiality. "But wasn't no way I'd ever be Paul D again, living or dead," he says (*Beloved* 86). Here, Paul D is pointing to the way that the black(ened) body and mind are twisted and contorted in a manner indifferent to structures of form, their integrity, and their limits. So, it is not only a body that is stolen but also the becoming of the slave: the slave's future perfect state of being. The black(ened) are, therefore, defined as plastic: impressionable, stretchable, and misshapen to the point that the mind may not survive—it potentially goes wild. We are well beyond alienation, exploitation, subjection, domestication, and even animalization; we can only describe such transmogrification as a form of engineering. *Slavery's technologies were not the denial of humanity but the plasticization of humanity.*

After all, as Paul D learns, slavery is not "like paid labor" (*Beloved* 165). Economic labor might actually be incidental to enslavement.[37] "Beast of burden" is one of the many forms that Paul D is forced to take but not the sole form; as *Beloved* depicts it, the slave's body is always subjected to something else, to forms of domination that are in excess of forced labor. "The slave" is paradigmatically that which shall be appropriated by emerging demands of the reigning order, as needed, with no regard for the potential irreparable effects of ontological slippage. Arguably, plasticization is the fundamental violation of enslavement: not any one particular form of violence—animalization or objectification, for instance—but rather coerced formlessness as a mode of domination and the *Unheimlich* existence that is its result.[38]

"Plasticity," as concept and thematic, has been differentially articulated and inflected by thinkers as diverse as Hegel, Lévi-Strauss, Darwin, and most recently the French philosopher Catherine Malabou. While my use of the term "plasticity" arose independently of Malabou's unique philosophical elaboration and development of "plasticity" as concept and reading practice in its distinction from and productive tension with Malabou's materialist-realist hermeneutics, my approach is, nevertheless, arguably responsive to what has become Malabou's signature concept.[39] Transformed by but also transformative of Hegelian, Derridean, Heideggerian, and contemporary neuroscientific thought, "plasticity," as taken up by Malabou, refers to a fundamentally immanent mutable, transformable, and indeed plastic understanding of thought, matter, and being whereby the plastic is defined as that which is able to receive and give form and assumes the destruction of form in this giving and receiving. In the words of Malabou:

> Existence reveals itself as plasticity, as the very material of presence, as marble is the material of sculpture. It is capable of receiving any kind of form, but it also has the power to give form to itself. Being the stuff of things, it has the power both to shape and to dissolve a particular facet of individuality. A lifetime always proceeds within the boundaries of a double excess: an excess of reification and an excess of fluidification. When identity tends toward reification, the congealing of form, one can become the victim of rigid frameworks whose temporal solidification produces the appearance of unmalleable substance. Plasticity situates itself in the middle of these two excesses. (*Plasticity* 81)

Malabou's philosophy is an attempt to think the dialectical process anew as a plasticity that governs the continuous or even explosive process of (de)formation of the real.

While an engagement with the fullness of Malabou's conceptualization of plasticity is beyond the scope of this project, for the purposes of this discussion I contend that with respect to Malabou's proposed structuring dualism—dialectics of reification and fluidification—"the slave" is that discursive-material instance where the givenness of structural form is denied or fluidified. What is in flux, in the first instance here, is not immanent metamorphosis or matter's self-regulation but antiblack bonds of ontological effacement or irresolution that produce blackness as a plastic way of being—a relational field whereby what Malabou describes as "the fragile and finite mutability" of being is effaced or fluidified (*Plasticity* 81). In other words, the slave is the discursive-material site that must contend with the demand for seemingly infinite malleability, a demand whose limits are set merely by the tyrannies of will and imagination. What is at stake is the definitive character of form, its determinacy or resistance, which is potentially fluidified by a willed excess of polymorphism and the violent wresting of form from matter.

In contrast to Malabou's approach, the plastic ontology described here is neither the thing-in-itself nor an immanent ontology of the real but representational or paradigmatic: an *a posteriori* virtual model of a dynamic, motile mode of antiblack arrangement. As ontologizing plasticization has been constituent to a mode of unfreedom and the history of antiblackness, plasticity is, therefore, inflected differently than in Malabou's work. My conceptualization of plasticity neither posits that human form can become "any kind of form" nor affirms such a potential; rather, it concerns the way potential can be turned against itself by bonds of power.[40] As Jayna Brown in "Being Cellular: Race, the Inhuman, and the Plasticity of Life" rightfully cautions:

> Remembering how a plasticity of life was imagined and scientifically practiced through race and ability is key as scholars go forward in the project of decentering the human. A trust in scientific knowledge must be interrogated, and the 'we' of new materialist thinking situated historically. Scholars must remember not to assume a universally shared positioning in relation to the material world. (327)[41]

Similarly, I suggest that the desirability and ruse of the "any kind" or optimization is embedded in and conditioned by an antiblack imaginary, in other words by the afterlife of slavery.[42]

Moreover, I am resistant to Malabou's theory of plasticity because of its commitment to Hegelian dialecticism. I remain skeptical of attempts to read both the "interior" of bodies or the organismic field in Hegelian terms and to elevate such thought to the level of an originary anterior principle, or even "systemic law," underpinning the organization of life, sense, and meaning (*Plasticity* 57). Even in its plastic presentation as the principle of fundamental mutability rather than totalizing movement toward identity, the constitutive operations of plasticity remain contradiction and synthesis, or negativity and reconciliation (*New French Philosophy* 87).

Beloved's refiguration of trans-species correspondence, rather than oppositional difference, disrupts the ontologizing plasticization I describe and Man's ability to cast "animal"—human or nonhuman—as the abjected referent in the production of the human Self. *Beloved* makes possible an intervention into an episteme, and not simply its application, by inviting an investigation of the potentially disruptive effects of trans-species correspondence—or more specifically, correspondence between actants—on the reigning order of being, knowing, naming, and its attribution of value. I use the term "correspondence," denoting connection, interplay, and communication, in place of and against the normativity that legislates intersubjectivity in the Hegelian terms of the Self–Other relation. In the Hegelian tradition, Paul D and Mister are neither Self nor Other but reciprocally and constitutively sub-Other. The animal as negative referent rests largely on the presumption that "the animal" lacks perspective or exists in a state of privation.[43] In this tradition, black people are situated as "animal man" (Hegel 177). In other words, the African is animal in the form of a human and is, thus, devoid of the achievement of feeling and Reasoned perspective. Attributes of body and character are presumed to provide evidence of black people's bestial nature. Here, I aim to think the relationship between Paul D and Mister in vocabularies and terms other than those of post- or neo-Hegelian thought, which tends to inform the theorization of "Self/Other" as the plasticization of the black(ened) forestalls definitive position as either Self or Other.

Paul D begins the telling not sure he "can say it. Say it right" (*Beloved* 85). "Definitions belonged to the definers—not the defined," and Paul D's ontology was denoted by an em dash, an emphatic gap between definition and the act of defining (*Beloved* 225). Aphasia rather than dissemblance more precisely characterizes Paul D's speech; rather than trying to spare the reader, Sethe, or the teller embarrassment or shield his interiority, Paul D's speech is paralytic, not unlike his tightly bound hands on that fateful day.[44] Signifying aphasia rather than dissemblance, the ellipses in Paul D's narration of his encounter with Mister—"I was . . ."—and the pregnant pauses in his speech emblematize lexical gaps in language; as Jennifer DeVere Brody describes, "visceral and elusive, enveloping and intangible, material and conceptual" (63). De-composing speech and the page by signifying an excess, the ellipses "labors to contra-dictory ends" (Brody 71). The ellipses testify to the impossibility of a grammar—predicated equally on domination as a particular mode of violence and foreclosure, rather than forgetting, as a particular imposition of erasure—to give voice to the severing of person from personality that Paul D attempts to describe as well as expressively infer elusive contra-dictory possibilities.

Whereas Paul D "was . . ." in his phantasy, Mister was definitively masculine, and he envied him for it. Yet, Mister is in many respects a phantasm: an emblem of the desired but denied pleasures of racial patriarchy. His comb is described by Paul D as "as big as my hand and some kind of red" (*Beloved* 85). Its size and red color makes him simultaneously a demonic apparition and a potent symbol of eroticism, as Mister has access to "at least fifty hens" (*Beloved* 85). Yet, Paul D's envy combines his incipient existential awakening with a myopic, patriarchal, Humanist entitlement (*Beloved* 85).

However, because Paul D's envy does not merely reflect misplaced resentments and patriarchal desires, we should resist moralizing and dismissing his envy outright. As Sianne Ngai points out, "envy" is not "a term describing a *subject* that lacks, but rather the subject's affective *response* to perceived inequality."[45] Moreover, Ngai observes, "[E]nvy lacks cultural recognition as a valid mode of publicly recognizing or responding to social disparities, even though it remains the *only* agnostic emotion defined as having a perceived inequality as its object" (128). Because it has been so thoroughly pathologized as an error of individualized passions, envy, whether pointing to phantasmatic or actual disparities, is undervalued as a political diagnosis.[46] Helmut Schoeck asks, "Why is a subject's enviousness automatically assumed to be unwarranted or petty? Or dismissed as an overreaction, as delusional or even hysterical—a reflection of the ego's inner workings rather than a polemical mode of engagement with the world?" (172). Even the imaginary sources of envy can be a form of oppositional consciousness to what are indeed actual asymmetries. That one so often feels shame as a result of one's envy points to how successfully envy has been pathologized and stripped of its critical value. Envy has been overdetermined as a passion that belongs to the individual psychological failures of the poor and especially the feminine; it is no coincidence that envy is so frequently rendered a symptom of hysteria. Once cast as feminine, representative of a disreputable economic class and the hysterical, envy is devalued for its critical implications (Ngai 126–173).[47]

Mister's freedom to move across the expanse of the plantation, juxtaposed to Paul D's tightly bound hands and forcibly mute tongue, makes Mister an object of Paul D's envy. However, this envy is not simply a passive condition or psychological flaw; it is the means by which he recognizes and responds to an actual relation of power, where antagonism may be an appropriate response. However, instead of directing his antagonistic feelings toward enslavement, he turns them in on the self before misdirecting them at Mister based on a rivalry engendered by white patriarchal slavery. That slavery could inspire such debilitating envy and traumatic desire is astounding given Mister's position as animal in the order of things. Mister's low rank in the Chain of Being makes him a surprising symbol of phallocentric power, but at Sweet Home, Mister would appear to enjoy a measure of freedom withheld from Paul D.

Paul D has been acutely dispossessed of his sexuality by sexual trauma and Garner's control. The slave's captive embodiment often placed his pleasure and his will at odds with one another; throughout the novel Paul D's pleasure does not temporally or spatially coincide with his desire, not only because desire's satiation is ultimately impossible but also because his will is "locked up and chained down," dramatically undercutting his ability to participate in the metonymic chain of desire (*Beloved* 21). The physical and psychical limitations constitutive of his enslavement expropriate and alienate him from his pleasure and desire. Paul D's seemingly intractable investment in a symmetrical, heteromasculine recognition that never arrives suggests normative manhood's racial exclusion. Nevertheless, Paul D's investments in that manhood blind him to the manner in which said manhood establishes itself based on his vulnerability to gendered and sexual violence whether in the context of Garner's control over his sexuality or the routinization of rape on the chain gang.[48] Tragically, he fails to see how such an investment places him in an ironic relation to freedom, obscuring the fullness of being. Not only is patriarchy itself inimical to freedom, but his investment in normative masculinity is also especially pernicious for at least two reasons. First, he does not yet understand that patriarchal desire is counterproductive to a politics of black freedom, in particular, as the pursuit of patriarchy binds black people to a model that can only reinforce black gender as failed or fraudulent. Not only are the discursive-material conditions absent for heteronormative genders and domestic arrangements, but attempting to embody such genders will entrench internecine violence among black people and be seen as reinforcing whiteness as their natural home and point of origin. Second, this purported fraudulence is predicated on the projection of animal lack—human and nonhuman—such that the slave will never experience ontologically level relationality without displacing this epistemic premise.

In short, while Paul D's traumatized envy suggests the highly problematic and ultimately self-defeating consequences of his identification with Garner and the master's conception of manhood, it also underscores a historical and existential truth: "the human" and "the animal" are not mutually exclusive ontological zones but rather positions in a highly unstable and indeterminate relational hierarchy, one that requires blackness as exception, as plasticity, in the establishment and reproduction of its code or representational grammar.[49] Blackness's ontological plasticity and the near formlessness of the violence that secures it do not and cannot rigidly observe strictures of human exceptionalism where blackness is concerned as blackness's plasticity acts as a safeguard against emergent conditions that threaten to disestablish its code. Thus, arbitrary inversions of anthropocentric hierarchy as well as absurd and paradoxical modes of human recognition are essential to the renewal and adaptability of liberal humanism's biopolitical logics.

Beloved facilitates a reconsideration of animal perspective's significance, and from this questioning, we can alter how we define our (human) being, black or otherwise. The scene underlines not only the questionable nature of Euro-patriarchal, anthropocentric constructions of the Self but also "the animal," and by doing so, it undermines "the human" ideal, one that claims that black people are representative of failed humanity, of being animals. In *Beloved*, Morrison narrates Mister and Paul D's traumatized correspondence neither as a sentimental romanticization of nature nor as a phantasy of dominion over nature, which would characterize so much of the Western humanist (literary) tradition, but as a rupture of the governing terms of social life and grammar of representation. Eye to eye with Mister, Paul D is traumatized by his identification with the rooster. The encounter fractures his sense of identity and radically destabilizes his sense of himself. Paul D, bit in mouth and in a traumatized state, cannot lay claim to a position of mastery that is supported by hegemonic orders of knowledge, culture, and being. Paul D has no epistemological, economic, or symbolic capital to do that. All he can do is try to hold on to his mind while carefully formed illusions of the self shatter. Embedded in that encounter is the incontrovertible specification of his existential predicament: he has not determined the meaning of (his) being; the manhood he claims is the property of an other, a Self-effecting phantasy.

The pain of the bit was certainly incalculably horrible, yet it was Paul D's traumatizing introduction into trans-species correspondence and the non-self-identical revelation that emerged in its wake that threatened a total loss of self. If Mister has a perspective authorized by something other than sovereign power, that supersedes sovereign recognition and disrupts its terms via an inexorable affectivity, how would Paul D define his manhood and (human) being? What *Beloved* establishes in this scene is that antiblack racialization exists within a biopolitical sphere that exceeds the master–slave relation and comprises also trans-species relations. However, human–animal binarism is, in turn, shaped by the historical development of slavery. The slave's plasticity neither conforms to a predetermined human exceptionalism nor maintains fidelity to the general principle of human privilege with respect to the animal. The arbitrary powers of the master (order) confound formulations that presume the coherence of humans' symbolic and material power over animals. The slave's status is uncertain and provisional with respect to animals even when slaves such as Paul D desire anthropocentric privilege and prerogatives. The interval effectuated by animal perspective is an interruption of the slaveholder's conception of humanity and manhood, a conception Paul D has inherited. However, what if this painful and traumatizing interruption is more than a personal crisis for Paul D? What if this crisis is the precipice of a conception of being that would rechart the fate of black masculinity, one where humanity would be defined in a manner other than as teleology or hierarchy? What would it mean for black(ened) humanity if (human) being was no longer binaristically or teleologically positioned with respect to "the animal"? On what basis would we then define black humanity as liminal, lacking, or absent?

Mister's gaze arguably haunts Paul D. However, if we limit our analysis to the *figure* of Mister, whereby his gaze is merely a symptom of Paul D's trauma, then we potentially miss that Mister's presence in the novel is also an invitation, an opening to question some of our most basic assumptions about who we are and what defines (human) being, revealing the fuller stakes of the ideal of "the human." Reading Mister deconstructively as a character in the novel calls into question the terms that have defined the antagonistic binarism subtending the human/animal distinction. Mister's gaze is a provocation inviting us to reconsider how we define ourselves especially with regard to the racialized, gendered, and sexual dimensions of our fleshly being. In place of reading Mister's presence as only a symbol of slavery's animalization of black(ened) humanity or as an emblem of the travestied manhood afforded to black men under conditions of a racially hierarchized "universal humanity," we can read Mister's presence as the onto-epistemo-ethical disruption that it is. Paul D sees Mister as a castrating figure, one that mocks him, showing him how low and unmanly he is. But not even Paul D, who is so thoroughly invested in normative codes of manliness, can resist wondering what is behind Mister's eyes: What phenomenological experience and meaning-making exist for the rooster—for this particular rooster?

Paul D's tortured speculation about Mister's smile and his constant return to it raise important questions about epistemology and being. Paul D is shaken by his own conviction that Mister has an authorized perspective and is not simply there mechanically recording but rather "sees." Mister is a spectator of his humiliation neither as human nor as Descartes's automaton but as one whose force and weight is registered as an affectivity that effects, and redirects, Paul D's experience of his gendered sexual being.

Moreover, Morrison's narration avoids the vexed problematics of anthropomorphism. Instead of purporting to transcribe or narrating Mister's mode of address and interiority, she alerts us to it, through Paul D's response to it, but does not represent it nor cast Mister as a transparency. Thus, Mister's mode of address and interiority are able to exist as a disruption of the onto-epistemo-ethical while honoring its opacity.[50] Morrison, therefore, could help us revise conventional interpretations of slave narratives in which the genre simply reinforces what Derrida describes as a presumed hierarchy of humanity over an already-known and unitary "animal" ("The Animal" 402). Morrison's text questions the terms on which we represent and define beasts, human or otherwise.

Paul D's near nullification in signification is what ails him. According to the ideology of slavery, the slave is human/animal/machine and more much more. Conceived as "animal man," reason, sentiment, morality, will, desire, or any of the exalted characteristics that putatively define humanity as not only species membership but also a cultivated achievement are either absent, pathological, criminal, wholly deficient, or wholly excessive. How might Paul D's pained correspondence with Mister the rooster, as fellow actants rather than subjects, problematize the very episteme and grammar of evaluation that animalize both? In that moment, Mister is no longer simply an animal, and if he is not simply an animal, then what does "animal" mean? Could slave–animal correspondence provide an entry point to another horizon of possibility or make way for another code or another mode of relating? Surely a different mode of relating and a different grammar of value is behind (and reflected in) Mister's eyes—one that might even disorder the ocularcentrism that underwrites the hierarchical arrangements of taxonomy and typology.

Instead of offering an elaboration of an alternative epistemological claim regarding the animal that would return us to foundational forms of authority rooted in scientific positivism or Scripture, *Beloved* queries without hastily concocting answers. In *Beloved*, because opacity is not to be overcome or domesticated, alterity remains open; it must be free to remain that which is present but is not fully apprehended. The text does not seek to definitively answer ethical questions; instead, it raises their profile as questions, problematizing regimes of knowledge rather than competing with them.

The text opens up a space for us to ask questions that may not have solutions, or else whose solutions may not be legitimated by hegemonic regimes of knowledge and liberal humanist ethics. The trauma of having a bit forced in his mouth may have been so great that it inhibited Paul D's ability to accept an address from another on any terms other than his traumatized own. Seeing Mister seeing him, Paul D is suspended somewhere between what used to be "the animal," what used to be "the human," and an entirely different arrangement of possibility. Paul D's traumatized identification with Mister is a caesura. No longer "the animal" or "the human," Paul D's plasticity potentially gives way to forms that would not turn "wild." The remainder of Paul D's story concerns his attempt to reconfigure his being, gender, and sexuality, not in pursuit of completion or wholeness but inside of conditions of irreparability and freedom's deferral.

In the text, Mister is not incapacity but instead is capacitated to situate and decenter Paul D's understanding of the Self. Crucially, the effects of correspondence are not predicated on granting permission or prior authorization; rather, to be affected is to expose the prerogatives of the Self as a beguiling fiction. If we consider that Paul D's perspective, his conception of himself, has already been intruded upon by Garner and

Schoolteacher's Eurocentric, patriarchal, and teleological understanding of the Self, where "animal" is the negative referent that defines Euro-humanity as an achievement and signifier of sovereign capacity, then the text's insistence on the situating power of animal perspective undermines one of slavery's most formative epistemic presumptions. But in order to problematize the sovereign "I," Morrison had to put the liberal humanist Self at risk.

Mister's capacity is occluded in the Chain of Being framework found in Douglass's 1845 *Narrative*. But what eludes anthropocentric humanism is not only that Mister has a perspective that does not await recognition but rather precedes and exceeds the limited terms of recognition; what also eludes it is that Mister's perspective requires that we rethink the limitations of our inherited views on "the animal" and examine how our presuppositions undermine thought on human identity. It is not that Morrison's text is suggesting that Mister, a male chicken, and Paul D, a male slave, are existentially the same; contesting the Chain of Being's (and related frameworks') ethico-onto-epistemological grounding does not require a disavowal of phenomenological differences of embodiment or existence. Instead, the text suggests the liberating potential, for Paul D and Mister as well as their avatars, both alive and dead, of a thoroughgoing questioning of the legacy of Enlightenment humanism.

Morrison's text suggests that slavery's violence is not the reduction of humans to the rank of animals but rather the transmogrification of the black(ened)'s being. More accurately, the black(ened)'s fleshly being, *in its humanity*, is turned into a form of infinitely malleable lexical and biological matter, a plastic upon which projects of humanization *and* animalization rest. This work is accomplished by the ontological position of blackness not as a sociological subjectivity or identity but as a matrix for forms of modern subjecthood and subjectivity.

Animal perspective, as an affectivity that effectively dislocated and redirected Paul D's conception of his gendered and sexual being by reminding him of what he knows but represses, may destabilize the prevailing grammar of "the human." Nevertheless, said disruption does not in and of itself topple hierarchical order: to do so would require a transformation of the terms and logics of correspondence and the institution of another mode of being/knowing/feeling. A shift in the valuation of animals, if it is to be transformative and not merely a reallocation of attribution within a racially hierarchical system of value, must be accompanied by a different mode of political social life and grammar of representation. In other words, a revaluation of "animality," or any other singular term ("objecthood," for instance) does not guarantee the revaluation of blackness; as in the example of Douglass, the elevation of the status of animals, especially their humanization, may reciprocally intensify the abjection or diminishment of black(ened) humans/animals due to some purported irrecuperable difference effected by rigged scales and retroactive justification. In short, *Beloved* not only questions the authority of the trope of "the animal" as applied to humans and animals but also offers an approach to the question "What is man?" that ultimately invites the dissolution of its terms.

2

Sense of Things

Empiricism and World in Nalo Hopkinson's Brown Girl in the Ring

The Door of No Return—real and metaphoric as some
places are, mythic to those of us scattered in the Americas
today. To have one's belonging lodged in a metaphor is vo-
luptuous intrigue; to inhabit a trope; to be a kind of fiction.
To live in the Black Diaspora is I think to live as a fiction—a
creation of empires, and also self-creation. It is to be a being living inside and outside of herself. It is to apprehend the
sign one makes yet to be unable to escape it except in radiant moments of ordinariness made like art. To be a fiction
in search of its most resonant metaphor then is even more
intriguing.
—Dionne Brand, *A Map to the Door of No Return*

The persistence of the question of blackness's resemblance to nothingness
reveals an anxiety about declension into a void.[1] Attempts to nullify blackness has a sexuating logic, I argue, one that figures black(ened) femaleness
and/or femininity as baleful, phobogenic fleshly metaphors of the void.
This predicament is signaled in *Brown Girl in the Ring* by Ti-Jeanne's vertigo, where the novel's main character's vertigo functions as a metaphor
for the "onto-epistemological" predicament of black mater, as mater, as
matter under conditions of imperial Western modernity or the conception
of Man within the terms of a taxonomical telos.[2]

To the extent that this ill-fated nothingness would appear to befall
black(ened) manhood and/or masculinity, it is via "the 'female' within"
that as Spillers reminds they will have to "*learn.*" Say "yes" to this power
within instead of attempting to displace or disavow it if there is to be
movement in and against history. Learning is in attending to the ways
they are situated to and by its matrixial weight and force instead of ig-

noring, rivaling, or under-attending to the sexuating logics of "race" or "blackness" or "the black" or "the slave." In "Interstices," Spillers draws our attention to a singularity in slavery by telling us the black female is "the principal point of passage between the human and the nonhuman world. Her issue became the focus of cunning difference—visually, psychologically, ontologically—as the route by which the dominant modes decided the distinction between humanity and 'other.'" (*Black* 155, emphasis in original) The predicament of black(end) female flesh's being that appears in the form of a question is what links Paul D to Sethe and Paul D to Ti-Jeanne and Sethe and Ti-Jeanne to each other.

In *Beloved*, Paul D's predicament occurs inside of the paradoxical and absurd *racial* logics of "manhood." In other words, patriarchal gender hierarchy is not so much precluded by antiblackness as it produces gender differentially along the ontologized lines of race. Thus, masculine entitlements are tentative and conditional and being sexed "male" or gendered "man" indexes a structural vulnerability to a racialized mode of domination whose gendered contours are productive of a manhood not disestablished by blackness but qualified by racial hierarchy among men. Thereby subjection and violation does not "unman" so much as constitute key sites of its differential production. That it is often suggested that violent prostration unmans suggests the casualness of our assumption that vulnerability to violation properly belongs to the female (slave), a mode of defining that, however, callously acknowledges "the 'female' within" yet fails to attend to the relational nature of violation (Spillers, "Mama's" 228). In other words, it is preoccupied by the homosocial relation while disavowing black men's relation to black women and the abjection of black womanhood and their contiguity to the existential predicaments of this problem space.

In the worldmaking Schoolteacher produced by letter and lash, it is Sethe who makes the ink. Schoolteacher liked the way Sethe mixed it although it was Mrs. Garner's recipe—Morrison further undercuts a temptation to read the Garners as benevolent characters. Sethe discloses to Paul D, "I made the ink, Paul D. He couldn't have done it if I didn't make the ink" (Morrison, *Beloved* 320). I take this admission to suggest she is a figure constitutive to Schoolteacher's transubstantiating pedagogy. The ink was made of "cherry gum and oak bark" recalling the chokecherry tree on her back (Morrison, *Beloved* 44). The ink and the notebook *need* Sethe and her avatars for its alchemy of being and world. The image of Mister stalks Paul D, and the smell of the ink stalks Sethe. Sethe overhears her name in one of his many lectures. Schoolteacher instructs his nephew, who was writing in one of his books, to "put her human characteristics on the left; her animal ones on the right. And don't forget to line them up." In doing so, Schoolteacher establishes the measure and metrics of being and world, indeed of being-in-the-world. This is an allegory of world history.

If the approach is to argue that blackness is nothingness and to demystify the machinations that falsely make blackness appear as something, my aim is the opposite: I maintain that blackness, and the abject fleshly figures that bear the weight of *the* world, is a being (something rather than nothing, perhaps even everything), and I aim to reveal and unsettle the machinations that suggest blackness is nothingness. Attentiveness both to the paradoxical gendering of blackness and the fundamental antiblackness of Western imperial gender as identity, presentation, and performative, or more accurately sexuation's antiblack production, reveals the fuller stakes of the debate on blackness and being that can be traced to key figures such as Du Bois, Fanon, and Césaire, among others. Blackness is not imperviousness to a politics of sex-gender but a site of its profound intensification. Black female flesh un/gendered arranges sex-gender and organizes the terms through which transgression and dis/order are perceived and defined. A blackness, in general, that is male and/or masculine by default can only serve to further obscure and obliterate. A comprehensive interrogation of racialized sexuation and gender takes us to the matrix-figure of "the human," black female flesh un/gendered.

As a commodified *object and scientific specimen*, black female flesh un/gendered is an indispensable precept of the linear taxonomical (ontological) thinking that scholars in animal studies, feminist new materialism, object-oriented ontology, and posthumanism are presently trying to displace. This study demonstrates that the icon of "black female body" has been an essential figure in the unfurling of the object, the thing, matter, and the animal in ontological discourses of Western philosophy and science and that there is a fundamental indefiniteness and opacity in projections and productions of blackness that troubles the ontological and its arrangements of world. In this chapter I examine the Heidegge-

rian metaphysical ordering of human, animal, and stone as world relation. In approaching the world-shattering claim of black female flesh un/
gendered's claim to being, I argue this is not an order to reify. This is an
order to destroy.

Subjects of all human orders once knew their physical environment
only in terms prescribed by their modes of subjective understanding and
cultural representational schemas. The revolution of imperial Western
humanism made possible the ongoing displacement of local knowledge
(or culture-specific orders) by a hegemonically (re)produced but no less
epistemically violent Western scientific conception of the cosmos.[3] A
transculturally verifiable image of the earth, or positivist knowledge as
aspirational horizon, has been pursued via a combination of material-
discursive force and a coercive (dis)possession of processes of sense perception and cognition on a global scale.

According to Sylvia Wynter, the novel form has played no small part
in this process. In "Novel and History, Plot and Plantation," Wynter
states, "The novel form and our societies are twin children of the same
parents" (95). That is to say, our contemporary racial, capitalist societies
and the novel form itself are both cause and effect of the market economy, "an emergence which marked a change of such world-historical
magnitude, that we are all, without exception still 'enchanted,' imprisoned, deformed and schizophrenic in its bewitched reality" (95).[4] Drawing on and augmenting György Lukács and Lucien Goldmann's theories
of the novel with Eric Williams's history of Caribbean slavery, Wynter
asserts that the emergence of the novel form is inextricably linked with
the historical developments of the conquest of the Americas and the
plantation societies of the Caribbean as the latter provided the "raw
material" for the extension and dominance of the market economy and
initiated a globally expansive reordering of aesthesis and imaginative
capacities. It is in this context that *Robinson Crusoe*, *Oroonoko*, and *The
Blazing World* in English and *Don Quixote* and *Sinapia* in Spanish, with
their imperial thematics and speculative elements, inaugurate a new literary form—the novel.[5]

In "The Ceremony Must Be Found," Wynter deepens the argument of
"Novel and History, Plot and Plantation" with the claim that not only are
"Literature" and racial capitalism mutually constitutive but also that by
the nineteenth century, literature was increasingly regarded as the "high-

est manifestation of language" and therefore considered to be an essential measure of the capacity for technological progress and scientific reason (46). Wynter argues that with the secularization of knowledge and the constitution of "man" in the post-Cartesian terms of Foucault's "empirico-transcendental doublet," "literature" came to function as the transcendentalized index of degree of "Culture" which a group, understood in the biologized terms of race and national identity, had achieved or could achieve based on their immanent "nature":

> Culture, in the new episteme, now took the place that Reason had played in the Classical episteme, as the index for determining the degree to which a particular group knew 'Self/World' in the metaphysical terms of the current order's 'rational' world view which by extension determined bio-ontological value and vice-versa. ("Ceremony" 46)

The reported presence (or absence) of the novel form coupled with textual and philological assessments of literature's aesthetic value along lines of race and/or national origin were embedded in the techno-scientific conception of progress that organized Man in the Hegelian terms of a teleology.

While this is not to say, as Wynter maintains (citing Valentin Mudimbe), that:

> African world views and African traditional systems of thought are "unthinkable and cannot be made explicit within the framework of their own rationality," the fact remains that "the ways in which they have been evaluated and the means used to explain them relate to theories and methods whose constraints, rules, and systems of operation suppose a non-African epistemological locus," and, in effect, suppose "a silent dependence on a Western episteme."[6]

However, the West itself is an iteratively dependent construction; its renewal depends on the ritual purification of knowledge produced by and expropriated from those indigenous onto-epistemic architects the West casts as benighted and, therefore, bereft of knowledge such that "the Western tradition" emerges as an imperious effect of adaptive processes and multiscalar mutations of matter and meaning.[7] Moreover, the upheavals of political and cultural thought most commonly attributed to the respective events of 1492 and the Copernican Revolution made possible that mutation at the level of sensorium, which led, in turn, to the rise of natural science and its racialized taxonomies and teleological mode of Reason and Universality. In this context, the idea of (national) literature and the novel, in particular, emerge as an imperialist technology, one that is the cause and effect of the (re)ordering of aesthesis and imaginative capacities. Hopkinson's 1996 Locus Award–winning novel *Brown Girl in the Ring*'s subversion and redirection of this order's inaugural literary form ruptures this sense of world.

Editor and speculative fiction writer Nalo Hopkinson draws from Greek myth and diverse Caribbean linguistic conventions, folklore, and spiritual practices in order to create fictive narratives and lifeworlds that often explore, allegorically, the vexed figure of "the black female body" in Western scientific discourse and metaphysics, rewriting the conventions of Western literary genres, in particular science fiction, realism, and fantasy, along the way. As Jessica Langer observes of postcolonial science fiction more generally, "There are levels upon levels of hybridity here: hybridity of form, of genre, of criticism, of concept" (109).[8] The observation that "postcolonial SF" introduces new complexity into literary theory may also require, as Luke Gibbons suggests, new methods of interpretation: "Theory itself needs to be recast from the periphery and acquire hybrid forms, bringing the plurality of voices associated with the creative energies of colonial cultures to bear on criticism itself" (27).[9] *Brown Girl in the Ring* provokes a reconsideration of theory and an experiment in method on at least two counts: (1) it centralizes the role of antiblackness and slavery in the postcolonial, inviting a reworking of prevailing postcolonial paradigms that disaggregate racial slavery from colonialism; and (2) it centrally stages and performs speculation as an intervention *into* and *as* theory, intensifying speculation's performance as theory and theory's performance by blackness.[10]

In a reading of *Brown Girl in the Ring*, I argue that as an enabling condition of an imperial Western humanist conception of *the* world *as such*, the black *mater*(nal) marks the discursive-material trace effects and foreclosures of the dialectics of hegemonic common sense and that the anxieties stimulated by related signifiers, such as the black(ened) maternal image, voice, and lifeworld, allude to the latent symbolic-material capacities of black *mater*, as mater, as matter, to destabilize or even rupture the reigning order of representation that grounds the thought-world relation.[11] In other words, the specter of the black mater—that is, nonrepresentability—haunts the terms and operations tasked with adjudicating the thought-world correlate or the proper perception of *the* world *as such* including hierarchical distinctions between reality and illusion, Reason and its absence, subject and object, science and fiction, speculation and realism, which turn on attendant aporias pertaining to immanence and transcendence.[12]

While the immanence-transcendence dualism has a long religio-philosophical inheritance, Hegel is perhaps the emblematic figure for the racialization of this prevailing dualism, providing raciality with what would become the essential touchstones of its logic: teleology and determinism.[13] At the incipiency of globality as an idea, Hegel argued that racial polarity is both the means and the ends of the universal-historical order, privileging transcendence over immanence and understanding the two principles in the oppositional terms of raciality.[14] Citing reports on African religion that claimed Africans worshipped nature or themselves, Hegel concluded that Africans are governed by the senses and, as a result, are incapable of acquiring adequate distance from nature, a distance that would allow them to oppose nature and the bestial dimensions of the self. For Hegel, opposing both is required for the achievement of Spirit, reason, and self-governance: "Inward freedom" is first attained through opposing one's immediate existence (natural environment) and one's natural existence (animal existence); this opposition then provides the condition of possibility for higher order thinking and self-governance. According to Hegel, one must rise above one's natural/sensuous existence via internal reflection to attain spiritual freedom, and this transcendence then becomes the basis of one's entry into the domain of culture and history. Ultimately, Hegel concluded, "the African" is *eternally* an "animal man" because Africans are trapped *within* immanence, or immediate experience, and are, therefore, unable to achieve transcendence or apprehend transcendent knowledge. In this, Hegel co-constitutes human–animal, nature–culture, and immanence–transcendence dualisms *within* the imaginary of global raciality.[15] The re-emergence of these dualisms, as I argue below, extends into Heidegger's highly influential conceptualizations of human, animal, world.

The final term "world" is what Hopkinson's text will rupture via black mater—the veil between worlds—and in doing so unmoors onto-epistemological claims that attempt to stably binarize *the* human and *the* animal, whiteness and blackness and even void the latter terms.

While it is crucial to demonstrate the perniciousness of Hegel's philosophical premises and vocabulary, given that Hegelianism remains the reigning framework of universalist historicity, it is just as necessary to engage onto-epistemological frameworks that challenge antiblack modes of worlding and epistemic authority. With *Brown Girl in the Ring*, Hopkinson makes it possible to read what is invisible (but nonetheless present) or what is constitutive yet absent at the manifest level of Hegel's text, namely the foreclosure of black *mater*, its latent capacities, and its effects on orbiting discursive-material formations of knowledge and being.[16] The term "nonrepresentability" as applied to the black *mater* in these pages alludes to a central and ever-present unsettling excess that nevertheless eludes representation.

If Wynter is correct that by the nineteenth century, "Literature" was understood as the incarnation of "Culture's" definition—the defining language of a collective impulse whereby poetry, drama, and fiction represented the "self-transcendence" of a people—then, in essence, *Brown Girl in the Ring* is both an effect and a critique of the very narrative processes and metonymic that have produced the Hegelian "myth of history" and (neo)Hegelian "aesthetico-ontology" ("Ceremony"). By turning on its head the (racial) teleology attributed to the novelistic form, Hopkinson reveals the function of myth in the poesis of racial teleology and harnesses the power of myth in a generative critique of antiblackness and its idea(l) of *the* world *as such*. To put it more pointedly, if a Manichean myth of history, reason, and "scientific fact" could produce a world-historical order predicated on the conjunctive abjection of black femaleness and nullification of black maternity, then Hopkinson's novel effectively counters this order by, in turn, performing its intervention at the register of myth. Writing in an allegorical mode, Hopkinson redirects Hegelian tropes of blackness, of "the African" in particular, in a manner that exposes the essential but invisibilized role of black *mater* in Hegel's system as well as the irreducible indistinction of scientific reason and myth.

Hopkinson's text recasts the metonymic of literature and blackness precisely by exploiting the equation of blackness, and in particular Africanness, with irrationality and teratology—by troping the trope of African religion. Though commonly apprehended in the narratives of Western science and philosophy through the terms of objective empirical fact, "the black female body" and her world are, as Hopkinson's text implies, better understood as enabling myths. In order to bring out the slippage between scientific empiricism and myth where black (maternal) female figures are concerned, Hopkinson turns the realist world of science fiction into one where myth and empirical reality not only coexist but also wherein myth is *embedded* in realism. By doing so, the protagonist Ti-Jeanne and the reader are provoked by "second sight" to confront the manner in which myth, in particular myths of history and of scientific fact, structure and obscure the black female figure—and therefore foreclose the comprehension of a perspective and comprehension from a perspective of black mater. In the novel, Ti-Jeanne's vertigo functions as a symptom and a metaphor for this predicament, as a disruption in vision, hearing, and proprioception or the felt corporeal sense of the body *in* space and *in the making of space*.[17] In using myth to counter "myths of history," the novel reveals that myth often shrouds "fact" and claims to objective reality, and for this very reason, myth—or, more precisely, a nonrepresentationalist mode of reason or onto-epistemology—may hold the potential to unsettle hegemonic modes of racist reality and their constituent myths. As such, the novel makes available a transvaluation of myth by investing representation differently and vice versa.[18]

The problem under consideration in these pages is not simply that of the gap between the referent and the sign—the classical problem of representationalism being the misalignment in spacetime of the thing and its representation—but rather that of a sublimity attributed to the signifier "black female" and the de*mater*ialization this attribution engenders.[19] The black *mater*(nal) serves an enabling function that although it can be *thought* of precisely as a condition of possibility—the racially sexuating movement of trace—in its all at-once-ness, it nevertheless exceeds what we can rightfully claim to *know*; it eludes both measurement and conceptualization, and the novel provides a way to read that approaches such *nonrepresentability*.[20]

I follow Hortense Spillers in this chapter by investigating two meanings of "representation" in the discursive practices of imperial Western humanism: representative and re-presentation. The black *mater*(nal) is non-represent-ability because the black *mater*(nal) gestures toward the foreclosed enabling condition of the modern grammar of representation: a space of nonsense or aphasia and correspondingly *without a representative* in the "I and thou" dialectical processes of recognition, value, and decision.[21] Regarding re-presentation, in the grammar described, there are "black (maternal) female" figures (or representations) that appear, but they function at the register of myth rather than indexicality and, therefore, reveal that representation *performs* rather than functions *mimetically* as the notion of "re-presentation" suggests.

In the pages that follow, I investigate both meanings of representation and trace how each works on the other in Hopkinson's text.[22] The approach here diverges from one that evaluates representation exclusively based on a representation's supposed accuracy or inaccuracy: in other words, its ability to re-present the real thing. While the text certainly problematizes calcified representations of black womanhood, the novel does not then reinvest in authenticity or the proper re-presentation of black women but rather performs representation in a speculative mode. The text does not (re)produce black women as an empiricist object or within the terms of her production as a transparent foundational object of science. Rather than functioning within the limited discourse of empirical facts or seeking the authority of scientific method, black female figures in *Brown Girl in the Ring* underscore the manner in which representation *performs* in worlds and in the (un)making of worlds rather than indexes *the* world *as such*.[23] Moving away from science fiction's defining investments in scientific fact, the novel provokes a consideration of the problem of representing a sublime function that necessarily exceeds any claim to knowledge but that can only be approached obliquely in a gesture of representation.[24] Moreover, one could argue that the long-standing black feminist preoccupation with representation, in particular the seemingly inescapable burden of paradoxical modes of visibility/invisibility, does not primarily gesture toward an assessment of the (in)accuracy of representations but rather toward a critique of the performative labor representation does in worlding processes—or the crafting and obliteration of worlds.

Brown Girl in the Ring contemplates the stakes and possibilities of a mode of non-self-identical onto-epistemology to emerge, some other relation of being to knowing to feeling to sensing than what organizes our antiblack present—not based on re-presenting "the voice" or "experience of the oppressed black woman" or simply affirming subaltern knowledge in the form of African religion—but by investigating the conditions of possibility for representation itself. In a reading that insists upon aesthesis and empiricism's inextricability, whether the epistemological context is the seemingly scientific or concerns perceptual knowledge that signifies otherwise, I will argue that the modern grammar of representation takes as its enabling figure (if "figure" is the appropriate concept here; "portal" is probably more accurate) that which is not only unrepresented but, more precisely, nonrepresentable—politicizing both the sense of commonality implied in the notion of common sense and sense perception itself. The regulating terms of the dominant grammar of representation (re)produce black(ened) *mater* as always and already trapped *within* immanence, burdening black (maternal) female figures in particular, but not exclusively, with functioning as a material metaphor that points to what Sylvia Wynter terms "demonic ground" or what is foreclosed from representability: the nonrepresentable beyond dividing what is sensible from what is nullified and precluded from representability ("Miranda" 110). This foreclosed space in discourse and dense material content, black *mater*, organizes and stabilizes the hierarchical arrangement of being. The foreclosure of black *mater* is what brings Heidegger's still highly influential thought concerning human, animal, and stone into legibility. My interest in this chapter concerns how our received conceptions of being hinges on our im/perception of black mater. I argue that Hopkinson's narrative topples Heidegger's hierarchical schema and the perception of world it generates.

Before the World

Martin Heidegger once wrote, regarding the relation between thought and being, "[1.] the stone (material object) is *worldless* [weltlos]; [2.] the animal is *poor in world* [weltrarm]; [3.] man is *world-forming* [weltbildend]" (*Fundametal Concepts* 177). Matthew Calarco comments on the meaning of this passage:

> if by "world" is meant accessibility to other beings, we can say that the animal has world; but if "world" is in some way related to having access to the being of beings, to beings *as such*, then the animal does not have world. (22)

Heidegger's initial analysis of the animal's relation to world is a "having by not having." However, as Calarco notes, in the same volume, Heidegger himself admits that the distinction between man and animal "is difficult to determine" (*Fundametal Concepts* 179).[25] I will show that Heidegger's theses, his attempt to parse this distinction, evokes and extends a racially sexuating and essentially antiblack tradition of thought and demonstrate how it becomes possible to transform the terms that authorize and cohere this "traditional statement" via the thought of Édouard Glissant and Sylvia Wynter and by way of Hopkinson's *Brown Girl in the Ring* in particular.

Despite admitting the difficulty in the distinction, Heidegger bypasses the need for a more exacting determination of the essence of animality and instead seeks to ensure that his guiding theses not be interpreted as hierarchical value judgment, advocacy of a continuist scale of being, or a misplaced effort to evaluate the animal based on a comparison to man or by the measure of man. Rather, he hoped that his thesis "the animal is poor in world" be understood as in accordance with the animal's own terms. The conclusion that the animal does and does not have world, Heidegger attempts to clarify by way of empirical examples drawn from the work of biologist Jakob von Uexküll, in particular, on insects. However, Heidegger ultimately rejects the conclusions of Uexküll and other ethologists because, in Heidegger's view, they grant *too much* world to those under the sign of what he termed *the* animal. Rather than follow their conclusions, Heidegger instead extrapolates a theory that the animal's relation to world is, in essence, captivation or fixation. Defined by instinct rather than cognition, while the animal enacts responsivity to external stimuli, there is no gap between an animal's activities and itself, only immediacy. The animal's instinctual behavior toward itself and the world, its specific capacity for being and essence thus "becomes and remains *proper to itself*—and does so *without* any so-called *self-consciousness* or any *reflection* at all, without any relating back to itself" (Heidegger, *Fundamental Concepts* 233).[26]

Despite such decisive claims, Heidegger occasionally equivocates, noting it is "only from the human perspective that the animal is poor with respect to world, yet animal being in itself is not a deprivation of world" (*Fundamental Concepts* 270–271). However, the animal's mode of being and relationality is voided at nearly the moment—within paragraphs—that Heidegger himself acknowledges a failure to understand the animal's mode of relationality on the animal's own terms. Setting his own uncertainty aside, Heidegger declares that "in accordance with its essence," "the animal behaves within an environment [Umwelt] but never within the world [Welt]" (*Fundamental Concepts* 238–239). The possibility (however limited) of world is withdrawn all together in the following:

> [I]n distinction from what we said earlier we must now say that it is precisely because the animal in its captivation has a relation to everything encountered within its disinhibiting ring that it precisely does *not* stand alongside man and precisely has *no* world. (*Fundamental Concepts* 269)

Calarco has described Heidegger's efforts as a "dead end" because Heidegger is forced to admit that his efforts reveal not the essence of animality and its relation to world but establish the terms of an "anthropocentric" comparison, where "the human functions as the measure of animal life" (Calarco 28).[27]

In a later work, *What Is Called Thinking*, Heidegger writes, "Apes, for example, have organs that can grasp, but they have no hand" (16).[28] What Heidegger is suggesting with this enigmatic claim is that the hand synecdochically figures a mode of being determined not by biological or utilitarian function—"does not let itself be determined as a bodily organ of gripping" (Derrida, "Geschlecht" 172)—but rather one that can serve as "a figure for thought" (Wolfe, *Animal Rites* 63). The particular mode of thought uniquely in possession of the *as such*, and the *as such*, for Heidegger, is the synecdoche for the capacity for worlding. Derrida will argue in Heidegger's thought there is an "abyss," between the animal and the human, between the grasping or "prehension" associated with the "prehensile" organs of the ape (Derrida, *Of Spirit* 11) and the hand of man, which "is far from these in an infinite way (*unendlich*) through the abyss of its being. This abyss is speech and thought" (Derrida, "Geschlecht" 174). "Only a being who can speak, that is, think," Heidegger writes, "can have the hand and be handy (*in der Handhabung*) in achieving the works of handicraft" (quoted in "Geschlecht" 174). Like *the* animal, Heidegger's *the* hand here is metaphysical. The empirical hand masking and acting as an alibi for metaphysics: "*The* hand of *the* man, of man *as such*, . . ." (Derrida, "Geschlecht" 183). In the Heideggerian synecdochic chain I describe "thought of the hand, but just as well the hand of thought, of a thought of the human" is in essence a thesis that rests, Derrida argues, on the shaky ground of an assured opposition of *giving* and *taking* (Derrida, "Geschlecht" 168):

> [M]an's hand *gives and gives itself*, *gives* and *is given*, like thought or like what gives itself to be thought and what we do not yet think, whereas the organ of the ape or of man as a simple animal, indeed as an *animal ratio-nale*, can only *take hold of, grasp, lay hands on the thing*. The organ can *only* take hold of and manipulate the thing insofar as, in any case, it does not have to deal with the thing *as such*, does not let the thing be what it is in essence. The organ has no access to the essence of being [*étant*] *as such*. (Derrida, "Geschlecht" 175)

Ironically, in thought that certainly aimed to be nonmetaphysical and withdraw *the* human from biological determinism, "this traditional statement" reinstalls "organico-biologic programs" and metaphysics at the center of its discourse (Derrida, "Geschlecht" 173–174). Heidegger's "animal" relies on no zoological knowledge but rather presupposes its object—a unitary object: *the* animal, for which the ape is mere example (Derrida, "Geschlecht" 173). "Nonknowing raised to a tranquil knowing" inscribed "not *some* difference but an absolute oppositional limit" (Derrida, "Geschlecht" 173–174).

As Cary Wolfe has noted, Derrida bridles against the reductiveness of the genre of the thesis in principle: the form of this thesis dogmatically presupposes "that there is one thing, one domain, one homogenous type of entity, which is called animality *in general*, for which any example will do the job" (Derrida, *Of Spirit* 57). Also noted by Wolfe, in Derrida's "Eating Well" and "The Animal That Therefore I Am (More to Follow)," the philosopher maintains "the Word, *logos*, does violence to the heterogeneous multiplicity of the living world by reconstituting it under the sign of identity, the *as such* and *in general*—not 'animals' but 'the animal'" (*Animal Rites* 66).

Ralph Acampora—after noting that most *domesticated* animals do, in fact, in the context of shared forms of life with humans, treat *x*-as-*x* whereby *x*'s cultural signification is understood and honored (certain surfaces are for sleeping, certain containers are for drinking vessels, etc.)—suggests sensitivity to metaphoric "*as*-ness" (even without the ontologic "*such*-ness") suffices to mark somebody as being-in-a-world—and some/many other (nonhuman) animals are thus attuned (Acampora 28, 29). Moreover, Acampora, stressing the importance of socialization and acculturation to *any concept* of world, elaborates further:

> [T]reating *x*-as-*x* can mean thinking through *x*'s identity and/or reflecting on *x*'s place as a being among other beings (or against the background of Being at large). But this would be too narrow a delimitation and tends in the direction of excluding worldhood from all but those whom we might call ontologicians. It seems to me that Heidegger here is captivated by the philosopher's prejudice of insisting that another being must approach the world metaphysically or ontologically in order to exist in it (at all). (29)

Similarly, Kelly Oliver concludes:

> Given Heidegger's analysis, we might imagine that in a sense, animals are by definition, creatures without a conception of world; that humans are, by definition, creatures with a conception of the world; and that these definitions refer more to how we use the terms *animal, human,* and *world*—to our concepts and language—than they do to the creatures themselves. (198)

Derrida extends the stakes of these criticisms of Heideggerian conceptualizations of *animal, human,* and *world* by arguing that in the process of figuring capacity for worlding "man," Heidegger links said capacity to a certain nationalist myth of language, and in doing so, he participates in "what deeply binds a certain humanism, a certain nationalism, and a certain Europocentric universalism" (Derrida, "Geschlecht" 168). Heidegger's thesis regarding the hand relied not on zoological knowledge but made recourse to the idea of *Geschlecht*—a German word that can be translated "sex, race, species, genus, gender, stock, family, generation or genealogy, community" (Derrida, "Geschlecht" 162). As Derrida notes, in the work of Heidegger's predecessor and founding figure of German Idealism Johann Gottlieb Fichte, the word pulled in competing directions; on the one hand, it held nationalist connotations, and on the other hand, Fichte's *geschlecht* opened onto a supposed but still to be constituted cosmopolitan "non-natural but spiritual" "we" that included in its humanism all that aspired to "spiritual freedom engaged toward the infinity of its progress" (Derrida, "Geschlecht" 163). Fichte is a figure that links Heidegger to two of the most influential philosophers of *(self)consciousness* and *world*, Immanuel Kant and Georg Hegel. Fichte is an influential theorist of self-consciousness and self-awareness, contributing the thesis-antithesis-synthesis structure to the Hegelian tradition.

In attempting to distinguish the *geschlecht* of man and *the* animal, Heidegger recalled, indirectly, a metaphysics predicated on the idea of a teleological essence in "humankind," "human species," "human race." How could a supposed difference in essence among man, animal, and stone stave off the assumption of a difference in degree and telos, as Heidegger had hoped, when difference is cast in terms of *relative* poverty? If as Heidegger suggests, "The world is always a *spiritual* world"—world is of spirit and therefore metaphysical—then his theses would appear to suggest relative degrees of spirit across his key terms (Heidegger, *Introduction* 34). Or as Derrida would put it, regarding the animal's purported privation of "world," "This is a thesis which, in its median character, as clearly emphasized by Heidegger (the animal between the stone and man), remains fundamentally teleological and traditional, not to say dialectical" (Derrida, *Of Spirit* 57). The two competing logics—degree versus kind—merge with the thesis that animal essence is a poverty. This confluence of competing values—lack and alterity—as we saw in the previous chapter and further elaborated in this one, is the logic of *racially hierarchizing* humanity, which crystalized in Hegel's conception of the African as "animal man" and as I will argue presages that of Heidegger.

We might press Derrida's critique further by inquiring into the reciprocal production of blackness and animality in Heidegger's thought, in particular, which can be gleaned from his defense of the pre-Socratics in *Introduction to Metaphysics*. Defending the "beginning of Western philosophy" from unflattering characterization—namely that of primitivity—he sought to clarify that the pre-Socratics were not merely "high-grade Hottentots" but that the origins of *the* Western tradition were great even in their putative "beginning." Remarking, according to some ill-informed critics:

In principle, the Greeks then become a kind of highgrade Hottentots, and compared to them modern science represents infinite progress. Quite apart from the particular *nonsense* that is involved in this conception of the beginning of Western philosophy as primitive, it must be said: this interpretation forgets that the subject here is philosophy, something that belongs among the few great things of man. Whatever is great, however, can only have had a great beginning. (Heidegger, *Introduction* 12, emphasis added)

Here the "Hottentot" is a trope, an antipodean figure, cast as Dasein's negative and oppositional term, signifying the limit case of the intentional attitude or comportment, of thinking *as such*, and the dimming of world.[29] By recalling this quote, I not only aim to expose the linkages of blackness and animality in Heidegger's thought, but I also suggest that there is perhaps an unmarked Hegelianism, a teleological myth of world history informing Heidegger's concept of the Hottentot here—indeed, the term "Daesin" was used most notably by Hegel, to refer to human existence or presence, prior to it becoming Heidegger's signature concept. We might well discern the antecedent of a Heideggerian "captivation" and world privation in Hegel's infamous summation of the African's lack in the following quote:

At this point we leave Africa, not to mention it again. For it is no historical part of the World; it has no movement or development to exhibit . . . What we properly understand by Africa, is the Unhistorical, Undeveloped Spirit, still involved in the conditions of mere nature, and which had to be presented here only as on the threshold of the World's History. (99)

Could Hegel's *the* African be the *metaphysical* antecedent of Heidegger's *the* animal? And what of the African's permanent and unchangeable stonelike state?[30] As in the case of Heidegger's "the animal," in Hegel's thought there is a familiar equivocation between lack and alterity: Is the African fundamentally of a different order of being or merely lacking? And if lacking an essential quality does that then make "the African" than of a different order of existence?[31] The figure of the African, as one lacking in self-consciousness and fixated in and by nature (or environment), was introduced in the previous section of this chapter and extended into the subsequent section.

We might press Derrida's critique further still, with the help of Glissant, by asking: How might Heidegger's rejection of mere grasping, in the name of worlding, relate to a "certain humanism, a certain nationalism, and a certain Europocentric universalism" that precisely relies on a myth of conceptual grasping, of *the* world *as such*? Glissant contends that when considering the development of Western imperialism—from "discovery" and territorial expansion to anthropological ethnography—the verb *to understand* in the sense of "'to grasp' [*comprendre*] has a fearsome repressive meaning" (26). Imperial "Myth," Glissant argues, approaches worlding via a "grasping" that demands "Transparency" and thus interdicts opacity—that which cannot be reduced and mastered by myth's system of intelligibility or is withdrawn from conceptualization itself—obscuring, potentially even forestalling, the movement of what he terms "Relation." The verb "to grasp," Glissant remarks, "contains the movement of hands that grab their surroundings and bring them back to themselves, a gesture of enclosure if not appropriation" (192). Contra "this version of understanding," Glissant declares, "Let our understanding prefer the gesture of giving-on-and-with that opens finally on totality" (192). Relation for Glissant is "an open totality evolving upon itself" (192). Clarifying further:

> That means that, thought of in this manner, it is the principle of unity that we subtract from this idea. In Relation the whole is not the finality of its parts: for multiplicity in totality is totally diversity. Let us say this again, opaquely the idea of totality alone is an obstacle to totality. (192)

Totality, here, should be distinguished from the idea of *the* world. Glissant's totality is speculative theory that resists the lure of the essentialisms I have just described. "Totality," in Glissant's work, is the poetic force of the putative referent of *the* world, obliquely—indeed, opaquely—gesturing toward what cannot be grasped or reduced to essence. Yet a certain idea of totality—*the* world *as such*—that presupposes graspability and preconceives totality in the mode of transparency is precisely what Glissant hopes to keep at a critical distance. Totality, veiled rather than graspable, *the* world *as such* proves to be a beguiling myth.[32]

I concur with Derrida's point regarding the confounding polyse-
mic valences of *geschlecht* in Heidegger's thought, as well as Derrida's
contention that Heidegger's evocation of *geschlecht* recalls a German
idealist myth of national literature: "ineradicable nature" and "national
imagination" (Fichte cited in Derrida, "Geschlecht" 165), and in light
of Sylvia Wynter's argument about the roles of the novel and speculative fiction in globality as concept and imperial practice, I argue that
a certain myth of essence and history is inaugurated and popularized
in philology and with the advent of the novelistic form itself, whereby
speculative fiction emerges as a privileged site for interrogating this
problematic.[33] Namely, the entanglement of literary form and genre
with an imperialist and racially sexuating mode of grasping, I suggest,
draws black mater into the orbit of *the* animal and animality into the
domain of *the* black.

In what follows, I argue that Nalo Hopkinson's 1998 speculative
novel *Brown Girl in the Ring* performs a critique that shatters the
globally hegemonic metaphysics of *the* world—indeed, of a world
relation—that transversally voids *the* black and *the* animal and their
respective worlding(s). I am interested in tracing how an injunction
against an avowed commonality *in* being, or humanity, by an ontologizing conception of racialized gender paradoxically provides access
to an alternative—a realm of reality (commonly disqualified and discredited by a racially exclusionary common sense), a sense-ability that
"operates or becomes manifest as an ability *in* the realities from which
this other realm or mode is excluded" (Scott, *Extravagant*, 175). The
mind-body-social nexus in *Brown Girl in the Ring* indicates a reality
discredited (a black[ened] reality) at once the experience of the carceral and the apprehension of a radically "redistributed sensorium."[34]
I argue that black mater holds the potential to transform the terms of
reality and feeling, therefore rewriting the conditions of possibility of
the empirical. If, as Darieck Scott instructs, blackness is "an embodied
metaphor, the lived representation that grants access to unlived possibilities," I seek to limn what vertiginous states introduce as possibility
in the narrative. I ask, if an essential feature of your existence is that
the norm is not able to take hold, what mode of being becomes available, and what mode might you invent (120)?

The Veil of the World

But can we escape becoming dizzy? And who can affirm that
vertigo does not haunt the whole of existence?
—Frantz Fanon, *The Wretched of the Earth*

They say I am 730, say I spaz out. FB is ill, she'll wild out.
Can y'all feel my pain? I can't let it slide. How could I smile
when I'm hurtin' so bad inside?
—Foxy Brown, "730"

[I] comforted myself that my sense of alienation and now-
heightened visibility were not inherent to my blackness and
my femaleness, but an uncomfortable atmospheric condition afflicting everyone. But at the gyroscopic heart of me,
there was and is a deep realization that I have never left the
planet earth. I know that my feelings of exaggerated visibility and invisibility are the product of my not being part of
the larger cultural picture. I know too that the larger cultural
picture is an illusion, albeit a powerful one, concocted from
a perceptual consensus to which I am not a party; and that
while these perceptions operate as dictators of truth, they
are after all merely perceptions.
—Patricia J. Williams, *The Alchemy of Race and Rights*

Hopkinson's story focuses on three generations of black Caribbean-
Canadian "seer women" and their struggle for physical and psychic
survival in the isolated, walled-off urban center of Toronto known as
"The Burn." The names of the women, Mami-Gros Jeanne, her daughter Mi-Jeannne, and granddaughter Ti-Jeanne, allude to the Derek
Walcott play *Ti-Jean and His Brothers*, which explores the epistemological problems wrought by slavery and colonialism, particularly the
loss of indigenous knowledge and the gap between colonial knowledge and its applicability in the lifeworld of a colonized person. In an
exploration of similar questions, *Brown Girl in the Ring* uses tropes of
"African religion," in particular spirit possession and aspects of "double-
consciousness" such as burdened "gift" and "second sight," to explore the

modern grammar of representation and its economies of value. In effort to limit my analysis to aspects of the text that most serve to elucidate its implications for the theorization of world, onto-epistemology, and representationalism at stake in my analysis, my reading focuses primarily on the scene when Ti-Jeanne initially experiences visions while on the streets of The Burn.

"The Burn" is the cordoned off, economically devastated, urban core of near-future Toronto. As gleaned from a series of newspaper headlines the narrative provides, colonialist and environmentally racist governmental policies underlie the city's collapse, one crises sets off another: the province of Ontario refuses to settle an ongoing land-rights dispute brought by First Nations Temagami peoples, then an international trade embargo, the Canadian government funding cuts to the province leading to unemployment, failures of mass transit, deadly rioting, and eventually roadblocks at the borders of the city (Stein 216). In the aftermath of the city's political, social, and economic collapse and the large-scale riot that emerged in its wake, with the city aflame and experiencing an extreme case of "white flight," those with the means and mobility to flee to the suburban perimeter did so (Wood 317). Such a state of affairs might be best read allegorically, a fictional underscoring of an insight of Rinaldo Walcott:

> A critical engagement with coloniality therefore demands that we see the mutual imprint and the overlap between the 'reservation,' the 'housing project,' and 'the priority neighborhood' (the latter is the name given to archipelagoes of poverty in Toronto), the project of deportation and the dispossession of people beyond Canada's borders. In each case the very terminology delineates a specific if limited space, and an out-of-place-ness for those marked as abject and waste within the boundaries of the nation-state of Canada. (Walcott 100)

Abandoned by public governance systems and commerce and economically at the mercy of centrifugal forces, inner-city Toronto has developed an alternative, informal economy based on interdependence and care, one that is nevertheless beset by a ruthless drug lord named Rudy. The premier of Toronto, suffering from heart failure, had recently become aware of something the public had not: the sudden emergence of a zoonotic virus is making it untenable to continue the porcine organ donor program. Rather than publicly admit the failure of the porcine program, the premier exploits the discourse of animal rights and promotes a volunteer program based on "people helping people" all while representatives of the ailing leader hire Rudy and his "posse" to procure a human heart from someone in The Burn by deadly means. Ever eager to capitalize on the city's decline, posse members include Crapaud, Crack Monkey, Jay, and Tony, all characters introduced on the streets of The Burn at the start of Ti-Jeanne's epic quest to defeat Rudy and his posse, but unfortunately, she is not able to do so before they claim her grandmother's heart for the premier.

No longer under the cover of rights and protection, and in an attempt to expropriate what resources remain in The Burn, such exploitative practices reveal the racialized and colonial dynamics that undergird "volunteer" donor programs. As Nancy Scheper-Hughes notes in *Commodifying Bodies*:

> [C]ommercialized transplant medicine has allowed global society to be divided into decidedly unequal populations—organ givers and organ receivers. The former are an invisible and discredited collection of anonymous suppliers of spare parts; the later are cherished patients, treated as moral subjects and as suffering individuals. Their names and their biographies and medical histories are known, and their proprietary rights over the bodies and body parts of the poor, living and dead, are virtually unquestioned. (4)

Capitalism, as Cedric Robinson teaches us, is always racial capitalism. Despite a preoccupation with concerns of the organismic body in the field of capital, this orientation to the problem of capitalist mechanization of the body is one the new materialists have failed to attend to and is the subject of the final chapter.

The analysis concerning race and animality is not as it might appear. This is a chapter exploring neither the racial politics of zoonosis nor a mode of capitalism that places under erasure distinctions among black(ened) humanity, land, and animality via an economy predicated on the racialized expropriation of life and mereology of extraction, subjects aptly handled by thinkers such as Nicole Shukin, Neel Ahuja, and

Rachel Stein; nor is it even an examination of how the ideal of animal rights and the humane becomes a pretext for the ontological dislocation of black(ened) people, a topic taken up in the previous chapters. Rather, it is about how the idea of *the* world *as such* makes such economies of value imaginable and hegemonic at the register of assumptive logic.[35] Expropriations of the flesh are as determined by metaphysics, or the idea of *the* world *as such*, as by capitalist logics, in truth, the assumption of world privation facilitates the deadly mechanization of life at the center of the text. Thus, Ti-Jeanne must open herself to supernatural powers and counterintuitive truths that exceed her sense of self and reality as well as challenge the coordinates of the given world in order to confront the tragic mystery surrounding her mother and grandmother.

When the reader is first introduced to the narrative's protagonist, Ti-Jeanne, we learn that "Ti-Jeanne could see with more than sight" (Hopkinson 9). Her spectacular visions of the premature deaths of others in The Burn threatened a total loss of self and initiated fear "like ice in her chest" (Hopkinson 19), followed by feelings of vertigo. Ti-Jeanne's burdened "gift" of "second sight" opens up the question of reality for Ti-Jeanne. "Ti-Jeanne hated the visions" (Hopkinson 9) not only because of their at times frightening content and overwhelming immediacy but also because no one else could see them. They threatened her sense of self and reality.

But Ti-Jeanne was not alone in experiencing visions. Other women in her family had the "second sight." As the story unfolds Ti-Jeanne learns "second sight" is a "gift," an ability inside of debility, and she must invent a way of being and knowing "world" that approaches this constitutive paradox.[36] Departing from Du Bois's highly influential formulation of double-consciousness, Ti-Jeanne's "second sight" is not deployed by Hopkinson in pursuit of recognition within the terms of mimetic reality. Rather the female subject of double-consciousness in Hopkinson's text explores the limits of representability itself, ultimately exchanging a bid for recognition for an exploration of the potential enabling powers of myth. The prelude to the narrative's first full account of Ti-Jeanne's prophetic yet terrifying vision is a scene of sexual street harassment immediately followed by a frightening encounter with her mother (Ti-Jeanne only knows her as "blind Crazy Betty") on the streets of The Burn while running a simple errand for her grandmother, Mami-Gros Jeanne.

While making her way through the streets of The Burn, Ti-Jeanne caught a glimpse of Rudy's posse, men she was accustomed to avoiding. Tony, a man we will come to learn is the father of the baby she held in her arms, was among them. Pulse thumping, gaze averted while edging past the men, Ti-Jeanne tried to appear very interested in picking her way through the garbage-strewn sidewalk (Hopkinson 16). A voice called out to her: "'Hey, sister, is time we get to know one another better, you know!' . . . 'Ah say,' Crack [Monkey] hollered, 'is time I get to know you better!' The men's mocking laughter spurred Ti-Jeanne to move faster. She hugged Baby closer to her and scowled at Crack" (Hopkinson 16). As a vision manifests, Ti-Jeanne is dislocated in spacetime: simultaneously taken out of herself and pulled deeper into herself, her voice, vision, and thoughts recede as an emergent sense takes over.

Ti-Jeanne, now immersed in "second sight," abruptly froze, "not trusting her eyes any longer to pick reality from fantasy" (16). She saw before her Crack Monkey, Rudy's "right-hand man" (Hopkinson 16), "*a wasted thing, falling to the ground and gasping his last*" (Hopkinson 16). For one of the other men, Crapaud: "*Metabolic acidosis. Cirrhosis of the liver. Rum*" (Hopkinson 16). The third man, Jay, killed "*running to the aid of his sweetheart*" (Hopkinson 16), a trans sex worker; her would-be attacker, a john with knife in hand, would eventually alter course with the gutting of Jay. Interspersed with folksongs and italicized, the shift in tense and references to rhymes and riddles inject the narrative's realism with the mythical quality of time suspended or a dreamlike or magical state.

Ti-Jeanne could not see her own death; that of her child, Baby; or that of her on-again, off-again boyfriend, Tony. She could not see the deaths of anyone close to her; she also could not see "blind Crazy Betty" until the woman was right in front of her, her mother's sightless eyes turned toward Baby exclaiming, "That is my child! He's mine!" (Hopkinson 17). Announcing the ambivalence that accompanied Baby's birth stemming from constrained circumstances, irreducible to the sum of socioeconomic factors, for a woman still young in age, Crazy Betty continued, "What you doin' with my baby? You can't make a child pretty so! You did never want he! Give he to me!" (Hopkinson 17).[37] The resonant quality of the woman's words sprang from the circumstance that, unbeknownst to Ti-Jeanne, the woman was in fact her mother, Mi-Jeanne, and like Ti-Jeanne she was a "seer woman." The "gift" of "second sight" ran along the maternal line, and the woman Ti-Jeanne had known as "blind Crazy Betty," or simply as a "bag lady," had not benefited from having her gift cultivated and supported by relations—psychic, spiritual, social—that would sustain her.

For most of the narrative, Mi-Jeanne's identity as Ti-Jeanne's mother is concealed by her ominous image as "blind Crazy Betty." Although Mi-Jeanne is presumed missing, as "blind Crazy Betty" she recursively appears in the narrative as the specter of madness and incommunicability. The mystery surrounding Mi-Jeanne's identity and the revelation of maternity is primarily relayed through the fragmented perspective and memory of others, especially that of Mami Gros-Jeanne and Ti-Jeanne. The precipitating events that led to Mi-Jeanne's disappearance are relayed through flashback and the exchange of traumatic memories between Ti-Jeanne and Mami. Like Ti-Jeanne, Mi-Jeanne was a seer, and like Ti-Jeanne, she refused Mami Gros-Jeanne's help but for different reasons. Mi-Jeanne's psyche was overcome by waking nightmares that presaged the violent traumatic events of the riots. By the time Mami realized her daughter was having visions, the enormity and intensity of the visions had already overwhelmed Mi-Jeanne, "[a]nd the powers of the visions had driven her mad" (48). Mami hoped that through the cultivation of Ti-Jeanne's "gift" of "second sight," Ti-Jeanne might be spared from what happened to her mother. But for that to be possible, Ti-Jeanne would have to reimagine the nature of her "second sight" and the coordinates of the given world. For the time being, Ti-Jeanne rebuffed: "What I was to tell you, Mami? I don't want to know nothing 'bout obeah, oui" (Hopkinson 47). Mami replied, hoping to clarify both the significance of Ti-Jeanne's visions and convey the urgency of Ti-Jeanne's predicament, "Girl child, you know better than to call it obeah. . . . Is a good thing, not a evil thing. But child, if you don't learn how to use it, it will use you, just like it take your mother" (Hopkinson 47). Now afraid, Ti-Jeanne could do nothing but stare at Mami (Hopkinson 47). In hoping that "if she ignored the second sight, it would just go way" and dismissing her grandmother's teachings as "old time nonsense," Ti-Jeanne clung to an empirical reality ordered by a teleological mode of Reason and Universality (Hopkinson 20, 37). But ignoring the visions was not diminishing their unsettling power. Ti-Jeanne worried: "Mami, this ain't the first time I see something like this. I going mad like Mummy, ain't it?" (Hopkinson

46). In moments when Ti-Jeanne suspected her own madness, memo-ries of her mother and of the frightening encounter with "blind Crazy Betty" alternated in her mind without Ti-Jeanne ever realizing that her mother and "blind Crazy Betty" were the same person.

In accordance with the modern grammar of representation, in Ti-Jeanne's memory, her mother inhabits a space in and as madness, non-sense, and chaos. In other words, the black maternal figure functions as a signifier that apportions and delimits Reason and the Universal.[38] In the aftermath of the riots, her mother became nearly synonymous with the disorienting enormity and chaotic origin of The Burn. For Ti-Jeanne, the riots "were mixed up in her mind with memories of her mother lying helpless in her bed, besieged with images of the worst of the rioting *before* it happened" (Hopkinson 48). Ti-Jeanne remembered that her mother had a vision back when the riots were just starting. In the days that fol-lowed, her mother appeared to go mad, "complaining that she was hear-ing voices in her head" (Hopkinson 20). Her mother disappeared soon after the voices had started, "run away into the craziness that Toronto had become. She had never come back" (Hopkinson 20).[39] Ti-Jeanne wor-ried, "Maybe it is hereditary?" This was an anxiety that overdetermined the apprehension of both her mother and grandmother as well as ob-scured the power and force of the abilities constitutive to the disorienting debility of her own "second sight" (Hopkinson 20).

When the visions started, Ti-Jeanne attempted, by the forces of Will and Reason, to dis-identify with that which would potentially sustain her and by implication elude the matrilineal mark of foreclosure as-cribed to black mater and related, racially abject worldmaking practices. Having already dismissed what Mami was trying to teach her as "old time nonsense," Ti-Jeanne initially refused to accept the disruption of common reality that her sense-ability both performed and symbolized, even as hegemonic reality attempted to foreclose the perception of her reality and of a shared being *in* a reality such as hers—a reality that nec-essarily could not be held in common; in truth, its foreclosure inaugu-rated the common sense (Hopkinson 37). In the case of her mother, a sense-ability without a spiritual (initiation and ritual practice) and social locus, Mi-Jeanne's psyche was in ruins. Her reality and the capacities her sense-ability roused were foreclosed by a common sense that ap-prehended her as monstrosity. Mythologized as "blind Crazy Betty," she became an anonymous feature of the generalized image of The Burn as antipodean dilapidation. When the black female (maternal) figure appears, if she appears, she appears as the work and revelation of myth.

There were many names for what Mami, Mi-Jeanne, and Ti-Jeanne were: "myalist, bush doctor, iyalorisha, curandera, four-eye" (Hopkinson 218); the supposed incontrovertible "truth" of black worldmaking as paradigmatic teratology and "nonsense" has the racialized exchange and circulation of the derisive term "obeah" (and related markers such as "mumbo-jumbo") as an essential exponent. The term "obeah" (and the lifeworld it is purported to represent) is a recurring flashpoint for characters in the novel: a dramatic contest over the meaning of "obeah" punctuates the narrative's arc, making it arguably the central conflict of the novel, one that emblematizes the unsettled convergence of the racialization of epistemic authority and sense perception with that of the time and place of Africa in New World blackness under conditions of imperial Western modernity. While Ti-Jeanne is undoubtedly the narrative's central consciousness, the recursive shifts in narrative perspective to that of Mami Gros-Jeanne—as a griot figure, healer, symbol of communalism—and the nonlinear work of time and memory function to place pressure on or introduce irony into Ti-Jeanne's perspective. Exploring the caesura between the grandmother's voice and the vital knowledge it both possesses and is possessed by and troubling an ocularcentric apprehension of reality that is similarly haunted by raciality, the novel resignifies double-consciousness wherein Ti-Jeanne's passage between the "two worlds" and its accompanying vertigo marks a desire for that which is anticipated but cannot be fully brought into legibility from *within* the terms of the modern grammar of representation in any form other than nonsense.[40] Like Mi-Jeanne before her, Ti-Jeanne risks her sense-ability—its anticipatory and transformative function, which is contiguous with its debilitating power—in an attempt to seek a place and an explanation within a science-fictional reality wherein all phenomena can be presumably explained within the terms of Western (scientific) rationality.[41] While Ti-Jeanne understands herself in the terms of a Hegelian "rational" subject, both the science-fictional world she seeks and the Hegelian (and Heideggerian) discourse that undergirds it position her and her grandmother in the same space as "blind Crazy Betty," a black and bestial space of privation of reason and world, a reality Ti-Jeanne is not yet ready to confront.

On that street and immediately following her immersion in "second sight," upon looking into her mother's face and its self-inflicted, dugout eyes, Ti-Jeanne saw the specter of her own (un)becoming: "The old fear of madness made Ti-Jeanne go cold. . . . Madwoman in front of her. Hard-eyed men just behind" (Hopkinson 17). She thought, "But at least the men had *something* behind their eyes, some spark of humanity" (Hopkinson 17). Face-to-face with dually gendered images of social death—in the forms of her mother's visage, which she no longer recognizes, and the huddle of men, a site of gendered violence's spatial and substitutive logics—Ti-Jeanne clung to a common reality and sense of humanity that she will eventually have to shed in order to, however provisionally, spark life on nonhegemonic terms and to keep her sense-ability intact. In the interval, Ti-Jeanne chose the men's "something" over her mother's seeming nothingness or, more precisely, vacuity. She attempted to turn and run back the way she had come only to find herself transported to a green tropical meadow, where, at the end of a narrow, downward-curving dirt path, a figure came over the rise, leaping and dancing up the path:

> *Man-like, man-tall, on long, wobbly legs look as if they hitch on backward. Red, red all over: red eyes, red hair, nasty, pointy red tail jooking up into the air. Face like a grinning African mask. Only is not a mask; the lips-them moving, and it have real teeth behind them lips, attached to real gums. He waving a stick, and even the stick self paint-up red, with some pick and crimson rags hanging from the one end. Is dance he dancing on them wobbly legs, flapping he knees in and out like if he drunk, jabbing he stick in the air, and now I could hear the beat he moving to, hear the words of the chant: "Diab'-diab'! Diab'-diab'! Diab'-diab'!"* (Hopkinson 18, italics in original)

Upon opening her eyes, she found Tony standing beside her in Roopsingh's roti shop. "In disorientation," Ti-Jeanne asked over a raucous sonic mix of soca and customers yelling their orders through aroma-filled air boasting of curry, frying oil, and stew peas with rice, "What happened? Is where we was?" (Hopkinson 19). While Ti-Jeanne had hoped "if she ignored the second sight, it would just go away," the visions overwhelmed her sense of self-willed ocularcentric agency and thwarted her attempts at backward movement. Her visions' sublime vertiginous disruption of proprioception creates an interval for Ti-Jeanne to move beyond representationalism and Western scientific empiricism in particular. But precisely because it is a threat to identity in the terms of "Self/World" described by Wynter at the beginning of this chapter, she initially resists its force and affect ("Ceremony" 46).

For Ti-Jeanne, the approach of the Jab-Jab is synonymous with the arrival of death in the form of atavism and disordered being: the Jab-Jab's wobbly legs and tail portend the threat of life out of order, a disabled life, a figure described as having a "face like a grinning African mask" (Hopkinson 18). As observed by many scholars, "the African mask," a fetish of nineteenth-century anthropology, exceeds mere representation, as the fetishized mask is perceived as the synecdochic-embodiment of the African's purported stonelike atemporal opacity and disordered metaphysics more generally, such that African masks and people are not merely correlates but appear interchangeable.[42] Whereas for Heidegger, the hand is the synecdoche for thought, which is the synecdoche for world-making rich in spirit, historically in the West, the fetishized mask is the synecdoche of Hegel's Africa or the spiritless impoverishment of thought and world. Michelle Wallace has described the fungibility of African (art) objects and African people in the following terms:

> The fate of African art objects was not unrelated to the fate of the human bodies also removed from Africa under less than ideal circumstances— some of them sold or just handed over and some of them kidnapped . . . The greatest difference then, between the bodies of our ancestors and these tribal objects is that the bodies were allowed to die (therefore enabling us to replace them), whereas the tribal objects can never die, given their curious half-life on the back shelves of Western art . . . It might be useful to think of them [museum and gallery collections] as ruins. (465, 467)[43]

The authorized disposability of black people that Wallace describes with the rather truncated phrase—"allowed to die"—sits somewhat ironically, even if not altogether unsurprisingly, next to her observation that "African objects were *salvaged* for exhibition or sale" (463) only to find a deadly synthesis in *the exhibition* and *sale* of black people: "entire villages were sometimes shipped over to Europe, England, and the United

States and placed on display in zoos and circuses" in the "general chaos" that accompanied the annexation and colonization of the African continent in the late nineteenth century (463).[44] Wallace concludes, "No doubt, many of the objects that made it either to the New World, Britain, and Europe were probably destroyed one way or the other" (463). No doubt, indeed. We know that the name "Venus," practically synonymous with the terror and pleasure of exhibiting people, does not index a single life, but many.[45]

Moreover, black people's relation to the world of objects cannot be properly understood in the terms of what Quentin Meillassoux calls Kantian correlationism or of the question of perceptual integrity between subject and object, *as black peoples' fungibility with objects* is a primary function of blackness in "the" world (in the making of "the" world) and forms an essential condition of possibility for both Kant's questioning of subject-object relations and the emergence of globality as a conceptual horizon.[46] So for black people it is not that the question of perceptual integrity is not a problem for contemplation; rather, the question of subject-object is thought in a world that *primarily* annunciates blackness as the fungibility of people and objects while steadfastly equating subjecthood with the possession and dispossession of objects (human and nonhuman)—objects that necessarily haunt the distorted perceptual terms of the Kantian-subject and thought-world relationship, whereby black mater signifies the formlessness of noise, and noise is produced as isomorphic to black mater, reciprocally.[47] Therefore, black contemplation of the question of subject-object, including thought that exceeds its logic, must contend with and cannot help but occur in a context effected by the indistinction and distortion race introduces into these very terms.[48]

Given Man's historical horizon of possibility—slavery, conquest, colonialism—the Western metaphysical matrix has race at its center in the form of a chiasmus: the metaphysics of race ("What is the 'reality' of race?") and the racialization of the question of metaphysics ("Under whose terms will the nature of time, knowledge, space, objecthood, being, and causality come to be defined?"). In other words, the question of race's reality has and continues to bear directly on hierarchies of knowledge pertaining to the nature of reality itself. Though the notoriously antiblack pronouncements of exalted figures like G. W. F. Hegel,

Immanuel Kant, or David Hume, for instance, mark neither the invention of metaphysics nor its conclusive end, the metaphysical question of race and that of the foreclosure of black mater in particular as race's status-organizing principle marks an *innovation* in the governing terms of metaphysics, one that would increasingly purport to resolve metaphysical questions in terms of relative proximity to the spectral figure of "the African female" or, more precisely, that of black mater. In probing and radicalizing the indefinite distinction between immanence and transcendence, their gendered and racialized prefigurement as the staging of the black *mater*(nal)'s nonrepresentability, Hopkinson's novel challenges the terms that ground both attempts to distinguish and combine science and fiction as well as speculation and realism.[49]

What I want to stress here is that both the reigning hegemonic conception of the human thought-world correlate as well as the idea that ontological unification is both desirable and attainable by means other than violence are essential onto-epistemic aspects of antiblackness historically and contemporarily. The dominant order of appearances and its representationalist logics are forged through and by what Denise Ferreira da Silva has termed the "global idea of race," yet this onto-epistemic violence is commonly understood as *merely* the proper apprehension of reality and justified on that basis.

Representationalism's ontological propositions and effects commonly rely on a problematic material reductionism that I argue is secured by the idea of race in particular. The mater of racial being and its "hieroglyphics of the flesh" have been the primary measure of being(human) and a principal site for maintaining and extending representationalist rationality.[50] The presumed primacy and transparency of (racial) mater is called upon to adjudicate "reality," "fact," and "truth," in general and as such. In the process, nonrepresentationalist systems of inquiry and modes of ontology are cast in the racialized terms of a teratology, whereby the so-called fetish is its signal anxiety.

Simon Gikandi has described the doubleness of the fetish as "a figure that is located at the heart of culture and ritual and yet seems to appear to us in its perceptual nature, against reality." Embalmed in a paranoid discourse that mystifies their ritualized forms and functions in the movement of West African religion and everyday life, whether in the explicit terms of "race" or the supplementary discourse of "culture,"

African objects, and masks in particular, appear, one could argue, as not only "against reality" but as the foreclosing of the reality principle—in this sense, masks become fungible or metonymic with the related signifiers of black mater.[51] The mask's frightening appearance stems from a selective, yet lawlike, figuration of anxiety in antiblack gendered terms, regarding "a dangerous potentiality in *all perception and representation*" that "reality itself is open to construction," such that the relation between observable experience and external reality is one of vast potentiality rather than determinism (Simpson 11, emphasis added).

Indeed, the world is not as it appears. It is revealed later in the novel that the Jab-Jab is a manifestation of Ti-Jeanne's patron spirit Papa Legbara or Eshu—in her consternation, she initially misrecognized him and the helpful messages he provided. Throughout the novel, the appearance of Eshu and possession by Eshu is one of her greatest sources of strength for defeating the ruthless drug lord Rudy and, more importantly, for her and her mother's survival (M. Coleman, 11). That her patron spirit is Eshu is significant at the very least because the Eshu in *Brown Girl* is a messenger and, like Ti-Jeanne, passes between worlds. Nevertheless, in Ti-Jeanne's attempt to confirm the integrity of her own relation of form to image, she necessarily has to pass, at the very least, through the gendered, antiblack associative links I have just described. The image of the Jab-Jab recalls the fungibility of African objects (masks) and people as well as the conflation of Africa, more generally, and West African religion, in particular, with mythic irreality and the teratological, associations that *precede* Ti-Jeanne's attempts to order her reality. It is no wonder that such circular logics and paranoid relations would induce misapprehension and the dread of vertigo.

In the passage above, vertigo—that sense of unhinged reality, a communion with death and that realm which exceeds life—seems to threaten a total loss of self as incommensurable metaphysical frameworks and sensory maps meet. This episodic experience is made possible by what Frank Wilderson has called a "paradigmatic necessity," namely that blackness is "a life constituted by disorientation rather than a life interrupted by disorientation" ("Vengeance" 3). A life constituted by disorientation has as its essential feature what Fanon diagnosed as an "aberration of affect"—autophobia and self-aversion—an effect of realizing selfhood in the terms of our present global hegemonic *mode of the subject*: its transindividual and systemic scales of value "woven out of a thousand details, anecdotes, stories" imposes an antiblack system of meaning and affective economy (Wynter, "1942" 45). In global hegemonic terms, *the* African is cast "out of the world" and is thus without standing in relation to the constitution of the reality construct.[52] It is not an absence of alternative metaphysical frameworks and perceptual matrices that produces the vertigo I describe; rather, vertigo is an effect of the inability of these alternatives to find footing *within "the world"* due to ever-renewed processes of foreclosure that take the nullification of black mater as the horizon of the reality concept and threshold of the sensible world.

For Ti-Jeanne, "to assume a culture, to support a civilization" under these terms is to be possessed by a metaphysics that produces egoic and filial conflicts and disintegration as well as a desire for "one human being who was totally dependent on her and would never leave her" (Hopkinson 25). Within the logic of the specific civilization in which she finds herself, within the language it speaks and that speaks it, as a "Negro" one will find herself biochemically altered, its physicalist correlation vertiginous (Wynter, "Sociogenic"). In a gloss of the work of physicist David Bohm, Wynter concludes, "Transformed *meanings* have led to transformed *matter*, to a transformed mode of experiencing the *self*" ("Sociogenic" 38). Assuming the rhetorics of possession, Wynter states further:

[A]nother mode of conscious experience takes over. This mode is one that compels her to know her body *through* the terms of an always already imposed 'historico-racial schema'; a schema that predefines her body as an impurity to be cured, a lack, a defect, to be amended into the 'true' being of whiteness. ("Sociogenic" 41)[53]

Thus, sensorium and its faculties are "culturally determined through the mediation of the socialized *sense of self* as well as the 'social' situation in which the *self* is placed" (Wynter, "Sociogenic" 37).

In *Being and Nothingness*, Jean-Paul Sartre describes existential vertigo in terms that return us to the site of an ominous narrow path, one whose feared balefulness is not understood as manifestly figural, as in the form of a Jab Jab, but whose causality is annunciated affectively. And yet its existential terms also recall the racialized, gendered, and sexual conditioning of anxiety:

> Vertigo announces itself through fear; I am on a narrow path—without a guard rail—which goes along a precipice. The precipice presents itself to me *as to be avoided*; it represents a danger of death. At the same time I conceive of a certain number of causes . . . which can transform that threat of death into reality . . . Through these various anticipations, I am given to myself as a thing; I am passive in relation to these possibilities; they come to me from without; in so far as I am also an object in the world, subject to gravitation, they are my possibilities. (Sartre 66)

Reading this canonical passage on existential vertigo in light of the gendered sexual history of conquest and enslavement makes perceptible the visceral nature of anxieties that orbit the status of objects. Framed in essentialist terms, blackness marks a violation of gendered and sexual norms such that race—once ontologized—fixes blackness, regardless of "sex," in the "feminine position" as that passivity and stasis ascribed to objecthood and death, or objecthood as a form of living death. In this frame, the predominant one—blackness, womanhood, female sex, passivity, objecthood, inertia, death, and matter—form an unbreakable chain and negative telos or declension. For a black woman, such as Ti-Jeanne, to be "riddin by spirits" is to be possessed by a gendered sexual redundancy, an intensification of death *in and by* objecthood. Paradoxically, here objecthood serves to feminize a womanhood considered to be of questionable feminine standing by way of placing her being *in* common under erasure; in other words, it genders black womanhood on the register of her object status only to dispossess her gender of the fullness of being (human). In sum, according to the ontologized, gendered metrics described, the object's nonbeing as blackened status figures black womanhood a superposition or the state of occupying two distinct and seemingly contradictory human and object worlds simultaneously—a predicament that underwrites both the separation of "subject" and "object" in Western ontological discourse and exposes the impossibility of consistently keeping these terms apart. Thus, I argue that rather than simply restore activity to matter or militate against the charge of passivity in the exclusive terms of defining agency by activity, an alteration of the object's blackened gendered status necessitates a transvaluation of the gendered symbolics of passivity and the inoperability of its sliding substitutions, which I will argue, in the following chapter, is modeled in Octavia Butler's "Bloodchild."

Brown Girl in the Ring is a novel that perhaps should be understood not as a mixing of genres but rather as a performance of their deconstruction—literary genres and those genres of the human that apprehend black mater as the precipice of nothingness. In posing the question of onto-epistemology at the register Hopkinson's text poses it, as an intervention into the modern grammar of representation, operative dualisms—science-fiction, fact-belief, observation-projection, realism-fantasy—are destabilized, problematizing generic codes and conventions, their terms of legibility and historical-national organization, and their bonds of signification and constitutive oppositions displaced. These narrative strategies underscore the manner with which *Brown Girl in the Ring* refuses to be an "object of anthropological desire" (Ferreira da Silva, *Toward* xxii). *Brown Girl in the Ring*'s philosophical inquiry into onto-epistemology and perceptual reality destabilizes the ground of "ethnographic authority" rather than invites it and deauthorizes not only Hegel's racial telos but also the foundational empiricism of Franz Boas as well.[54] Ferreira da Silva has shown that as a knowledge project that addresses man as an object, Franz Boas's cultural anthropology tied certain bodily and mental configurations to different global regions as Boas's conceptualization of "the primitive mind" sought to explain sense perception in terms of the "laws" of "cultural development" that relied upon and extended a logic that made globality and raciality coextensive.[55]

Rather than read *Brown Girl in the Ring* through the imperative of anthropological translation or map its proximity to some ideal of Western secular scientific rationality, I am most interested in the way Yoruba and related cosmological systems function in the novel as tropes in service to a generative critique of the racialized, gendered, sexual fictions of ontology and subjectivity I have just described. Diasporic practices of world-making potentially act as a mode of redress for onto-epistemic violence to the extent that said praxes preclude the monopolization of sense that authorizes antiblack (Euro)modernity. Ti-Jeanne ticked them off on her fingers: "Shango, Ogun, Osain, Shakpana, Emanjah, Oshun, Oya, and

Eshu" and would need to call upon them, the "old-time stories," and even Crazy Betty/Mi-Jeanne to possess and aid her in her battle with Rudy, ultimately recovering her mother in the process (Hopkinson 204).[56] Troping *rather than rehearsing Yoruba religious practice*, in *Brown Girl in the Ring*, the invocation of the orishas does not so much act as a guarantor of Africa as the "essential base" of New World cosmological praxis. Rather, it marks the process of altering terms and objects *from* that of "Africa" as a paranoid discourse *to* that of blackness as an existential predicament such that Africa is understood and problematized as an *invention* of imperial Western modernity and its grammar of representation.[57] This is a vertiginous circuit whose vicissitudes and paradoxes must necessarily include both the anticipation *and* indeterminacy of alternation between paranoid and deliberative modes of onto-epistemology.

Awaiting neither "the science of culture" (anthropological historicity) nor the authentication of what is or is not "Caribbean" or "African" ("ethnographic authority"), this altered course reveals that blackness is an existential predicament that precisely and decisively unmoors the fictions of origin and integral (human)being. The Middle Passage is neither place nor historical past but statelessness, a processual (un)becoming, the (dis)continuous iterative unsettling of origin and being, and a challenge to the question and terms of origin writ large; therefore, it confounds rather than permits the compensatory gestures discourses of "hybridity" and "syncretism" offer to (racial) ontology.[58]

Even when it is to their great detriment, or perhaps even especially in those instances, the novel's characters of different racial, gender, age, and class positionalities participate in a signifying process that negates, rejects, misapprehends, and misnames what has already been prefigured void. Mami-Gros Jeanne's empiricist praxis and interventions—her onto-epistemology—lie buried under the signifiers of superstition and nonsense. The author's use of dramatic irony performs and exposes the impossibility of black mater to be either re-presented or known in the modern grammar of dialectical subjecthood and authority; what emerges from this narrative strategy is not an affirmation of the positive value of either "immanence" or "transcendence" but rather a (re)valuation of deferral, the ongoing pursuit of a praxis that is not already determined by those terms, fails to signify in those terms, and mutates those terms and their grammar beyond recognition.

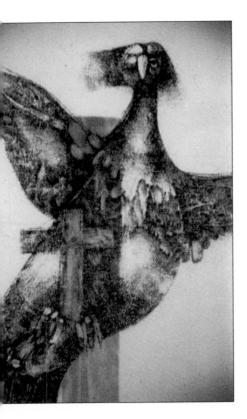

Figures P.1a and b. Ezrom Legae. *Chicken Series* (details), 1977–78. Drawing on paper. Courtesy of South Africa National Gallery.

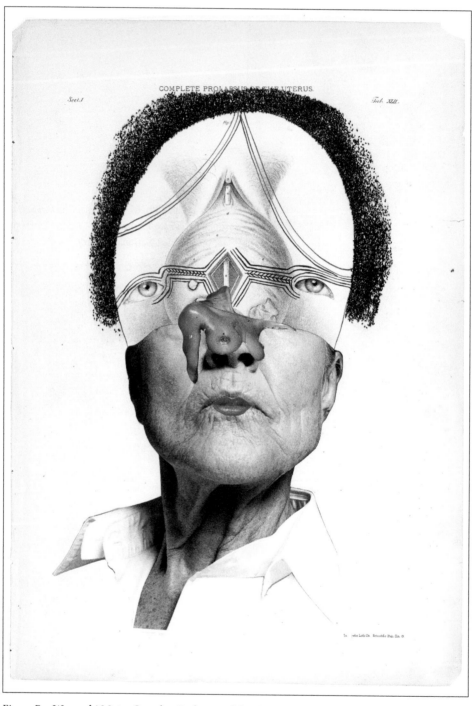

Figure P.2. Wangechi Mutu. *Complete Prolapsus of the Uterus*, 2005. Glitter, collage, ink on found medical illustration paper, 18 × 12 in. Copyright Wangechi Mutu. Courtesy of the artist and Vielmetter Los Angeles.

Figure P.3. Wangechi Mutu. *Histology of the Different Classes of Uterine Tumors*, 2005. Glitter, collage on found medical illustration paper, 18 × 12 in. Copyright Wangechi Mutu. Courtesy of the artist and Vielmetter Los Angeles.

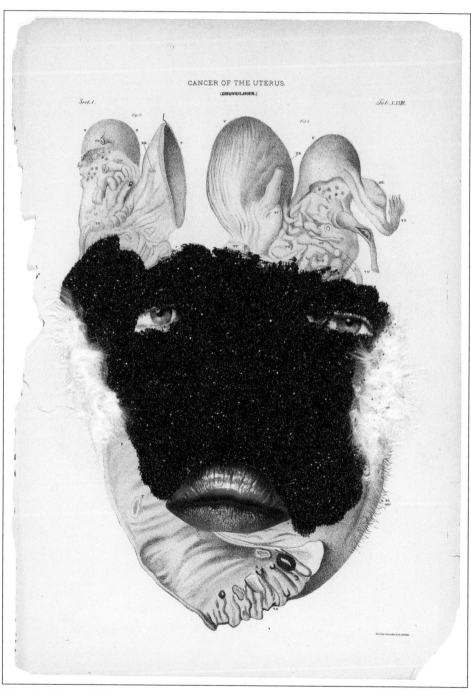

Figure P.4. Wangechi Mutu. *Cancer of the Uterus*, 2005. Glitter, collage, fur on found medical illustration paper, 18 × 12 in. Copyright Wangechi Mutu. Courtesy of the artist and Vielmetter Los Angeles.

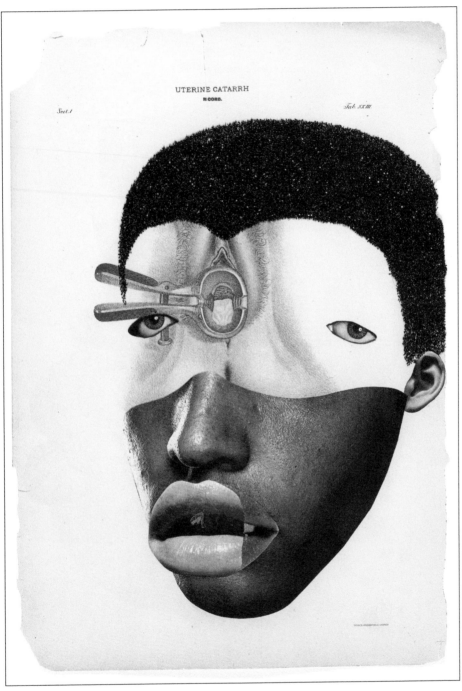

Figure P.5. Wangechi Mutu. *Uterine Catarrh*, 2005. Glitter, collage on found medical illustration paper, 18 × 12 in. Copyright Wangechi Mutu. Courtesy of the artist and Vielmetter Los Angeles.

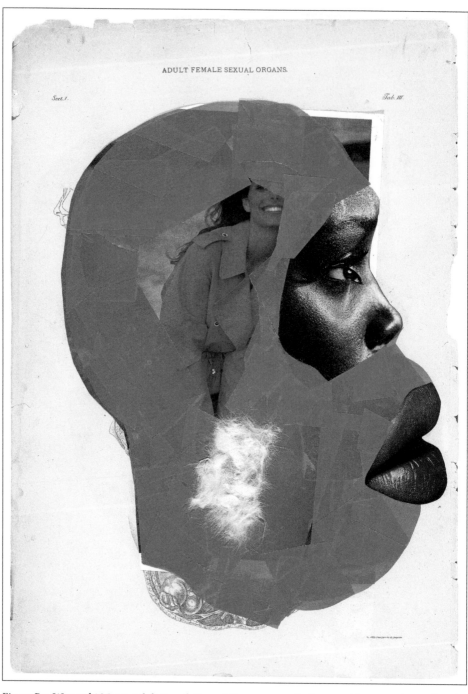

Figure P.6. Wangechi Mutu. *Adult Female Sexual Organs*, 2005. Collage, packing tape, fur on found medical illustration paper, 18 × 12 in. Copyright Wangechi Mutu. Courtesy of the artist and Vielmetter Los Angeles.

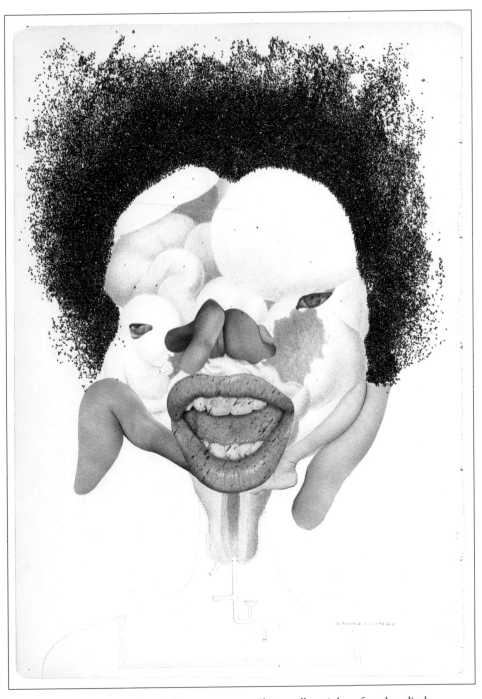

Figure P.7. Wangechi Mutu. *Ectopic Pregnancy*, 2005. Glitter, collage, ink on found medical illustration paper, 18 × 12 in. Copyright Wangechi Mutu. Courtesy of the artist and Vielmetter Los Angeles.

Figure P.8. Wangechi Mutu. *Tumors of the Uterus*, 2005. Collage on found medical illustration paper, 18 × 12 in. Copyright Wangechi Mutu. Courtesy of the artist and Vielmetter Los Angeles.

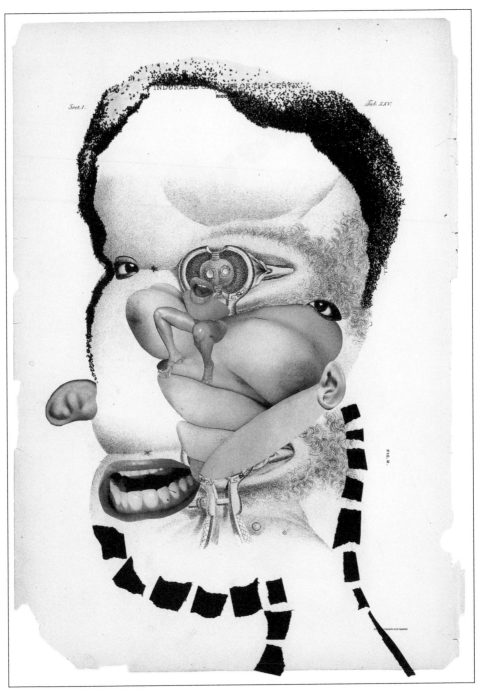

Figure P.9. Wangechi Mutu. *Indurated Ulcers of the Cervix*, 2005. Glitter, collage, ink on found medical illustration paper, 18 × 12 in. Copyright Wangechi Mutu. Courtesy of the artist and Vielmetter Los Angeles.

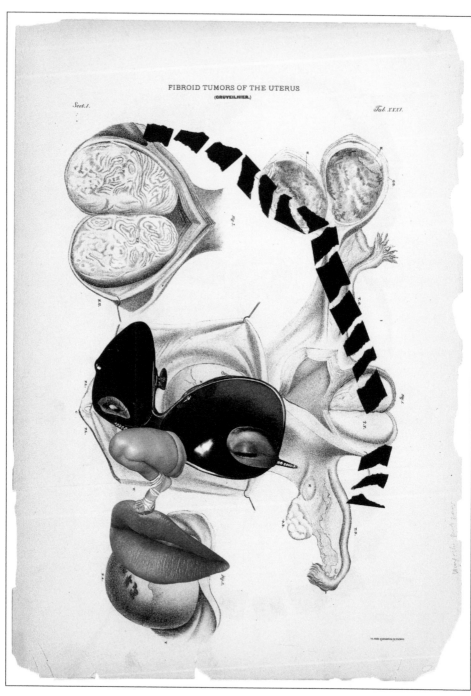

Figure P.10. Wangechi Mutu. *Fibroid Tumors of the Uterus*, 2005. Collage on found medical illustration paper, 18 × 12 in. Copyright Wangechi Mutu. Courtesy of the artist and Vielmetter Los Angeles.

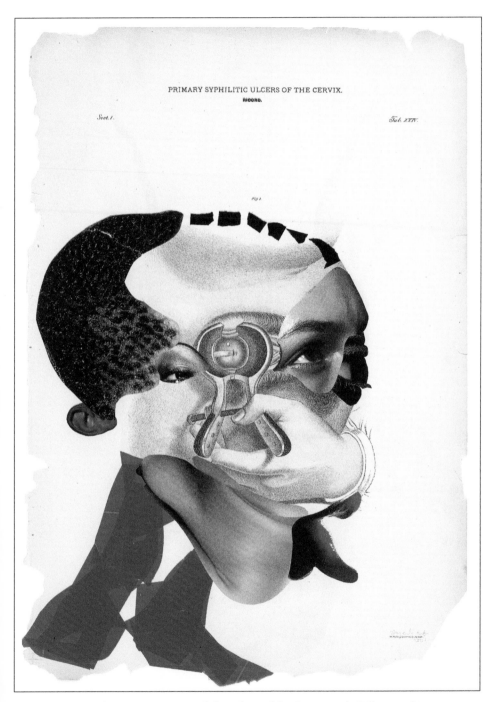

Figure P.11. Wangechi Mutu. *Primary Syphilitic Ulcers of the Cervix*, 2005. Collage, packing tape on found medical illustration paper, 18 × 12 in. Copyright Wangechi Mutu. Courtesy of the artist and Vielmetter Los Angeles.

Figure P.12. Wangechi Mutu. *Cervical Hypertrophy*, 2005. Glitter, collage, ink on found medical illustration paper, 18 × 12 in. Copyright Wangechi Mutu. Courtesy of the artist and Vielmetter Los Angeles.

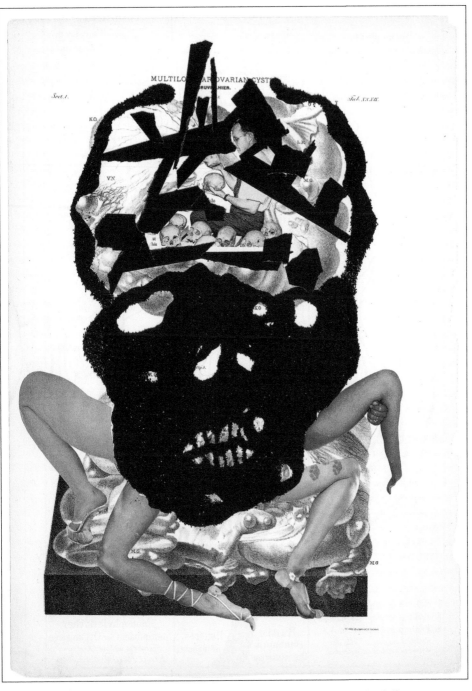

Figure P.13. Wangechi Mutu. *Ovarian Cysts*, 2005. Glitter, collage on found medical illustration paper, 18 × 12 in. Copyright Wangechi Mutu. Courtesy of the artist and Vielmetter Los Angeles.

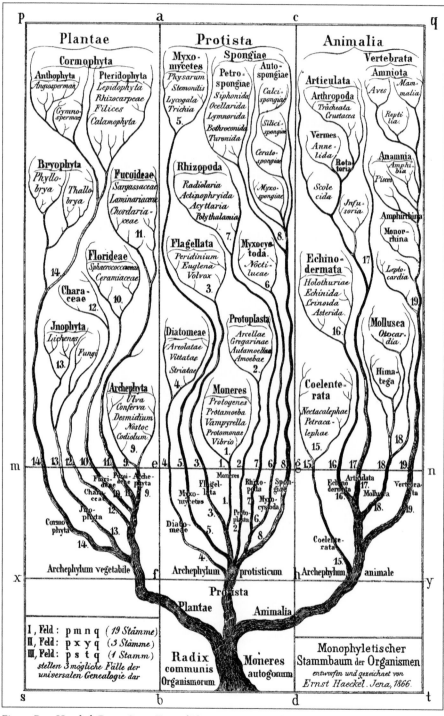

Figure P.14. Haeckel, Ernst. Stem-Tree of Plants, Protists, and Animals (1866). *Generelle Morphologie der Organismen*, 2 vols. Georg Reimer, 1866.

Discomedusae. — Scheibenquallen.

Figure P.15. Haeckel, Ernst. "Discomedusae.Scheibenquallen, 1904" Haeckel, Ernst. "Kunstformen der Natur (1904)." *Prestel, München* (1998).

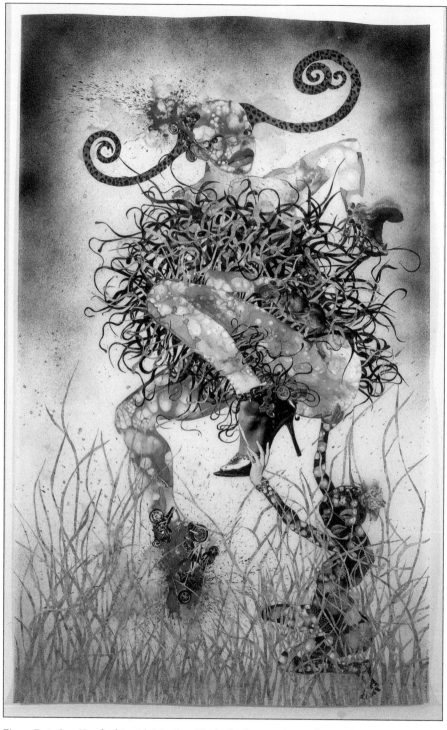

Figure P.16. *One Hundred Lavish Months of Bushwhack, 2004.* Cut-and-pasted printed paper with watercolor, synthetic polymer paint, and pressure-sensitive stickers on transparentized paper, 68.5 × 42 in. Copyright Wangechi Mutu. Courtesy of the artist and Vielmetter Los Angeles.

As the novel unfolds, Ti-Jeanne gradually relinquishes a phantasy of the will (unified and rational, self-directed subjectivity), or sovereignty, as the seat of agency, a phantasy perhaps all the more beguiling because of the ways abandonment, disposability, and segregation act to ensure life's irresolution in The Burn, an irresolution that extends into existence as the ever-presence of dreadful anticipation, psychic diremption, and (dis)possession of the flesh. Ultimately, Ti-Jeanne discovers that receptivity to and assumption of the orishas as ontological co-constituents may not only provide a means for survival but may offer a sense of life beyond mere survival. Thus, Ti-Jeanne's (dis)abling predicament, or vertiginous state, provides Ti-Jeanne some other mode of relating where the other is neither an agent of your aggrandizement nor of your diminishment but the arrival of the inoperability of the binary between the two and a suspension of relation on those terms, thus making way for the unforeseen. Going deeper into blackness rather than fleeing its trace, *Brown Girl in the Ring* is an allegory for unsettling modes of cognition and sense-making that authorize antiblack metaphysics, including those of Heidegger and Hegel.

Antiblack metaphysics, as foreclosure, positions the existence of blackened reality beyond the conceptual borders of the dialectical encounter that underwrites representationalism's hegemonic processes of worlding. However, the novel does not simply advocate one representationalist schema that is presumed to be more comprehensive or offer more accurate re-presentations of existing entities over another; rather, it allegorizes the potential enabling effects of disordering the hegemonic mode of reality and self–world relation. The idea of a unitary, finite "reality" and "world" is an imperial invention.

In *Brown Girl in the Ring*, Ti-Jeanne must forgo faith in the idea that there is an all-encompassing transcendental structure—"reality," "the world," "truth"—that settles matters of existence once and for all. Instead, she measures claims to existence based on their metaphorical resonance and ontological effects upon *a* world rather than *within* "the world." In ineluctable co-constitution, where self and world are internal (but not reducible) to each other, what arrangement of existence, modes of relationality, and agential possibilities emerge? Rather than assume that the epistemic purchase of inquiry into ontology resides in the measurable distance between representation and referent, Ti-Jeanne asks instead what worldings do particular ontological claims (dis)enable? In this important sense, Ti-Jeanne's reorientation to the question of world serves as an analytic for interrogating what representationalism claims to do.[59]

In conclusion, in *Brown Girl in the Ring*, vertigo functions as the precipice of a new consciousness and "inchoate theoretics" (Scott, *Extravagant* 64)—where "sense and non-sense have yet to be differentiated" (Marriott, "No Lords" 522).[60] Vertigo provides an alternative to "the tyrannies of our common reality," where positivist knowledge is forged through epistemic coercion, expropriation, and relations of direct domination (Scott, *Extravagant* 26). I have argued that Western science and philosophy's foundational authority and the reproduction of the scientific matrix of classification necessitates and is maintained by the recursive symbolic foreclosure of black mater and dislocation of black(ened) gender, maternity, and sexuality in hegemonic ontology or the idea of *the* world *as such*. Vertigo, here, is a measure and means for the disordering and inoperability of a metaphysics that takes the black *mater*(nal)'s nonrepresentability as its enabling condition. In vertigo, we may limn the potential to disarrange metaphysics via a transvaluation of (human) being and a reconfiguration of gendered sexual embodiment by means of an emergent sensorium. Disordering metaphysics and metaphysics disordered: "Ti-Jeanne felt the gears slipping between the two worlds" (Hopkinson 19). In this, Ti-Jeanne's vertigo is both the apprehension of unlived possibilities and the salvific irruption into consciousness of discredited sensation, of other ways of living, other modes of life that provide a dizzying sense of vivifying potentiality.

3

"Not Our Own"

Sex, Genre, and the Insect Poetics of Octavia Butler's "Bloodchild"

Sexual reproduction is only one, and arguably not even the
most predominant, kind of reproduction that is found in
nature; bacterial budding, rhizomic replication, spore production, viral infection, symbiosis, bacterial recombination—
such reproductive models challenge not only our *humanness*
but also (and perhaps more profoundly) our *animalness*.
—Susan Squier, "Interspecies Reproduction"

Species reeks of race and sex . . .
—Donna Haraway, *When Species Meet*

A guiding conviction of *Becoming Human* is that we must attend to the
material histories of our categories, as they are given shape and vitality
by way of, and inside of, organismic bodies, even if (or especially if)
ultimately our aim is to be rid of received categories because of their
world-wrecking capacities and death-dealing effects.[1] Otherwise, we
will most likely build on foundations we would be better off destroy-
ing. If species divisions and membership have fundamentally been a
question of reproduction, whereby the scene of birth is determinant
of taxonomy, then this chapter asks: What could be gained from the
cognitive estrangement of reproduction and birth? How might estrangement ironically facilitate contact with flesh, a discursive hapticality, the
meeting of matter and meaning, on different terms and guided by an
alternative orientation to the flesh? What unexpected sense of freedom
could be gained by passing through possibilities just beyond the edge of
the given world?

This chapter underscores the reach of antiblackness into the nonhuman—*as (anti)blackness conditions and constitutes the very nonhuman*

disruption and displacement recent scholarship invites. I discuss how racial slavery, conquest, and colonial ideas about gender, sexuality, and "nature," more generally, have informed *evolutionary discourses on the origin of life itself* and our ideas of cellular biology by looking at the racialized history of the theory of symbiosis in relation to Octavia Butler's "Bloodchild." I demonstrate that the racialized controversies and anxieties, concerning the fortification of the sovereign body, accompanying the development of the theory of symbiosis reveal the extent to which categories of "race" and "species" are homologous such that antiblack and colonialist histories have informed the very forms scientific discourse can take.

In a reading of "Bloodchild," I draw out a materialist conception of the body that upends the conception of the organismic body as *terra nullius*, or empty, vacant space appropriable for the Self that many want to defend and idealize.[2] "Bloodchild" reestablishes fleshly embodied subjectivity as a multispecies processual environment characterized not by Self-control but the transfer of control rather than a sovereign "I."

This chapter joins the final chapter of this book in meditating on the possibilities of mutation. This one focuses on the mutation of literary forms and idea(l)s of the body while the other looks to the mutation of bodily forms and considers what mutational possibilities reveal about the autopoesis of antiblackness as well as the scientific and philosophic discourses concerning species.

One could argue that Octavia Butler is best conceived as a singularity. She is a writer that invites reconsideration of how conventional literary histories and generic categories fare when confronted with randomness or the aleatory. I open a discussion of Butler, genre, and tradition with an evocation of mutation, the *generative* failure of transcription, as a way of suggesting that Butler's fiction invites reimagination of that which goes under the heading of "African American literature." This tradition should be imagined not as a single vertical, linear line or chronological teleology but as literary history's mutation, the generation of new forms—or even as a rhizomatic, horizontal multiplicity and dynamic process with multiple genealogies.

Another way to approach the questions of genre and tradition might be to think about Octavia Butler's fiction as an asignifying rupture.[3] In other words, we should think of her fiction as a black feminist and

queer reassembly in an elsewhere and else-when of early black speculative works such as W. E. B. Du Bois's *The Comet*, Charles Chesnutt's
The Goophered Grapevine, and George Schuyler's *Black Empire*.[4] I draw
upon Deleuze and Guattari's conception of "asignifying rupture" because the emplotment of Butler in a traditional, arborescent genealogy
of African American literature has far too often led to readings that miss
too many of her thematic concerns and interventions into both African
American literature and science fiction. And perhaps these readings especially obscure her interventions into African American literature via
the science fictional and the unsettling of realism as a privileged mode
of political critique.[5] Arguably, Robert Heinlein's Hugo Award–winning
military science fiction novel *Starship Troopers* and James Tiptree Jr.'s (or
Raccoona Sheldon's or Alice B. Sheldon's) Nebula Award–winning "The
Screwfly Solution" are the most resonant intertexts for the short story at
the center of my analysis: "Bloodchild."[6]

In my reading, "Bloodchild" is thematically linked to the African
American literary tradition not so much through its intertextual reexamination and revision of identifiable African American literary predecessors but in *how it takes up and revises the motifs and conventions
of science fiction*, offering up for examination the way science fiction's
genre strictures are shaped by racialized, gendered, and sexual histories
of conquest, slavery, and colonialism. One of the achievements of the
African American literary tradition is that, in the main, it has displaced
the oppositional hierarchy of aesthetics and politics, making the critique
of racialization, conquest, slavery, and colonialism central thematic
preoccupations coextensive with its artistry, creativity, and generative
imagination. Indeed, it is in African American as well as postcolonial
literature that conquest, slavery, and colonialism have persistently been
revealed as determinant of the Western literary imagination writ large.
With "Bloodchild," Butler broadens both traditions, African American and postcolonial, by poignantly challenging Eurocentric (andro)
anthropocentricism, as well as the imperialist dimensions of terrestrial
and extrasolar narratives of exploration, discovery, conquest, and settlement. Her story tarries with dislocation and loss of identity not simply
as defeat or the loss of tradition but also as a processual opening to un-
foreseeable, emergent modes of belonging and existence.[7] I find myself
in agreement with Mathias Nilges that Butler's novels are "less about the

value of embracing change than about the struggle with the necessity of *having* to do so" and "the psychological struggle that arises out of confrontation with change" (Nilges 1337).

Octavia Butler's "Bloodchild" also horizontally extends genealogies of feminist science fiction, which include such works as Ursula Le Guin's Hugo and Nebula Award–winning *The Left Hand of Darkness* and Marge Piercy's *Woman on the Edge of Time* by questioning the Cartesian dualistic thinking that grounds gendered and sexual colonial fantasies of subjectivity, sovereignty, and agency and assigns social value to sexual difference, linking these feminist concerns to queer and trans contestation of the inflexible terms through which sexual difference is understood. Patricia Melzer has argued that "To read science fiction in conjunction with feminist theories can . . . foster a new and more intimate understanding of the theories, their limits, and their co-option by dominant culture" (10). In *How Like a Leaf*, Donna Haraway takes this argument one step further with the assertion that "science fiction is political theory" (120). Moreover, "locating feminist theory in cultural texts contests the separations of cognitive realms, such as creativity and abstract thought, on which the Western-defined concept of theorizing rests," shifting discourses away from a hierarchical structure of theory-building and toward more open, multimodal, and interdisciplinary approaches within feminist inquiry (Melzer 10–11). Similarly, in *Queer Universes: Sexualities in Science Fiction*, Wendy Gay Pearson, Veronica Hollinger, and Joan Gordon locate the radical potential of "queer SF" not solely in the estrangement of gender, sexuality, and corporeality, issues commonly thought to be the sine qua non of queer theory but more fundamentally in SF's potential "to think thought itself differently" or to "queer thought itself," "defamiliarize and denaturalize taken-for-granted constructions of what it means to be, and to live, as human," and to "imagine alternative ways of living in the world as a sexual/ized subject" (3–4, 6). The result, according to Pearson, Hollinger, and Gordon, "is a field that is coming to understand that knowledge of social systems and ontological questions is as necessary to any conception of alternative (future) societies as is knowledge of science and technology per se" (7).

Critics have often underappreciated the role of ontological questioning or speculative thought in the work of black writers, instead favoring sociological readings of African American literature. My particular interest, in this chapter and in this book as a whole, lies in a question that has heretofore not been pursued: In light of a history of antiblack raciality that has equated speciation with racial taxonomy, how might a latent theoretical analysis and critique of what Cary Wolfe has termed the "discourse of species" exist inside of African American literature? The contiguity of discourses of racialization and speciation, I argue, is a central, if not *the* central, thematic preoccupation of Butler's fiction in particular. What I hope to show is that by reflecting on and revising the conventions of science fiction and the fictions of science, Butler brings to light how the science fiction genre performs in relation to *the logics* of conquest, slavery, and colonialism and invites a reexamination of the role of the biological both as a regulatory scientific discourse and fleshly archive of the productivity of the organismic body in the (un)making of imperial Man. Thus, the politics of subjectivation, the movement of difference in and as speciation, matter, and materiality emerge as persistent thematic concerns in Butler's fiction.

Sticking with the conceptual metaphor of the asignifying rupture, it could be argued that with Butler we see the emergence of a new lateral shoot of black feminist and queer science fiction. It is difficult to imagine how the work of Nnedi Okorafor, Nisi Shawl, Nalo Hopkinson (discussed in chapter 2), and on and on would have emerged without the queer reproduction of mutation and the rhizomatic.

New Worlds Old

[I]n the beginning, all the world was America.
—John Locke, *Second Treatise of Government*

In his log entry for November 23, 1492, Christopher Columbus coined the term "cannibal," a word that purported to both serve as a descriptor of the Taino and identify the threat that they represented (in Hulme 83–84, 86).[8] As Kyla Tompkins notes, "cannibalism has signified the total primitive otherness against which [white] Western rationality—and its installation of the putatively ungendered and deracinated 'human' as its subject—measures itself" (*Racial* 94). This signifier set in motion both the ontological disfigurement of the "Native" in the Americas and presaged the absurd constitutive contradictions of "universal humanity," namely human recognition with and as racial hierarchy and violence—which is to say human recognition with and as enslavement and colonial terror. Columbus and his crew's abjection of the Taíno and the Caribbean natural environment, viscerally embodied as fear, disbelief, excitement, and repulsion, establishes the centrality of both "the body" and aesthetico-affective experience in "universal history." A cultural phantasy that extends into science fiction, the dread of antipodal threat was and continues to be principally one concerning the monstrous recombination of orifices and appetites that both establish and elide the human–animal distinction that Tompkins might term *queer alimentarity*—filed teeth, ferocious maw, all-devouring womb, gaping mouth, and "toothed vaginas" (Creed 27, 28, 122).[9] "The New World" would be discovered in mythic time.[10]

Colonial power and its affective schema reorganize and renew themselves through the subversion of both distinctions between indigenous peoples and the ontologized border between the human and the animal, Man and environment, even when these distinctions and borders are erected under the auspices of colonial authority. Not unlike "universal history," science fiction's representational strategies are indebted to a colonial mode of aesthetico-affective-cognition. The genre's historical resonances and elisions commonly rely on alternating practices of substitution, conflation, and redaction. John Rieder, in *Colonialism and the Emergence of Science Fiction*, maintains:

> It is not a matter of asking whether but of determining precisely how and to what extent the stories engage colonialism. The work of interpreting the relation of colonialism and science fiction really gets under way, then, by attempting to decipher the fiction's often distorted and topsy-turvy references to colonialism. Only then can one properly ask how . . . science fiction lives and breathes in the atmosphere of colonial history and its discourses, how it reflects or contributes to ideological production of ideas about the shape of history, and how it might, in varying degrees, enact a struggle over humankind's ability to reshape it. (3)

Thus, science fiction, as a genre, has both revealed and obscured the erasure of histories of colonialism in the production of the fiction of universality.

Octavia Butler's 1984 short story "Bloodchild" evokes in order to turn to new ends a colonial representational and affective schema.[11] The colonial specter of being devoured is embedded in a representational politic that both racializes animal appetites and animalizes human appetites. Butler's critical awareness of the organismic body as a historical agent inspired the author to use her fiction as a vehicle to ceaselessly interrogate and transform the onto-theological asymmetry and (meta)physical violence that authorized Columbus's hyper-visceral encounter with the Taíno and the incalculable primal scenes that follow its example.

I want to suggest that it is precisely the nonteleological relation of political commitments and viscera, no doubt commonly shared, that makes Butler's highly evocative and highly theoretical meditation on the discursive-material body and subjectivation in "Bloodchild" so complex and important. For colonialism is not merely an opening up of new possibilities, a "new world" becoming available to the "old" one—it also provides the impetus behind "cognitive revolutions in the biological and human sciences that reshaped European notions of its own history and society" (Rieder 4). However, this chapter is not merely interested in revolutions of thought but also revolutions of being, affect, and desire; it also asks how science fiction might do something other than "transpose and revivify colonial ideologies" by disrupting and redirecting economies of being/feeling/knowing at a gut level. If as Derrida suggests, metonymy is essentially (and perhaps even inevitably) what happens at the edge of orifices, in other words, the capture of alterity by a "sacrificial symbolic economy" of "infinitely different modes of conception-appropriation-assimilation of the other," whereby the literalness or symbolicness of the eating is ethically appositional rather than dualistic and ultimately undecidable, the question is indeed "*how* for goodness sake should one *eat well?*": the question comes back to "determining the best, most respectful, most grateful, and most giving way of relating to the other and of relating the other to the self" (Derrida, "Eating" 114).[12] Kyla Tompkins tells us, "Eating is an act through which the body maintains the fictions of its materiality, both discursively and biologically."

Evoking Judith Butler: eating is performative, a "ritualized repetition . . . through which physicality and political subjectivity coalesce in the flesh as it is ritualistically constituted through the repetitive ingestion of materials" (Tompkins, "Everything" 206, 207). In "Bloodchild," there is an attempt to establish another performative, to transform ritual. This chapter concerns the practical fact of being a feast for others as an ontological opening and ethical problem.

Butler's fiction persistently examined the biopolitical stakes of colonial histories of conquest and contested colonial imaginaries and affective economies in science fiction.[13] Most frequently, this examination took the form of a protracted investigation that parsed different modalities of symbiosis and questioned presumed irreconcilabilities between parasitic and mutual symbiosis, often contemplating the promise and perils of symbiogenesis for the evolution of the human species. Symbiosis was initially a term used to describe people living together in a community; the term was adopted in the 1870s by German biologists to describe a long-term relationship between two (or more) different species to the relative benefit or detriment of each evolutionary partner. After over a century of debate, the theory of evolutionary association has been further divided into four classes: mutualism (benefit for both), commensalism (benefit for one; neutral for the other), amensalism (costly for one; neutral for the other), parasitism (benefit for one; costly for the other) and synnecrosis (costly for both). However, even these distinctions struggle to account for the complexity of evolutionary association that can shift over time. The biologist Lynn Margulis, famous for her work on endosymbiosis (i.e., where one evolutionary partner lives inside the other), advanced a theory called symbiogenesis, which argues that the origin of life itself is symbiotic and that mutual interaction, cooperation, and dependence among organisms is as important if not more evolutionarily significant than Darwin's natural selection (Margulis and Sagan, *Symbotic* 6).

Butler offers an extended meditation on the possible forms organismic and societal symbiosis can take in "Bloodchild" in light of enslavement and colonial histories. In fact, the term "colonialism," Eric C. Brown explains in *Insect Poetics*, "replays one of the most visible ways in which humans and insects have been compared: insect 'colonies' take their name from the Latin verb *colere*, meaning 'to cultivate,' especially agriculturally." This poetic Latinization of the zoological world extends the bygone Roman Empire into the realms of contemporary biological science and political theory (Brown, Introduction xiv). In Butler's fiction, and in "Bloodchild" in particular, interspecies relations open up the question of what it means to be (human), rather than neatly map onto intrahuman relations and histories.

This chapter aims to critically examine the stakes, possibilities, and problems of trans-species metaphors at the interface of Butler's fiction and its criticism. To this end, I advance three related arguments regarding Butler and "the discourse of species." Firstly, Butler's fiction does not annul species distinctions; neither does it simply abandon the category "human," as both the establishment and the abandonment of species distinctions have been integral to racism and colonialism. Rather, it *radicalizes and transforms* the aesthetico-affective-cognitive politics of embodied difference rather than attempt to overcome (the movement of) differentiation. To accomplish this, Butler exposes how received ideas about species are *always* a question of power, which as Donna Haraway puts it, "reek of race and sex" (*When* 18). In other words, this chapter investigates how logics of antiblackness and colonialism have preconditioned and prefigured the development of debates and theories regarding the origin of life itself and across the scales of biological discourses. Secondly, in investigating how Butler goes about unsettling a theory of the subject and subjectivity grounded in imperial histories of conquest, slavery, and colonialism, I conclude her oeuvre is not an unqualified endorsement of symbiosis, as some feminist posthumanists have claimed but rather a complex meditation on the promise and perils of symbiogenesis, symbiosis, and parasitism under conditions of unequal power and between beings with radically different subjectivities and corporeal semiotic logics. Thirdly, some readers have interpreted "Bloodchild" to be about slavery. Rather than engage in an interpretive act that overrides the centrality of speciated difference in the story by substituting species for race, potentially reifying the idea that race *is* speciation, instead I read "Bloodchild" as a meditation on the possible conditions and terms of mutual adaptability, communicability, and reciprocal responsibility across lines of radically discontinuous speciated embodiments and sensoria.[14]

Science fiction is a highly metaphorical genre and has historically been a productive site of intervention, where extrasolar narratives analogically critique terrestrial human conflicts, and Butler's narratives frequently possess the explicit and metaphorical dimensions of slavery and colonialism. Butler's *Kindred* and *Wild Seed* include direct comments on histories of enslavement in the United States and Africa, and the *Xenogenesis* series considers the question of colonial intrusion and settlement as well as nationalist resistance to that process.

However, it's worth considering what we might find if we were to resist the anthropocentric tendency to read nonhuman representations *exclusively* through the metaphorical terms of intra-human histories. What if we read the story in light of and with an eye for the politics of species? Rather than evacuate the nonhuman from the narrative, might it be possible that slavery metaphors and intra-human analogy obscure recognition of the unique form Butler's critique takes and why it matters? After all, the plot of "Bloodchild" as well as its character development, symbolism, and themes are articulated through a detailed and committed articulation of speciated difference as it emerges in and through encounter with discontinuity. What if it is not by analogy or metaphor but *through* the semio-material production of species that the text reveals its analysis of unequal and asymmetrical power relations?[15]

The emphasis in "Bloodchild" on the interspecies encounter is the specific route through which the narrative challenges the racialized, gendered, and expansionist conception of "the human" that underwrites Eurocentric human exceptionalism and its fraudulent universalism. Critics' metaphoric readings often bypass the difference species makes for understanding the stakes of those very histories and undercut a fuller appreciation of the disruptive potential of Butler's intervention. Ultimately, it is through a critique of the relational politics of species, rather than by recourse to the substitutional logic of human–animal metaphor, that Butler is able to disrupt racialized, gendered, and colonial hierarchies instituted by what Denise Ferreira da Silva terms the "transparency" thesis, whereby Europe's affectability is transferred elsewhere—to other peoples, species, and spatiotemporal environments.[16] Butler imbeds her critique of the relational politics of species in a transformative philosophy of subjectivation and embodied subjectivity.

To the extent that the Western (literary) tradition and its critics imagine freedom in the terms of what Ferreira da Silva calls "the transparency thesis," then Butler's critical rewriting of the body and subjectivation will continue to trouble such an imagination. According to Ferreira da Silva, the "transparency thesis" is the idea—produced in Western philosophy and science—of a knowing subject that is not primarily determined by exteriority but rather determines itself. The "transparent I" is underwritten by the privileging of the notion of interiority over exteriority and fantasies of "self-determination" as self-sufficiency, "the will" as self-discipline, and rationality as "self-regulation" such that the "transparent I" defines itself in opposition to the "affectable I" or the historical-cultural phantasy of the racial other as outer-determination, or lacking capacities of interiority that enable one to decide his essence and existence (Ferreira da Silva, *Toward* 40).[17]

According to Ferreira da Silva, philosophical and scientific discourse have instituted both "transparent subjectivity," associated with self-determination, temporality, and interiority, and "affectable subjectivity," associated with outer-determination and spatiality in the terms of a racially hierarchical universality. As Alva Gotby notes, in a reading of spatiality in Ferreira da Silva's *Toward a Global Idea of Race*, transparent subjectivity becomes racially coded as white, while affectability is located in the bodies of those who are not white and thus seen as coming from "elsewhere" in space. The body is then figured as a central signifier of the racial and one that is connected to other forms of spatiality, such as nature. In representations of race, the body can be understood as a link and mediator between subjectivity, as "interiority," and the world, as "exteriority" (Gotby 8).[18] As Gotby further notes, for Ferreira da Silva, race is not simply "a negative category, and it is not a category that works by excluding various groups from the notion of humanity. Rather, it is a productive category, a substantive, if fragmented, set of ideas that are instituted through implicitly or explicitly racialized representations of modes of subjectivity" (Gotby 6). Eurocentric human exceptionalism and imperialism render non-Western environments, creaturely life, and peoples as simultaneously biological threats and abject figures of affectability or outer-determination rather than self-determination and interiority. This is a biopolitic Butler would challenge by creating a story that disrupts its gendered, sexual, and ontological presuppositions by rejecting three interrelated cultural phantasies: the Self as sovereign, (self) consciousness as "Proprietor of his own Person," and what I am describing as the conception of the organismic body as *terra nullius,* or empty, vacant appropriable space.[19]

I believe "Bloodchild" is best understood as an examination of the co-constitutive nature of embodied subjectivity and environment. Thus, from the outset, the human organismic body is a multispecies processual environment characterized not "by centralized fixed control, but the transfer of control" rather than a sovereign "I" (Oyama 186). Similarly, human history and politics are also reimagined as a processual unfolding, where humans might not hold the balance of power. Moreover, "Bloodchild" invites the reader to consider the possibility that intra-human desire, affect, and unequal relations of power are mutually imbricated in the dynamics and processes of nonhuman bodies and worlds including those of insects and microorganisms, such as parasites, viruses, protoctists, fungi, and bacteria. Butler asks us to consider, in a moment when we are contemplating the apocalyptic end of the species, how might we parse what is harmful transmutation versus what is merely different or unrecognizable or strips one of a certain phantasy of mastery and control?

A Future Beyond Immunity?

The moral question is thus not, nor has it ever been: should one eat or not eat, eat this or not that, the living or the non-living, man or animal, but since *one must* eat in any case and since it is and tastes good to eat, and since there's no other definition of good (*du bien*), *how* for goodness sake should one *eat well* (*bien manger*)? And what does this imply? What is eating? How is this metonymy of introjection to be regulated? And in what respect does the formulation of these questions in language give us still more food for thought? In what respect is the question, if you will, carnivorous?
—Jacques Derrida, "Eating Well"

"Bloodchild" tells the coming-of-age story of a young man, Gan, faced with a difficult decision. He must decide whether he will incubate the eggs of an alien species or offer his sister in his place. This decision is especially vexing due to the entangled history of the two species: After fleeing from slavery and death on Earth, his people, Terrans, have found themselves on a planet populated by an insectoid people called Tlic.[20] Initially, humans respond to the Tlic with hostility and mass murder, killing them "as worms" (O. Butler, "Bloodchild" 25). Despite direct conflict, the Tlic are now hosts for a hostile people, and they have established the Preserve for human settlement. The Preserve is a highly contained community; its human occupants are restricted to its borders, and it is governed in a top-down fashion by the Tlic.

The Tlic loosely share features with the centipede and a family of insects called Oestridae—often referred to as a parasitic fly. Some species grow in the flesh of mammalian hosts, others grow in the gut. Enticed by body heat, their larvae hatch under the skin. The ongoing growth and development of the larvae requires the flies to feast on their hosts. If any segment is left behind, say in the process of attempted removal, it dies and rots, introducing a bacterial infection in the body of the host. Conversely, when left undisturbed in the host's body, the larvae are relatively painless and have bacteriostatic properties, keeping wounds free of infection. The fly typically finishes the larval part of its growth cycle in four to eighteen weeks, upon which it will unceremoniously crawl out of the flesh and fly away.[21]

The shadow of past interspecies war looms: many humans continue to view the Tlic as an alien and oppressive species, and many Tlic have deep ambivalence about whether they should seek compromise with a hostile species. Nevertheless, both peoples have something to gain from accommodating the other. The humans, having escaped enslavement and genocide, have gained a new livable world, and the Tlic larvae grow stronger, larger, and more numerous when human bodies incubate their fertilized eggs.

Due to the Red Queen effect,[22] where evolutionary partners' adaptations become incompatible, the Tlic can no longer rely on local hosts. The local animals that were once host for their eggs are now poisoning their young, killing them before they can complete the larval stage of development. This leaves the Tlic desperate and near extinction. Human surrogacy enables the Tlic to be a "healthy and thriving" people again (O. Butler, "Bloodchild" 25).

Gan must decide whether hosting the eggs in exchange for a new start on another planet is mutually symbiotic or a parasitic compromise of his humanity. The answer to his dilemma largely rests on the definitions of "host" and "compromise" that the two peoples are able to effect. Both terms can imply pernicious parasitism or, conversely, mutual accommodation or adaptation. Historically, both peoples have committed horrific crimes against the other. Humans, upon arrival, made an attempt at conquest but ultimately failed. The Tlic, having discovered the benefit of human hosts, established breeding programs, which some Tlic want to revive, where humans would be kept as breeding stock in pens. The "Preserve," the tightly controlled and bordered Terran community, is the outcome of these events.[23] To complicate matters further, the Tlic who wants to impregnate Gan is T'Gatoi. She is both the top-ranking official that governs the Preserve and a close friend of his mother, Lien, since childhood. T'Gatoi helped raise Gan and was herself incubated and born from the body of Gan's father. Indeed, whether "host" implies one who provides what is needed and desired or one who is parasitized will be decided based on the delicate and subtle maneuverings of risk and accommodation in a symbiotic relationship of unequal power and asymmetrical subjectivity: Terrans have bio-reproductive power, and Tlic have military might. While some feminist critics have mistakenly understood symbiosis as incompatible with asymmetry and hierarchy, as explained above, symbiosis does not actually imply the absence of incommensurability and hierarchy; rather, symbiosis is a theory that considers the different forms interdependent relations can take.[24]

In my view, "Bloodchild" is a meditation on the embodied mind's encounter with other species, particularly insects, parasites, bacteria, fungi, protozoa, and viruses, which are the dominant forms of life composing our world and bodies. It explores how we, at the registers of affect, desire, and the organismic body, accommodate other species; the story also shows how the organsmic body adapts with and as other species. It asks: Is our embodied subjectivity a site of accommodation and cooperation among different species, or will we immunize ourselves from the alien, the stranger, and the unknown?[25] Embodied subjectivity is reimagined as a site of both mutual symbiosis and struggles for dominance as well as modes of conviviality that exceed the terms of this binary.[26]

In "A Symbiotic View of Life: We Have Never Been Individuals," Gilbert, Sapp, and Tauber demonstrate that genomic individuality or the "one genome/one organism" view is not only misleading but erroneous, as "neither humans, nor any other organism, can be regarded as individuals by anatomical criteria" and are instead complexly holobiont or an "integrated organism" composed of host elements and symbionts (327). They argue the prominence and medical successes of the "germ theory of disease" has effectively obscured the life-giving properties of microbial infections and antagonistically cast microorganisms in general as disease-causing "germs" and an "enemy of man" (329). Indeed, the discipline of immunology has been called "the science of self/non-self discrimination," whereby the immune system is portrayed "as a defense network against a hostile exterior world": "In this view, the immune system is defensive 'weaponry,' evolved to protect the body against threats from pathogenic agents: worms, protists, fungi, bacteria, and viruses. Accordingly, if it were not for the immune system, opportunistic infections would prevail (as they do in cases of immune deficiencies) and the organism would perish" (Klein, quoted in Gilbert, Sapp, and Tauber 330). However, recent studies suggest that an organism's immune system is in part created by the resident microbiome and is less a weapon and more a mediator.[27] Moreover, the authors go on to suggest that evolution likely selects not for individuals (host or symbionts) but for holobionts. For instance, the mitochondria suffusing every cell of the human body have their own independent genome. Mitochondria live in the body and are essential for such vital functions as converting food into energy (Adenosine triphosphate or ATP), cell growth, and cell death, yet they are genetically "nonhuman" despite being passed along the maternal line. Moreover, within the body of a healthy adult, microbial cells are estimated to outnumber human cells ten to one.[28] These communities, called microbiome, are so crucial to the cells that host them that some have called them the "second genome."[29] Similarly, in "Bloodchild," skin is no longer perceived as a limit to so-called alien or external forces but a contact zone for interspecies encounters and accommodations characterized by risk and compromise.

In "Bloodchild," skin is reimagined as a two-way door to one's "home": a door that can be opened inward and outward. Home is simultaneously an edifice, a body, a planet, and a sense of belonging to a heterogeneous whole. Gan states with respect to his sister, "We had always been a unit, she and I" (O. Butler, "Bloodchild" 7). A family inhabits a home, where family includes more than human agencies housed by and living beyond the skin. These agencies, in this case Gan's—so-called biological—family members, take different positions with respect to the Tlic generally and to the prospect of impregnation in particular.[30] Gan's older brother Qui believes impregnation is a repulsive and intolerable compromise of his masculinity and identity as a human while his younger sister, Xuan Hoa, unquestionably views it as an honor—we are to assume as a result of an uncritical acceptance of the conflation of womanhood with motherhood. Lien, Gan's mother, is deeply resentful of the terms and conditions of the Terran–Tlic partnership, but the nature of her resentment, like resentment itself, is left somewhat irresolute by the author. But it is implied that it is rooted in a sense of protectiveness of Gan and an unwillingness to compromise her sense of identity even despite an awareness of the necessity of doing so. These characters represent different positions one could take with respect to hospitality. Ultimately, Gan will renegotiate the assumptive terms of compromise so that risk and reciprocal responsibility are acknowledged rather than rejected, stressing the value of mutual adaptation for all parties involved.

When Butler introduces T'Gatoi, we learn that she shares some important features with Oestridae or parasitic flies: T'Gatoi "liked our body heat and took advantage of it whenever she could" (O. Butler, "Bloodchild" 3). Butler continues, "She simply came in, climbed onto one of her special couches, and called me over to keep her warm" (O. Butler, "Bloodchild" 4). The Tlic provide their host their sterile eggs for food, which enhance vigor and prolong life, potentially even doubling the average human life span (O. Butler, "Bloodchild" 3). Tlic eggs, like those of parasitic flies, have properties that protect the body from disease.[31] According to Gan, his father "who had never refused one in his life, had lived more than twice as long as he should have. And toward the end of his life, when he should have been slowing down, he marries my mother and fathered four children" (O. Butler, "Bloodchild" 3). Gan's mother, Lien, knows at least one of her children will be called upon by the Tlic, by T'Gatoi in particular. She resents the terms of the relation, which she expresses initially by refusing T'Gatoi's offer of her sister's sterile eggs. Eventually, "unwillingly obedient" she swallows its contents with an "It's good. . . . Sometimes I forget how good it is" (O. Butler, "Bloodchild" 4–5). To complicate matters further, the eggs are not only regenerative but also a powerful narcotic. As is typical in Butler's fiction, "Bloodchild" presents a world that complicates its asymmetries of power by comingling benevolence and coercion, generosity, and self-interest.

The kinship bond uniting T'Gatoi and Gan is by no means equal and symmetrical. The Tlic generally and T'Gatoi in particular dominate the arena of political power. Not only is she the official that governs the Preserve, she also protects the Terrans from the Tlic who would just as soon parasitize humanity without providing humans any accommodation, potentially to the point that it put their own survival at risk yet again—a survival they had only just recovered with the arrival of Terrans. At the very least, for this reason, Lien demands that her children respect and take care of T'Gatoi:

> T'Gatoi was hounded on the outside. Her people wanted more of us made available. Only she and her political faction stood between us and the hordes who did not understand why there was a Preserve—why any Terran could not be courted, paid, drafted, in some way made available to them. Or they did understand, but in their desperation, they did not care. (O. Butler, "Bloodchild" 5)

The Tlic could easily be likened to the insects, parasites, viruses, fungi, and bacteria that challenge the very notion of human dominance. The following exchange between Lien and T'Gatoi implies that, as on Earth, human dominance and control should not be assumed. Lien responds to T'Gatoi's coercive power (albeit tacit) over her and her children bitterly: "I should have stepped on you when you were small enough" (O. Butler, "Bloodchild" 7). However, this "old joke between them" is an empty threat between lifelong friends and asymmetrical rivals. During Lien's lifetime, T'Gatoi was never small enough for Lien, or any other Terran, to step on. Furthermore, T'Gatoi would still be young after Lien dies from old age, despite already being three times Lien's age (O. Butler, "Bloodchild" 7). Dominion in this scene becomes an "old joke"; conviviality and rivalry comingle.

Myra Hird has called into question the ideology of what Margulis called "big like us," which concerns "concentrating on creatures that easily bear human ocular scrutiny—creatures we can see unaided by technology as though creatures 'big like us' resemble the majority of life" (*The Origins of Sociable* 21). Hird argues that the ideology of "big like us" has left three million years of living organism activity in the Proterozoic and Archean underresearched: "This effects a double privileging of organisms as autonomous individuals and sexual reproduction" (*The Origins of Sociable* 66). Hird adds, "Perhaps we could imagine, as no doubt science fiction writers have already, our eyes to have microscopic vision, enabling us to focus immediately upon the microbial world unimpeded by what must then be unfathomably oversized species. Perhaps then we might overcome the myopia that defines our natureculture border to be with animals" (*The Origins of Sociable* 21). What if human domination is provisional, circumscribed, and contingent upon nonhuman agencies—in other words, a ruse? Consider the following excerpt:

> [T'Gatoi] parceled us out to the desperate and sold us to the rich and powerful for their political support. Thus, we were necessities, status symbols, and an independent people. She oversaw the joining of families, putting an end to the final remnants of the earlier system of breaking up Terran families to suit impatient Tlic. . . . It was a little frightening to know that only she stood between us and that desperation that could so easily *swallow us*. My mother would look at her sometimes and say to me, "Take care of her." And I would remember that she too had been outside, had seen. (O. Butler, "Bloodchild" 5, emphasis added)[32]

His mother's admonishment to "take care of her" qualifies both human and Tlic agency in the story. For both Terran and Tlic, agency would only be relational and therefore not a matter of individual autonomy. The Tlic cannot biologically reproduce without hosts, and this sets inescapable limits on their agency—interdependency. Terrans, having escaped enslavement and genocide, gain a "new livable world" that hastens them to abandon the phantasy that identity and autonomy are the source of agency (Jacobs 91). For Terrans, the Tlic symbolize the limit of such a phantasy: affectability. "Bloodchild" seems to suggest that human agency is always compromised and is always simultaneously a form of subjection on dual registers—language and biology. Here the body is not only subjected by the intra-human politics of culture: the "intra-human" relation is itself the effect of trans-species encounters. Butler challenges readers to confront the fact that the sovereign "I" and the human body's integrity are already breached and violable.

Naomi Jacobs notes that in the classic dystopian novel the world is "drained" of agency—"of an individual's capacity to choose and to act, or a group's capacity to influence and intervene in social formations" (Jacobs 92). In a dystopia, the capacity "to choose" and "to act" are undermined because the spheres of "thought" and "action" are so severely controlled (Jacobs 92). Jacobs elaborates, "The realm of subjectivity is such a regime's primary locus of social control; without a clear sense of self, a citizen of a dystopia will feel no need to rebel, even if means of rebellion were available" (Jacobs 92). The classic dystopian text presumes that a clear sense of self is derived from an inviolable sense of individual identity, self-definition, and self-determination. Thus, classic dystopias speak "from and to the humanist perspective, in which the unique, self-determining individual is the measure of all things" (Jacobs 93). Without these attributes one does not have a "truly human" life: "Indeed, such self-determination is sometimes offered as a characteristic that sets humans beings apart from (other) animals" and, I would add, primitivized peoples (Jacobs 93). The *primitive community* has long been imagined as the obverse of the *sovereign individual*, held to be the bedrock of a Western civilization that has left behind the prehistorical primitive mind and primal horde with one notable caveat: in a recapitulation of one of anthropology's archetypal themes, Freud, in *Group Psychology*, once again casts individuality as the mark of civilization and collectivity as the mark of primitivity. As noted by Celia Brickman in *Aboriginal Populations of the Mind: Race and Primitivity in Psychoanalysis*, Freud equates group mind and the unconscious, presenting both as tantamount to the mind of so-called primitives

> out of which modern individuality is seen to have emerged at a certain point in evolutionary history but into which it can be resubmerged when in the presence of a crowd. Through this identification of primitivity with the crowd and with the unconscious, the primitive—racially other—human is once again shown to be the past of modern, civilized society, still present in the unconscious as in the colonies, always threatening to overcome modern European civilization should its members let down their rational guard. (Brickman 94)[33]

In "Bloodchild," the self-determining and self-defining subject is "dismantled" and "demolished" (Hurley 205).[34] However, rather than lament this existential predicament or try to recuperate a spurious notion of individuality, Butler replaces it with a radical conception of subjectivity that sees generative possibility in *relational* subjectivity and agency emerging from "these very ruptures and violations" (Jacobs 91, 92). In effect, Butler suggests that agency can only be exercised interdependently. In the following scene, Gan is unexpectedly introduced to live childbirth, and his sense of his own humanity pivots on how he interprets what he saw.

En route to a call box, a pregnant man, or N'Tlic, named Bram Lomas accidently stumbled into Gan's family's lives. He had hoped to contact T'Khotgif, the Tlic whose grubs he incubated, but unexpectedly began the advanced stages of labor before reaching T'Khotgif. The transition from the breeding pens of past generations to the interspecies joining of families in the present carried with it the stipulation that Tlic were responsible for easing the passage of their young. T'Khotgif had the responsibility of supporting and facilitating Lomas's labor; she would provide an egg that would dull pain and promote healing. Qui goes in search of T'Khotgif as Bram would soon give birth. The grubs were releasing poison, and as they ate their way out of their egg cases, their movement under the skin was visible. Soon, they would begin to consume their host if birth was delayed any further. The time between sickness and removal is a crucial determinate of whether incubation is a lethal parasitism or a potentially mutual, yet bloody, symbiosis— equally determinant, of course, are the social conditions, between the two peoples, initiating and surrounding birth. T'Gatoi immediately steps into T'Khotgif's role. With her stinger, T'Gatoi eases the birth as much as possible, but despite her best efforts, the absence of T'Khotgif's egg makes this an unusually difficult birth. T'Gatoi recruits Gan's help. He must slaughter an animal, an achti, and return with its flesh so it can be fed to the grubs in exchange for Lomas's life. Despite being a member of an agropastoral family, Gan had never killed an animal and only begrudgingly shoots an achti before he returns to his living room only to witness what he imagines is his fate as T'Gatoi performs a surgery reminiscent of a cesarean.

The entire episode is a bloody affair. Despite having seen drawings and diagrams of birth his entire life, Gan is unprepared for the viscera of the live birthing scene. As he watches T'Gatoi bite away the egg case and lick away the blood, he wonders, "Did she like the taste? Did childhood habits die hard—or die at all?" (O. Butler, "Bloodchild" 17). Now confronted with the full potential of birth that can lead to a painful death, Gan is no longer willing to accommodate T'Gatoi's larvae. What he once regarded as mutual symbiosis, he now views as "wrong, alien":

> I had been told all my life that this was a good and necessary thing Tlic and Terran did together—a kind of birth. I had believed it until now. I knew birth was painful and bloody, no matter what. But, this was something else, something worse. (O. Butler, "Bloodchild" 16–17)

Two events happen in succession that produce opposing feelings about the developing human–Tlic partnership, forcing Gan to confront the decision that awaits him. When T'Khotgif finally arrives, her concern for Lomas, and not just her children, temporarily restores Gan's faith in the Tlic–human partnership. She expresses concern about Lomas's health, as well as her children's well-being. She had planned to be by Lomas's side, despite the possibility that her attendance might exacerbate her deteriorating health, as she is dying from illness. Her name had been the last thing Lomas said before he lost coherence. But Gan's faith in interspecies partnership was shaken once again by his brother's admission that, while out of sight, he had seen years before a man killed by the Tlic who had the responsibility of caring for him during childbirth. Without an achti or neighbors nearby, the man in his painful desperation begged for death. Preventing him from enduring further pain, his Tlic slit his throat. The grubs, even then, continued to eat.

Gan, now ambivalent and terrified, contemplates suicide. T'Gatoi enters the kitchen and finds a distraught Gan. She offers reassurance: "That was bad. You should have not seen it. It need not be that way." She regrets what Gan has witnessed, and she expresses gratitude for what Lomas made possible—another generation (O. Butler, "Bloodchild" 23). Looking at her, Gan wonders "how much I saw and understood there, and how much I only imagined" (O. Butler, "Bloodchild" 23). He protests, "No one ever asks us, You never asked me." Initially unresponsive to his protest, she eventually responds with a question. She asks if he used the rifle to shoot the achti and "do you mean to use it to shoot me?" (O.

Butler, "Bloodchild" 24). His response is equally indirect: "What does Terran blood taste like to you? . . . What are you? What are we to you?" Initially saying nothing, T'Gatoi eventually offers an enigmatic response: "You know me as no other does. You must decide." When Gan demands once again that she ask, she replies with a question: "For my children's lives?"[35] (O. Butler, "Bloodchild" 24).

This dialogue is necessarily cryptic. One of the most challenging dimensions of the story is that it suggests communicability across speciated worldings is possible while also foregrounding that communication is marked by opacity: Gan and T'Gatoi's communicability exists outside of a shared framework of perception and meaning yet is collaborative and reciprocal. Thus, for Gan and T'Gatoi, shared meaning ultimately lies beyond speech despite being unquestionably interactive. Through their relation, Butler reveals that parasites and microorganisms mark the limit of liberal humanist conceptions of subjectivity characterized by autonomous agency and consent. However, does such a limit necessarily foreclose the possibility of mutual symbiosis, or is abject parasitism the only interpretive frame available? This is what Gan must decide.

Here is where I believe the story emphatically stresses its deconstructive impulse with regard to liberal humanist touchstones—sovereignty, agency, choice, diplomacy, reciprocal obligations, and especially self-determination. For Butler, self-determination is ultimately self-defeating, particularly when it becomes synonymous with self-ownership, a concept in and of itself indebted to slavery.[36]

In attempting to demonstrate that there is an "intrinsic association" of *self* and *own* in John Locke's thought, Etienne Balibar in "My 'Self' My 'Own': One and the Same?" suggests Locke "appeared to have inaugurated and actually invented a conception of individual subjectivity that places it within the realm of consciousness and practically identifies it . . . with the possibility of self-consciousness" (23). Balibar argues that Locke "progressively creates or elaborates" an equation of self and own, a metaphysical event that arises at the semantic and syntactical level in the *Second Treatise of Government*, by taking advantage of the double meanings of "my self" and "my own;" both terms, by making them separate words, invite them each to be read as pronouns and possessive expressions. For instance, "my self" can be read either as "the self that is mine, that is my own self, or simply that is my own" but also by analogy, *it self* as in "*its self*, the self that belongs to it, that is its own self, or that is its own" (Balibar 24). These "grammatical subtleties," Balibar writes, inaugurate what Crawford Brough MacPherson has called "possessive individualism" (24).[37] Such a metaphysical fact or event rests upon the idea that consciousness is the operator of a mental system that appropriates the self to itself, "where 'appropriate' at the same time means to identify with and to make a property, a separated or private property of, and where also itself should be heard as it(s) *self*, in a mirror construction: consciousness appropriates *my* self to my *self*" (Balibar 26–27). Similarly, the word "own," which is both adjective and verb, signifies either to acknowledge or confess, as well as to possess or both, further cementing a metaphysical fact that functionally make *self* and *own* near equivalents, whereby the circularity of the argument places identity and identification on one side of an equation and appropriation and property on the other such that the two sides continuously exchange their functions: "So what I can consider as me, myself, is *my self*, and "my" *self* is some "thing" that I *own*, or that I must own (confess) is mine, was done or thought by me, has become my own because I appropriated it to me by doing it or thinking it consciously" (Balibar 27).

Thus, claims to self-ownership are paradoxical in that they reject the master's authority but not the property relation. Such a speculative identity casts the Self as "Proprietor of his own Person," ironically conscripting being to the domain of competitive markets and proprietary claims, which naturalize the oppositional hierarchical relations of their production and suppress the heterogeneous agencies that shape market events.[38] The social contract's speculative identity is, therefore, haunted by a sovereignty it theoretically aimed to dethrone but ultimately only appropriates for its Self.

Gan seeks reassurance that he is not simply an "animal," biological matter sans avowed relationality, significance, and agency (in other words, an object [of property]) by exclaiming: "Ask me, Gatoi . . . I don't want to be a host animal. Not even yours . . . You use us" (O. Butler, "Bloodchild" 24). T'Gatoi, somewhat reassuringly, responds, "We do. We wait long years for you and teach you and join our families to yours. You know you aren't animals to us" (O. Butler, "Bloodchild" 24). However, this answer is more indirect and obscure than it seems. Butler's fiction consistently exposes and sharply criticizes the assumption of human superiority and the exploitation that results from it: in particular, the deadening objectification that accompanies the tropological designation of beings as "animal."[39] T'Gatoi's protest "You know you aren't animals to us" suggests that theirs is not a relation limited to unidirectional dominance and objectification, whereby the fundamental role that the animalized play in (re)producing the Self is denied. An essential feature of objectification is that the relational tie itself does not even register as a form of relationality at all. Thus, such an objectification proceeds as if "the animal" lies outside the sphere of influence that generates the conditions of one's agency. Tlic *need* hosts for reproduction; they are symbionts, a companion species for humans.[40] This grants humans forms of power and agency stemming from interspecies co-evolutionary relationality, albeit beyond a liberal humanist frame, which the Tlic are, out of necessity, beginning to appreciate. As host "animals" began killing Tlic young prior to the arrival of Terrans, the arrival of the Terrans was the beginning of a new way of relating to hosts—as partners. As a result, the Tlic have been revivified, the use of host animals has been brought to a near standstill, and exceedingly bloody, painful births like Lomas's are becoming increasingly rare.

Butler's alternative account of the "subject" and "agency" in the interspecies evolutionary encounter exceeds consciousness and self-determination: Gan or the human host might be an object of the Other's agency but in the absence of objectification; on a biological register, beyond speech, the reproduction of the species is dependent upon the host's cooperation. Such a notion of "object" beyond "objectification" places pressure on the presumed inertia thought to cohere to "objects" because, in this case, the object—the host—makes renewed subjectivity possible. Without the host's cooperation, the species' futurity is foreclosed, and the Tlic would return to a state of impending extinction. For the Tlic, humans do have agency and significance; they engender Tlic that are "healthy, and thriving." In exchange, the Tlic, like many other nonhuman life forms that affectively vex us, provide sanctuary—"a livable space on a world not our own" (O. Butler, "Afterward" 32). The "not our own" here is important. Ownership of "the world" and even of "the self" is being outright challenged. T'Gatoi returns the charge of objectification: "your ancestors . . . they survived because of us. We saw them as people and gave them the Preserve when they still tried to kill us *as worms*" (O. Butler, "Bloodchild" 25, emphasis added).[41] Butler troubles the imperialist impulse that underwrites the scientific exploration of terrestrial and extrasolar outer space and the inner space of the organismic body simultaneously as well as the science fiction genre such explorations inspire by disestablishing its subject. In "Bloodchild," human attempts at colonial settlement of an alien planet rebound such that humans find their colonial ambitions thwarted, and they themselves become not colonized, or in an inverted role but located in an uncharted social position rather than territory: partnership. Here T'Gatoi asks Gan to be accountable to the genocidal telos humans attempted to impose on Tlic upon arrival.

This impasse is reconciled by the mutual acceptance of risk and vulnerability that comes with interdependence and symbiosis. Gan could have been selfish and offered his sister in his place. After all, rather than abject T'Gatoi's young, Xuan Hoa would be "proud" to give birth to them. T'Gatoi assures him that she would take Xuan Hoa as a substitute. However, Butler forcefully suggests that the rejection of interdependent relations, even with their risk and vulnerability, is self-destructive: When T'Gatoi asks "Would you really rather die than bear my young, Gan?" and later if "you would have destroyed yourself?," questions as much existential as they are practical, Gan responds, "I could have done that. I nearly did. That's Qui's 'way.' I wonder if he knows" (O. Butler, "Bloodchild" 29). Ultimately, Gan assumes the vulnerability and risk that comes with symbiosis out of a surprisingly emerging affection for T'Gatoi's affection and desire for what he had previously feared and abjected. Gan affirms his decision to gestate T'Gatoi's young both verbally ("Yes") and to himself: *"Take care of her,* my mother used to say. Yes" (O. Butler, "Bloodchild" 29). The standalone sentence, as Laurel Bollinger suggests, represents a full affirmation of the decision he has made ("Placental" 334–335).[42] T'Gatoi must adapt and accept compromise as well. When T'Gatoi insists that Gan surrender his gun (as the Tlic have outlawed human possession of guns), Gan replies, "Leave it here! . . . if we're not your animals, if these are adult things, accept the risk. There is risk, Gatoi, in dealing with a partner" (O. Butler, "Bloodchild" 26). Gan accepts the risk of death involved in bearing T'Gatoi's young in exchange for T'Gatoi's assumption of the risk of Terran violence, including that Terrans could potentially kill the children implanted in their bodies.

What is significant here is not only Gan's *conscious* acceptance of risk or Gan's negotiation of shared risk but also (and perhaps more importantly) the revelation that mutual risk had been there all along. The significance of this compromise lies in the revelation that affectability and mutual vulnerability had always already been constitutive to their relationality. Gan's family had that gun the whole time and would have had it whether or not it was ever brandished in front of T'Gatoi. Mutual symbiosis can potentially become a deadly parasitism, but symbiosis potentially carries this risk as symbiosis is a process of "becoming with," not a guarantee of a pregiven arrangement. Gan learns that if he were to reject this vulnerability or his affectability, he would become the phantasmagoric parasite Terrans project onto Tlic. Thus, sovereignty, in the form of absolute freedom, is a dangerous ideal as it stands in opposition to the recognition of relationality (in this case, a relationality that crosses boundaries of species).

In Butler's narrative, absolute human autonomy is not presented as a viable alternative to accommodation and adaptation. This revision of activity *as* receptivity and agency *as* other than sovereignty is a provocative call for a radical politics of accommodation that challenges the forms of dominance the text evokes, including but not limited to slavery, colonialism, and imperialism. While this receptivity is a form of vulnerability, Butler suggests that attempts to reject interdependence and the abilities of adaptability are self-defeating (even self-destructive) and thwart potentially mutually beneficial symbiosis. Butler presents a picture of embodied subjectivity that is not unitary, wholly autonomous, and impenetrable but is characterized by receptivity and context-dependent agency. Both the Tlic and Terran must adapt and accommodate the other or else face mutual extinction (Green 172). In Gan's case, it is an "unusual accommodation"—male pregnancy.

In Butler's story, men share the burden of societal expectation to bear children as well as the pain and physical risks of childbirth, challenging the often-unquestioned presumptions of heteropatriarchal culture. "Bloodchild" departs from the rivalrous tone of traditional male pregnancy narratives, in which they commonly seek to penetrate and master a female domain. Emblematized by Mary Shelley's Dr. Frankenstein, historically, these characters have tended to privilege the powers of procreation and disavow the pain and burden of sexist societal expectations.

In the following scene, egg implantation is reimagined as interspecies lovemaking, when T'Gatoi impregnates Gan:

> I undressed and lay down beside her. I knew what to do, what to expect. I had been told all my life. I felt the familiar sting, narcotic, mildly pleasant. Then, the blind probing of her ovipositor. The puncture was painless, easy. So easy going in. She undulated slowly against me, her muscles forcing the egg from her body into mine. I held on to a pair of her limbs until I remembered Lomas holding her that way. Then I let go, moved inadvertently, and hurt her. She gave a low cry of pain and I expected to be caged at once within her limbs. When I wasn't, I held on to her again, feeling oddly ashamed.
> "I'm sorry," I whispered. (O. Butler, "Bloodchild" 28)

The queer and feminist criticism on "Bloodchild" has suggested that it is perhaps this scene of interspecies lovemaking, rather than the theme of male pregnancy, that more profoundly disrupts heteronormative gender assumptions.[43] Elyce Helford argues that T'Gatoi recalls both "female and male [sexual] positions" and further states, "T'Gatoi's action embodies both possession of the female egg and male penetration" (264).[44] Similarly, scholars have argued that T'Gatoi has "masculine" powers and "patriarchal authority" as she is the official in charge of the Preserve. Some have even suggested that in "Bloodchild," "masculine" social power, penetration, and ejaculation coincide in the character T'Gatoi, and, thus, the proliferation of these "masculine" symbols inescapably point to a male referent.

I would argue that she has *masculinized* powers in that she pursues and penetrates Gan in a context where she holds the balance of "phallocentric" power—generally imagined to be a male domain. Furthermore, I maintain that in this scene it is species difference rather than the drama of metaphorical exchange and substitution that unsettles gender and sexual essentialism. For instance, in the insect family oestridae, it is the female that scouts the host; it is her "ovipositor" that penetrates the skin and releases the fertilized egg into the pierced host. However, the female fly's ovipositor does not conform to the anthropocentric logic of dimorphism, which problematically purports to faithfully identify human forms and subjectivities *and* is problematic with respect to insects as well.[45] It is only by way of an (Euro)(andro)anthropocentric logic of substitution that one can interpret T'Gatoi as a "masculine" character or indexes a male referent. Such a reading reduces the story to a simple reversal of gender and sexual roles that can only be appraised for their success or failure to reject patriarchal heteronormativity. Yet, T'Gatoi is neither reducible to a metaphor for "man" nor "male penetration" as penetration is not something only males can do, an observation her ovipositor incites. Departing from a heteronormative anthropocentric mapping of the organism, her ovipositor vexes the imagination and invites the reader to reimagine the organ of sex, reproduction, and ejaculation.[46] The ovipositor unsettles the presumption of dimorphism and underscores that signifiers such as "masculine" and "feminine" as well "female" and "male" are other than ontological pregivens.[47] Oestridae do not adhere to heteropatriarchal presuppositions of sexuated embodiment and sexuality.

"Bloodchild" unties reified notions of sex and reproduction in order to knot them in an unfamiliar way in the narrative: a way that suggests sexual difference is, to evoke Eva Hayward, dispersion rather than binary—and I would add, troubling even the notion of sex difference as a continuum. Such an insight underscores that sex is superabundant with respect to reproduction. Moreover, in "Bloodchild" reproduction is more than a biological imperative but also encompasses suprahuman evolutionary processes and a dynamic life history—the subject of the subsequent chapter.[48] Thus, "Bloodchild" breaches the terms of dominant logic's tethering of sex/gender and reproduction rather than reinforces limiting and misleading notions of biological essentialism and determinism. Such logics have, of course, been primary to the poesis of antiblackness that casts black(ened) people as inverted and/or alternately excessive and deficient vis-à-vis sex and gender.[49]

Similarly, Gan's "male pregnancy" is *not* an exploration of *the feminine position but a feminized position*—that of being subjected to the Other. Gan is not "feminine" because his body is an incubator for T'Gatoi's children but rather because pregnancy is one of the more prominent symbols of affectability and interdependence in a culture that equates interdependence, compromise, and accommodation with castration. And for that reason, these attributes have been feminized and/or deemed unmanly. Like T'Gatoi, the figure of Gan does not map neatly onto gender stereotypes.

"Bloodchild" encourages the reader to examine and challenge common assumptions of womanhood—including the equivalence of woman with female, feminine, biological reproduction, sexual reception, and motherhood—through the introduction of a nonmimetic reflection or recalcitrant analogy that emphasizes difference as much or if not more than similarity between terms. Here Butler reveals that "nature" does not mirror human constructions, undercutting the solipsism that often underwrites animal metaphors. Thus, "Bloodchild" problematizes the solipsistic metaphorism it would appear to invite: the theme of "male pregnancy" provides an uncanny reflection that unsettles rather than stabilizes the anthropocentric logic of nature analogies. Indeed, as Elizabeth Wilson notes, it is too reductive to transpose our subjectivities and identity categories onto the nonhuman. If we assume the nonhuman simply mimics human, cultural and social forms, now routinely marked "queer" or "trans" for instance, then we miss the possibility for "nature" to work on us "contrariwise, to render those familiar human, cultural, and social forms more curious" as a result of their affiliation with "nature," not as "knowable through its association with familiar human forms, but because it renders the human, cultural and social guises of queer less familiar and more captivated by natural and biological forces" (284).[50]

As Amanda Thibodeau notes, "the desire to encounter aliens is almost always accompanied by a desire to demonstrate human strength, ingenuity, and ambition—three traits often appropriated by a masculine imperial ideology that penetrates unknown or virgin frontiers," but "Bloodchild" upends rather than inverts the heteronormative constructions of subjectivity, empire, exploration, and genre that rely on, to use Anne McClintock's phrase, "imperial thrust" (263).[51] Anne McClintock has argued that British imperialism erected a patriarchal narrative on colonized lands thought to be "passively awaiting the thrusting, male insemination of history, language, and reason," and in so doing the so-called virgin lands of Africa, Asia, and Americas were "libidinally eroticized" (22, 31). One of the more striking features of Butler's scene of penetration and impregnation is that it not only parodies and upends this relation but also that the narrative as a whole exposes impenetrability and inviolable masculinity as a phantasy inimical to the phenomenal experience of Man's embodiment. Pressed against each other, through improvised precepts and intertwined with each other they experience a hapticality where Gan is neither engulfed nor defeated and as a result feels oddly ashamed that he found this provisional togetherness so threatening.[52]

What is at the center of "Bloodchild" is an articulation of embodied subjectivity that is typified by receptivity rather than mastery. Receptivity here should not be confused with passivity. Receptivity is the processual experience of embodied humanity—the active, but not always conscious, process of receiving and participating in an encounter—not the totalizing identity implied by the term "passive."[53] Thus, Butler can provide incisive, critical commentary on the Anthropocene while also suggesting that the Anthropocene stems significantly from a futile rejection of the fundamental receptivity of embodied experience. Suggesting that embodiment entails receptivity does not imply that the organismic body is inert, inactive, or non-agential; rather, it clarifies the agency of the body by situating the organism's agency within an "interactive model of causality," which includes not only the embodied mind but also its environment and nonhuman agencies, evolutionary history, and culture—all in a network of relationality (Birke 22). Butler's articulation goes beyond a conception of the body awaiting the inscription of culture by narrating the body as agential in the shaping of corporeal vulnerability. Biology and culture are, to use Karen Barad's term, agentially "intra-active" (Barad, *Meeting the Universe* 210). Thus, to have a body is to be enmeshed in a network of relations where humans are not always in control or even conscious participants. Thereby, human agency is not the practice of centralized fixed control but the transfer of control (Oyama 186). Derrida has argued that "language" has served as a kind of armature with respect to the vulnerability of embodiment, but paradoxically, this very armature produces a second "vulnerability" as humans are vulnerable to the caesura between language and meaning.[54] Receptivity is what links the organism to its existential predicament.

Butler exposes and confronts (hetero)sexist, male anxiety about the specter of submission to the Other. Such submission often carries with it the specter of slavery and the annihilation of the self. Butler seems to suggest that the body's receptivity is more accurately viewed as an invitation to turn toward, rather than away from, co-adaptation and improvisational identities. (Fe)male reception need not be equated with inaction, a lack of agency, or dispossession. "Bloodchild" diagnoses the colonial and sexual crisscross of this anxiety, which often equates passivity with sexual reception. That Man equates virility with impermeability in a zero-sum game of power not only forecloses the pleasures of reception but also mistakes accommodation for parasitism, symbiosis for slavery, and symbiogenesis with extinction.

In this sense, social contract philosophy and scientific discourses of symbiosis are analogues, or better yet, they co-produce fictions of the Self that underwrite the transparency thesis in that they establish, unquestionably, freedom (understood as mastery and self-possession) as the privileged value over and against the black(ened) and queerly gendered figure of the slave.[55] In so doing, Kant and Locke not only prefigure "self-possession," "sovereignty," and "self-determination" as effectively property in whiteness, but Locke equated the drive toward such a notion of freedom and simultaneous movement away from the black(ened) figure of the slave with the preservation of life itself: quoting Locke, "freedom from absolute, arbitrary power is so necessary to and closely joined with a man's preservation that he cannot part with it but by what forfeits his preservation and life together" (quoted in Ferreira da Silva, "Toward" 52).[56] While some feminist, posthumanist critics have looked to the scientific theory of symbiosis as a possible antidote to neo-Darwinian depictions of "Nature, red in tooth and claw," I argue that the liberatory possibilities of symbiosis and its metaphoric use in posthumanist theory must be carefully considered alongside critical reflection on the antiblackness that has historically accompanied developments in scientific discourse and biotechnology. Those that accompany the theory of symbiosis include Lockean ideals of freedom as they travel with and are extended into the realm of the biological.

I argue that racial discourse is not simply a by-product of the discourse of species, but rather race and species discourses are homologous and symbiotic. To this point, even the notion of the symbiosis of race and species I reflexively and critically deploy here cannot fully escape the racialization embedded in the very discursivity of symbiosis. As I will demonstrate, biologist Lynn Margulis's theory of symbiosis emerged against a backdrop of hierarchical racialization, and at times her theorization, and that of other scientists, reintroduced tenets of popular and scientific racism, where black(ened) people are imagined as of another order than "the human" species, even if only by implication.

One could get the impression that for pioneering biologist Lynn Margulis bacteria are the most interesting life on Earth and that all other life is merely an embellishment. According to Margulis and her son, American science writer Dorion Sagan, "The creative force of symbiosis produced eukaryotic cells from bacteria. Hence all larger organisms—protoctists, fungi, animals, and plants—originated symbiogenetically. But creation of novelty by symbiosis did not end with the evolution of the earliest nucleated cells. Symbiosis still is everywhere" (*Acquiring Genomes* 55–56). To put it another way, Margulis argues that multicellular life began with the eventual fusion of independent prokaryotic cells and microbes drawn into a symbiotic relation, and this fusion generated the first eukaryotic or multicellular organisms. All species, including humans, originate from symbiosis and continue to perpetuate the symbiotic relation. For instance, microorganisms in our stomach eat food we cannot digest in exchange for a place to live and reproduce, and those in our intestine emit critical vitamins (Bollinger, "Placental" 326). In Margulis and Sagan's view, increasingly complex life forms are the result of intricate and multidirectional acts of association with other life forms (Haraway, "Encounters" 112). Therefore, complexity emerges where organisms from different taxa comingle. Bacteria disrupt our sense of stable, recognizable taxonomy as they constantly swap genetic material, frustrating any notion of bounded species (Haraway, "Encounters" 112).[57] An organism like the human body comprises forms that partner with, fuse with, or parasitize other forms; this symbiotic enmeshment then engenders ever more intricate associations. This continual but directionless process of protracted symbiotic association is the "engine" of biological diversity.

One consequence of this symbiosis is symbiogenesis: the introduction of a new species that results from the merger of two distinct species. Perhaps Margulis's most radical argument is that symbiogenesis likely produces evolutionary novelty; in other words, symbiogenesis is speciation itself (*Acquiring Genomes* 8). Margulis and Sagan stress that the cell rather than the genome is "the crucial knot of structure and function in the biological world" (Haraway, "Encounters" 114). Symbiosis, this once controversial theory, has become biological orthodoxy.[58] However, not

all symbiosis is the same, as it may be more or less mutually beneficial, or it could lead to the absorption of one entity by another, which is
termed "endosymbiosis." Scientists have been divided over whether or
not endosymbiosis is a form of parasitism. For those who view endosymbiosis as parasitism, they have often rendered it analogous to slavery, a figuration that at times explicitly recalls the historic enslavement
of black(ened) people in the Americas. From its earliest introduction
on, some biologists likened symbiogenesis to slavery, as noted by Lynn
Margulis and Dorion Sagan:

> In both merged and free-living forms, the descendants of all four kinds
> of bacteria still live today. Some say the four types are mutually enslaved,
> trapped in plant and as plant. Today each of the former types of bacteria
> provides clues about our ancestry. (*Symbiotic* 34)

When advocating for the theory of symbiogenesis (therefore arguing
against reactionary readings of Darwin), it seems to have gone unnoticed
that Margulis and Sagan also present their theory in highly racialized
terms, even occasionally referring to symbiotic cells as "miscegenated":

> [T]he co-opting of strangers, the involvement and infolding of others
> into ever more complex and *miscegenous* genomes . . . The acquisi-
> tion of the reproducing other, of the microbe and genome, is no mere
> *sideshow. Attraction*, merger, fusion, incorporation, co-habitation,
> recombination—both permanent and cyclical—and other forms of *for-
> bidden couplings*, are the main sources of Darwin's missing variation.
> (*Acquiring Genomes* 205, emphasis added)

Here, Margulis, in defending mutualism, actually extends, however
ironically, the slippage between race and species by relying on a term
("miscegenation") coined by a proslavery, prosegregationist Civil War
propaganda pamphlet, to illustrate the value of her theory and of mutualism itself. Margulis and Sagan's elaboration of their theory implicitly
hints at the racial anxiety and apprehension that met the introduction of
their theory while also instantiating the theory's long-standing historic
racial logic.[59] "Miscegenation" draws its etymology from the Latin *mis-
cere* "to mix" and *genus* "kind." Now, *genus* is a rubric that can include

organisms of different species—organisms are generally thought to be of different species if sexual reproduction cannot produce a fertile offspring. The etymology of *genus* developed in the context of an evolving conception of "race." In Latin, *genus* can mean "family, gender, type, and descent" and in Greek *genos* designates "kin, stock, race." The term "miscegenation" was coined at a time when the country was vexed by debates concerning the Civil War. "Miscegenation" and the specter of the disappearance of a "distinct" "white race" was a source of anxiety for some. The term's origin has been tied to an anonymous antiblack and anti-Republican political tract from 1863 called "Miscegenation: The Theory of the Blending of the Races, Applied to the American White Man and Negro."[60] Initially attributed to the Republican Party, the pamphlet was a hoax but was widely distributed in the US North and South, popularizing the term (Kaplan, 273–343). Thus, the notion of "race mixing" and "miscegenation" was a technology of antiblack politics.[61] The notion of "miscegenate" cells instantiates what I have argued is the homology and symbiosis of "race" and "species" and exposes how the racial politics of human sexual reproduction has shaped scientific discourse concerning symbiosis, including nonsexual reproduction.

Margulis and Sagan's elaboration of symbiosis relies on the all-too-readily available metaphor and even metonymic link between race and species, including the one posited between animals and black(ened) humans.[62] Such affiliation has historically implied that "miscegenation" was coterminous with zoophilia. The resultant child born of such a union was thought to be of indeterminate racial, or ontological, status. Indeed, in centuries prior to the Civil War, some doubted that such a child would be fertile, hence the shared etymology of "mule" and "mulatto." The particular import placed on sexual reproduction by this drama of substitution and exchange, as discussed in the subsequent chapter, establishes black maternity as an object of scientific scrutiny and figured black(ened) wombs as the *cause* of a crisis of taxonomy. Thus, black(ened) wombs were endowed with a peculiar kind of agency, one where the womb sexually reproduced disorder and indeterminate taxonomical forms.

Margulis and Sagan's "miscegenate" cells place race on the evolutionary scene prior to the emergence of the human species and at the introduction of (multicellular) life itself. It is curious that this scientific discovery is couched in the language of the sideshow, considering the "sideshow attraction" turned the conflation of blackness and animality into an industry that drew on virtually all branches of the life and social sciences. The fabulation of African slaves and colonial subjects with tails and fur were the objects of sideshow attraction.

Bacteria are racialized, even thought to be enslaved, and as Bonnie Spanier has noted, also gendered.[63] This is perhaps unsurprising given the historical development of the theory of symbiosis (Spanier 56). It continues to rehearse anxieties about individualism, self-ownership, and the nature of freedom. In this case, conceptions of the pure, bounded individual have been tethered to ideals of the pure, bounded race. This history exposes the manner with which antiblack slavery shapes scientific conceptions and debates concerning the significance of symbiosis for narratives of evolution. Because evolutionary theories are so often framed and freighted with gendered, reproductive, and sexual anxieties about racial slavery, this often shapes their reception and may even delay their acceptance, as in the case of symbiosis. It is only recently that it has been understood as fundamental to a modern scientific viewpoint.[64]

Posthumanist feminism has also quite frequently exchanged species for race, even, or perhaps especially when they have attempted to counter spurious evolutionary claims. For instance, Donna Haraway states in *Primate Visions: Gender, Race, and Nature in the World of Modern Science*, "At the end of *Dawn*, [Octavia] Butler has Lilith . . . pregnant with the child of five progenitors, who came from two species, at least three genders, two sexes, and an indeterminate number of races . . . Butler's fiction is about miscegenation, not reproduction" (378–379). However, *Dawn* is from a series, *Xenogenesis*. Xenogenesis is defined as the production of offspring that are entirely and permanently unlike either parent. It is a form of (re)production that produces offspring that fail to reproduce the parents. In other words, xenogenesis is novel speciation rather than genetic variation within a species.[65]

Haraway's praise and criticism of the *Xenogenesis* trilogy has shaped and continues to inform critical reception of the writer. For instance, Cathy Peppers in her interpretation of *Xenogenesis* builds on Haraway's formulation:

Where the African-American narrative of slavery finds its origin in miscegenation, rather than the "purity" of the races, the cyborg narrative of human identity might find its origin in a sociobiological determinism. But rather than reinforcing the story of the "pure, bounded individual" who "evolves" through competitive "survival of the fittest," it finds our origins in genetic "miscegenations"—mutations, symbiosis. Perhaps we are "biologically determined" ("our fate is in our genes"), but not in the ways we usually think. (52)[66]

In this case, fluid borders and subversion of taxonomic distinctions affect further racialization. Thus, the subversion of binaries need not be seen as in opposition to establishing them. Instead, both their establishment and transgression are possible routes for the monopolization of power as power's subversion may very well be its reorganization.[67]

Thus, raciality is not a derivation of "species" but is homologous and contiguous with biological constructions of species and evolution and, therefore, not simply a by-product of "speciesism" but rather an interdependent, coterminous, co-articulator of "the animal question." Considering that black(ened) people have been represented historically as the fusion of the human and animal, history would caution us against a quixotic celebration of hybridity or the transgression of species boundaries. The transgression and subversion of speciated boundaries is at least as central, if not more fundamental, to the production of animalized blackness and blackened animality as the semblance of an absolute distinction between human and animal. In fact, antiblackness does not require choosing one strategy—strict boundaries or hybridity—over the other; provisional designations, contradiction, absurdity, and arbitrariness are antiblackness's stock-in-trade. As I have demonstrated throughout this book, the fields "human" and "animal" are populated based on the ever-shifting needs of Eurocentric (andro)anthropocentricm.

"Bloodchild" ends on a hopeful note. Gan and T'Gatoi's relationship suggests that mutual adaptability could potentially transform being, including parasitism, into preservation, albeit of a different and unexpected nature. Affirming her commitment to the Tlic–Terran partnership and to Gan, specifically, who is now pregnant with her children, the final words of the story are T'Gatoi's: "I'll take care of you" (O. Butler, "Bloodchild" 29). Thus, the story ends with what appears to be a social contract, but it is not a social contract that rehearses the racialized and colonial terms in which freedom and the political society have been defined in both the philosophical and scientific discourses I have just recalled, but rather it is a contract with affectability itself and, thus, deconstructs and displaces these terms: a willed *Self* dispossession. At the end of the story, Gan breaks with the patriarchal tendency to substitute Man's vulnerability by displacing it onto "woman," namely his sister Xuan Hoa. Xuan Hoa has been socialized to assume the physical and symbolic vulnerabilities of childbirth and motherhood, but rather than exploit this socialization, Gan turns toward rather than away from affectability.[68] When T'Gatoi states, in an attempt to reassure Gan, "Terrans should be protected from seeing," Gan "didn't like the sound of that" (O. Butler, "Bloodchild" 28). The physical vulnerabilities of childbirth and sociogeny on a multispecies planet more generally should not be cast as abject or loom as a specter; they should be confronted outright. As Gan states, "Not protected. Shown. Shown when we're young kids, and shown more than once" (O. Butler, "Bloodchild" 28–29). "Bloodchild" is a bildungsroman but perhaps not only in the usual sense in that it tells the story of Gan's coming of age but also in another important and urgent sense: it may even inspire maturation in the reader in relation to received racialized and colonial ideas about the social contract, subjectivation, and the terms through which freedom is imagined.

In conclusion, for Butler power is immanent to and inseparable from "the body," which she suggests materializes at the intersection of biology and culture. Rather than present a unitary human body that is the summation of discursive effects, in Butler's fiction the body is a contingent and mutable unfolding. With the emphasis placed on interactivity rather than mastery, it is ineluctably affectable and interdependent. Butler's corpus identifies the multiple exchanges among human and nonhuman bodies, generatively acknowledging that humanity and nonhuman species are part of a wider pattern of relationality and not discrete, unitary monads that preexist interspecies exchange. While affectability is a form of vulnerability, Butler suggests that attempts to reject interdependence are self-defeating (even self-destructive) and thwart potentially mutually beneficial symbiosis. As a consequence, the subject of politics is estranged from precepts of liberal humanism predicated on the assumption of sovereignty and self-directed agency. The political is now the ever-expanding processual field of the relational dynamics of life in ceaseless flux and directionless becoming.

In Butler's narrative, absolute human autonomy is not presented as a viable alternative to mutual accommodation. The (social) body is reimagined as a discursive and multiscalar complex system of bodies inside of bodies that have differential capacities, powers, activities, and aims. Butler's revision of human embodied subjectivity as multispecies interactivity is a provocative call for a praxis of being/feeling/knowing that can accommodate accommodation and challenges the forms of dominance the texts evokes including but not limited to slavery, conquest, colonialism, and imperialism. Such a praxis might very well leave "the human" behind. Imagining a new world, then, demands the reimagining of the human body.

4

Organs of War

Measurement and Ecologies of Dematerialization in the
Works of Wangechi Mutu and Audre Lorde

Is a metaphysics of race more or less serious than a naturalism or biologism of race?
—Jacques Derrida, *Of Spirit*

I felt the battle lines being drawn up in my own body.
—Audre Lorde, *A Burst of Light*

Gendered and sexual imperial discourses on "the black female body"
provided the conditions of possibility for the historical emergence of
the generic construction of "the animal"—a term elastic enough to
include humans and nonhumans. The transcultural adoption of our current hegemonic and specifically *biocentric* conception of "the human,"
in its distinction from "the animal" as defined in the onto-teleological
terms of natural science and philosophy, articulated black female abjection, in particular, as a prerequisite of human qualification in the newly
conceived globalizing terms that occasioned "Discovery." This history's
preoccupation with sexual difference and maternity is often evoked by a
Latin phrase: *partus sequitur ventrem* (delivery follows the womb). But
as I will show, this could just as easily be evoked by contemporary racial
reproductive health inequity.

I demonstrate that racism not only posits cleavages in womanhood
such that black womanhood is made to be a gender apart, an other gender, but also that antiblackness itself is sexuating, whereby so-called
biological sex is modulated by "culture." In other words, at the registers
of both sign and matter, antiblackness produces differential biocultural
effects of gender and sex. Such a frame raises the stakes of recent feminist materialism's inquiry into both the inter(intra)actional relations of

discursivity and materiality as well as the gendered politics of hylomorphism, or the form-matter distinction. Thus, antiblack formulations of gender and sexuality are actually *essential* rather than subsidiary to the metaphysical figuration of matter, objects, and animals that recent critical theory hopes to dislodge.

The operations of racialized sexuation and maternity are essential to what Giorgio Agamben calls the "anthropological machine," or the recursive attempt to adjudicate, dichotomize, hierarchize, and stage a conflict between "the human" and "the animal." Agamben stresses that while it is commonly and devastatingly exteriorized, this conflict is first and foremost a conflict within Man. While Agamben fails to do so, we might name this conflict within Man: race. Yet, the ordering of nonhuman nature is also not reducible to a demand for racial hierarchy, as the domination of environs and nonhuman forms of life was a privileged expression of conquest as well. Neither "race" nor "species" is merely symptomatic, but rather they are contiguous and interdependent. To make matters more confusing, this abutting is often the case at the register of semantics. As Darwin would state in *Descent of Man*, "race" and "species" are virtually synonymous and thus parsing "race's" heteroglossia or various meanings is perhaps only perceptible by its contextual appearances.

The final chapter of *Becoming Human* concerns the interrelation of scientific and philosophical discourses of race and species as well as continues the previous chapter's investigation of mutation, speculating on both its potentiality pernicious and vitalizing force by examining figurations of the black female body in genetics, evolutionary discourse, and works by Audre Lorde and Wangechi Mutu. I argue that Mutu's alternating aesthetic strategies of exposure, allegory, and mutation articulate the potentiality for the inoperability of biopolitical calculations of personhood and the forestallment of antiblack economies of life. In other words, her aesthetic strategies reveal a potential (with neither guarantee nor a manifest horizon of possibility—but a potential, nonetheless) for mutation beyond a mode of thought and representation that continually adheres to predefined rules and narratives that legitimate antiblack ordering and premature death.

It would appear that speculation regarding the (im)materiality of *genetic race* has overshadowed the more fundamental (and materially pertinent) question of how racialized environments are embodied. Or as Clarence Gravlee succinctly notes, "The common assertion that 'race is not biology' may be correct in spirit. But it is too crude and imprecise to be effective. It does not adequately challenge the reductionism and genetic determinism of biomedical science or popular culture, and blinds us to the biological consequences of race and racism as socio-cultural phenomena" (53).[1] In other words, the controversy surrounding the "reality" of genetic race has forestalled a fuller recognition of the biopsychological consequences and somatic materialities of antiblack racism. An exclusive focus on the domain of DNA undercuts what could be a fuller consideration of both the agentic capaciousness of somatic processes and the life-and-death stakes of that capacity.[2]

Sylvia Wynter would argue that this overinvestment in DNA is a symptom of biocentrism. A purely biological definition of what it means to *be*, biocentrism is undergirded by a genomic principle: that "the human" is a purely biologically determined mode of being. Biocentrism is characterized by Wynter as the belief that we are "biological beings who then create culture" ("Biocentric" 361).

According to a biocentric logic, human cultural practices are linearly determined by groups' bio-ontological composition. "Racism," Wynter argues "is an *effect* of the biocentric conception of the human" ("Biocentric" 364, emphasis added).[3] She contrasts this belief system's reductive investment in DNA as substratum and mechanistic causation with an alternative:

My proposal is that we are bioevolutionarily prepared by means of language to inscript and autoinstitute ourselves in this or that modality of the human, always in adaptive response to the ecological as well as to the geopolitical circumstances in which we find ourselves. ("Biocentric" 361)

Wynter has expanded upon this view, which she calls the *sociogenic principle*. Sociogeny defines (human) being in a manner that is not reducible to physical laws. In fact, said laws are redefinable as sociogenetic or nature-culture laws because culture is not only what humans create but also what creates human being. However, sociogeny differs from previous and contemporaneous theories of nature-cultures in that desire and affect play a decisive role in the concept. Wynter argues that a "culturally imposed symbolic belief system" serves as the internalized sanction system that motivates behavior, biochemically affirming or negating in dynamic relation to societal norms and values prior to any reflective process. A species-specific opioid (reward and punishment) system serves to induce its appropriate behaviors through the mediation of each person's subjective experience of what feels good and what feels bad to and for each person (Wynter, "Sociogenic" 54). If the organismic body delimits the human species, then the body is itself culturally determined through the mediation of the socialized *sense of self* as well as through the "social" situation in which this *self* is placed. The transformation of subjective experience is culturally and, thereby, socio-situationally determined with these determinations in turn, serving to activate their physicalist correlates (Wynter, "Sociogenic" 37). Thus, subjectively experienced, visceral processes take place such that their functioning cannot be explained in terms of *only* the natural sciences, of only physical laws. Alex Weheliye rightly distinguishes Wynter's sociogeny from sociobiology, cautioning: "Wynter does not focus on the origins and adaptive evolution of race itself but rather on how sociogenic principles are anchored in the human neurochemical system, thus counteracting sociobiological explanations of race, which retrospectively project racial categories onto an evolutionary screen" (Weheliye 27).

Inspired by Frantz Fanon's famous axiom in *Black Skin, White Masks* "beside phylogeny and ontogeny stands sociogeny," a reworking of Ernst Haeckel's theory of evolution, Wynter's sociogenic principle draws on Fanon's observation that the individual (ontogeny) does not simply emerge and unfurl via species membership (phylogeny) in its natural scientific conception but in dynamic relation to a sociocultural situation (sociogeny). Fanon speaks of how the social situation, in this case, implicit knowledge of a "historico-racial schema" (40) alters the psyche and the nervous system's biochemical dynamism prior to the reflectivity of "consciousness" ("Sociogenic" 36). In the case of the human species, the sociogenic principle is the information-encoding, organizational principle of each culture's criterion of being/nonbeing that functions to *artificially* activate the neurochemistry of the reward and punishment pathway *as if it was instinctual*, doing so in terms needed to institute the human subject as a culture-specific and thereby semiotically defined, if physiologically implemented, mode of being and *sense of self*. In contrast to a biocentric view of the species, Wynter argues, "We can experience ourselves as human *only* through the mediation of the processes of socialization effected by the invented tekhne or cultural technology to which we give the name culture" ("Sociogenic" 53, emphasis added).

Wynter once stated, "For me, Black Studies is about enabling the exit from the substitute religion 'evolution,' a substitute religion which represses the fact that once language has co-evolved with the brain, the process of evolution was followed by the Event of human auto-institution, of autopoesis!"[4] In other words, the technology that is culture, Wynter argues, is evolutionarily significant such that with the emergence of semantic technologies humans gained a technology that developed the power to direct the specific terms of the nervous system's order of perception and categorization, harness its drives to its now culturally defined sociogenetic own, and even override the genetic-instinctual sense of self where necessary, activating, by their semantic reprogramming, the opioid system (reward and punishment) in culture-specific terms *as if it were instinct.* Thus, semiosis plays a determinant role in the adaptive processes of both culture and biology, meaning and biochemical affect. Wynter argues that racism deploys "coercive semantic technologies" and "systemically imposed role[s]" that reify bodies into types or prescriptive categories, and these types and prescriptive categories, in turn, trigger affects, sensations, and behaviors reflexly, activated by pervasive associations that predefine and assign responsibility to those made representative of a type ("Sociogenic" 48, 58, 42).

In this chapter, thinking with Wynter's argument that this choreography has evolutionary significance and against a biocentric conception of the species, I want to push her theory of sociogeny beyond an exclusive focus on the nervous system and problematize the question of the "auto" of poesis by reinscripting the embodied self as a kind of openwork produced by a lattice of agencies rather than primarily self-authored closed system. In particular, I want to investigate how breast systems and reproductive systems more generally are also sociogenic. In other words, I argue that the matter of sex itself, the very biologic stuff of sexual difference, is imprinted, altered, and transmuted in dynamic relation to the antiblack technologies of culture and explore antiblackness's potential evolutionary significance via the epigenome. In turning to the epigenome, I query how might we register distinctions in the quality of being, stimulated and directed by antiblack ecologies, without reintroducing racial difference or speciation in/as racial difference and its hierarchies.

Departing from an *exclusive* focus on structure, whether it be that of the double-helix or scaled up to the symbolic order, I argue that the matter of black female sex(uality) and reproduction are better understood via a framework of emergence and within the context of iterative, intra-active multiscalar systems—biological, psychological, environmental, and cultural. Wangechi Mutu's *Histology of the Different Classes of Uterine Tumors* crucially reveals the stakes of this intra-activity as it pertains to the semio-material history of "the black female body," reproductive function, and sex(uality) as opposable limit and linchpin of "the human" species in scientific taxonomies and medical science. Mutu's art provides insightful commentary on systematicity in general, but for our purposes, it is notable for its constructive reorientation of the theorization of race via a reflexive methodological practice of collage, one that reframes the spectatorial encounter from that of a determinate, Kantian, linear, teleological drama of subjects and objects to that of interactive processes and indeterminate feedback loops. Thus, this is not a study of a reified object but of an interactional field that includes material objects but is not limited to them. Moreover, I assume diverse (im)material agencies and affectivity without pretending to exhaust causality.

While Mutu's *Histology of the Different Classes of Uterine Tumors* presents an art object for interpretation, the nature of that object may perhaps surprise because, as I will demonstrate, the object is tripled, interactional, and chiasmatic—a material and immaterial interactant. In other words, the material object is offered for interpretation but so is the process of interpretation itself—hence, the art object is best conceived neither solely in its material existence nor in the actualization of symbolic interpretation but rather in the chiasmatic and seemingly infinite interactive meeting of matter and systems of representation in the semio-affective field of visuality. The collagist work(s) might thus be described as *mise-en-abyme*. Like *Histology*, this study is equally concerned with the material object, its corresponding "politics of representation," and the very *process* that produces the material object as both an effect of discourse and an actant that exceeds and perturbs the operability—cognition and affective resonance—of the governing system of representation.[5]

After opening with a consideration of Mutu's work, this chapter turns to Audre Lorde's insights to achieve a fuller appreciation of Mutu's artistic practice. Lorde's *The Cancer Journals* was one of the first critical treatments of female reproductive cancers to put forth an understanding of the body as an emergent and discursive-material inter(intra)actional system and to emphasize that semio-affective-psychic relations are crucial determinants of physiological processes. The disjunctive co-presence of Mutu's provocative exploration of the possible social determinants of reproductive illness with its converse, our difficulty in speaking about racialized disease frequencies without naturalizing them (in the terms of speciated difference, however convoluted, or portraying them as inevitable) invites a reevaluation of Lorde's contention in *The Cancer Journals* that carcinogenesis is a feedback loop encompassing biological, psychological, environmental, and cultural efficacies. Therefore it is neither a matter of individualized disease nor inferior biology but rather a somaticization of politics. Lorde's work is edifying for our thinking in that she was able to broaden our conception of politics— and by politics, I mean war—to include gross health-related inequities in mortality and debility while also noting that the frame of war resides both within and beyond the subjectivist domain. Perhaps most crucially, Lorde theorizes nonsubjectivist modalities of agency without losing the acuity of her critique of the social power differentials endemic to war's exercise. These aspects of her critique, I will argue, are instructive for reframing and expanding our understanding of the parameters, operations, and stakes of necropower for the theorization of sex-gender and natality and vice versa.

In the pages that follow, I intend to investigate how Lorde's *Cancer Journals* and Mutu's *Histology of the Different Classes of Uterine Tumors* elucidate antiblackness as it pertains to at least three interrelated systems—biology, temporality, and semiosis—and are generative for clarifying the complex nature of their mutual production. First, specifically in light of Carl Linnaeus's *Systema Naturae* and Ernst Haeckel's iconicity as an artist as well as an architect of the science of species, Mutu's art exposes how the performative epistemological mechanisms of both classical aesthetics and biocentric, scientific taxonomical systems and the limits therein are problematized and (op)posed by objects themselves, human and nonhuman alike. As shown across the chapters of this book, "species" and "race" have never been fully disaggregated. In fact, logics of race are determinate of logics of species, and ecologies of antiblackness shape epistemologies of scientific thought and their taxonomies that purport to divide human from animal. In what follows, the line dividing Man from animal is blurred such that the plasticity of un/gendered black(female)ness permits objects to converge and/or be substituted across received orders of animacy and species. With Mutu, there is a working through that repeats this movement but with a critical difference. Employing aesthetic strategies of exposure and allegory, Mutu mutates these system's received logics and aesthetic hierarchies. Racism is an aesthetics and a politics of aesthetics. It debilitates and seeks to transmogrify and produce blackness as grotesque: the material embodiment of abeauty. And, thus, racism targets the beauty of blackness. What Mutu and Lorde are invested in is a counterclaim of beauty in what would otherwise be perceived as antithetical to beauty: the grotesque. Second, Mutu unflinchingly exposes both the racialization of female reproductive systems in the field of representation and the embodied systemic inequities that have materialized as a consequence through the unique prism of female reproductive disease including its perhaps most devastating form—cancer. If *the* body remains purely a discursive abstraction, we potentially lose our ability to gauge the consequences of racism for the *organismic* body. *Histology*, ironically, abstracts from the flesh only to return us to it anew, such that we may limn the stealth anatomical pathways of terror made mundane and interpret quotidian violence's "hieroglyphics of the flesh" that would otherwise remain undecipherable. Third, Lorde's *The Cancer Journals* and Mutu's art are productive for reconceptualizing antiblackness as the processual unfolding of an iterative and inter(intra)active system without a predetermined terminus, encompassing human and nonhuman agencies.

I contend that while antiblackness is terrifyingly persistent and ongoing as a system, antiblack racism and its (somatic) effects nevertheless unfold processually, bearing the capacity to take form as "event" and within the ontological expanse of "emergence" rather than reflect a passive "legacy" emanating from a reified foundation or immutable structure.[6] An event is primarily identifiable by its effects, which cannot be precisely known in advance but rather *emerge* in time, in the making of time. Whether be it the extraordinary that retroactively introduces its causes or that which nonspectacularly organizes possibilities, an event disrupts a progressivist realization of possibility and creates new possibilities by changing or displacing the limit between possibility and impossibility. To put it another way, my precise interest concerns the restoration of event to history, how antiblack conditions of possibility are shaped by emergent contexts, and how this process occurs within the fold of the iterative assembly of semiotic, environmental, and biological systems, both antiblack and radically ahuman, in a manner that is nondeterministic in its teleology.

I close both this chapter and this book with a coda that considers recent developments in the biological sciences and biotechnology that have turned their attention to narrating the problem of "racial health disparity" in reproductive health. This work on the epigenome, mostly housed in the regulatory sciences—epidemiology and public health—possesses contradictory potential and thus uncertain possibilities with respect to (dis)articulating the antiblack logics that have conditioned the symbiosis of racialized teleological determinism and evolutionary thought (whereby a developmental conception of "the human" is only one of its most obvious instantiations).

Genealogical Mutations

Kenyan-born, Brooklyn-based Wangechi Mutu is known for her mixed-media collages featuring ink and paper drawings or watercolor paintings of gelatinous black female figures. Mutu's works are set in fecund, imagined landscapes, exploring postcolonial paradoxes and technological possibilities. In the case of *Histology*, her work investigates black women's alienation in US-based globalizing circuits of media and representation. Mutu's technique of collage—the alternation of discordant juxtapositions with seamless transitory states—catalyzes the irresolute becoming of what Deleuze calls assemblage.[7] Mutu's collages invite viewers to reflect on their aesthetic judgments as the perceived harmony or discordance of elements is undergirded by historically situated taxonomies and typologies (often scientific). More to the point, Mutu's collages reveal the extent to which Western science and visual art share and mutually constitute what is a racialized, gendered, and sexualized imperial economy of aesthetics, desire, and affect.

In *Histology*, three traditions of photography are juxtaposed—ethnography, pornography, and fashion—highlighting their homology, bespeaking their commonalities, mutual constitution, and tangled roots. Here, popular scientific magazines such as *National Geographic* are implicated in the fetishistic voyeurism of pornographic magazines such as *Black Tail*, which are nevertheless rather arbitrarily divided on newsstands in accordance with the ritualistic enactment of genre.[8] As Amber Musser reminds us in *Sensual Excess*, "the scientific/pornographic gaze's desire" is that of "visual knowledge as 'truth'" (49). The inclusive slash linking "pornographic" and "scientific" echoes a confluence of desire for what Glissant critically refers to as "transparency" and Musser, elsewhere, calls "flatness," whereby black female figures function as "a homogenous signifier of the flesh" (*Sensational* 155). Not unlike the surgical glove, the plastic wrap that sheathes pornography attempts to regulate touch and the presumed contaminations therein. But the plastic wrap is rather belated even hypocritical, a sleight of hand that seeks to mystify an intertextual sexual cross-pollination that has already occurred, promiscuous and still flourishing in these genres' tracing, cutting, and pasting of forms. Alessandra Raengo notes that the use of materials such as rabbit fur in works like *Histology* act as a materialization of desire for a tactile encounter with porno/ethnographic figures "that was already present, but also disavowed, in the glossy aesthetics of the female figure of pornography or advertising. Yet, as much as Mutu's surfaces are seductively glossy, they are also exceptionally moist: splattered with blood and other bodily fluids coming from improbable places and received with improbable pleasure by the subjects in the works themselves" (Raengo 79).

In *Histology*, a proliferation of provocative visual phrases suggests the generic promiscuity I have just described. A squatting leg becomes a nose, a stereotypic pose grafted onto a stereotyped feature; parted legs and the triple play of bush—coiffure, pubic, and wild, uncultivated territory in black glittery opalescence (Figure P.3, P.5, P.7, P.9, P.10, P.12). Black, no longer mythologized as white's opposite—absence; here, black is dichroic, an anamorphic abundance of color (Figure P.4). The black glittered hair situates the full spectrum of color as constitutive to blackness rather than emblematizing a pregiven yet visualizable cut in the human. Cephalopod and serpentine forms, fur, smoldering eyes, and packing tape create incongruous countenances superimposed on found nineteenth-century medical illustrations of vulvas and tumors (uterine, ovarian, and cervical), cancers, ulcers, cysts, catarrh, prolapses, hypertrophy, and ectopic pregnancy (Figure P.4, P.9, P.10, P.11, P.13). Before these sprawling decentering images, viewers are provoked into examining how they define and measure humanity, theirs and that of others.

Mutu's work is not that of natural history—cataloguing types or artifacts thought to represent types—an approach Bridget R. Cooks has described, in *Exhibiting Blackness*, as "the compulsion to place Black artists within a framework of discovery and primitivism" (2). Instead it examines histories of biocentrism in the field of visuality and their sociogenic material-discursive consequences or, in this specific instance, the way raciality's taxa intrudes upon what it has already conditioned: the operations of biological reproductive systems—whereby the efficacies of the body must contend with what they are entangled with: racism's debilitating and deadly force (Cooks 1–2). Yet, in *Histology*, not unlike biological systems, antiblackness and spectatorship are reconceived as iterative, processual, interactional systematicity that while totalizing is neither absolute nor bound by the spatiotemporalized fiction of foundation or an origin proper to the past but an open-ended, looping indeterminacy, one whose terminus must necessarily remain unknown.

What we find in Mutu's visions of zoology and botany is a return, not so much a recapitulation but rather a mutation of German biologist Ernst Haeckel's foundational aestheticized evolutionary theory. In the history of Western imperialism, geologists, archeologists, surveyors, and mapmakers (among others) employed ink and watercolor media for taxonomizing "foreign" people and environments as well as to generate an artistic industry that documented European "discoveries" for scientific and popular consumption—these two domains, the popular and the scientific, never quite being separate. In privileging watercolor and ink drawing as media of critique, I will demonstrate that Mutu turns the medium against the very taxonomical imagination that gave rise to its prominence as a technology of representation. Mutating the aesthetic philosophy and artistic practice subtending Haeckel's evolutionary thought, Mutu's art highlights the efficacy of randomness, offering something other than the foundational and prevailing antiblack depictions, created by Haeckel and his contemporaries.

Haeckel was a preeminent architect of scientific taxonomical thinking. He described, named, and illustrated thousands of species before
placing them in a genealogical tree, guided by the aim of relating all
life forms (Figure P.14). Additionally, Haeckel identified the cell nucleus
as the carrier of hereditary material; described the process of gastrulation; and was an important, if controversial, contributor to embryology
(Richards 4).[9] He provided initial formulations of concepts such as an-
thropogeny, phylum, phylogeny, and stem cell. Haeckel even established
an entire kingdom of creatures, the Protista—representing them visually
in stunning detail, in what are now canonical images in the history of
Western visual culture. Haeckel was a scientist of well-known theoretic
and artistic acumen. In 1866, he coined the term "ecology," the study of
relations among organisms and their environment.

By the end of the nineteenth century, Haeckel was possibly the world's
most famous evolutionary theorist. According to Haeckel's biographer,
philosopher and historian of science Robert J. Richards, more people at
the turn of the century were carried to evolutionary theory on the tor-
rent of Haeckel's visually arresting and theoretically rich publications
than through any other source, including those authored by Darwin
himself (Richards xviii). Known internationally as a promoter and pop-
ularizer of Darwinian theory, Haeckel's own expertise lay in marine in-
vertebrate biology. To this day, no other investigator has named as many
creatures—radiolaria, medusa, siphonophores, sponges—as Haeckel
(Richards xviii). Drawing inspiration from the Romantic Naturphilosophie of Goethe, Humboldt, and Schleiden—thinkers who insisted that
the understanding of organic forms required not only theoretic consideration but aesthetic evaluation as well—Haeckel honed his considerable artistic talent in keeping with these principles, illustrating all of his
books by brush or ink, believing that a proper assessment of the development and function of organic forms necessitated a studied attentiveness to their artistic qualities (Richards 8–9). In the words of Richards,
"Haeckel's talent with the artist's brush served him no less than his dex-
terity with the scientist's microscope" (8).

Haeckel believed that his theory of recapitulation, which he termed
the "biogenetic law," was evidenced in an inherent and apparently transparent progressivist taxonomic order, captured in his succinct axiom,
"ontogeny recapitulates phylogeny." Haeckel's cardinal principle held

that the embryo of a species goes through the same morphological stages as the phylum went through in its evolutionary history; thus, the embryo in its development chronologically passes through the successive morphologies of its nearest and most distant ancestors. In the case of the human embryo, one begins as a single-celled organism, just as biologists presume life on earth began in a unicellular mode; upon passing through a stage of gastrulation, a cuplike form is produced, similar (Haeckel believed) to a primitive ancestor that plied the ancient seas; then, the embryo takes on the structure of an archaic fish with gill arches and then that of a primate, before acquiring the form of a specific human being (Richards 502).

Despite the objections of those who take issue with the progressivist orientation essential to Haeckel's thought, I argue that in terms of somatic theories of race, Naturphilosophie and evolutionary theory were less a cacophony of irreconcilable opinions and more a chorus.[10] In a set of specific examples far too long to relate, biocentric hierarchy either cast what were purportedly preexisting (yet ever changing in number) biological races in the terms of a (perpetually shifting) taxonomy of species; or conversely, when theory posited a singular origin of humanity comprising what was presumably a single human species, it was nonetheless presumed that the species was occasioned with immutable divides which could ultimately justify the postulation of amalgamated or intermediate "types." Thus, the question of "race" was never conclusively separated or disengaged from the question of "species." For instance, Darwin used both terms, "species" and "race," interchangeably in *The Descent of Man*, at times even using the term "sub-species" to refer to people.[11] To put it another way, the disaggregation of a conception of race as "type" within a presumably shared humanity from the positing of race *as* "species" in a discontinuous (in)humanity, was never fully completed—nor could it be—in discourses dependent upon the promiscuous use of the term "race"; instead, the issue of race's ontology was indefinitely deferred. Therefore, I would argue that in sum these positions, polygenesis and monogenesis respectively, were more of a threshold effect than opposing positions: what they lacked in logical clarity they more than made up for in complementary social and political agendas. Identifying a core of agreement at the center of early biological science's branching thought, Stephen Jay Gould claimed that taken as a whole both schools of thought maintained that "however flex-ible in future movement, the scale of human races could still be ranked from lower to higher—and recapitulation provided the major criterion for ranking" (Gould 127).

When applied to the morphology of humanity by a burgeoning sci-ence that anticipated, and indeed pursued, validation of its metaphysical order in observable somatic phenomena, Haeckel's signature articula-tion of progress in evolution asserted directly that the telos of evolution was evidenced in an observable and, Haeckel maintained, progressivist hierarchy of the races. Haeckel maintained that the laws of nature re-vealed their evolutionary aims and organizational structures in a gradu-ated achievement of civilization. Haeckel surmised that the role of the scientist was to hone skills of discernment necessary for delineating the metrics and scales given by nature. Believing it possible to relate all of humanity according to relative degree of intellectual and cultural advancement, Haeckel's metrics placed human "races and species" in a stem-tree that ranged from "simple" to "complex" forms and societies.

While the occupants of the various branches shifted considerably, moving higher or lower with each successive edition of *Generelle Mor-phologie*, the text never wavered from its low estimation of blackness. The tiers occupied by American Indians and the Japanese, for instance, shifted up or down with developments in popular culture—the wide popularity of literary depictions of the American Indian as "Noble Savage" in nineteenth-century Germany—or with developments in di-plomacy such as Japan's concerted effort at "modernization," which in-cluded a new constitution directly modeled on Germany's in 1889. But each edition remained remarkably stable in its decisive and emphatic antiblackness (Richards 248–250). Haeckel's depiction of blackness did not conform to the model of vertical movement I have just described but was dependent upon the operations of addition or subtraction—more or fewer black groups. This racial arithmetic taken as a whole effectively produced "blackness" as incomparability and discontinuity—ultimately revealing a static otherness that defines blackness as a genealogical iso-late and unassimilable in relation to all others (Richards 75–77).

Perhaps this hierarchical and teleological view of race on Haeckel's part is unsurprising since, as Gould notes in *Ontogeny and Phylogeny*, the "very first sustained argument for recapitulation in morphology was cast in a racist mold" (Gould 126). In his 1797 work, German physician and specialist of forensic medicine Johann Heinrich Ferdinand von Autenrieth argued that completed forms of "lower" animals are merely earlier stages in the ontogeny of "higher" forms. Autenrieth then spoke of "certain traits which seem, in the adult African, to be less changed from the embryonic condition than in the adult European" (quoted in Gould 126). In fact, several of the leading pre-Darwinian recapitulationists ranked humanity according to what Gould has termed "the-primitive-as-child argument" (128).

As *Histology*'s proliferation of lips, breasts, hair, noses, and vulvas framed by speculums and nineteenth-century medical drawings suggests, comparative anatomists utilized "[a]ll parts of the body . . . minutely scanned, measured, and weighed," in an effort to claim a material basis of race so that they might "erect a science of comparative anatomy of the races" (Brinton 48). It is commonly presumed that conceptions such as recapitulation are the exclusive products of eighteenth- and nineteenth-century comparative anatomy, yet Gould has shown such views were not singularly evidenced in sciences laying claim to the materialist ground of the body. As evoked in *Histology*, skulls were indeed collected and compared, perhaps most infamously by craniologist Samuel George Morton, but "the primitive-as child argument" performed better for theories claiming insight into the *immaterial and ephemeral* dimensions of human personality, such as intelligence, character, personality traits, moral faculties, criminality, and aesthetic value—relying more on inference than on direct empirical observation (Figure P.13). The purview of the immaterial liberated scientists from an ill-fated quest predicated on an undeliverable promise—the discovery of incongruous yet transparent material forms that would prove an innate racial scale organized the species rather than racism.

What I claim is that imperialist racist rationale drove a demand for a material basis of scientific evidence *in general* and was the engine of species designations in both humans and nonhumans. The pursuit of an observable and comparative basis of racial taxonomy and typology is central to the rise of empirical science, an organizing principle, not a matter merely incidental to it. In light of a dauntingly elusive material basis for their imperial rationale, speculative theories concerning mental traits would allow recapitulationists to rely more on products of the mind than on physical criteria for ranking in a matter now relieved from the constraints of data: paleontologist and zoologist E. D. Cope argued, "Some of these features have a purely physical significance, but the majority of them are . . . intimately connected with the development of the mind" (293). Founder of Social Darwinism Herbert Spencer claimed that "the intellectual traits of the uncivilized" recur in "the children of the civilized" (89). Lord Avebury (John Lubbock), the English leader of child study, compared "[m]odern savage mentality to that of a child," stating, "As we all know, the lowest races of mankind stand in close proximity to the animal world. The same is true for infants of civilized races" (4). Of course, that the purportedly immaterial—mind, mentality, morality, intelligence, character, personality traits, moral faculties—as embodied practices have a quotient of materiality is actually an inconvenience to measurement's rationale because matter does not conform to the dictates of racial logic.

Claims of knowledge of the so-called *immaterial* properties of the "savage," "the uncivilized," and "the lowest races of mankind" relied upon the imperial expedition and its—literary and visual—representational maps for navigation, which commonly maintained a coextensive relation among African humans, animals, and territories. Social Darwinist Benjamin Kidd contended:

> The evolution in character which the race has undergone has been northwards from the tropics. The first step to the solution of the problem before us is simply to acquire the principle that [we are] dealing with peoples who represent the same stage in the history of the development of the race that the child does in the history of the development of the individual. The tropics will not, therefore, be developed by the natives themselves. (51)

As in the example of Kidd, recapitulation was commonly cited as a rationale for the conquest of Africa. Similar ideas are perhaps most immediately recallable in light of the canonical first verse of Kipling's most famous hymn for colonialism:

> Take up the White Man's burden—
> Send forth the best ye breed—

Go send your sons to exile
To serve your captives' need
To wait in heavy harness
On fluttered folk and wild—
Your new-caught, sullen peoples,
Half devil and half child
Take up the White Man's burden (Kipling, "The White Man's
    Burden")

Friedrich Schiller, godfather of Naturphilosophie and Haeckel's favorite poet, exposes that Western scales of being and their representational modes (modeled in the Kipling verse) relied upon the might of an
imperial fleet: "The discoveries which our European sailors have made
in foreign seas . . . show us that different people are distributed around
us . . . just as children of different ages may surround a grown-up man"
(qtd in Gould 126).

In the early 1870s, Charles Wyville Thomson, a naturalist at the University of Edinburgh, proposed an expedition to sound the oceans of
the world in order to discover the chemical composition, temperatures,
and depths of their various waters as well as survey their marine life.
A fighting ship was dispatched by the Royal Navy, HMS *Challenger*, as
the research trip was fully within the purview of the military. The ship
was graphically depicted in paint and ink (Figure 4.1). Upon removal of
most but not all of its guns, the ship was fitted with dredging and other
equipment needed for the accomplishments of the expedition's goals.
In December 1872, the three-mast ship with Captain George Nares and
his crew of two hundred men aboard, along with six scientists headed
by Thomson, embarked on a three-and-a half year voyage. In all, the
ship traveled to the Canary Islands, Brazil, the Cape of Good Hope,
Australia, New Zealand, Fiji, the East Indies, Japan, the Sandwich and
Society Islands, Chile, and Argentina before returning to England in
May 1876 (Figure 4.2). An international team of chemists, physicists, and
marine biologists were commissioned and charged with the task of describing the composition of seas, the seabeds, and the animals procured.
Haeckel, by then already an established systematist, was asked to work
on cataloguing the radiolarian, medusae, siphonophores, and sponges.
Ten years, 1,803 pages, and 140 plates later, Haeckel completed his *Re-*

Figure 4.1. HMS *Challenger* from Charles Wyville Thomson's *Report on the Scientific Results of the Voyage of HMS Challenger During the Years 1873–76*. Thomson, Sir C. Wyville, ed. *Report on the Scientific Results of the Voyage of H.M.S. Challenger During the Years 1873–76*. 6 vols. Her Majesty's Stationery Office, 1878–1895.

port of the Radiolara, which detailed systematic relations, morphology, the locality where taken (latitude, longitude, and the nearest land), the abundance of creatures, the depth and temperature of the waters, and the nature of the sea bottom. Haeckel's *Challenger* research formed the basis of his taxonomical system of radiolarian—in large measure still in use today (Richards 75–77).

Haeckel also initiated approximately twenty solo expeditions, a number that Richards notes seems "almost superfluous for the sheer purpose of acquiring new materials and for advancing a career," as after 1870 Haeckel had solidified a reputation as a premier researcher and could have obtained organisms through the work of other naturalists or assistants. The acquisition of new materials would always be a justification, but with Haeckel there was usually more at stake (Richards 213).

For scientists like Haeckel, the "danger" and "hardship" of "exotic travel" potentially served as a means of sealing the importance of any discoveries made:

> The model of great voyages of the past suggests that any findings or new ideas derived from a journey would have their significance elevated by the degree of difficulties suffered during the excursion. The assumption is easy: that the importance of results achieved would be commensurate with dangers chanced. (Richards 214)

And, in fact, as Richards notes, Humboldt and Darwin had made their intellectual fortunes by "exotic" travel, a context Haeckel was well aware of; the hazard of great danger and hardship in "alien travel," or at least the appearance of it, set the standard for scientific greatness and paved the path to immortal fame (215). Haeckel's ambition and appetite for adventure impelled him to the western coast of Africa and the Canary Islands in search of "biological riches" and the land of supreme beauty he had read about as a youth in in the evocative travel writings of his hero Alexander von Humboldt (Richards 173). Moreover, Richards has noted that Karl Haeckel, Ernst's father, had a keen interest in "geology

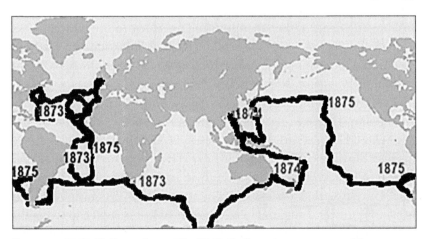

Figure 4.2. HMS *Challenger* Route: The HMS *Challenger*'s voyage spanned four years and covered close to seventy thousand nautical miles. "Then and Now: The HMS Challenger Expedition and the Mountains in the Sea Expedition." NOAA Ocean Explorer Podcast RSS oceanexplorer.noaa.gov/explorations/03mountains/background/challenger/challenger.html. Retrieved March 5, 2013.

and foreign vistas"; similarly, his son devoted himself to the travel literature of Humboldt, Goethe, and Charles Darwin, "which set the deep root of a lasting desire for adventure in exotic lands" (Richards 20). Richards's observation that young Haeckel's dreams arose out of reading works like Daniel Defoe's *Robinson Crusoe* invites not only a recollection of the historical intermingling of science and travel literature—in other words, the uneven imperial representational politics authorizing claims to scientific "discovery"—but also prompts a reopening of the question of the roles of aesthetics, literature, and visual art in empirical racial science in particular. Haeckel never set sail toward any new research horizon without his sketchbooks and canvasses, and "during his last travels, the implements of the aesthetic life became even more important than his microscopes, dissecting blades, and spirits of wine" (Richards 60, 215).

Haeckel attempted to capture with his mind's eye the archetypal structure of an organism—and thus he did not purport to faithfully capture empirical reality. It is not that Haeckel's studies were without empirical foundation; his studies of the radiolarian, for instance, undoubtedly were initiated on empirical ground. Rather, he believed the conveyance of evolutionary processes required a theory that exceeded the dictates of an exacting or experimental science (Richards 313). Following Goethe, he sought essence rather than limiting his study to the particulars of empirical evidence. In his view, mathematical induction and methods privileging the terms of mechanistic causality were not sufficient for the revelation of essence (Richards 75).

Haeckel's commitment to "exotic" and idealized depictions of forms would play a decisive role in persuading readers of the evolutionary theory behind Haeckel's art. Haeckel is canonized as an artist largely due to his lush drawing of Cnidaria in his *Art Forms in Nature*. The seductive appeal of Haeckel's theory lay mainly in the splaying of "untamed nature" (Richards 214). Haeckel's exploitation of Kantian metaphors linking femininity and sublimity can be gleaned in his choice to name the "Discomedusae" after the black(ened) sexed myth of the Medusa, also known for her venomous lethal sting and looks that could turn a man to stone (Figure P.15).[12]

Mutu is known to borrow freely from marine biology, zoology, and botany but in a manner that gathers critical attention and directs it toward gendered aesthetics that imply facile connections between female bodies, femininity, and nature. Her collaged figures conspicuous made-ness, their artificiality is embraced and integral to their beauty. As Malik Gaines and Alexandro Segade put it, her figures "do not fear technology, because they are made of it" (146). *One Hundred Lavish Months of Bushwhack* alludes to Haeckel's canonical gelatinous figures in a manner that problematizes colonial hierarchies of sex/gender, and in so doing, reveals that the iterative aspects of culture are "mutational, autopoetic, performative" (Figure P.16).[13] *One Hundred* figures both the enormously weighty aspects of hierarchies of sex/gender as well as their precarity as a much larger figure rests upon the genuflection and exploitation as well as caprice of one much smaller. The two chimerical figures are sheathed in mottled skin, one light and one dark, and framed by a sparse grassland and ominous cloud that is either lifting or moving closer. The central and much larger golden figure has spiraling leopard-printed horns, hippopotamus heads for hands, and an exploding foot releasing motorcycle fragments—or perhaps flying motorcycle shrapnel is what initially caused the rupture. The larger golden figure's blasted head seemingly burst open by a hurled motorcycle and the accompanying bleeding stump are suggestive of an ongoing conflict. From her perched vantage point, the golden woman's oversize *discomedusae*, or sea anemone–reminiscent skirt, obscures the darker feminine figure that sustains her—the shadowy figure adorned with a flower behind her ear, narrowly holding off her plunging stiletto or perhaps lifting her, exposing the golden figure to harm's way.[14] In *One Hundred*, the black(ened) myth of Medusa is inherited mutationally; her petrifying gaze takes on new gendered meanings, even suggesting alterations to meaning itself. In other words, in the process of reinscription—the replication of historical metaphors—the structures of meaning that license Medusa's racialized sexed metaphoricity, informing Haeckel's "Discomedusae," become mutational. However, this mutation is not attributable solely to "artistic genius" but exceeds subjectivist claims—mutation relying as it does on the meeting of fortuity and the autopoesis of a system. Mutation is that radical alteration in the interstice of chance and design, "a process that is not 'ours' because it necessarily involves a degree of randomness"; in other words, mutation exploits the unpredictable and the limits of human control (Rutsky 103). Thus, mutation, given its implied randomness, cannot be narrativized or, more precisely, can be narrativized only by subordinating its "unpredictability" to the bias and parallax inherent in human perspective.[15] In the words of R. L. Rutsky, "Mutation, one might say, serves to figure a notion of change that seems to have taken on an uncanny life of its own" (103).

If we interpret Mutu's strategies of ironic appropriation and pastiche merely as evidence that historical change has occurred, a subversive sign heralding the arrival of a postmodern critique of race, we potentially miss the ways that her work announces not so much a change in "cultural-historical period" (the arrival of the "post" in its viral variability, post this, post that), but rather, her work *performs* "a change in the *conceptualization* of history" (Rutsky 102, emphasis added). History, here, is re-conceptualized such that it defies dominant conceptions in a manner particularly unsettling for the presumption that history belongs to the (human) subject and that it "moves towards an end" (Rutsky 102–103). Progressivist and developmental historical narratives conceptualize "history" as the "passage from one era to another," propelled by the achievements and designs of human self-directed agency; yet, as I maintain, historical movement is a more-than-human inter(intra)actional process rather than human-directed sequential action. Humans participate in history, but we can only know history, and thus ourselves, partially and obliquely. While the transference of history encompasses human action, it is an irresolutely ahuman process that resists the teleological narrative closure ascribed to it.

In *Histology*, one particular visual phrase both denaturalizes "nature" and humanist progressivist history simultaneously, the titular image, *Histology of the Different Classes of Uterine Tumors*, a doubling down of double entendre: a monkey's face with shellacked, painted, red lips, the mouth of a vulva agape overlain on a gynecological medical drawing; a dark breast becoming a chin, a brain a uterine tumor; the skull sprouting an afro. This is an image that gathers legibility against a backdrop of publicity linking the icon of the black female body and sexuality to that of orangutans. During the eighteenth century, in an attempt to settle the long-standing question of whether continuity or fissure organized species hierarchy, the terms of the Chain of Being's dualistic, *divided yet united*, hierarchization are transformed by a transcontinental debate regarding the plausibility of African females' sexual congress and procreation with orangutans.[16] However, there are, of course, no orangutans in Africa. In fact, in many if not most cases, naturalists never set eyes on either Africans or orangutans but nevertheless purported to depict them based on ideas from the rather fanciful teachings of the ancients combined with the untutored observations of voyagers.

Eighteenth-century representations of monkeys and apes sought to address a gap in knowledge: the precise operations of sexual reproduction and by extension the intractable enigma of human origins. As Elizabeth Liebman observes:

> Without demonstrable scientific laws for sex and love, the unexplained biological status of the monkey revived the ancient fear of exogamy—the union of unlike entities, specifically, mating outside of a recognized group. In social and biological spheres, and in an increasingly diverse and mobile population, exogamy threatened Enlightenment aspirations for collective and individual perfection. (139)

Under the guise of new empirical knowledge, African and Asian apes as well as Polynesian and African females were incorporated into the litany of ancient divinities—satyrs, fauns, sylvan, and faeries—the familiar roles and devices of ancient fiction and popular tales—including, or especially those exploring mythic passions and appetites (Liebman 140).

The Dutch physician and naturalist, Jacob Bontius's 1631 work "Historiae naturalis et medicae Indiae orientalis" introduced the term "Orang Hutan" into Western languages, where he claimed that the orangutan "was born of the lust of the women of the (East) Indies who mate with apes and monkeys to satisfy their detestable desires." By the eighteenth century, the question of human species (dis)continuity rested primarily on fabulations of African female bodies and appetites, yet I mention Bontius's 1620 discussion of the East Indies (Indonesia and Malaysia) to underscore that the ontologizing vocabularies and scales under construction here were produced in the context of imperial appropriation not only of territories and their inhabitants but also of narrative fabulation where narrative drifts, deletes, and substitutes its objects and characters.[17] In the passage from Malay sources to Dutch colonial natural history, what was once a relatively circumscribed yet dubious seventeenth-century Dutch imperial phantasy intensifies and transmutes into a transcontinental debate, a century later, concerning the peculiarities of the African female's sex difference, appetites, and reproductive capacity, whereby the African female functions as the delimiting measure of human species membership in the context of an emerging global imaginary.[18]

While this chapter of comparative anatomy has often been discussed, what typically gets lost is not only the transnational context but also the extent to which European, male naturalists identified with apes and the correlative efforts taken to foreclose identification with African females, and black people more generally. This debate concerned not only the degree to which black(ened) females were properly human but also whether or not the orangutan was superior to her. In this debate, black(ened) females variously occupied all positions: human, animal, animal human, human animal, unknown quantity, cipher.

Beginning in the second half of the seventeenth century, according to naturalists, female apes were distinguished by their "great modesty." Jacob Bontius, the first to impute demureness to the female orangutan in his *Historiae naturalis* (1658, originally 1620), wrote that the young female inspired admiration by hiding her "secret parts" with great modesty from unknown men. Hiding her face with her hands, she wept copiously, uttered groans, and expressed sentiments so humanlike that Bontius concluded she lacked nothing human but speech (Schiebinger 99). Monboddo, Edward Tyson, and Linnaeus also produced reports of female apes' modesty. Londa Schiebinger argues,

> In this, naturalists followed newly emerging ideals for middle-class European women. . . . What is surprising in the portrayals is that female apes were *not* depicted as closer to nature than were the males. Even in the state of nature, female apes were chaste, modest, soft, sober, considerate, attentive, and tranquil—qualities Linnaeus attributed to civilized humans. Portrayals of male apes, by contrast evoked Linnaeus's descriptions of uncivilized "man": foolish, lascivious, imitative. (99, 105)

In an attempt to naturalize hierarchy, speculations about female apes great affection and bounds of attachment for their young and companions were also not uncommon. Toward the end of the century, the female apes depicted in European natural history (for instance, see Linnaeus's

1801 *Histoire Naturalle*) were figured in accordance with contemporaneous European standards of female beauty.

Perhaps the most notable modification was the lifting and rounding of breasts, given the role of breast shape in the naturalization of racial hierarchy. Late nineteenth-century anthropologists classified breasts by their perceived beauty in the same way that they measured skulls for intelligence. The ideal breast was the compact "hemispherical" type, found, it was said, only among whites and Asians. In contrast, female African women were purported to have flabby, pendulous breasts similar to the udders of goats (Schiebinger 64). Pendulous breasts were long perceived as a distinctive marker of the African female, and as signifiers of her savagery and cannibalism. Early depictions of apes superimposed this feature on female apes thus racializing them in the same bestializing, sexuated terms that they initially imputed to African females (Schiebinger 91, 161). It was not until the end of the eighteenth century, in accordance with Europeans' increasing identification with apes or identification of elite European women with female apes, that apes' breasts were given a demurely feminine shape.

While naturalists imputed to female apes the narrow-gendered prescriptions and aesthetic qualities they expected of middle-class European women, they continued to depict African females in grotesque and prurient terms. In the eighteenth century, in studies of female anatomy, what was invariably at issue was some aspect of their sexuality, the peculiarities of their breasts, genitalia, menstruation, parturition, or suckling. Thus, it is not surprising that studies of female anatomy designed to reveal the exact boundary between humans and apes interrogated aspects of their sexuality (Schiebinger 89). As Londa Schiebinger concludes, "for eighteenth–century male naturalists, that which distinguished female humans from animals was not reason, speech, or the ability to create culture, but rather distinctive forms of sexual anatomy" (94). Moreover, as Liebman argues:

> The peculiar new ape resembled the human, and by projection it bore the mien of the polymorphous and irrational gods of antiquity who sojourned on earth, frequently to couple with mortals. Thus early life scientists and social theorists were confronted with the task of rescuing the monkey from the realm of mythology. (140)

In this chapter and the earlier one on Hopkinson and "world," while I direct attention to the role of mythology in domination, the aim here is not principally that of rescuing black womanhood from the function of myth; rather the primary aim is to investigate the potential liberatory use of nonrepresentationalist inquiries into ontology.

Histology's monkey situates the history of the body in the body of history wherein one's taxonomic carcerality, as in the examples of Linné's and Haeckel's respective systems, is determinant of an ill-fated singularity in the order of matter itself that, I will show, precisely *emerges* via the agentic capacities and efficacies of bodily process. In the next section of this chapter, I want to tarry with the question of measurement. If as Karen Barad suggests, measurement is a mode of knowing that is also a means of doing/making or worlding, then I want to consider how the apparatus of measurement in parsing and ontologizing distinction introduces its cause. Barad clarifies, "Measurements are agential practices, which are not simply revelatory but performative: they help constitute and are a constitutive part of what is being measured" (Barad, *Nothingness* 6). In other words, the means and modes of measuring are inseparable from the iterative material-discursive phenomena they claim to identify. Measurement and mattering, metric and object, are inextricable and co-constitutive, or to use Barad's term, "intra-active within phenomena," not interactions: "Measurements are world-making: matter and meaning do not pre-exist, but rather are co-constituted via measurement intra-actions" (*Nothingness* 6). Measurement is agential and constitutive with what is measured rather than disinterested; thus, it matters how some *thing* is measured. Take the case of the famous wave/particle experiment: when electrons (or light) are measured using one kind of apparatus, they are waves; if they are measured in a complementary way, they are particles. As Barad explains, "What we're talking about here is not simply some object *reacting* differently to different probings but *being* differently. What is at issue is the very nature of nature" (*Nothingness* 6). Regarding bodily differentiation, what this suggests is that there is no preexisting "black female body" with determinate boundaries and properties that precede measurement.[19]

Like a collage, the orgasmic body "is always making itself as it is being unmade" in intra-action with (sociogenic evolutionary) history's discursive-material means of measurement and cutting a figure (Martin, "Fracture" 50). Mutu's collages and the technical skill required to make these are certainly disruptive of narrative genres, in particular those foundational to evolutionary theories of race, but this critique, as important as it is, nevertheless overlays a more fundamental structural critique not just of a particular set of representations but of an entire mode of representation that underwrites racial representation(alism). Mutu's use of collage to underscore the irresolute borders of assembly and disassembly that history performs suggests that any representation that defines itself in the terms of a pregiven developmental ontology can only do so by effacing the processual conditions, and indeed conditional contexts, that produce its peculiar mode of representation. The open-ended processual nature of history itself, its contingency and continual change, can only mutate the linear narrativity of thinkers like Haeckel. "Implying a shift in the notion of change itself—in how cultural change comes about," Mutu's collages, their performance of the contingent, recombinant, and the aleatoric dimensions of history thereby poses a challenge to the very nature of historical genre and its privileged terms: linear teleology and stagist development (Rutsky 102).

The organismic body's directedness, not unlike that of history itself, is marked by stable replication as well as chance and the aleatory; thus, neither history nor the organism's effects can be known in advance. What I want to consider in what follows is how measurement, including the logics of taxonomy and typology as well as economies of desire and the affect(ivity) of raciality that accompany them, are sociogenically determinant of the materiality of sexual difference and reproduction. In other words, I want to consider how the logics of taxonomy and typology, the singularity of black(female)ness previously identified in the history of evolutionary thought, is potentially intra-actional with the matter we call "the black female body" and the incomparable and confounding health indicators entangled with this material metaphor.

The speculum is a rather ignoble technology. Its weaponization lies in how the methodical parting of female lips established racially ontologizing divisions of sex and gender in gynecology. This instrument proliferates across the twelve serialized frames that comprise *Histology*— matted and sharply separated into black and white. Yet, emblems of white femininity—blue eyes, ruby lips—superimposed on images of black women suggest the discursive-material entanglement of black and white, *divided yet united*, at the registers of gender *and* sex. Dr. Marion

Sims, who many consider "The Father of American Gynecology," bought and raised female slaves for the express purpose of using them for experimentation (Washington 55). Slave quarters and backyard shacks were the setting for his reproductive experiments pertaining to vesicovaginal fistula, cesareans, bladder stones, and ovariotomy, for example. The pervasiveness of such practices persuaded historian of medicine Harriet Washington to conclude that "forced medical experimentation was the scientific personification of black enslavement in the U.S." (54).[20]

It was commonly professed, by men of letters and the uncredentialed, that African females did not feel pain or anxiety in the way white women do. In "Some Could Suckle over Their Shoulder: Male Travelers, Female Bodies, and the Gendering of Racial Ideology, 1500–1770," Jennifer Morgan argues that the European imaginary equated African females' purported fecundity and propensity for easy birth and breastfeeding with their projected astonishing capacity for manual labor; painless, meaningless, and mechanical childbirth in their estimation was the measure of black female gender and of blackness, more generally (186). African womanhood as a discursive formation materialized in the context of England's need for productivity; in response to this need, utilitarian feeding and mechanistic childbirth would ultimately become located in the English economy (187). By the time Sims appears on the scene in the nineteenth century, these tropes of "the black female body" were oft repeated.

An admission of suffering in black(ened) people was effectively bypassed by theories such as these to the extent that commonplace exaggerations of black females' purported capacities for endurance offered assurance that *black* pain was not *really* pain. Regarding forced gynecological experiments on enslaved women in particular, Dr. James Johnson, editor of the *London Medical and Chirurgical Review*, comments on the "wondrous" capacity of the "Negro" to bear what would be insurmountable pain in whites: "When we come to reflect that all the women operated upon in Kentucky, except one, were Negresses and that these people will bear anything with nearly if not quite as much impunity as dogs and rabbits, our wonder is lessened" (qtd. in Washington 58). What has typically gone unremarked is that René Descartes's ticking-clock-animal-automata thesis, which held that animals felt pain but that pain was merely a mechanical response to stimulation, was historically coincident with theories about African women and childbirth discussed by Jennifer Morgan.

Descartes's bête machine theory and the theory that black people were impervious to pain recall and reinforce each other (*Discourse on Method*).

Contemporary research on race and pain reports quite different findings. In the first study to examine the link between perceived discrimination and pain, researchers concluded that for whites, one's particular history of physical ailment was the chief predictor of pain, and perceived discrimination was found to be unrelated to report of pain. For black people, it was the opposite: perceived discrimination was actually a better predictor of pain than physical health variables, suggesting that the experience of racism itself modulates how one experiences pain.[21] These results confirmed what others have long suggested—the domain of experienced pain is the somaticization of an intra-actional field that includes biological, psychological, and cultural actants (Turk and Monarch 6–8).

As Washington notes, in the context of forced experimentation, the mandate was profit rather than cure; profit came in the form of restoring the slave's body as vital property, notoriety, or the recovered health and life of whites that directly benefited from these experiments while not being subject to them. The semio-material profiteers of such experiments would justify their practice largely based on the notion that black people's purported low intelligence and hypersexuality was evidence of their animality. But as Harriet Washington notes, doctors themselves mandated the very immodesty that purportedly defined *the* black female sex. During the Victorian period, layers of dress symbolized sexual chastity. While doctors maintained white femininity's modesty by covering white women during gynecological surgeries, averting their eyes from even modestly dressed women (relying on their sense of touch beneath voluminous Victorian skirts), it was common to ask black(ened) women to undress completely in front of multiple male doctors. Beliefs about black women's sexuality provided doctors the opportunity to explore new forms of looking at women's disrobed bodies and to peer inside the female body (Washington 64).

Histology's layers of women's bodies are coated by the overlay of sexologists' causal theories of queer erotics on sexual practice, which they typically attributed to purported genital irregularity. As Aliyyah Abdur-Rahman asserts,

Sexologists and medical scientists alleged that supposed genital irregularities (e.g., enlarged labia or an elongated clitoris) that predisposed white lesbians and prostitutes to sexual deviance were standard features of black women's sexual organs. . . . It is important to note here that black women's sexuality symbolized in nineteenth-century scientific discourses only the excesses of white women's sexuality, whereas it figured black women's and men's sexuality as a whole. (14, 11)

"The criminalization of lesbianism and prostitution," Abdur-Rahman maintains, "was effected in part through sexologists' claim of their bodily and behavioral kinship with black women, the archetypes of sexual deviance" (14, 11).

Histology's superimpositions of genitals on faces also recalls a history Rahman alerts us to: the conflation of female genitalia with the faces of women. The face, or rather the stereotypic caricature of black women's faces, has been held to index the nature of the anatomies of women (Abdur-Rahman 13). Within such logics, "Black women are wholly genitalized, visualized . . . as manifestly sexual and debased" (Abdur-Rahman 13). To facialize the medical text, to build a face around the original text's illustration of a vagina, as in *Primary Syphilitic Ulcers of the Cervix* and *Uterine Catarrh*, is also possibly to, as Alessandra Raengo describes, resituate "the vagina so that it occupies the position of the Third Eye" (77), returning the gaze with what Chelsea Mikael Frazier brilliantly characterizes as a "side-eye" (Figure P.5, P.11).[22] Crucially, one of the questions at stake in this work is how one knows one is looking at a female face and, relatedly, what role race plays in this determination. Raengo continues, "As much as colonial discourse constructs the native woman synecdochically *as* a vagina, Mutu empowers that bodily opening with an inquisitive, challenging, and knowing look" (77). *Histology* is not simply, or exclusively, an interrogation of how black female forms are measured but more pointedly, *Histology* underscores how sex difference, which is always raced, more generally, gathers legibility and materializes in the entangled relational field of racial domination.

Whereas a *naturalism* of sex and sexuality arose with the incipient racialized comparison of breasts and appetites, a century and a half later a maturing *science* of sex emerged out of the experiments on the captive population by J. Marion Sims and his contemporaries in the nineteenth century. Histology calls to mind this history: speculums and the partition of legs expose vulvas and cavernous cavities. The brain is alternately overlain with a series of evocative and interrelated images: an archeologist and his collection of human skulls recall the spectacle of craniometry—an erupting volcanic salvo suggests the culmination of a prurience that masks itself as disinterested authority (Figure P.8, P.13). Behind the eyes is a fashion model, an emblem of Eurocentric standards of beauty (Figure P.6). And with this cameo, Du Bois's double-consciousness takes form not only on the register of the ethereal psyche but of a tumorous doubling of an organ at war with an other that, as Fanon noted, is nevertheless the self. The "African female's" putative lack of legible feminine gender, the disfiguring withholding of the symbolics of sentient personhood afforded normatively gendered humanity, is lived as a multiplication of the organ—a tumorous breast (Figure P.9). In contrast to Haeckel, Mutu evokes images of nature in order to denaturalize the subject of sex-gender and challenge the alienation from the body invited when many of the conditions cited in *Histology* are noted for their "masculinizing effects." An inverted fennec fox head is recast as a moustache, turning the sexually patronizing moniker "foxy lady" upside down (Figure P.12). In *Histology*, the appearance of morphological incongruity is not an accomplice to ableism but an indictment of the disfiguring and debilitating effects of power as well as a questioning of the aesthetic devaluation of abject forms.

The motif of hyperbolic mouths alludes to the meeting of aperture and the pleasure of stereotype, highlighting that mechanistic, technological forms are just as integral to the maintenance of a racialized, gendered order as media traditionally framed as subjective (such as painting, drawing, and sculpture) rather than objective—*objectif* being the French word for lens. In the context of the West, mouths and tongues perform a kind of double-speak in the field of signification. On the one hand, they provide speech, understood to deliver indisputable evidence of Man's justifiable authority—language, an achievement thought to offer testimony to a "natural" hierarchy among species and races (or races as species), whereby "proper" speech purports to guarantee mastery and justifiable authority over "nature." On the other hand, mouths are also irresolute figures of porosity, vulnerability, pleasure, and contamination that evoke racialized, gendered specters with respect to sexuality—"the feminine position," the locus of the erotic and devouring womb—as Sigmund Freud infamously put it, "the dark continent of female sexuality."

With her characteristic wit and satirical humor, Mutu explores the link between violence and ecstasy: extracted from pornographic magazines, such as *Black Tail*, oversized pulpy painted red lips with outstretched tongues and piercings are grafted onto disassembled forms, suggesting that the privileged significatory production of language, its assumed teleological and intersubjective powers, can all too easily be annulled by economies of pleasure that presuppose black women's animality and the animality of sex. Perhaps this is to be expected, given that the establishment of credentialed speech and the assurance it offers, has been predicated on an antiblack weaponization of sexuality in and beyond the field of the symbolic: in the discourse of Man, black womanhood is understood in terms of a bestializing, serialized negation, whereby seriality's characteristic deferral operates to negate terms in successive order of their appearance—(black) race, (black) gender, (black) sexuality, (black) sex, (black) maternity—when one term appears another recedes. Black women's sexuating vulnerability to weaponized language coupled with the permeability and fragility of the body led feminist critic Hortense Spillers to exclaim, with similar wit, "Sticks and bricks *might* break our bones but words will most certainly *kill* us" (*Black, White, and in Color* 209). That Mutu named each cameo after disease types draws our attention to the problematic nature of naming in medical science, insisting that technomedicine's tools are constitutive with the symptoms that serve as points of access (Stanford 31). Mutating breasts form a tumorous mass, the breasts' maternal *function and pleasures provided for the flesh* give way under the weight of the layers of accumulated meaning ascribed to black women's breasts in an antiblack world (Figure P.9).

Battles in the Flesh

[T]hose of us who live our battles in the flesh must know
ourselves as our strongest weapon in the most gallant struggle of our lives.
—Audre Lorde, *A Burst of Light*

In *The Cancer Journals*, Audre Lorde also provides an analytic treatment of the interrelation of language and debility, including her own, which took the form of breast cancer and the experience of mastectomy before her death in 1992. Lorde critically reframed her experience from that of *being* sick (cancer) to that of *becoming* sick (carcinogenesis) in order to explore the *politics* of health. By shifting the frame from cancer to carcinogenesis, Lorde announced her rejection of biomedical conceptions of cancer viewed either as individualized disease or as ultimately attributable to an immutable division in raced and gendered bodies. Alternatively, Lorde's framework emphasized that the *process* of carcinogenesis is a political matter and a matter of politics.[23] I have argued that Mutu's work de-essentializes "the body" as the "cause" of disease in order to draw attention to the biological, psychological, environmental, and cultural interactions that perturb organ systems and disrupt physiological function, producing disease as palimpsest. Similarly, Lorde describes breast cancer as a "preventable" death, one that is bound up with patterns and networks that encompass human and nonhuman actants—food, natural environment, psychic structures, and the fields of pleasure, desire, language, and aesthetics.

For Lorde, breast cancer is not simply a matter of malignant and recalcitrant cells; it *is* that, but it is also a physical index of patterned social relations that pollute physical, psychological, environmental, and social worlds. As Marcy Jane Knopf-Newman contends, Lorde's radicalization of breast cancer takes "bodies and the environment into account. Cancer is not political because either subject—bodies or environment—is inherently political, but rather because of the silence and secrecy surrounding the overlapping intersections of these subjects" (134).[24] Regarding her decision to not wear a prosthetic breast and re-aestheticize her mastectomy scars (rather than see them as something private, shameful, and dis-aesthetic), she sees them as "an honorable reminder that I may be a casualty in the cosmic war against radiation, animal fat, air pollution, McDonald's hamburgers and Red Dye No. 2, but the fight is still going on" (60). Arguing "a clear distinction must be made" between the affirmation of the self and "the superficial farce of looking on the bright side of things," Lorde states:

The happiest person in this country cannot help breathing in smokers' cigarette fumes, auto exhaust, and airborne chemical dust, nor avoid drinking the water, and eating the food. The idea that happiness can insulate us against the results of our environmental madness is a rumor circulated by our enemies to destroy us. (77)

By directing the reader's attention to an assemblage of agencies that produce disease effects, Lorde's and Mutu's works render the causality and concept of disease problematic and productively irresolute. In *Histology*, the interior–exterior binary nearly collapses as Mutu's figures are turned inside out. The body is diffuse im/materiality, a bursting star; each particle interacts with external actants and forces.

In the face of the pressing reality of mortality and physical pain, Lorde argued that one must consciously—and critically—incorporate the reality of pain, abjection, and mortality into one's consciousness. From there, mortality and pain can be a source of strength, propelling one to fight for the transformation of the pattern but only if one allows "mortality" and "difference" to alter how one lives. To avoid this confrontation with one's mortality and abjection is to undercut one's strength by remaining attached to a phantasy that one does not have to "fight" in a world patterned by the differential manufacture of death (Lorde 76). For Lorde, such avoidance may even thwart the potential for livable possibilities to emerge.

That Lorde framed her "fight" by laying claim to the symbolics of war has been a source of controversy among feminists, some of whom claim that Lorde's "metaphorics" reinforce the dominant culture's tendency to frame war as justifiable and inevitable due to a reductive and ideologically driven biologism (Khalid 701, 710; Jain 521). Moreover, they suggest, Lorde's invocation of war relies upon and extend the "masculinist" cultural postures, or "militarized masculinity," she claims to abhor.[25] What these feminist critics miss is not only that it is possible to reconfigure established metaphorics, including those that militarize disease, but also that such a potentiality is a matter of survival as language is a crucial terrain upon which war is fought.[26] Lorde's metaphorics acknowledge a recent observation of Jasbir Puar, the debilitation of bodies is, in part, how populations come to be populations as such in the first place: "[t]he body that is seen as consigned to death is the body that is already debilitated in biopolitical terms" (*Right to Maim* 69, 86). In an antiblack world, the relations of force that cohere the symbolic order and its sexuating racial hierarchies are mutually imbricated in the biological domains of racial domination.

As Dorothy Roberts has noted, it is now well established that "dividing people into races has biological *effects*," a fact that is not a matter of immutable biological difference but of systemic societal violence enacted on the scale of a population (*Fatal Invention*, 5). It is also well documented that in comparison to other US racial populations, black people have the highest rates of morbidity and mortality for almost all diseases; the highest disability rates; the shortest life expectancies; the least access to health care; and startlingly low rates of use of up-to-date technology in their treatments.[27] Moreover, even as the overall health of the US population has improved, these racialized inequities in health and mortality have increasingly widened (Williams, "Race, Socioeconomic Status, and Health" 176). With respect to race and reproductive health in particular, black(ened) females have the highest rates of preterm birth, infant mortality, low birthrate, and reproductive cancers.

In her now classic essay, Hortense Spillers articulates a distinction between "flesh" and "body" as foundational to respective modes of captive and liberated subject-positions:

> [B]efore the "body" there is the "flesh," that zero degree of social conceptualization that does not escape concealment under the brush of discourse or the reflexes of iconography. Even though the European hegemonies stole bodies—some of them female—out of West African communities in concert with the African "middleman," we regard this human and social irreparability as high crimes against the *flesh*, as the person of African females and males registered the wounding. If we think of the "flesh" as a primary narrative, then we mean its seared, divided, ripped-apartness, riveted to the ship's hole, fallen, or "escaped" overboard. ("Mama's" 206)

"Before the 'body' there is the 'flesh'" Spillers writes. Here, the *before* has spatial as well as temporal significance, as *before* recalls that the master class gains a sense of proprietary embodiment and sovereign "I" retroactively, whereby the ekphrastic scenes of enfleshment she describes act as a mirror stage such that the other is spatially before the lash and her ensuing corporeal fragmentation hypostatizes (by that I mean "converges" literally and figuratively) in the abstractions made of flesh.

But what happens when recognition of a whole self-possessed body does not take hold and the flesh as dispossession becomes the sine qua non of existence? Or to put it more pointedly, what if the very notion of a sovereign, integral, self-possessed body is intrinsic to the production of the slave's existence as its privileged obverse? Spillers's "before" is often interpreted as affirming the notion that the biological matter of the flesh can and does exist prior to cultural inscription, but this is precisely what I am arguing against. I argue that the conception and *mater*ialization of the organismic body itself is already sociogenically entangled with culture, and indeed, informed by culture—culture itself being determinant of matter and evolutionarily significant. In probing the relation between epigenetic "marks" and Spillers's transfer of marks, epigenetic marks might be akin to what Kimberly Juanita Brown calls "afterimage," "the puncture of the past materializing in the present" and "the history of corporeal imperialism" manifesting as intergenerational debility and reproductive disease (Brown, *Repeating* 18). For Lorde, like Mutu, black female bodies are disfigured, seared, lacerated, and dispossessed not only by the historical uses of the lash but also by the afterlife of slavery's ongoing semio-affective-psychic deployments of systemic antiblackness, which as I will show precede and intrude upon the event of conception. Their portraits of cancer suggest that racialized disease frequencies and inequitable reproductive outcomes are best understood as material accompaniment to the color line's dichotomization of "body" and "flesh" (Spillers, "Mama's" 206).

Moreover, and this is key, the matter of war for Lorde is not in any simple terms metaphorical. Lorde replaces the popular biomedical concept of "war" as symbolic analogy with an analysis of antiblackness *as* systematized war, one that takes the form of a bio-psycho-eco-cultural feedback loop, whereby matter and symbol are contiguous and mutually productive. To presume that Lorde is *merely* drawing an analogy between a culture's antiblack, gendered violence and "war" is to miss how "war" is being redefined according to the lived sexuating conditions of Lorde's black womanhood. Lorde's attempts at resignification must contend with racialized, gendered dialectics of discursivity—the threat and even imminence of foreclosure and appropriation—in the context of a language structured by black women's lack of discursive power:

> We were never meant to speak together at all . . . When language becomes most similar, it becomes most dangerous, for then differences

pass unremarked. . . . Because we share a common language which is not of our own making and which does not reflect our deeper knowledge as women, our words frequently sound the same. But it is an error to believe that we mean the same experience, the same commitment, the same future, unless we agree to examine the history and particular passions that lie beneath each other's words. (*Burst* 70)

While it is true that in working inside the existing rhetoric of "war," Lorde risks concealing that the predicament she seeks to scrutinize is powered by what Frank Wilderson terms "gratuitous violence" rather than tactical deliberation.[28] However, Lorde's expansive redefinition of war neither licenses prior biopolitical conceptions nor obscures the violence of war; rather, the term's temporary loss of definitiveness exists for the express purpose of a critical reframing—exposing and clarifying the antiblack *relations of power* that attend the dominant conceptualization's prematurely narrowed scope. Moreover, I argue that the war Lorde describes *conditions* prior conceptions of war, both those precipitated by formal declarations and those biomedical wars inspired by them—in particular the "war on cancer" with its promise of biotechnological "intervention"—as the antiblack mereological conversion of corporeal existence into flesh provides the epistemological and economic conditions of possibility for globality and its attendant hierarchization of empiricist knowledge.[29] Rather than uncritically reiterate genocidal, biopolitical logic, Lorde is identifying a wider field of relations that are only now coming to be recognized as biopolitical. By doing so, Lorde raises and opens up the *question* of "war," its scope and meaning, to renewed investigation.[30]

In my view, Lorde's combative language is neither masculinist nor at odds with her transformative vision of societal reorganization. As Lorde suggests, the violence that attends the disproportionate rates of breast cancer incidence, morbidity, and mortality among black women is, in fact, militarized and targeted: the breast cancer survival differences between black and white women are among the most striking and consistent of racial "health inequities."[31] A growing bioscientific literature now suggests that racial discrimination raises both the risk of the development of breast cancer and a higher incidence among black women.[32] In other words, antiblackness is determinant at the stage of the disease's initiation, one's susceptibility to the disease, and in its prevalence within a population, how likely are you to get it; if that were not enough, antiblack racism is also determinant of how long you will live once you have it and whether you will ultimately die from it.[33] This destructive power on the part of antiblack racism has principally been attributed to its distinctiveness as a stressor. It is not that other forms of stress are not harmful; rather, antiblack racism appears to have an incomparably debilitating impact on psychological, cognitive, and allostatic systems, introducing disequilibrium in the integration and regulation of endocrine, immune, cardiovascular, and metabolic functioning.[34] In terms of breast cancer specifically, it has been hypothesized that chronic stress from racism introduces dangerous amounts of inflammation into the body, increasing black women's "allostatic load" or the "wear and tear" on the body that occurs when exposed to a stressor.[35] As Quach explains, chronic and severe social stress prompts the stress-response system, activating adaptive physiological mechanisms, which over time degrade the body's ability to properly regulate systems. The overcirculation of stress hormones, among other outcomes, is linked to an uninhibited inflammatory response, and chronic inflammation has been associated with breast cancer recurrence and mortality (Quach et al. 1027).[36]

Moreover, racialized inequities in mortality across a spectrum of cancers, including but not exclusive to breast cancer, are growing despite rapid advancement in detection and treatment. An identifiable pattern has emerged—perhaps for some a counterintuitive one—that as cancers become more amenable to medical intervention, racial survival inequities widen (Tehranifar et al. 2701). While overall breast cancer mortality has declined with improvements in screening and treatment, black–white patient inequities in breast cancer mortality rates have instead increased since 1980—the year *The Cancer Journals* was published (Odierna et al. 669). In 1980, breast cancer mortality rates were reportedly similar across the color line, but whereas white women experienced a decrease in breast cancer mortality rates between 1980 and 2007, black women did not (Odierna et al. 669)—a reality arguably presaged in Lorde's *The Cancer Journals* and *Burst of Light*.

Moreover, studies have begun to suggest that the growing availability of gene-expression profiling and other forms of personalized medicine will likely not benefit all population groups equally; the interrelationship between technological development and racialized somatic processes serves to heighten racial inequities in treatment response, morbidity, and survival. Tumors that develop in breast systems are variegated and can have fundamental differences in their biological features. Given the variegation and corresponding distinctive molecular features of cancers occurring in breast systems, some clinicians speculate that molecularly dissimilar cancers originate from separate cell types and should be treated as separate diseases (Odierna et al. 670). While any of these genetically differentiated tumors can and do exist in all population groups, it appears that anti-black racism increases the probability that black(ened) females will develop tumors that are harder to treat, result in shorter survival time, and increase chances of recurrence and mortality. The development of gene-expression profiling technologies, which include the tests currently available, has privileged molecular presentations of the disease that are correlated with whiteness and increased odds, or more precisely, forms not correlated with blackness and its depreciated odds (including the particularly fatal "triple negative" breast tumors which are nonresponsive to current hormonal therapies).

Personalized medicine promises "targeted" diagnostic and prognostic tests, but in practice, the development and diffusion (design, testing, and availability) of these technologies has not remedied racial health inequities; instead, they have only created new pathways for inequity because such tests are developed, marketed, and consumed in accordance with existing social inequalities, in particular race (Odierna et al. 669, 670, 672). Thus, biotechnological intervention "targets" black and white women in inverse relation to racial inequities in morbidity and mortality, not as individuals but, in the words of Roberts, as hierarchically racialized "populations." While these technologies are presumed to be purchasable by any individual of means, the design and development of the technology itself is preceded by, and becomes an agent in, the perpetuation of a racially exclusionary economy of life. In other words, while it places a price tag on white life, it prefigures and preauthorizes black(ened) female debility and premature death, making black(ened) life untenable despite the interest of profit.[37] In sum, in a racialized system, to delay or avoid death from disease requires something in excess of technological innovation and even equitable access to medical care; it requires symbolic capital such that in the economy of life, it would appear that life is principally purchased by means of bio-ontological currency.

As Lorde suggests, if black women were to opt out of this battle, they unwittingly leave themselves unarmed and open to a militarism that is there whether they recognize it or not and whether they self-consciously engage in battle or not. To label this experience of embattlement "masculinist" erases the critical reconceptualizations of gender that black women and/or trans people and/or queer men have adopted in order to resist the very real forms of occupation and brutality they experience—a reimagining of feminine gender that does not place militancy and femininity at odds. The work of feminist and queer criticism is to reveal the limitations of rigid gendered semiotics, not reinforce them by presuming we know what forms the properly feminine or masculine can take outside of the racialized contexts that introduce complexity and variance into gendered experience and symbolics. To presume preemptively that "militarized" expressions of one's experience and efficacy are masculinist potentially reinforces the very patterns and networks that Lorde asks us to confront and combat. And there is a significant literature suggesting that black people's unconscious, and therefore impersonal, identification with antiblack attitudes and affects bears directly on black(ened) people's physical health.

In short, the establishment and maintenance of pro-black attitudes among black people, even where there are repeated experiences of racism, may help to mitigate (but not fully avoid) the physiological and psychologically debilitating effects of antiblackness.[38] For these very reasons, Lorde's resignification of war with its attentiveness to semiotics, affect, aesthetics, and desire was that much more incisive and prescient. In Mutu's *Histology*, a skull is nestled between two pairs of black women's splayed legs—cross bones (Figure P.13). The skull, tumorous overtakes the trunk of the body and head. The body visually restates the metaphor of openwork employed here. Inside the lattice where a head would be, the white male scientist surrounded by his collection of skulls. The image recalls that black female flesh's death and debility historically and contemporarily arranges and capacitates Man and powers empirical science—Henrietta, Lucy, Anarcha, Betsey, Saarjite . . .

Coda

Toward a Somatic Theory of Necropower

Lorde's and Mutu's contention that racial domination has a direct impact on bodily states and somatic processes challenges prevailing biocentric theories in the life sciences that have historically suggested that social and environmental (f)actors were distal to manifestations of disease. However, to underscore the linguistic power of racist culture is not to discount the agencies or efficacies inherent to the organismic body; Lorde and Mutu reveal that biology's agency is not prior to or independent of the biopolitical order but *embedded* in biopolitical systems that not only inscribe the surface of bodies but also penetrate the skin. Rather than deny the agentic capaciousness of matter, in this view, the very agency of the body produces the conditions of possibility for the racially disparate gutting of bodies by reproductive tumors and cancerous cells. This sociogenic production of antiblackness, which I will describe as necropolitical, extending Achille Mbembe's original formulation, anticipates and radicalizes emergent theories in the burgeoning biomedical field of epigenetics (Mbembe, "Necropolitics"). I argue that epigenetics' claim that the body is emergent, mutable and protean potentially can be interpellated by racism such that black maternity is further tasked with the responsibility to observe cultural norms held to reproduce norms of reproductive health and bodily outcomes that are themselves antagonistic to blackness. It suggests that prior hierarchical biologized conceptions of race could be recast in epigenetic terms. Epigenetic race like "biological race" potentially extends and dissimulates forms of governmentality that need race and maintain antiblackness.

With biological determinism now on the decline in the life sciences, epigenetics is currently unsettling genetic dogmatism with the contention that genes never act alone but always "in concert" with social and environmental partners. Reviving mid-twentieth- century embryologist

Conrad Waddington's model of the "epigenotype," epigenetics emphasizes that biology is socially meaningful and the social is biologically
meaningful (Waddington 10). According to epigeneticists, environment
and social processes have the ability to modulate gene expression without changing the underlying structure of DNA—on both the scale of mitosis (cellular reproduction) and meiosis (sexual reproduction).[1] We not
only inherit genes from our parents, we also inherit a system that regulates their expression, revealing or concealing our genetic potential. This
system is called an *epigenome*, and it is commonly likened to volume
controls for our genes (Roberts, *Fatal Invention* 142). The controls, called
marks, can turn on or off, to quiet or amplify genetic potential. *Therefore, our genetic potential is not determined by any preset or fixed program
but is instead modulated by an epigenome which is highly responsive to
social and environmental prompts.* Moreover, our genes possess potential, including pathogenic potential, that may very well go unexpressed
depending upon our social and environmental experiences; the reverse
is also true, as social and environmental toxins may initiate disease processes that could have otherwise gone unexpressed. That we inherit an
epigenome and its structure of marks suggests that we are affected by
the social and environmental experiences of our recent ancestors; while
these marks are durable, they are also reversible precisely because they
rely upon social and environmental cues.

Genetic reductionism, or the idea that genes dictate the form and
function of organisms (captured in the simplistic notion that "DNA
makes RNA makes protein"), lost esteem with the conclusion of the
Human Genome Project, which not only demonstrated that humans
have fewer genes than predicted—some twenty thousand rather than
the hundred thousand expected—but also revealed that less than 3 per-
cent of those genes code for protein (Barnes and Dupré 65). Shaking the
confidence of stalwart genetic determinists and raising questions about
what other functions the genome might perform, the Human Genome
Project's findings catalyzed desire for a more complex model, making
way for our moment's "interactionist consensus" (Kitcher 411).

While epigenetics unsettles long-held ideas in genetics, in particular
genetic reductionism and determinism, it thankfully does so "without
the immediate resettling of doxa—the primacy of the gene as *causal
foundation* of life phenomena and the vehicle of heredity" has by and

large been eclipsed by theories of "causal cascades" and "chains of causation" (Landecker and Panofsky 342, 343, emphasis added). This more complex theorization of "cause" halts nature-nurture debates that "pose genes and environment as separate and opposed causes" (Landecker and Panofsky 349). Epigenetically relevant environmental (f)actors are both internal and external to the organism (Meaney 50). As Landecker and Panofsky note, "This broadens the scope of "environment" to a net of interconnected molecules and processes to which the boundary of the skin is of little significance" (339). Nonteleological and dynamic, epigenetic models allow not only for stability but also nondeterminacy and even unpredictability with respect to gene expression.

The interactant supersedes genetic metaphors such as "the blueprint" and "the book of life" along with the false certainty they imply—the epigenetic references complex systems of bio-psycho-cultural-environmental interactivity and a corresponding *range of potential* genetic outcomes therein. Epigeneticists depart from approaches that seek to establish a 1:1 relationship between DNA and phenotype, proposing that we depose the "iconic double helix" in exchange for a flexible system of interactants where the body is active in its own iterative developmental unfolding. Social and environmental exposures incite hormonal response, which then initiate cellular processes that affect the structure and function of the body, which then responds anew to the environment in a dynamic and ongoing interactive relationship between the body and environmental agencies (Guthman and Mansfield, "Implications" 497). Genetic logic seeks the sequence variation that underlies different physical and behavioral outcomes; in contrast, epigenetic logic asks how different outcomes arise from essentially similar genetics (Landecker and Panofsky 336).[2] In short, epigenetics concerns how environments and social structures "come into the body" and attends to how the interactive process of penetration and internalization modulates the genome, rather than positing genetic variation as the "underlying" cause of biological difference or racial health inequities (Landecker and Panofsky 348).[3]

Epigenetics' proponents suggest that the field's arrival spells the end of biocentric conceptions of race, even as paradoxically the epigenome gains its purchase against the backdrop of the biopolitical cult of the gene: the double-helix acquired much of its intransigent iconicity as a result of the desire for a sturdy theory of biological race. The prominence of reductions and faulty expectations such as "Genes as biological atoms, and genes as carriers of information," created anticipation (and funding) for the Human Genome Project, exposing, as much as they relied on, the interpellative power of the desire for an empiricist and, indeed, molecular (im)materialization of race (Müller-Wille and Rheinberger 217). If we consider that the epigenetic study of "racial health disparities" has been key to elevating the status of, and ensuring confidence in, the field's potential to effectively research and create new *biomedical solutions to social-induced racial inequities* in health, then we must critically consider the field's insights as well as its biopolitical, and even necropolitical, implications and consequences. Like the Human Genome Project, the field's insights may very well be bound up with its biopolitical objectives.[4]

Drawing from developmental biology theories, which emphasize the importance of fetal and early childhood development for the lifetime health of a person, epigenetics maintains that social and environmental impacts experienced by the maternal parent have consequences for fetal development and may even contribute to adult health outcomes: epigenetic marks and gestational processes have consequences for biological processes and responses across the life cycle (Barker 27). For instance, early life and prenatal undernutrition have long been thought to help explain racialized patterns of adult cardiovascular disease risk, wherein low birth weight is a crucial indicator of the potential for adult cardiovascular disease as well as preceding conditions like hypertension and diabetes (Kuzawa and Sweet 4). Studies aver that a fetus faced with undernutrition might make adjustments to rate of growth, reduce nutritional requirements, and even modify the structure and function of organs and other systems involved with metabolism and physiology; such fetal modifications are believed to have effects that linger on into adulthood, influencing the development of chronic disease (Kuzawa and Sweet 4).

While there is little doubt that black women globally, in particular impoverished black women, commonly experience a redundancy of exposure to harm from the environment and undernutrition, many now believe that—as is the case with breast cancer recurrence and mortality—psychosocial stress stemming from systemic racism is the most representative factor in the determination of black women's reproductive health outcomes. This phenomenon is sometimes referred to as "weathering" (Geronimus 207). In *In the Wake: On Blackness and Being*, Christina Sharpe takes inspiration from Morrison's *Beloved* in defining her concept of weathering in ecological terms: "The weather is the totality of our environments; the weather is total climate; and that climate is antiblack . . . it is the atmospheric condition of time and place; it produces new ecologies" (Sharpe 104, 106). The weather is particularly pernicious with respect to low birth weight and infant mortality—black infants' mortality rates are almost three times that of white infants (National Center for Health Statistics 114). Regarding low birth weight, Kuzawa and Sweet note, "The most important predictors of compromised birth outcomes include factors such as self-perceived discrimination, racism, and chronic stress" (10; see also Giscombe and Lobel 669, and Mustillo et al. 2128). Given the intransigence of structural racism, it is likely that low-birth-weight children could very well experience similar psychosocial stressors in adulthood as their mothers, predisposing them to have low-birth-weight children as well. As a consequence, certain biological or metabolic states theoretically have the potential of cycling intergenerationally across matrilineal generations (Kuzawa and Sweet 9).[5] While epigenetics implies that stressors not experienced firsthand can have biological consequences for successive generations, if these stressors were to disappear entirely, blackness' deathly prefiguration could still intrude upon and overtake forces of life for generations; as such, the somaticization of antiblackness, its physics, carries the potential to unmoor the time and spatial constraints of "historically situated" modalities of racial terror.[6]

In Achille Mbembe's formulation, necropower is power over death, acts of killing that exceed state regulatory capacities: the onward march of war in the absence of a formal declaration or army. Might the forms of deadly power I have described be necropolitical? Might Mutu and Lorde be pointing us to a mode of war that Sharpe describes as "total climate" (Sharpe 104)? With the history of Western colonialism as a starting point, in "Necropolitics," Mbembe calls into question the normative theory of democracy by troubling its privileged term—politics. Mbembe goes on to redefine "politics" as an idiom of war before announcing that war is the primary driver of Western sovereignty. Mbembe casts doubt on the presumed sufficiency of Foucault's theory of biopower—that domain of life intruded upon and held hostage by state power—by ultimately arguing that the regulation of death rather than life is the essential objective of Western sovereignty, an objective that collapses distinction between means and ends (Mbembe, "Necropolitics" 12). In light of Mbembe's reconsideration of Western sovereignty's telos as that of death rather than life, it follows that biopower would be deposed in an effort to provide a closer examination of the contours of necropower—its technologies and mechanisms. As Mbembe sets forth, necropower's "concern is those figures of sovereignty whose central project is not the struggle for autonomy but the generalized instrumentalization of human existence and the material destruction of human bodies and populations" (14).

My interest in extending Mbembe's theorization of necropolitics here concerns how necropower's antiblack "relations of enmity," which are in fact a nonrelational form of relationality, not only instrumentalize human existence but also weaponize the biological field such that the black(ened) body, the very materiality of the organism, yields and redirects its energies to the destruction of black vitality (16). Biopolitics defines itself "in relation to a biological field" which it "takes control of and vests itself in" so that it might regulate the life of those who matter and dispose of those that prefiguratively do not through war and genocide (17). Conversely, the necropower I describe "displays no weapons" because war as described here is im/materialized, concealed in the bodily processes of the nullified as a kind of suicidal telos or self-detonation and even internecine in utero toxicity (36). This idiom of war in its nonspectacularity and nontheatricality thwarts biopolitics' gendered calculus of those wounded, fallen, and vanquished by war. While civil society largely disavows the existence of this war, it nevertheless insistently appears in the "scopic regimes" of medicine's diagnostic technologies and algorithms, where we might argue that the HeLa cell is a kind of cipher.[7]

While I share Mbembe's contention that humanity is embedded in the technological and coevolves with technicity, my reformulation of necropolitics necessarily departs from Mbembe's conceptualization of the relationship between space and technology as it pertains to the embodiment of race, in particular his spatialized theory of prosthesis. As in Foucault's original formulation, Mbembe describes a social power that merely objectifies a presumably inert body, such that the body like the environment is mere setting (Guthman and Mansfield 489). Moreover, in "Necropolitics," the technological object, or weapon, is thought to reside in a space exterior to the body. Upon the usurpation of the weapon-ized object, it becomes an extension of your self-conscious will—a tool that extends the reach and capabilities of a self-possessed body, aiding in the navigation of worlds and manipulation of matter.[8]

In the contrasting framework elaborated here, the black(ened) ma-ternal body's endocrine system, organ systems, neuropsychological pathways, and cellular functioning are essential agencies in antiblack necropower, such that the distinction between the body and war's weap-onry no longer rests on a solid boundary between human subjectivity and external environment, nor that of subject and object. Here, acts of war are not exclusively directed by intentional human action, and the har-nessing of war's weaponry exceeds the subjectivist domain. While I share Mbembe's concern regarding the manner with which colonial racializa-tion produces and is produced by the spatialization of populations into "cells," my emphasis is different. I want to query how social processes—the prison "cell," the political party "cell," and the military "cell"—interact with somatic cellular processes, producing alterations to the immediate cellu-lar environment and cellular functioning in a manner that we might also describe as necropolitical. Privileging the colonial modality, Mbembe's spatial reading describes a necropower that compartmentalizes life and death into geographic zones "epitomized by barracks and police stations," but in what I describe necropower's "boundaries" and "internal frontiers" are not so much spatialized but corporealized and are therefore nomadic, traveling with black(ened) subjects even when they are able to transgress geopolitical-spatialized borders (Mbembe, "Necropolitics" 26).

This nomadism on the part of antiblack violence, both in its corpore-alization (traveling with black subjects) and in its ubiquity and oppor-tunism (waiting for a black subject to arrive), has required researchers working in the areas of "racial health disparities" to reconsider their baseline suppositions about the relationship between socioeconomic status and health. It has become increasingly difficult to justify contin-ued investment in the belief that the assumption of increased economic mobility can provide the sufficient conditions necessary to rectify dis-parate reproductive health inequities for black women; rather, trends in the findings cast doubt on the appeal of regulatory authority and policies aimed primarily at black attainment of upward mobility in the form of increased educational access and class ascendancy.[9]

One particular statistic has captured the attention of the media likely due to the way it shatters the commonly held belief that class mobility and educational access can provide shelter from the pernicious effects of antiblackness: black women with graduate degrees have been reported to have higher infant mortality rates than white women who did not finish high school; in fact, the health inequity between black and white women is higher among women who are more educated and therefore presumably more advantaged.[10] Some have interpreted this divergence with general findings as providing proof of genetic racial difference (Cooper et al. 1166). As Clarence Gravlee notes, such a view rests on two reductive and mutually constitutive equations: "race" equals "genes" and "biology" equals "genes" (Gravlee 49).[11] Such genetic deterministic thinking forestalls reflection on what should otherwise be obvious; as Dorothy Roberts notes, "It would seem strange for a large group of people as genetically diverse as African Americans to have such a concentrated genetic susceptibility to so many common complex diseases . . . A more plausible hypothesis, given the persistence of unequal health outcomes along the social matrix of race, is that they are caused by social factors" ("Fatal Invention" 116–117). Moreover, what racially deterministic reasoning forecloses is the possibility that upward mobility does not provide sufficient shelter from the health burdens of systemic racism for black women.[12] On the contrary, systemic racism, I contend, exceeds the health safeguards class mobility would presumably provide and regulation purports to protect—introducing irony into our conception of upward mobility.[13]

Systematic research into racial health inequities, only really begun in the 1990s, has challenged some of the initial guiding assumptions informing not only genetic approaches to race but also constructivist approaches. As I will argue, this recent research has actually exposed what they share in common. Both perspectives adhere to a teleological approach to the theorization of race and attribute a problematic materiality to race, suggesting that race resides in bodies, rather than in the (im)material effects of interactional systems.

It appears that most researchers prematurely assumed that racial health inequities are primarily attributable to economic class discrimination (black people's disproportionate representation in economically disadvantaged classes) and access-related factors thereto such as insurance status, income, education, access to medical care, residential segregation, and neighborhood-level poverty.[14] Similarly, even when re-searchers thought racial health inequities were likely attributable to an aggregate of socioeconomic variables, and not simply reducible to class discrimination, they also imported a bias by erroneously presuming that these amalgamated factors would take a linear and additive structure in the lives of black people (Kaplan and Kell 1993). This interpretation shares with the class reductive approach the assumption of an overly simplistic, gradational structure of privilege, and thus wellness, in the lives of black people by too readily equating the relative achievement of income, education, and/or occupational prestige among some black people with the assured *embodiment* of privilege.

While studies typically attempt to test their presumptions by estab-lishing socioeconomic "controls" as a matter of course, quite often they confront the twinned aspects of an impasse: the impossibility of estab-lishing "control" in the arena of experience and blackness' irreducibility and opacity—in other words, its resistance to representation. Moreover, as Calvin notes, even when indices of socioeconomic status are thought to "explain" differences, "findings suggest that there may be a very differ-ent experience of SES [socioeconomic status] among ethnic groups . . . the processes by which these differences occur are not uniform among or within ethnic groups" (Calvin et al. 319). Researchers presumed that black lives would mirror those of whites—once socioeconomic adjust-ments were taken into account, of course—whereby wellness would typically stand in positive linear relation to upward mobility; however, often what they found instead was more indicative of an inverse correla-tional matrix—confounding initial expectations.[15, 16] Precisely because both approaches underestimated the extent to which antiblackness is an "antecedent and determinant" of socioeconomic scales as well as an integral component of the "causal pathway" for health among groups—irrespective of racial identity—they missed that *(anti)blackness structures the racially differential operations of socioeconomic status and therefore cannot be reducible to socioeconomics.*[17] In other words, their presuppo-sitions obscured the fact that antiblackness is ecological or total climate.

Moreover, as David R. Williams et al. note:

[T]he conceptualization and measurement of SES is limited. SES is too often used in a static, routine and atheoretical manner . . . [The] persistence of racial differences after adjustment for SES emphasizes that race is more than SES and that additional research attention is required to understand the ways in which unique experiences linked to race, such as non-economic forms of discrimination[,] can adversely affect health. ("Racial Differences" 337)[18]

It is not that socioeconomics is unimportant or irrelevant to racial health outcomes; it is undeniable that SES bears directly on health, but it would appear that in the lives of black people SES impacts health in ways that are often surprising, contravening rather than reinforcing presumed causal or correlational links between socioeconomics and health.

As racial health inequities research studies have begun to suggest that blackness is far from a metonym for socioeconomic status (whether a single factor or compounded factors), the shift in attention from poverty to racism not only underscores the distinctive health burdens posed by racism, it also raises a related question with regard to how one might account for or "measure" racism. Specifically, it calls into question whether any standardized measure of "discrimination" or "perceived discrimination" could be sensitive enough to capture "the same construct for [all] women" given divergence and relational hierarchy in how the societal structure mediates the relation between racially divergent paradigmatic constructions of "woman" and subjective experiences of "womanhood" (T. Lewis et al. 363).[19]

If a metric, by definition, attempts to delimit and monopolize the terms of a phenomenon's intelligibility and even provides the terms through which we might conceive of a problem such as "discrimination," this also means that our metrics simultaneously suggest parameters for our solutions and, in the case of regulatory science, may even be a determinant of the terms of social policy. If measurement is the sine qua non of regulatory science and is contiguous with state policy, what metric is adequate to measure the ubiquity and chronicity of antiblackness?

The point I am trying to make is that antiblackness is an ecology of violence—pervasive and chronic. Although antiblackness relationally distributes differential material effects across the color line, in the making of the color line, the experience of "race" confounds comparative study rather than provides a comparable standard of measure.[20] To put a finer point on it, the matter of black womanhood, as universality's nullified referent, stands in nonanalogous relation to normative womanhood on both the registers of experience (embodiment) and paradigm (structural relation); consequently, and as should be unsurprising by now, the white woman standard reveals its fraudulence as universality. For black women, socioeconomic upward mobility, when attainable, is nevertheless enfolded by racial immobility—a stasis at the heart of their mobility that often takes the form of a downward telos, a negative correlation in the context of (re-productive) health.[21] This constituent contradiction, stasis in mobility, stems from the targeting of a population in their blackness. That this de-clivity travels with black people, like a second skin, distinguishes it from economic discrimination and targeting of the poor in their poverty.

What this suggests is that the very tools of regulatory science have ex-posed a crisis at their center. Fields such as public health, epidemiology, and epigenetics are now confronted with both the limits of their tools' explana-tory powers and the stakes of their function in the ongoing maintenance of the regulatory apparatus, especially with regard to the state's sleight of hand: socioeconomic access and reform. These fields have discovered and documented the conditions of their ongoing crisis and revealed the poten-tial, and even necessity, for regulatory science to fundamentally question its partnership with the state, in other words, for science to extricate itself from the regulatory apparatus. If the "interactional consensus" surfaces in popular media via depictions of black female sex/uality and reproduction as peculiarity, it behooves us to ask to what extent this mediatization is other than pornotroping: yet another occasion to terroristically marvel at and/or spectacularize black female sex/uality and reproduction for public consumption. This crisis of purpose must be confronted if the "interac-tional consensus" is to be other than the subjection of Man's limit case to further antiblack experimentation and genealogical isolation at the hands of self-appointed experts or a prelude to black maternity's censure and punishment. To put it another way, if these fields are the research arm of policy, what policies do the findings discussed above suggest? What policy initiatives are sufficient to intercede on behalf of black life?

Two key concerns, in particular, have been raised regarding the fu-ture of epigenetic research: One, it is troubling that researchers continue to essentially ignore paternal pathways to reproductive health.[22] Two, studies that attend to sex difference tend to bypass "gender," namely how gender dynamically and nonteleologically interacts with the sex.[23]

However, if epigenetic developmental theories, with their emphasis on fetal health and intergenerational transmission, continue to precipitately gain acceptance, then epigenetics' contention that certain ages and/or developmental stages are particularly sensitive to environmental and social influence raises the disquieting specter of biopolitical reproductive regulation. It is not hard to imagine that purported concern for the development of fetal biological systems will likely increase as the content of epigenetic research enters public consciousness. Might such concerns for the fetus eclipse the contextual conditions of black women's maternity? Will the public travel the well-worn path of black maternal abjection, negation, and criminalization?[24] One might recall the criminalization of crack-addicted mothers in the 1990s. The view of undeserving black motherhood provided the rationale for restricting fertility and unrestricting carcerality. As noted by Dorothy Roberts, the mediatized image of "diabolical pregnant crack addicts and irreparably damaged crack babies" was based on spurious data. Despite the medical, developmental, and behavioral problems reported to be caused by maternal crack use, recent studies have shown the methodological flaws of initial studies, which tended to not only exaggerate findings but also ignore other causal pathways that might better explain findings and were better supported by evidence (Roberts, "Unshackling" 951).

If in an epigenetic framework race is seen as an emergent quality of the body rather than an essential one, then an epigenetic understanding of biology as mutable and protean "can intensify race by relying on-and ascribing responsibility for upholding—racialized norms of behavior and bodily outcomes" which are presumed to be healthy and "normal" (Mansfield 353). Despite the views of those who maintain that epigenetics boosts a social constructivist conception of race and heralds salubrious futures, Becky Mansfield questions if epigenetics' linkage of "social regulation to gene regulation" portends not the end of biological constructions of "race" but rather recasts the biopolitical operations of biologized race in epigenetic terms:

> Biology may be mutable—life epigenetic—but *because of this* it becomes not just the individual opportunity but individual responsibility to manage that. The ability to choose is taken for granted. In this liberal project, the problem is non-white women, who do not properly

protect themselves and their offspring. If they fail in their choices—fail as liberal subjects—they cause harm to themselves and their children ... It is because biology is not given but made that race becomes more important. In a world in which biological outcomes are made (they are our own responsibility), then differences in outcomes show that we are in fact different, and it is that difference that constitutes race. (369)[25]

Mansfield's insightful query is a pressing one considering that biopolitical regulatory power and disciplinary power go hand-in-hand; discipline and regulation are interdependent and mutually reinforcing forms of governmentality.

The discovery of the broad mutability of the body and its intergenerational pathways has the potential to subvert the gains made by the scientific nullification of genetic conceptions of race, especially if epigenetics is understood in biologically reductive terms and in an uncritical relation to antiblack misogynist depictions of black women's maternity. If antiblack racism's biochemical and neurophysical pathways predispose both *mother and fetus* to bio-neuro-social imposition in a manner primarily impervious to consciousness; this inescapable somatic vulnerability for both *fetus and mother* might nonetheless be subject to censure by a biopolitical state power that continues to invest in structures that conscript potentials and impose harm. Cloaked by the pretense that black women are able to consciously "choose" otherwise, the censure and even criminalization of black motherhood, in the nightmare scenario I describe, would only serve to renew commitment to the perpetuation of biological racism.

Such a perilous existential horizon requires a response that both exposes biopolitical regulation's inadequacy with respect to the inequitable burden antiblackness places on developmental processes (fetal and otherwise) and challenges regulation's emphasis on "personal responsibility." Such notions extend and dissimulate structures of power that need racism in order to maintain their regulatory authority. Rather than take Western sovereignty's self-representation for granted, we must foreground the practice of sovereignty, and when examining sovereignty in action, sovereignty's normative claims of regulatory "protection" must be reconsidered. As Mansfield succinctly notes:

Individualized optimization is not a post-racial promise, but rather a gendered and racialized demand. . . . Nor does this sort of individual optimization require that we choose between inclusion or exclusion (as liberal subjects, part of the population to be protected) or exclusion (as exception, that part of life dangerous to itself and so sacrificed). Here we see that—through race—we have both, intimately tied, and in the same body (individual and collective). Not only in the name of protecting "others," but in the name of protecting themselves, racialized subjects are assumed to be full liberal subjects capable of securing the population through their behavior, and are shown to be incapable of such: to be a threat . . . as the one who is given the chance to be the liberal subject and fails, and as biologically different, producing offspring who bear the biophysical signs of her failures. (369)

Subversion of genetic race, like regulatory intervention, is only meaningful to the extent that the system of racism is made inoperable. The subversion and reintroduction of racialized codes of bodily difference has been central to biopolitics; thus, we need not only the subversion of racialized codes but also the mutation of ordering logics and their structures of signification to forestall the reintroduction and dissimulation of racialized logics. In other words, our disruptions must exceed subversion, specifically by dismantling racism's sociogenic autopoetic structures, or self-perpetuating systems, if we are to make antiblackness inoperable.

A framework critical of the meeting of epigenetics, biopower, and necropower might proceed via an inquisitive practice of description that neither presumes we already have an adequate epistemological model for comprehending the nature and stakes of the *kind* of force I describe nor presupposes that a sufficient political framework for intervention already exists. One might ask: What are the methods and delineations of a violence that has the capability to impinge on black women's bodily agentic capacity and appropriate the mutability of bodies, such that the body submits—materializing social rather than genetic categories? Do we know how to conceive of a socially constructed principle, specifically "racial blackness," that despite its fraudulent foundation is nevertheless able to "drive developmental processes?" (Kuzawa and Sweet 11). How might an abstraction—race—become a biological pattern? If each introduction of regulation or policy holds the potential to expand disciplinary power, how might we disarticulate state authority rather than re-inscribe it?

Moreover, how might one practically propose regulatory "protection" from the "nebulous concept" of "stress"? What language of "equal protection" and "life, liberty, and the pursuit of happiness" could one avail themselves of that does not prefigure racial blackness and preauthorize antiblack violence? If one were to nevertheless seek regulatory "protection"—cessation and redress, for instance—then one would necessarily vest authority in the regulatory apparatus and thereby risk reinforcing its legitimacy. If Mbembe is correct and racial injury is Western sovereignty's condition of possibility and ongoing effect—even its sign of legitimation—then the severe limits of this strategy are obvious, even if disappointing for some. In light of this predicament, what are the consequences of pursuing something that falls short of systemic social and environmental transformation? Is it any wonder that the landmark essay of David R. Williams et al., "Racial Differences in Physical and Mental Health: Socio-economic Status, Stress, and Discrimination" concludes with the assertion that ending these inequities will "require changes in the fundamental social systems in society"? Taking heed, at the very least, would require the pursuit of ever-increasing complexity in our understanding of the problem systemic antiblackness poses for the form and function of life systems, their nature, and their varied temporalities and scales (349). In other words, it would require a *sociogenic* confrontation with the ontological plasticity and even formlessness imposed on black people.

While "[e]pigenetic changes are defined as alterations in gene expression that are self-perpetuating in the absence of the original signal that caused them," this does not imply narrative closure or a predetermined end (Dulac 728).[26] As Kuzawa and Sweet note, it would be a mistake to view epigenetics as simply

> replacing genetic race with an essentialized concept of epigenetic race; instead, it shows how social environments, defined along lines of constructed and socially imposed racial identities, can drive developmental processes, thereby becoming embodied as biological patterns that influence health and disease. (11)[27]

Thus, while the social consequences of racism can have durable effects on biology and health, as Kuzawa and Sweet note, "durable" need not

equate with "permanent" (11). Even as we note the potential dissimu-
lative dangers of epigenetic insight, biological systems are much more
flexible than racial social structures have proven to be. Studies demonstrate the continued flexibility of biological systems into later stages of
development and hold open the possibility that strategies can be introduced to limit disease risk and even reverse epigenetic influences prior
to birth (Kuzawa and Sweet 11).[28]

I began this coda by discussing an error in the predictive capacities of empiricist (social) science; such an error, I argue, stems from an
incomplete break in logic governing the conversion of a genetic theory
of race to a social constructivist conception. In the transition from genetic code to social construction, "race" was still imagined as a variable
rather than a system of terrifying yet contingent inter(intra)actions: to
the extent that blackness is an identity, that identity is not complete
in itself—it points to an evolving multiscalar field of inter(intra)acting
systems (human and nonhuman), not a discrete entity or compound.[29]
While the structure of blackness may assume a significant measure of
coherence as systemic antiblackness has certainly enjoyed a remarkably stable telos of redundant and premature death, nevertheless it is a
telos that in its very *iterative* structure defers ontological finality. Antiblackness—if it is a system rather than a ground—will have to confront
that which exceeds its structure of stable replication and confounds its
adaptive operations, which are the very conditions that generate mutational possibility.

Becoming Human was underwritten by the belief that if history is
processual and contingent, then art holds the potential of keeping possibility open or serving as a form of redress. In other words, art can be
a remedy and may be a means of setting right a wrong. The expressive
works in this book, like those of Mutu and Lorde, perform this intervention by defying the rules of given literary and visual artistic genres and
traditions, performing innovative philosophizing and contrary aesthetics using what Saidiya Hartman has once called "the visceral materials
of history."[30] These novels and visual works "break forms, breaking them
open so other kinds of stories are yielded" and other philosophies of
being can be felt and known (Hartman).

ACKNOWLEDGMENTS

I owe immeasurable gratitude to my teachers: Ms. Turpeau, Tommie Shelby, Paulette Pierce, Saidiya Hartman, Abdul JanMohamed, Kaja Silverman, Samera Esmeir, Kristen Whissel, Paola Bacchetta, and Nelson Maldonado-Torres. I have benefited tremendously from learning from you. Thank you!

I would also like to thank the following people for their words of encouragement and support over the years: Carla Trujillo, Katherine McKittrick, Alex Weheliye, Rinaldo Walcott, Roshanak Kheshti, Christina Sharpe, Kimberly Juanita Brown, Jared Sexton, Kyla Wazana Tompkins, Dinesh Wadiwel, Frank Wilderson III, Stephanie Batiste, George Lipsitz, Julie Carlson, Jeffrey Stewart, Axelle Karera, Cedric Robinson, Courtney Baker, Christina León, Dana Luciano, Rebecca Wanzo, Robin Hayes, Simone Browne, Janine Jones, Jayna Brown, Jasbir Puar, Mel Chen, Marlon Bailey, Calvin Warren, Xavier Livermore, María del Rosario Acosta López, Keguro Macharia, Sora Han, Charis Thompson, Kyla Schuller, Mireille Miller-Young, Brandi Catanese, Darieck Scott, Donna Jones, Neel Ahuja, Aimee Bahng, Anne Pollock, Harlan Weaver, Banu Subramaniam, Susan Squier, Alvin Henry, Irina Aristarkhova, Kim TallBear, Ruha Benjamin, David Marriott, Kelli Moore, Sheri Davis-Faulkner, Treston Faulkner, La Marr Jurelle Bruce, Dionne Brand, Kara Keeling, Jules Gill-Peterson, Greta LaFleur, Jennifer DeVere Brody, Cary Wolfe, John Deckert, Samantha Frost, Claire Jean Kim, Timothy Morton, Vanessa Agard-Jones, Rizvana Bradley, Patrice D'Agostino, and Moya Bailey. I cannot thank you enough for your generosity, guidance, and professional advice.

Much gratitude to the English Department at the University of Southern California for inviting me to join the department and guiding me toward success, especially David St. John, Karen Tongson, Elda María Román, Melissa Daniels-Rauterkus, David Román, Alice Gambrell, Meg Russett, Dana Johnson, Ashley Cohen, Devin Griffiths, Robin Coste

Lewis, Viet Nguyen, Maggie Nelson, John Rowe, Hilary Schor, Danzy Senna, Rebecca Lemon, Christopher Freeman, Joseph Boone, Daniel Tiffany, Thomas Gustafson, Lawrence Green, and William Handley. I am also grateful for the opportunity to get to know and build community with people at USC beyond my home department, in particular Natalie Belisle, Ronald Mendoza-de Jesús, Neetu Khanna, Veli N. Yashin, Elaine Gan, Erin Graff Zivin, Nayan Shah, Sarah Banet-Weiser, Chris Finley, Edwin Hill, Sarah Kessler, and Reighan Gillam. I appreciate former colleagues at George Mason University, especially Noura Erakat, Keith Clark, Stefan Wheelock, Craig Willse, Paul Smith, and Steve Holmes, for their generosity and support.

I want to thank the following people for their camaraderie and friendship: Kai Green, Siobhan Brooks, Kwame Holmes, and Eva Hayward. I thank the members of the Sexual Politics, Sexual Poetics collective for laughter and fellowship: Amber Musser, Jordan Stein, Ramzi Fawaz, Damon Young, Roy Pérez, Kadji Amin, Jennifer Row, Uri McMillan, Katherine Brewer Ball, and Shanté Paradigm Smalls. I want to especially thank Shanté Paradigm Smalls for being the best possible friend I could ask for and for being everything that's right in this profession.

I have had the privilege of being in queer and trans community with people who have modeled modes of worlding, critical thinking, ethics, care, and love beyond the violence and indifference of the present: Tisa Bryant, Amina Cruz, Tchaiko Omawale, Janaya Khan, Gabrielle Civil, Rebecca Ruiz-Lichter, Ill Nippashi, Wild Tigers Kendrick, Macio Kendrick, Amir Rabiyah, María Cherry Rangel, Leah Lakshmi Piepzna-Samarasinha, Kenyon Farrow, Quo Judkins, Marques Redd, Adee Roberson, Irina Contreras, Jyvonne Haskin, Elokin Orton-Cheung, Ryan Sinclaire Davis, Urooj Arshad, Taising Chen, Sam Feder, Myra Boone, Tiffany Mott, Almas Haider, Sadie Crabtree, Ebony Dumas, Miriam Zoila Pérez, Ki Mack, Kat McKyle, Abby, and Lynnée Denise. Your friendship has sustained me. Although the ebb and flow of life as well as the realities of gentrification and neoliberalism have, at times, made our connections tenuous and transient, know that I cherish your friendship. I am the history of my relations, and I thank you for your loving praxis.

Working with NYU Press has been simply wonderful. I thank them for believing in this project and for their steadfast commitment to bringing it to fruition. Many thanks to my editor, Eric Zinner, his assistant Dolma Ombadykow, and the Sexual Cultures series editors, Tavia Nyong'o, Ann Pellegrini, and Joshua Chambers-Letson. My thanks to Wangechi Mutu and Vielmetter for permission to reproduce *Histology of the Different Classes of Uterine Tumors* and *One Hundred Lavish Months of Bushwhack*. Thanks also to Nandipha Mntambo and Stevenson for permission to reproduce *Europa* on the cover. I am grateful to the anonymous readers of this manuscript. I appreciate your care and thoughtful reflection.

This book could not have been completed without the support of the following fellowships: The Erskine A. Peters Dissertation Year Fellowship at Notre Dame, the Department of Black Studies Dissertation Fellowship at UC Santa Barbara, and the Carter G. Woodson Institute Postdoctoral Fellowship at University of Virginia. My thanks to LaMonda Horton-Stallings for her comments on chapter 4 and Karla Holloway on chapter 3 while I was a Woodson postdoctoral fellow.

Portions of chapters 1 and 2 were developed in earlier essays: Jackson, Zakiyyah Iman. "Losing Manhood: Animality and Plasticity in the (Neo) Slave Narrative." *Qui Parle: Critical Humanities and Social Sciences*, 25.1–2, 2016, pp. 95–136; and Jackson, Zakiyyah. "Sense of Things." *Catalyst: Feminism, Theory, Technoscience*, 2.2, 2016, https://catalystjournal.org.

NOTES

ON BECOMING HUMAN: AN INTRODUCTION

1 For more on Césaire's concept of thingification, see Césaire, *Discourse on Colonialism*.

2 The idea that the enslaved's humanity was plasticized, at the register of ontology, initially arose out of the following series of phrases "the chameleon capacities of racism, the various registers of domination, exploitation and subjection traversed by racism, the plasticity of race as an instrument of power, and the divergent and sundry complex of meaning condensed through the vehicle of race" in Hartman's *Scenes of Subjection* (119). I was struck by the term "plasticity," and in my dissertation, "Beyond the Limit: Gender, Sexuality, and the Animal Question in (Afro)Modernity," I created a theory of the slave's plasticity in light of Hartman's critique that slavery operated most commonly, in practice, if not word, through the recognition of humanity rather than by means of the denial of humanity. The theory I developed there was deepened in an article of mine titled "Losing Manhood: Animality and Plasticity in the (Neo) Slave Narrative." Within the structure of much thought on race there is an implicit assumption that the recognition of "human being" will protect one from (or acts as an insurance policy against) ontological violence. See Jackson, *Beyond the Limit* and Jackson, "Losing Manhood." My thanks to Patrice Douglass for the phrase "everything and nothing" as a descriptor of the plasticity I describe (P. Douglass 116).

3 See also Richard Wright's "Blueprint for Negro Writing" and Gates's reflection on the literary genealogical conditions that facilitated Wright to "broadly characterize Negro writing as an effort to demonstrate the writer's full humanity and equality with white human beings" (Gates 129). Gates, *The Signifying Monkey*. For an argument about how literature functions as a tool for liberal multiculturalism's discipline and regulation of difference see Melamed, *Represent and Destroy*.

4 While this area of the philosophy of race is certainly edifying and formative for my thinking, there is a striking lack of attention to the role of sexual difference even despite its central role in the historical discourse of reason. On Kant and reason see Eze, *On Reason* and Mikkelsen, *Kant and the Concept of Race* for a learned review of recent scholarship on the topic and translations of the primary sources. On Hegel and reason see Park, *Africa, Asia, and the History of Philosophy*; Valls, *Race and Racism in Modern Philosophy*; Smith, *Irrationality*; Mbembe, *On the Postcolony*.

5 For the phrase "afterlife of slavery," see Saidiya Hartman's *Lose Your Mother*. For a recent and innovative work that thinks the terrible longue durée of slavery beautifully see Christina Sharpe's *In the Wake*.

6 See Sharpe, *In the Wake*; Scott, *Extravagant Abjection*; Ferguson, *Aberrations in Black*; Jackson, "Waking Nightmares—On David Marriott."

7 See Butler, *Bodies that Matter; Gender Trouble*; Fausto-Sterling, *Sexing the Body; Sex/Gender*.

8 While our notions of plasticity are distinct and take different approaches to the question of the racialization of sex/gender, what I do strongly agree with is Schuller's problematization of binary sex and the assertion: "What we need is theories that account for the coconstitution of material and cultural processes over time." Schuller, *The Biopolitics of Feeling* 27. This book is my contribution to these shared projects. To observe how my concept of plasticity has developed, see the second note of this chapter and Jackson, "Losing Manhood." In addition to Schuller, "plasticity" has been conceptualized by a range of thinkers including Hegel and most notably Catherine Malabou. I take up these alternative usages in chapter 1.

9 See also Jules Gill-Peterson's important new book which also explores the possibilities of plasticity as a mode of optimization vis-à-vis normativizing clinical discourses of sex/gender and trans* subjectivity; Gill-Peterson, *Histories of the Transgender Child*.

10 For considerations of this point as it concerns the early modern Americas, see for instance: Morgan, *Laboring Women*; Sublette and Sublette, *American Slave Coast*. Regarding the nineteenth century, a few key but divergent approaches to slavery's paradoxes of sex difference and gender: Hartman, "Seduction and the Ruses of Power"; Abdur-Rahman, *Against the Closet*; Somerville, *Queering the Color Line*.

11 For an introduction to this line of inquiry see: Henry, *Caliban's Reason*; Bogues, *Black Heretics*; Mannoni, "Prospero and Caliban." For a consideration of the antiblackness of the sex-gender matrix and its implications for the Caliban figure, see also: Wynter, "Beyond Miranda's Meanings."

12 See Henry and Wynter on the historical context of European expedition and voyage to the New World: Henry, *Caliban's Reason*; Wynter, "1492."

13 See Wynter for an important work that initiated my thinking on this topic. Wynter, "Beyond Miranda's Meanings."

14 See Wolfe, *What is Posthumanism?* and *Animal Rites* and Derrida, "Eating Well."

15 For critical work in this area, read: Wolfe, *Animal Rites*. Derrida, *The Animal That Therefore I Am*; Seshadri, *HumAnimal*.

16 See TRAFFIC, "What's Driving the Wildlife Trade?" and Vince, "Organised Gangs Target Wildlife Trade."

17 Recent scholarship is beginning to trouble this tendency, see for instance: Chen, *Animacies*; Ahuja, *Bioinsecurities*; Kim, *"Dangerous Crossings"*.

18 See: Fanon, *Black Skin, White Masks*; Gordon, *Existentia Africana*; Hartman, *Scenes of Subjection*; Spillers, *Black, White, and in Color*; Wilderson, *Red, White & Black*; McKittrick, *Sylvia Wynter*; Moten, *In the Break*; Césaire, *Discourse on*

Colonialism; Sharpe, *In the Wake*; Ferreira da Silva, *Toward a Global Idea of Race*; Mbembe, *On the Postcolony*; Weheliye, *Habeas Viscus*; Wynter, "Unsettling the Coloniality."

19 By Wynter, see "1492," "Is 'Development' a Purely Empirical Concept . . . ," and "Unsettling the Coloniality."

20 The phrase "genre of the human" was developed by Sylvia Wynter in order to provincialize Enlightenment-based humanism, despite its claims to "universality."

21 For more on how this debate has been discussed from either a philosophical or historical perspective, see: Jordan, *White Over Black*; Goldberg, *Racist Culture*; Gordon, *Fanon and the Crisis of European Man*; Mbembe, *On the Postcolony*; Eze, *Race and Enlightenment*; Mehta, *Liberalism and Empire*. Enlightenment thinkers were not univocal in their views on imperialism. Arguably, there are many Enlightenments rather than a singular imperial modernity. For texts that highlight anti-imperial tendency within Enlightenment see Muthu, *Enlightenment Against Empire* and Pitts, *A Turn to Empire*.

22 For an excellent introduction to Aristotelian theories of human animality, see MacIntyre, *Dependent Rational Animals*.

23 See Linne, *The System of Nature*; Buffon et al., *A Natural History, General and Particular*.

24 See Wynter, "1492" 7.

25 I argue that this is the case even in Aristotle's conception of dependent and rational animals, as Aristotle developed his theory of human animality in the context, and as a justification, of his society's practice of slavery.

26 Hegel critiques African rationality for its "arbitrary" nature, but this is because he conflated his conception of rationality with Reason.

27 See Dyer, *White*; Hollander, *Moving Pictures*.

28 See Hill, "Iconic Autopsy." I am thankful for John Peffer's excellent *Art and the End of Apartheid* for bringing my attention to Legae's *Chicken Series*. My engagement with this work draws considerably from Peffer's astute contextualization of Legae's art practice. See Peffer's "Becoming-Animal" for his argument that there is common ground in "Christian and African narratives of regeneration and birth" (Peffer 72).

29 For recent scholarship that explores these aspects of Sylvia Wynter's theory of sociogeny, see Ambroise, "On Sylvia Wynter's Darwinian Heresy;" McKittrick, O'Shaughnessy, and Witaszek, "Rhythm." I extend Wynter's theory by considering bios's implications and efficacies beyond the neurological.

30 I would like to thank one of my anonymous readers for this observation.

31 See Haraway, *The Companion Species Manifesto*; Frost, *Biocultural Creatures*; Alaimo, *Bodily Natures*; Barad, *Meeting the Universe Halfway*.

32 Linnaeus, *Systema Naturae*; Haeckel, *Generelle Morphologie* and *Natürliche Schöpfungsgeschichte*.

CHAPTER 1. LOSING MANHOOD

1 An earlier version of this chapter was published in *Qui Parle: Critical Humanities and Social Sciences* and has been revised and extended here. Jackson, "Losing Manhood."

2 My use of the term "conscription" in this chapter is inspired by David Scott's thought-provoking *Conscripts of Modernity*.

3 See Orlando Patterson's description of the "constituent elements of slavery": violent domination, dishonor, natal alienation, and chattel status. Patterson, *Slavery and Social Death*.

4 Hartman, *Scenes of Subjection*. In the course of her study, Hartman demonstrates the manner with which the purported peculiar properties of humanity became the pathways for the intensification of domination. This project extends Hartman's pathbreaking intervention. On the pitfalls of the concept of "dehumanization" in particular, see Samera Esmeir's "On Making Dehumanization Possible."

5 I have adopted "being/knowing/feeling" from Sylvia Wynter, "On Disenchanting Discourse."

6 The neo-slave narrative is commonly defined as a modern or contemporary fictional work that draws on antebellum slave narratives, postbellum slave narratives, abolitionist fiction, and the sentimental novel in order to fictionally recreate a narrative of New World slavery's past and/or consider the continuities and implications of history for the present. See this foundational text for a representative approach to the genre: Rushdy, *Neo-Slave Narratives*.

7 For instance, René Descartes (*Discourse on Method*) and Thomas Jefferson (*Notes on the State of Virginia*).

8 For a fuller discussion of the historical context and development of the Chain of Being, see Archibald, *Aristotle's Ladder, Darwin's Tree*.

9 For a great book that explores this topic historically, see Salisbury. She argues that during the Middle Ages a culture that once considered humans as absolutely distinct from animals began to adopt the view that the animal was within, and one's humanity was measured by behavior not species membership. This corresponded with the humanization of animals. Humans began to identify with animals, especially in literature, but the anxiety caused by shifting borders led to the animalization of Jews and other marginalized populations. Salisbury, *The Beast Within*.

10 Hereafter cited as *WH*.

11 Cary Wolfe coined the phrase "discourse of species" in order to critically intervene in the semio-material twinned and oppositional constructions of "human" and "animal." Wolfe, *Animal Rites*.

12 For an excellent discussion of the raciality as geopolitics, see Ferreira da Silva, *Toward a Global Idea of Race*.

13 Ring, "Painting by Numbers" 126–127. Ring provides an excellent exposition of how Douglass embraces "Christ-based values" while rejecting the hermeneutical

warping of its pro-slavery adherents. She also underlines the problems of elevating Douglass's narrative as authentic or original.

14 For differing but highly generative accounts of how white racial anxiety, in particular, structured transatlantic debates concerning the interrelation of political sovereignty, humane reform, race, and animality as they pertain to white heteropatriarchal reproductive futurity and salvation during the nineteenth century, see Hartman, *Scenes of Subjection*; Grier, *Pets in America*; Mason, *Civilized Creatures*; and Pearson, *The Rights of the Defenseless*.

15 Deborah E. McDowell, in the introduction to Frederick Douglass, *Narrative of the Life of Frederick Douglass, An American Slave*, 101.

16 McBride 3, 5.

17 An actant is that entity or activity which "modif[ies] other actors." Latour, *Politics of Nature*, 75. On "noise" see Michel Serres's cybernetic approach in Serres, *The Parasite* and *Hermes*, 123–124. For a different take on noise see also Moten, *In the Break*. In Moten's highly-influential text, his interest is in the scream or what is in excess of speech as disruption and fugitive action. The emphasis in this chapter is different. Exploring and naming noise's other potentials, I am concerned with the way the orator's speech and the verbal quality of the slave are interpellated, in such a manner that forecloses the interruption of meaning. Moreover, as in the case of Douglass, one's speech could be considered a performance of eloquence and experienced as unintelligible simultaneously, precisely where its political demand is unsettling and especially where it is cataclysmic. Here, as in the subsequent chapter, I am also concerned with where speech itself commonly does not even register as utterance or is coercively rearranged into consent to the terms of domination. As in chapter 2, I describe (channeling Spillers) this as the predicament and the mark of black mater that conditions not just that of Douglass's speech but of modern globalizing discourse more generally. Michel Serres argues that noise or the parasite is constitutive of communication; all communication is vulnerable to interruption by the noise that is constitutive to it. Thus, what is at stake is not primarily whether a disruption has occurred but whether a disruption actually interrupts or forestalls communication. As noise is a relational quality or affect rather than inherent; it can therefore emerge while being inaudible due to habituated unlistening.

18 Texts that historicize and analyze the conditions of early African American autobiography with respect to the conventions of abolitionist discourse and other literary modes and forms include Foster, *Witnessing Slavery*; Foreman, "Manifest in Signs"; McBride, *Impossible Witnesses*; Andrews, *To Tell a Free Story*.

19 Douglass, "Frederick Douglass" 4, emphasis added. Douglass is not proposing that all farming is brutalizing. Rather, he argues that slavery is brutalizing to both humans and animals as it coarsens humans' treatment of life. However, Douglass's humanism does have him privileging particular aspects of humanity that are seen as uniquely human, such as reason and affection, even if he seeks to recognize these traits in animals. But his recognition of animal reason and affection still

positions animals as lacking "to a limited degree." Animal studies scholars such as Derrida question how securely "the human" possesses these very characteristics, and others such as Vicki Hearne argue that the comparisons do not take difference seriously. As a dog's nose is its strongest sense and the average dog's nose is exponentially stronger than the typical human's, critics such as Hearne ask: on what basis do we compare humans and animals? For thinkers such as Hearne, the presumptive politics of comparison is the problem as it tends to take presumed human attributes as the norm from which to compare animals. Arguably, by privileging the gaze, *Beloved* also participates in Western, anthropocentric ocularcentrism even while contesting the terms of its logic. Derrida, *The Animal That Therefore I Am*; Hearne, *Adam's Task*.

20 It is difficult to suggest that theoretical, ethical, and political questions should be coterminous with a species distinction with the human on one side and everything else on the other. Nevertheless, for a sampling of recent scientific research on animal intelligence and emotion, see Dawkins, *Through Our Eyes Only?*; Griffin, *Animal Minds*; Bekoff and Jamieson, *Interpretation and Explanation*; Bekoff and Pierce, *Wild Justice*; Bekoff and Goodall, *The Emotional Lives of Animals*; Peterson, *The Moral Lives of Animals*. While these texts foreground a world of multiple intelligences and communicative beings, they do so at the risk of reinforcing scientism and anthropocentrism by preserving "the human" as norm. In my work, indeed in this chapter, I have tried to trace the limitations of both scientism and identification (with all its vicissitudes) as the grounds on which one bases an ethics.

21 Fragments of this speech are often circulated in animal rights literature. For an example of a prescriptive approach see Spiegel, *The Dreaded Comparison*.

22 For an alternative reading of the "humane" and of Douglass in *My Bondage and My Freedom*, see, Boggs, *Animalia Americana*, esp. 138–140 and 77–107.

23 See *Scenes of Subjection* on the question of empathetic identification, 17–25.

24 Although the event was held at the "Colored Fair Grounds," the *Tennessean* gives a detailed account of the whites in attendance: their anticipated and actual numbers, their societal standing, and their projected responses to Douglass's "address, and the manner and style of delivery, and the sentiments which it contained." See Douglass, "Frederick Douglass," 4.

25 For a discussion of these issues during the Progressive Era, see Lundblad, *The Birth of a Jungle*.

26 The literature here is long. For a critique of sentimental identification as a mode of ethics, perhaps start with Lundblad (*Birth of a Jungle*), Hartman (*Scenes of Subjection*), Pearson (*Rights of the Defenseless*), and Grier (*Pets in America*). For variations on the subject of affect(ability) and affect(ivity), see, respectively, Ferreira da Silva (*Global Idea of Race*) and Mel Y. Chen (*Animacies*).

27 While not directly referencing or quoting the work of Giorgio Agamben, this chapter is informed by his highly influential contributions to animal studies and posthumanism. The psychoanalytic theory and criticism of Jacques Lacan and

Hortense Spillers also loom large as influences. Agamben, *The Open*; Lacan, *Écrits*; and Spillers, *Black, White, and in Color*.

28 Articles that underline the manner in which *Beloved* undermines or complicates empathy between reader and characters as the novel's approach to ethics include Travis, "Beyond Empathy"; Hale, "Fiction as Restriction"; Phelan, "Sethe's Choice"; Wu, "Doing Things with Ethics."

29 For an article on *Beloved* that stresses the narrative's contradictions and aphorisms as central to its ethics, see Harding and Martin, "Reading at the Cultural Interface."

30 Morrison, *Beloved*. Again, Morrison is fictionalizing and exploring the racialization of the Oedipal relation at the register of the paradigm rather than making a historical point or for the sake of pursuing historical accuracy. However, on questions regarding the enslaved's gendered, familial, and sexual relations as they existed under slave law, I would suggest Margaret Burnham's important work: Burnham, "An Impossible Marriage" 187.

31 Saidiya Hartman has identified the slave's fungibility, which is both economic and legalistic, as a major characteristic of the institution. Hartman describes fungibility as the "abstractness and immateriality of blackness characterized by the replaceability and interchangeability of black people within the logic of the commodifying practices of enslavement" (*Scenes of Subjection* 21).

32 Mae G. Henderson provides an excellent discussion of Schoolteacher's empiricism with respect to the fields of history and ethnography as opposed to science and medicine.

33 My discussion of invention riffs off of Darieck Scott's examination of the concept in *Extravagant Abjection*.

34 Freud, *The Uncanny* 14.

35 Darieck Scott does a great reading of this shaking as tied to the feminized conceptions of hysteria and female orgasm. Orgasm and the hysteric system are metonymically related in Freud's early theory of hysteria. For Scott, this shaking is the bodily notation of the distance between Paul D's actual male embodiment, his sense of failure, and a broken ideal (Scott, *Extravagant Abjection* 142).

36 In *The Death-Bound-Subject: Richard Wright's Archaeology of Death*, Abdul JanMohamed defines the death-bound subject as occupied by the zone between Spillers's *flesh* and *meat*, or "insensate flesh" (JanMohamed 10). On the production of blackness as meat, see also Gray, "Necrophagy at the Lynching Block" 13–15; Marriott, *On Black Men*. For an approach that further considers these two modes of meat production in their distinction see Wadiwel, "Chicken Harvesting Machine."

37 See *Slavery and Social Death*, where Orlando Patterson argues that "laboring" for the master's economic wealth is only one form that slavery takes. Not all slaves increased the master's economic profits, but all slaves labored for the symbolic accruement of the master's status.

38 We must think critically about the enthusiastic fetishism of ontological slippage in much recent posthumanist, ecocritical, and speculative-realist work. Not only

does the erection of ontological dualism necessarily entail contradiction and aporia, but for these very same reasons, they also require an exception, and black people have been burdened with those contradictions. Fred Moten's work is essential reading for serious thinking on the question of objecthood. Moten, *In the Break*.

39 In *Plasticity at the Dusk of Writing*, Malabou variously describes plastic reading as "a new reading method," a "new transformed type of structural approach," or, more specifically, as "the metamorphosis of deconstructive reading": "*The plastic reading of a text is the reading that seeks to reveal the form left in the text through the withdrawing of presence, that is, through its own deconstruction. It is a question of showing how a text lives its deconstruction.*" Malabou 51, 52. Ian James argues that plastic reading attempts to "discern how the destruction or deconstruction of the metaphysics of presence leads to a mutation of form, and, indeed, arises necessarily from a fundamental mutability of form per se. In this sense, plastic reading is, like plasticity itself, defined as movement or passage between the formation and dissolution of form" (James 85).

40 I share Samantha Frost's concern about imaginings of the organismic body as limitless unfolding and want to affirm her insistence on the evolutionary constraints and delimitations of somatic potential. While ultimately indeterminable embodiment's procession—its emergent quality as it is entangled with an environment—is limited by what its evolutionary history introduces into the realm of possibility. My argument is that the imagination of limitless morphology is conditioned by slavery. Frost, *Biocultural Creatures*.

41 Brown's essay provides an important historical analysis of discourses of plasticity in the influential theories of eugenics and transhumanism while remaining optimistic about what the plasticity of life introduces into possibility—an optimism I share even if it is not the focus of the argument presented here.

42 More recently, Malabou's conception of plasticity has extended to an engagement with neuroscience. "Neuroplasticity," Malabou explains, means the brain is modulated by the unfolding of our experiences—and these modulations do "not just" document "that the brain has a history but that it is a history" (Malabou, *What Should We Do with Our Brain?* 4). The neurobiological concept of "neuroplasticity" commonly describes the brain's ability to reorganize itself by forming new adaptive neural connections across the life course, allowing neurons (nerve cells) in the brain to compensate for injury and disease and to adjust their activities in response to new situations or to changes in their environment. Contrasting sharply with its predecessors, which characterized the brain in genetically deterministic terms, as a static control center, the discourse of neuroplasticity emphasizes, instead, the dynamic modulating function of experience and the continuous development of the brain over the life course. Neuroplasticity has been heralded in the popular press as a promise of salubrious futures, enunciated in an ableist key: cures for autism and ADHD, for instance. Since the 1990s a more expansive conception of neuroplasticity has also been put forward, neurogenesis,

one that Tobias Rees contends Malabou largely ignores. Neurogenesis challenges the idea of adult cerebral fixity, suggesting that the dynamism of the adult brain is not limited to synaptic communication and that the development of new neurons extends into adulthood. By marginalizing neurogenesis, Rees argues, Malabou's "synapse-centered conception of the brain" is actually "a pre-plasticity conception. And her notion of cerebral plasticity is a relic of a time in which the brain's main feature was not plasticity—but its fixity" (Rees 266).

Moreover, in her recent turn to neuroscience, or the discourses of neuro-plasticity, Malabou risks charges of material reductionism and scientism in constructing an ontology of the real based on the flux of experimental research and recent findings. In an attempt to map the interrelations and effects of social networks of power and neural networks, Malabou argues in *What Should We Do with Our Brain?* that capitalistic society is isomorphic to neuronal organiza-tion. I would argue it is a *racial* capitalism and the not-yet-past of slavery that conditions biotechnological and biocapital imaginaries, including those that shape the history of neuroscience. I thank Cameron Brinitzer, Gabriel Coren, and Mel Salm for bringing Rees's critique to my attention.

Lastly, Victoria Pitts-Taylor's new work is crucial to this discussion. *The Brain's Body: Neuroscience and Corporeal Politics* provides an urgent and necessary rejoinder to contemporary discourse that often assumes binary sex difference, such as neuroplasticity, overdetermining their findings. See also Jordan-Young, *Brain Storm* and Fine, *Delusions of Gender.*

43 On the figuration of animality (human and otherwise) as a state of privation, see Seshadri, *HumAnimal.*

44 On dissemblance see Morrison, "Unspeakable Things Unspoken", and Hine, "Rape and Inner Lives." On aphasia see Jakobsen et al., "Two Aspects of Lan-guage." See also Frank Wilderson's important discussion of antiblackness and aphasia, "The Vengeance of Vertigo."

45 Ngai 126.

46 Jameson 202, 268.

47 For more information, see Stearns, "Gender and Emotion," esp. 135.

48 See Darieck Scott for a reading of male-on-male rape on the chain gang in *Beloved* (*Extravagant Abjection* 126–152). Paul D once tries to escape from slavery, only to be sold to a new owner, who he eventually tries to kill. Foiled in his at-tempt, his ankles and wrists are shackled before being tethered to a buckboard by rope. Paul D subsequently finds himself on a chain gang. The chain gang quarters that greet Paul D are "wooden boxes." The convicts have "a door of bars that you could lift on hinges like a *cage* [emphasis added]" which "opened into three walls and a roof of scrap lumber and red dirt" (Morrison, *Beloved* 125). The "grave" is two feet over his head; Paul D is five feet underground in a ditch (Morrison, *Beloved* 125).

The jailer's placement of Paul D *in* the earth potentially implies that he has descended below the rank of animals and has become insect—his cage, an exoskeleton. But the cage does not fulfill vital functions, as the exoskeleton typically does, including excretion, sensing, feeding, protecting the muscles, and acting as a barrier against predatory organisms. For Paul D, the cage as exoskeleton fails in its essential function: it is not a form of protection at all. Literally lower than dirt, Morrison notes, "anything that crawled or scurried" can join him; and what can join Paul D would likely feast on him and/or the excrement Paul cannot remove from the cage that has now become part of his body (Morrison, *Beloved* 125). This skeleton, instead of protecting his muscles, actually atrophies his bodily strength along with his mind. Commonly for arthropods, when the time comes, if they do not shed their exoskeleton, they will die from suffocation. For Paul D, his exoskeleton is a redundant symbol of and means by which he would experience his "captive embodiment" and living death (Hartman, *Scenes of Subjection* 86).

49 Alex Weheliye, in *Habeas Viscus*, makes a similar point in the following:

The concentration camp, the colonial outpost, and slave plantation suggest three of many relay points in the weave of modern politics, which are neither exceptional nor comparable, but simply relational. Although racial slavery and the Holocaust exhibit the state of exception, they do so in different legal and political ways, since slavery's purpose was not to physically annihilate, at least not primarily, as much as to physiologically subdue and exploit, erasing the *bios* of those subjects that were subject to its workings. (37)

In doing so, Weheliye quite directly and persuasively problematizes the Nazi concentration camp as "ultimate incarnation" and the mandate of "zone of indistinction" in Agamben's theory of biopolitics (34). However, what is paramount, in this chapter, is the plasticity of black(ened) people at the register of the paradigm rather than the instance of the historical slave. In the process of developing such a theory, or by implication, plasticity unsettles and displaces both "suspension" and "zone of indistinction" as the sin qua non of biopolitics. This is not to say that history is not important here, but rather that as Hartman states, slavery is "yet to be undone."

50 My thinking on *transparency* and *opacity* is shaped by the work of Glissant (Glissant and Wing, *Poetics of Relation*).

CHAPTER 2. SENSE OF THINGS

1 Portions of this chapter appeared in *Catalyst: Feminism, Theory, Technoscience*. Jackson, "Sense of Things." For further thought on the question of void in my work, please see Jackson, "Theorizing in a Void."

2 My use of the term "onto-epistemology" is an attempt to think with as well as depart from Barad's work on entanglement and the problematics of representationalism. Barad states, "onto-epistem-ology—the study of practices of knowing in being—is probably a better way to think about the kind of understandings that are needed to come to terms with how specific intra-actions matter" ("Posthumanist" 829).

3 I use the term "local" not to signify "isolation" or a lack of politically complex encounters with discontinuous onto-epistemologies near and far; rather, the use of
"local" here is meant in the relative sense given the relatively recent emergence of
the global scale introduced by processes of enslavement and imperial domination.
See, for instance, Jayasuriya and Pankhurst, *The African Diaspora in the Indian
Ocean* and Alpers, *East Africa and the Indian Ocean*. I thank LaMonda Horton
Stallings for bringing these texts to my attention. See Gayatri Spivak's *A Critique
of Postcolonial Reason* for her use of "epistemic violence."

4 See Robinson, *Black Marxism* for thought on "racial capitalism."

5 *Robinson Crusoe, Oroonoko,* and *The Blazing World* in English and *Don Quixote*
in Spanish have been variously described as the first novels in either English or
Spanish. *Sinapia* is generally regarded as the first Spanish utopia, and *Blazing
World*, similarly, is often considered the first work of science fiction.

6 Wynter, "'Genital Mutilation' or 'Symbolic Birth,'" 503.

7 To take but one example, in a process that contemporarily often goes by the
name of biopiracy or bioprospecting, Western biomedicine and pharmaceutical
corporations "discover," expropriate, and recast indigenous knowledge of plant
and animal species. Through the enactment of purportedly secular rituals of
copyright, patent, and commercialization, indigenous knowledge is cleaved from
the onto-epistemologies with which it is embedded, and once purified this newly
repackaged knowledge is then prepared for sale and distribution in accordance
with market logics. See Mgbeoji, *Global Biopiracy* and Shiva, *Biopiracy*. Arguably,
Mami Gros Jeanne is a symbol of the confluence of African and Western biomedicine and science on two counts: 1) As a nurse, spiritual healer, and seer, she is
comfortable moving between indigenous and Western science, bridging the two;
2) her story recalls the way Western medicine has historically expropriated and
repackaged indigenous knowledge and mined black women's bodies and biomedical knowledge, for instance, under slavery and prior to the professionalization of
medicine, enslaved women's knowledge of midwifery, inoculation, and medicine
more generally was essential to preserving all classes on the plantation.

8 Many thanks to Amanda Renée Rico for bringing to my attention the Jessica
Langer text.

9 Gibbons 27.

10 Definitions of "postcolonial SF" vary. For instance, Andy Sawyer's foreword
to *Science Fiction, Imperialism and the Third World* suggests that "an explicitly
postcolonial science fiction not only has to be written from outside the traditional
strands of Western science fiction . . . but explained and criticized from outside
them too" (Sawyer 10), and Hoagland and Sarwal's "Introduction" more broadly
defines postcolonial SF as "texts that draw such explicit and critical attention to
how imperialist history is constructed and maintained" (10). On postcolonial SF,
see Raja et al., *The Postnational Fantasy* and Hopkinson and Mehan, eds., *So Long
Been Dreaming*. David Higgins's review of *Science Fiction, Imperialism and the*

Third World provides a productive introduction to some of the issues regarding definition. Higgins, "Postcolonial Science Fiction."

11 Black mater, as mater, as matter, gestures toward a web of interconnected signifiers such as materiality and black femininity, maternity, natality, and relation to the mother. The black *mater*(nal) as I describe it here is closely related to what Fred Moten in *In the Break* describes as the "silenced difference" of "black *mater*iality" at the meeting point of discursivity and materiality: "In a fundamental method-ological move of what-has-been-called-enlightenment, we see the invocation of a silenced difference, a silent black *mater*iality, in order to justify a suppression of difference in the name of (a false) universality" (205). I am also invigorated by recent work by Denise Ferreira da Silva that examines questions of black mater for the question of "world," in particular "Toward a Black Feminist Poethics." The ap-proach here is informed by the Lacanian Real rather than Leibniz and focuses on the particular problem of the definite article "the," as a qualifier of "world." In light of the work by Quentin Meillasoux and other realist approaches to "world" and an-ticorrelationist stances (i.e., some new materialist approaches), I have argued for a disenchantment of the idea(l) of "the world" as a knowable concept, while holding on to the notion of incalculable and untotalizable worldings. "The world," and es-pecially "the world as such," I argue, fails as a concept (at knowability) but succeeds as an idea(l) of imperialist myth predicated on the absent presence of what I call the black *mater*(nal). This critique is not limited to any particular representation of "the world" but is a rejection of the concept of "the world."

My use of the term "common sense" is informed by Antonio Gramsci's use of the term in his *Prison Notebooks*. For another important use of the term, drawing from and expanding Deleuzian thought, see Keeling, *The Witch's Flight*.

12 My argument about "nonrepresentability" is in conversation with and indebted to a tradition of black feminist and queer theorizing on the problem of representa-tion: Evelynn Hammonds's formulation of "black (w)holes," Hortense Spillers's analysis of "body-flesh" and "mythic time," Sylvia Wynter's "demonic ground," and Kimberlé Crenshaw's "intersectionality." They have also produced indispensable analysis of the modern injunction against the black *mater*(nal)'s representability as an enabling condition of the modern representational grammar. See Wynter, "Beyond Miranda's Meanings." More recently, Kara Keeling and Rizvana Bradley have produced energizing work on the relation between black femininity and capacity through a critical engagement with black women's filmic representa-tions. Keeling, *The Witch's Flight* and Bradley, "Reinventing Capacity." Lacan uses the term "foreclosure" to investigate the possible psychical causes of psychosis. Lacan, *The Seminar*. He locates the cause of psychosis in the absence of the (symbolic) father from the scene of Oedipal family, thereby limiting the fam-ily to the mother-child dyad. He concludes that the absence of the father or the Name-of-the-father is the central causal factor for psychosis, which is understood as a severed connection or disjuncture between the Symbolic, Imaginary, and the Real. I am not using the term "foreclosure" in this strict Lacanian sense. My

use is more informed by the aforementioned black feminist investigations of the burdened sublimity of the black *mater*(nal).

13 For more on the racialized distinction between immanence and transcendence, "belief" and "scientific fact," see Bruno Latour's "On the Cult of the Factish Gods," 1–66.

14 For a fuller discussion of raciality in Hegel's arguments on world history, please see Denise Ferreira da Silva's superb reading of Hegel in *Toward a Global Idea of Race*.

15 Andrews and Colucciello Barber's respective Deleuzian approaches to immanence attempt to think the fullness of immanence and problematize historical, hierarchical dualisms between transcendence and immanence. However, this chapter seeks to identify the powerful and seemingly inescapable ways that the reciprocal productions of race and gender haunt both the ongoing perpetuation of this dualism and its critiques as the very terms themselves are racialized and gendered. L. Andrews, "Black Feminism's Minor Empiricism"; Barber, *Deleuze and the Naming of God*.

16 This argument is informed by Jacques Derrida's important work in *Of Grammatology* and *Margins of Philosophy* concerning "structure of absence" and "différance."

17 I thank Vanessa Agard-Jones for urging me to think more about what space is doing in this work.

18 My use of the term "myth" is primarily informed by Hortense Spillers's concept of "mythic time" in "Mama's Baby, Papa's Maybe," which reworks the concept of myth in Roland Barthes's *Mythologies*. In Spillers's deployment of myth, black femaleness is the iterative and recursive material-discursive site, where the dominant system of values variably (re)produces itself in "mythic time" rather than in a temporally and/or socially progressivist manner. However, a number of scholars have written about myth in *Brown Girl* primarily as it relates to folklore and religious studies, works that do not emphasize the social regulatory function of myth in the sense that Spillers does and I extend. Spillers, "Mama's Baby, Papa's Maybe." See, for example, Coleman, "Serving the Spirits"; Baker, "Syncretism"; and Anatol, "A Feminist Reading."

19 Besides Spillers, Morrison, Crenshaw, Wynter, and Hammonds's indispensable engagements with the problem of black(ened) female sexuation in the field of representation, namely that "she" is both essential to the dominant mode and grammar of representation and necessarily invisible, Meg Armstrong provides an excellent introduction to race, gender, and sexuality in Kant and Burke's theorizations of the sublime. See Morrison, "Unspeakable Things Unspoken"; Hammonds, "Black (W)holes"; and Armstrong, "The Effects of Blackness." This is a topic I take up at great length in work in *South Atlantic Quarterly* (*SAQ*): see Jackson, "Theorizing in a Void." On blackness and Kantian thought, see Judy, "Kant and the Negro."

20 As the black *mater*(nal) cannot be comprehended as a unified object with definite identifiable endpoints, it invokes the infinite in size and power, appearing

boundless on both registers and, therefore, resists a mental *form* in the mind or imagination as well as understanding or conceptualization. Moreover, one could not "know" the serialized, empirical content of the black *mater*(nal) in its all at-once-ness or as it presumably *exists* but only in its serialized conception, which due to processual capacities of thought and human finitude would always remain incomplete. A book that names and engages this challenge via the question of "the world" and the infinity of things is Markus Gabriel's *Why the World Does Not Exist*. This chapter invokes the aesthetic experiences of the beautiful and sublime as they are read in Kant's *Critique of Judgment*. While I am neither strictly adhering here to Kant's philosophy nor the influential philosophical inquiries into the sublime offered by Edmund Burke and Jean-François Lyotard, the question of how the black female figure constitutes and disrupts these powerful analyses is taken up in an article in *South Atlantic Quarterly*. Jackson, "Theorizing in the Void."

21 The phrase "modern grammar of representation" indexes my attempt to think with and alongside Hortense Spillers's "American grammar" and Denise Ferreira da Silva's "modern grammar" and "modern representation."

22 On the notion of performance/performativity, here I am thinking with Karen Barad who states the following: "[T]he representationalist belief in the power of words to mirror preexisting phenomena is a metaphysical substrate that supports social constructivist, as well as traditional realist, beliefs. . . . A *performative* understanding of discursive practices challenges the representationalist belief in the power of words to represent preexisting things. . . . The move toward performative alternatives to representationalism shifts the focus from questions of correspondence between descriptions and reality (e.g., do they mirror nature of culture?) to matters of practices/doings/actions" (802). Barad, "Posthumanist Performativity."

23 See Bruno Latour and Steve Woolgar's *Laboratory Life: The Construction of Scientific Fact* for a critique calling into question the presumed primacy of the scientific method in the *practice* of science. Latour and Woolgar find that representation is constituted alongside practice at every level and that experiments are not rigidly performed or regulated in accordance with "scientific method." On the contrary, experiments typically produce inconclusive results, and much scientific fact is constructed during the subjective process of deciding which results to include and exclude. Latour and Woolgar, *Laboratory Life*.

24 See Robert Heinlein's definition of science fiction, for instance: "Realistic speculation about possible future events, based solidly on adequate knowledge of the real world, past and present, and on a thorough understanding of the nature and significance of the scientific method. To make this definition cover all science fiction (instead of 'almost all') it is necessary only to strike out the word 'future'" (Heinlein "Science Fiction" 9).

25 For critiques and extensions of Heidegger's metaphysics, see Mel Chen on the concept of stone and Graham Harman on the concept of object.

26 Heidegger, *The Fundamental Concepts of Metaphysics*. Hereafter cited as *Fundamental Concepts*.

27   Additional important exegeses on animality in Heideggerian thought include: McNeill, "Life Beyond the Organism"; Franck, "Being and the Living"; Kuperus, "Attunement"; Oliver, *Animal Lessons*, esp 193–207; and Krell, *Daimon Life*.

28   Heidegger, *What Is Called Thinking?* 16. Hereafter cited as *Thinking*.

29   This is the quote in its entirety: "[T]he beginning of Greek philosophy makes the impression which alone is, according to the everyday understanding, suitable for a beginning: it appears, to use another Latin root, primitive. In principle, the Greeks then become a kind of highgrade Hottentots, and compared to them modern science represents infinite progress. Quite apart from the particular nonsense that is involved in this conception of the beginning of Western philosophy as primitive, it must be said: this interpretation forgets that the subject here is philosophy, something that belongs among the few greats things of man. Whatever is great, however, can only have had a great beginning. Indeed, its beginning is always what is greatest. Little is only the beginning of little things, and their dubious greatness consists in belittling everything; little is the beginning of decay which can also become great in the end, but only in the sense of vastness of complete destruction" (*Introduction* 12). For Heidegger, what starts off small will stay small, even if it "progresses"; even if it aspires to greatness, it will never achieve greatness and remain small because 'greatness' must be present at its origin. As Vycinas puts it, "The decline of the great is the beginning of the small which starts small even though it may 'progress'" (135). A number of scholars working in the area of philosophy of race have offered considerations of racism in Heidegger's work; see the following notable critique: Maldonado-Torres, "On the Coloniality of Being."

30   As Mel Chen has rightly insisted, to oppose humanness to the stone or inanimate, as Heidegger does in his metaphysics, is to misrecognize that embodied humanity, in contrast to his idealized metaphysical concept, is capable of composing stones, such as calcium deposits. Moreover, Chen asserts, "Stones themselves move, change, degrade over time, but in ways that exceed human scales." So as it turns out stones do not mirror received representations. Chen, *Animacies* 210, 235.

31   My thanks to Ronald Mendoza-de Jesús for encouraging me to linger on this point. Hegel's contradictory statements on African religion, the equivocation and reversals pertaining to lack and alterity are mirrored in Heidegger statements regarding "the animal."

32   Markus Gabriel has written an important new book challenging the idea of *the* world as graspable, finite totality. In *Why the World Does Not Exist*, Gabriel rejects the metaphysical concept of a domain of all domains or an all-encompassing object called *the* world. The pursuit of such a domain leads to infinite regress, as every account of *the* world would introduce something new into it such that a new domain would have to be introduced in order to accommodate the totality of totality ad infinitum. In other words, Gabriel is not simply arguing "the world" is nonempirical; Gabriel also maintains it does not appear anywhere at all. There is no domain of domains that houses "the world." If there were, what of the house?

Is the house in "the world" or not? One implication of Gabriel's argument is that it interdicts the idea of a unifying metaphysical presence.

If we assume totality, as Glissant does, I do not think we can access it; it would not be determinable. I agree with Gabriel, *the* world is problematic as a concept, not because of its ontological invalidity but its epistemological spuriousness. While we can conceive of and contemplate *the* world as a unitary whole or totality as Glissant puts it, but we cannot know it. Any claim to knowledge of *the* world *as such* is tantamount to imperialism. Moreover, because we cannot know it and appears in no context does not necessarily imply its ontological in-existence but rather this contextlessness should interdict any definitive—rather than speculative—claim about it, including affirming or precluding its existence.

33   Regarding philology and the so-called Hottentot, Shane Moran draws on the work of Jacques Derrida, Edward Said, and Martin Bernal to show how the study of language was integral to the formation of racial discrimination in South Africa. Moran demonstrates the central role of literary history to the cultural racism and ideology that fed into apartheid by tracing the ethno-aesthetic figuration of the Bushmen. Moran, *Representing Bushmen.*

34   My thanks to Kyla Wazana Tompkins for this felicitous phrase. Michel Foucault is famous for his conceptualization of power's lability and distributed agency. Here, I am interested in theorizing that which Michel Foucault would not, namely domination (Foucault, "The Subject and Power"). Foucault famously equivo-cated before ultimately sidestepping the question of agency under conditions of domination. Prior to quickly shifting and remaining with the question of power's relational forms and dynamics, Foucault vacillates: he argues in one place that domination is the *calcification* of relation and therefore can neither be the proper site of an inquiry into the *dynamics* of power nor of relationality but rather their disablement. But elsewhere he allows for some modicum of relational capacity and distributed agency to exist in domination. Foucault, "The Ethics of the Con-cern." My aim is not so much to settle the question of capacity and/or relational-ity; rather, what I am more interested in exploring concerns how movement at the ontic register of experience does or does not alter the nature of domination and its ontologized terms in *Brown Girl in the Ring.*

35   See Stein, "Bodily Invasions;" Shukin, *Animal Capital*; Neel, *Bioinsecurities.*

36   See Jasbir Puar on "debility" in "Prognosis Time." In an extended work on debil-ity, Puar offers the following distinction: "debilitation" is distinct from the term "disablement" because it foregrounds the slow wearing down of populations instead of the event of becoming dis-abled (Puar, "Right to Maim" xiv). I mobilize the term "debility" as a needed disruption (but also expose it as a collaborator) of the category of disability and as a triangulation of the ability/disability binary. . . . [D]ebilitation is a necessary component that both exposes and sutures the non-disabled/disabled binary ("Right to Maim" xv).

37   Giselle Liza Anatol has noted, "One of the great strides that Hopkinson makes in her narrative is not only subverting the idea of the innately maternal woman,

but specifically debunking the contradictory European constructions of African-descended women as (a) hyper-maternal mammies and (b) genetically apathetic, cold-hearted, and emotionally distant mothers: stereotypes generated during the slave era and continuing into the present day in various forms" ("A Feminist Reading" 33).

38 See Wynter's "Miranda" and "Ceremony" for an articulation of black people's signification as chaos and irrationality in the discourses of Man.

39 Black maternity and madness had become nearly synonymous for Ti-Jeanne. Ti-Jeanne even initially wonders about her own "waking dreams," if they were brought on by "the stress of learning how to cope with a newborn baby" (20). Hopkinson, *Brown Girl in the Ring*.

40 I co-organized a panel on race and sensoria with Kyla Wazana Tompkins, where I presented a part of this chapter, for the American Studies Assciation's 2015 annual conference. On that panel, Kelli Moore offered a presentation on black womanhood and vertigo, the ear, and proprioception in light of Spillers's concept of "vestibularity." Moore's emphasis on the gap between voice and vision in black women's testimony in domestic violence cases inspired me to at least begin to think about how said gap might function in Hopkinson's text. That presentation has now generated a publication: see Moore, "Affective Architectures."

41 While Ti-Jeanne's development as a character pivots on this conflict, it is starkly conveyed in how Ti-Jeanne saw Mami's "bush medicine" in comparison to Western bioscientific medicine. While Mami used both as a healer and a formally trained nurse, "Ti-Jeanne didn't place too much stock in Mami's bush doctor remedies." . . . Ti-Jeanne would have preferred to rely on commercial drugs. . . . Ti-Jeanne didn't understand why Mami insisted on trying to teach her all that old-time nonsense" (Hopkinson 36–37). But it was commercial, Western medicine's imbrication in commercial networks and state power that threatened to dissolve the already fragile familial relations she had. I thank Darius Bost and Alvin Henry for helping me develop this point and for being such great sounding boards for this work.

42 For synthetic and critical engagement with this topic, see Strother, *Inventing Masks* and Gikandi, "Picasso."

43 Wallace's essay is productively riven with deep ambivalence and unsettled conclusions. But in addition to this view, she expresses a conviction that it is indeed possible (and even desirable) for these collections to be made available to black artists in the West, who may (and arguably already have) discover(ed) generative models in the ruins. Wallace, "The Prison House of Culture."

44 See also Gikandi's discussion of the meeting of Guyanese painter Aubrey Williams and canonical artist Pablo Picasso. Upon being introduced to Williams, Picasso looked at him and remarked that he had "a fine African head" that he would like to use as a model. Gikandi notes the following about that encounter: "Williams was disappointed that he was appealing to Picasso merely as an object or subject of art, not as an artist, not as a body, not even as a human subject" (455–456).

45 See Hartman, "Venus in Two Acts."

46 In *After Finitude*, Quentin Meillassoux defines correlation as "the idea according to which we only ever have access to the correlation between thinking and being, and never to either term considered apart from the other" (5). I am thinking here not only of Kant on the different races of man and on national characteristics but also of Hegel's thoughts on the geographical basis of world history and their elaborate and fallacious reasoning, whereby geography, reason, and time become the watchwords of an emergent, racially teleological conception of "universality" and "world." See Eze's *Race and the Enlightenment* for excerpts from these thinkers on these topics.

47 Eduardo Vivieros de Castro also contends that the terms through which Kant raises the question of "correlationism" must be de-transcendentalized because the self–other frame through which the question is cast is not universal but particular (de Castro, *Cannibal Metaphysics*). With Vivieros de Castro, my argument is related. I agree that Kant's mode of questioning is neither universal nor should it be transcendentalized, but more than that, I seek to explore the manner in which his mode of inquiry is an effect of an imperial history and rationality. Moreover, Meillasoux, in a critique of correlationism, defines it as "the idea according to which we only have access to the correlation between thinking and being and never to either term considered apart from the other" (5). While not the aim of this chapter, I hope one consequence of these pages is a disruption of the "thought vs. world" frame of the debate about correlationism. On noise, see Serres, *Hermes*.

48 Fred Moten's work is indispensable on the question of blackness and object-status, see in particular "The Resistance of the Object: Aunt Hester's Scream" in *In the Break*.

49 This paragraph is taken almost in its entirety from an article I wrote entitled "Outer Worlds."

50 The phrase "hieroglyphics of the flesh" is borrowed from Hortense Spillers's "Mama's Baby, Papa's Maybe."

51 See the following works that question eighteenth-century Eurocentric aesthetic standards for "art" and that centralize the internal forces of change producing formal dynamism rather than attributing innovation to relations with the West (especially Strothers, who cites other scholars working in a similar vein): Achebe, *Hopes and Impediments*; Arnoldi, "Playing the Puppets;" Strother, *Inventing Masks*. See Ferreira da Silva's *Towards a Global Idea of Race* for the insidiousness of the "culture" concept in the human sciences:

> [T]he racial, the nation, and the cultural—fulfill the same signifying task of producing collectivities as particular kinds of modern subjects. Each, however, has very distinct effects of signification: (a) the racial produces modern subjects as an effect of exterior determination, which institutes an irreducible and unsublatable difference; (b) the nation produces modern subjects as an effect of historical (interior) determination, which assumes a difference that is resolved in an unfolding (temporal) transcendental essence; but (c) the

cultural is more complex in its effects because it can signify either or both. (xxxvii)

52 The phrase "out of the world" is taken from Mbembe's *On the Postcolony*.

53 This quote is drawn from Wynter's reading of Fanon's reading of black(ened) men on the occasions when they had "to meet the white man's eyes" (110), as a prelude to the failure of intersubjectivity, at least one that would be occasioned by the black's ontological resistance. Wynter, "Towards the Sociogenic"; Fanon, *Black Skin, White Masks*. Here, I altered gendered assignations to accord with the focus of my analysis. Wynter also notes in the preceding page the gendered specificity of Fanon's narration of black(ened) men's experience of antiblackness, as well as what is shared across lines of gender:

> While the black man must experience himself as the *defect* of the white man—as must the black woman vis a vis the white woman—neither the white man or woman can experience himself/herself *in relation to the* black man/black woman in any way but as that fullness and genericity of being human, yet a genericity that must be verified by the clear evidence of the latter's lack of this fullness, of *this* genericity. The qualitative aspects of the two group's mental states with respect to their respective experiences of the *sense of self* are not only opposed, but dialectically so; each quality of subjective experience, the one positive, the other negative, depends on the other. (40)

In these pages, I am interested in how the black *mater*(nal)'s nonrepresentability enables this entire field of antinomic dualisms.

54 See Boas, *Race, Language, and Culture* and Boas, *The Mind of Primitive Man*.

55 It is more interesting, and perhaps more relevant, to investigate the racial logic of Boas's empiricism here, given both the common assumption that the "science of culture" established a decisive break with scientific racism as well as the pride of place anthropological translation holds in the scholarship on Hopkinson's writing. However, this investigation could easily extend to the empiricism of David Hume, commonly described as the founder of empiricism, and perhaps does so by implication as Hume is well-known for the likening of a multilingual black man to a parrot. Michael Hanchard comments upon the infamous analogy in the following: "Hume's cryptic commentary has dual significance, for it implies that the only civilizational possibilities for people of African descent were reactive and imitative. The act of mimicry itself, its subversive and infra-political implications notwithstanding, entails a temporal disjuncture. In historical and civilizational terms, Africans in the aggregate could—at best—aspire to caricature. They could only mimic the aggregate European" (Hanchard 252).

56 A number of critics have noted that the depiction of the orisha in *Brown Girl* does not appear to re-present any practicing tradition but rather the "blending," "fusing," and "dissolving of the boundaries in religious practices" as a "basis for a unique pan-Caribbean identity" (see M. Coleman). Or as Wood has noted, "tracing specific religious references seems to become an academic enterprise" as the novel's religious pantheon appears to perform in such a way as to undermine our

"ability to 'place' or locate these deities and practices" (319). Wood, "Serving the Spirits."

57 In contrast, please see Robert Farris Thompson's *Flash of the Spirit: African and Afro-American Art and Philosophy* for his highly influential argument mapping cultural continuities and what are called "survivals" between West African religion, particularly Yoruba religion, and "New World" religious and cultural practice. This process of transcription is mapped in spatiotemporal terms—from a putative African past to a (presumably Western) modernity—such that when Africans, even "ancient" Africans, possess cultural properties ascribed to "modernity," those properties are still framed in comparative terms that presume the "modern" is proper to the West. Furthermore, in framing its intervention in terms of a disruption of a commonly held assumption that finds Africa lacking vis-à-vis signifiers of "modernity," its corrective misses an opportunity to fundamentally call into question the mode of thought that seeks to distinguish and order a relational hierarchy between "primitive" and "modern" technologies and lifeworlds. In short, it recasts rather than forestalls a hierarchical binary between "modernity" and "tradition," bestowing the "traditional" with a positively inflected alternative value—that of transcendence. Moreover, in building an argument about the Yoruba's "transcendence" over the violence of the Middle Passage and colonial violence, for instance, it fails to adequately account for the disruptive and creative power of history, thus obscuring the dynamics of change that accompany "Yoruba" practice (Thompson, *Flash of the Spirit*). For a related set of critiques of anthropological claims to continuity, see Scott, "An Obscure Miracle of Connection," (*Refashioning Futures* 106–127) and "That Event, This Memory." And, of course "invention" here alludes to Mudimbe's important book *The Invention of Africa*.

58 Here I am in agreement with Scott's (*Refashioning*) contention, in a gloss of his first book, *Formations of Ritual*: "The argument (one, it seems to me, still not sufficiently recognized) was that anthropological objects are not simply given in advance of anthropological projects, but are constructed in conceptual and ideological domains that themselves have histories—very often *colonial* histories. My point, therefore, was that unless anthropology attends, in an ongoing and systematic way, to the problem of the conceptual-ideological *formation* of the objects that constitute its discourse, it will not be able to avoid the reproduction of colonialist discourse" (13). See also Omi'seke Tinsley's "Black Atlantic, Queer Atlantic" which also calls into question the Middle Passage as "origin" (192). The term "science of culture" is taken from the often-described founder of cultural anthropology, Edward Burnett Tylor. His highly influential *Primitive Culture* developed the thesis of "animism" and is known for being the first-systematic empirical study of the topic. Tylor describes the reformist mandate of anthropological science as follows: "[W]here barbaric hordes groped blindly, cultured men can often move onward with clear view. It is a harsher, and at times even painful office of ethnography to expose the remains of crude old cultures which have

passed into harmful superstition, and to mark these out for destruction. Yet this work, if less genial, is not less urgently needful for the good of mankind. Thus, active at once in aiding progress and in removing hindrance, the science of culture is essentially a reformer's science" (Tylor 453).

59 Other critics in (feminist) science studies have raised different but related concerns about representationalism. Notable works include Hacking, *Representing and Intervening*; Rouse, *Engaging Science*; Barad, "Posthumanist Performativity." See also Holbraad, who, like Barad, has rearticulated ontology in the terms of the performative and whose term "production" informs and shares aspects with the approach I develop in these pages. Holbraad, "Definitive Evidence, from Cuban Gods."

60 Scott, *Extravagant Abjection*; Marriott, "No Lords A-Leaping."

CHAPTER 3. "NOT OUR OWN"

1 The full Haraway quote in the epigraph is as follows, "Species reeks of race and sex; and where and when species meet, that heritage must be untied and better knots of companion species attempted within and across differences. Loosening the grip of analogies that issue in the collapse of all of man's others into one another, companion species must instead learn to live intersectionally. Donna Haraway, *When Species Meet* 105–106.

2 Making a different but related point, Neel Ahuja has argued that the American Indian body has been cast as the paradigmatic natural victim of disease: "a viral *terra nullius*." In the context of the Iraqi war, Ahuja argues, the state of the "non-immune Indian" was the ominous figure underwriting fear and intervention in the imperialist discourse of bioweaponry and emerging disease (Ahuja 141–142).

3 It is the process by which the rhizome breaks out of its boundaries (deterritorializes) and then reassembles or re-collects itself elsewhere and else-when (reterritorializes), often assuming a new or shifted identity. If you break a rhizome, it can start growing again on its old line or on a new line. Connections are constantly breaking (deterritorialization) and reforming. Giger, *Conversation and Figuration*.

4 Du Bois, *The Comet*; Chesnutt, *The Conjure Woman*; Schuyler, *Black Empire*.

5 Deleuze and Guattari use the term "arborescent" to characterize "thought" marked by essentialist totalizing principles, binarism and dualism. In *A Thousand Plateaus*, the term's counterpoint is Deleuze's model of the rhizome. Derived from the way genealogy trees are drawn, arborescence is characterized by centrifugal unidirectional growth. Rhizomes, on the contrary, are noncentralized and not regulated by any structure. Rhizomes mark a horizontal and nonhierarchical conception, they do not work via dialectics and subsumption but by ceaseless expansive connection, with no respect whatsoever for established categories or boundaries and thus generate heterogeneous links that are indifferent to the taxonomic thinking. For a concise explanation of key Deleuzian terms, see Parr, *Deleuze Dictionary*.

6 While some have read "Bloodchild" through the lens of the African American slave narrative, Butler was vocally set against those readings. However, I do not

agree with Butler that those readings should not be pursued; I believe they have yielded persuasive textual analysis, most notably Karla Holloway's reading of "Bloodchild" in *Private Bodies, Public Texts*. However, I do believe *Starship Troopers* and "The Screwfly Solution" are much more resonant intertexts.

Starship Troopers tells the story of a soldier Rico and the development of his military career set against the backdrop of an interstellar war between mankind and an arachnoid species known as "the Bugs." In Heinlein's coming-of-age story, the human characters, or Terrans, unquestioningly believe that humans are superior to "Bugs" and that humans are destined to spread across the galaxy, which some have interpreted as a quest for racial purity. However, Robert A. W. Lowndes argues that the war between the Terrans and the Arachnids is not about a quest for racial purity but rather an extension of Heinlein's belief that man is a wild animal. According to this theory, if man motivated by the will to survive rather than morality were to be confronted by another species, similarly motivated, and with war-waging technology, then the only possible moral result would be warfare. See "In Contrary Motion."

In the "The Screwfly Solution," a Nebula Award–winning story, Tiptree also takes up the question of the role of the biological in human societal and cross-species motivations of violence. However, in "The Screwfly Solution," an epidemic of organized murder of women by men has emerged. Some scientists, based on laboratory animal research, suspect the violence has its basis in a sex-selective insanity, but the murderers themselves think of it as a natural fulfillment of instinct and have formed a new religious movement, Sons of Adam, that justifies their actions based on an elaborate misogynistic onto-theology. The story centers on Alan, a scientist working on parasite eradication in Latin America, and his family's response to the plague of murders. Eventually, Alan succumbs to the murderous impulses he initially tries to resist, killing his daughter and leaving his wife, Anne, one of the last female survivors to be hunted by a swelling mob. At the close of the novel, Anne, pursued by an entire society bent on femicide, discovers the source and motivation behind the plague of murders: an alien species is intentionally causing the human race to destroy itself so that the aliens can have Earth for themselves.

7 See Rieder, *Colonialism*; Kerslake, *Science Fiction*; and Seed, "The Course of Empire" for critiques of imperialism in the science fiction genre.

8 Hulme argues, "What is at issue is not just an idea (of eating human flesh) but rather a particular *manner* of eating human flesh—ferociously—that is denoted in the European languages by the specific term 'cannibalism.' . . . Cannibalism is a term that has no meaning outside the discourse of European colonialism: it is never available as a 'neutral' word." Cannibalism "gained its entire meaning from within the discourse of European colonialism" (83–84, 86). Hulme, *Colonial Encounters*. Beth Conklin's *Consuming Grief* is an intervention into common misconceptions of funerary cannibalism.

9 "Vagina dentata" is locally and historically variable. "The myth generally states that women are terrifying because they have teeth in their vaginas and that women must be tamed or the teeth somehow removed or softened—usually by a hero figure—before intercourse can safely take place" (Creed 2). Tompkins defines queer alimentarity as "a presexological mapping of desire, appetite, and vice" whereby "eating functions as a metalanguage for genital pleasure and sexual desire. But eating is often a site of erotic pleasure itself, what I call, as a means of signaling the alignment between oral pleasure and other forms of nonnormative desire, *queer alimentarity*" ("Racial" 5).

10 Barthes's notion of mythic time suggests a temporality that troubles "before" and after;" thus, its ritual enactment appears to efface historicist lines of dividing one epoch from another. Barthes, "Mythologies."

11 Butler's "Bloodchild" shares many motifs with James Tiptree Jr.'s (Alice B. Sheldon's) 1977 Nebula Award–winning short story, "The Screwfly Solution," such as penetrating parasites and male sexism. "The Screwfly Solution" tells the story of an epidemic of femicide. It exposes sexism's bestialization of women, explores the danger of animalizing sex, and implies that being labeled "animal" potentially carries a lethal threat for all beings:

> We discussed the book, how man must purify himself and show God a clean world. He said some people raise the question of how can man reproduce without women but such people miss the point. The point is that as long as man depends on the old filthy animal way God won't help him. When man gets rid of his animal part which is woman, this is the signal God is awaiting. (Tiptree)

"Animal" analogies appear throughout the text and underwrite the realist dimensions of the story's medical explanation. Not only is the epidemic thought to be rooted in the biological locus of sexual reproduction, but it is also manifest in the Great Apes. In a communication penned by Professor Ian MacIntyre, the story explains the epidemic as follows:

> A potential difficulty for our species has always been implicit in the close linkage between the behavioural expression of aggression/predation and sexual reproduction in the male. This close linkage involves (a) many of the same neuromuscular pathways which are utilized both in predatory and sexual pursuit, grasping, mounting, etc., and (b) similar states of adrenergic arousal which are activated in both. . . . In many if not all species it is the aggressive behaviour which appears first, and then changes to copulatory behaviour when the appropriate signal is presented (e.g., the three-tined sickleback and the European robin). Lacking the inhibiting signal, the male's fighting response continues and the female is attacked or driven off. It seems therefore appropriate to speculate that the present crisis might be caused by some substance, perhaps at the viral or enzymatic level, which effects a failure of the switching or triggering function in the higher primates. (Note: Zoo gorillas and chimpanzees have recently been observed to attack or

destroy their mates; rhesus not.) Such a dysfunction could be expressed by the failure of mating behavior to modify or supervene over the aggressive/ predatory response; i.e., sexual stimulation would produce attack only, the stimulation discharging itself through the destruction of the stimulating object. In this connection it might be noted that exactly this condition is commonplace in male functional pathology, in those cases where murder occurs as a response to, and apparent completion of, sexual desire (Tiptree).

12 For a similar approach, see Haraway's *When Species Meet*, where she maintains a belief that ethical veganism bears crucial witness to the extremity of the quotidian brutality directed toward animals while adding,

> I am also convinced that multispecies coflourishing requires simultaneous, contradictory truths if we take seriously *not* the command that grounds human exceptionalism, 'Thou shalt not kill' but rather the command that makes us face nurturing and killing as an inescapable part of mortal companion species entanglements, namely, 'Thou shalt not make killable.' There is no category that makes killing innocent; there is no category or strategy that removes one from killing. Killing sentient animals is killing someone, not something; knowing this is not the end but the beginning of serious accountability inside worldly complexities. (Haraway, *Species* 105–106)

Similarly, on the question of symbolic anthropophangy, see hooks, "Eating the Other" and Derrida, "Eating Well."

13 Her earliest novels such as *Survivor*, midcareer *Xenogenesis* series, and "Bloodchild" all attempt to problematize some of the more imperialist dimensions of the science fiction genre. This chapter will provide a more detailed discussion of colonialism and SF in relation to "Bloodchild." See Ahmed, "Affective Economies."

14 The study of nonlinguistic sign making and interpretation (communication, meaning, habits, and regulation) in biological living processes is biosemiotics. Biosemiotics proposes that signification, meaning, and interpretation are intrinsic to biological life. The field aims to shed light on unsolved questions in the study of semiotics, such as the origin of signification in the universe. Biosemiotics challenges purely mechanistic interpretations of the organism and a reductive notion of instinct as sufficient causation by indirectly investigating the co-evolution of an organism's dynamical semiosis (its informational quality and sign action) with its physicality as situated by environmental interaction, including that which occurs between other living signs. Jakob Johann Baron von Uexküll (discussed in chapter 2) is considered a progenitor of the field, but the term was coined by Friedrich Salomon Rothschild. See von Uexhüll, *A Foray*; Hoffmeyer, *Biosemiotics*; Wheeler, *The Whole Creature*; and Barbieri, *Introduction to Biosemiotics*.

15 Unlike Butler, I believe that the disagreement between critics and the author as well as among critics about what "Bloodchild" is "about" is generative. I believe that Butler's fiction is a philosophical event of such magnitude that critics have only begun to grasp the depths of its complexity and interventions. Uninterested in confirming or countering Butler's claims concerning what the work is "about,"

here I pursue a line of investigation that considers the function of "species" in "Bloodchild," which extends to Butler's oeuvre more generally. My inquiry by no means exhausts the philosophical potential of Butler's fiction but approaches the politics of colonialism and raciality through the logic of species that reinforces it.

16 Ferreira da Silva, *Toward a Global Idea of Race.*

17 I would agree that the transparency thesis is a *phantasy* of autopoesis rather than grounded in a rigorous cybernetic theory of autopoesis where a system is always situated and thus mutually constitutive with determinants internal and external to its "self" regulation and "auto" institution. Phantasies of autopoesis or "self-unfolding, self-representing," suggest the self decides upon its own essence and existence and has the "the ability to design, decide on, and control one's action" (*Toward* 39, 42).

18 Alva Gotby has written a dissertation on the work of Ferreira da Silva titled "Body, Geography, Exteriority: Race and Spatiality in the Writings of Denise Ferreira da Silva." Gotby's reading of Ferreira da Silva is highly instructive. Gotby, "Body, Geography, Exteriority."

19 The history of the idea of and the term *terra nullius* is hotly debated. Fitzmaurice dates the idea to the 1888 Berlin Conference and the "Scramble for Africa," others much earlier (Reynolds 3). Some frame it as a "legal fiction" (Connor), whereas for others it is an organizing logic whether uttered during the early period of European colonial expansion and settlement or not. Nevertheless, there are some touchstones of the idea: Locke subscribed to the belief that God gave the world "to the use of the Industrious and Rational." The presumption that indigenous economies did not improve the land was taken as justification for regarding their claims to the land nonexistent and perceived as evidence that indigenous peoples were in a so-called state of nature: in other words, in a state prior to rationality and self-governance. Europeans, already thought to have left the state of nature behind, were then imagined to add value with the appropriation of land, and in fact presumably no appropriation could be said to have rightfully occurred according to the circular logic of terra nullius. The clearing away and extermination of peoples in the name of civilization, development, and progress is inseparable from this idea. Both genocide and territorial expansion and settlement are upheld by the twinned myth Francis Jennings has described as "virgin lands and savage peoples" (*The Invasion of America*). For the implications of the concept, see Mills, *The Racial Contract.* For the history of the concept, see Connor, *The Invention*; Rowse, "Terra Nullius"; Borch, "Rethinking"; Fitzmaurice, "Geneaology"; and Reynolds, *The Law of the Land.*

20 As Theodora Goss and John Paul Riquelme note, in referring to the Oankali as a "people" in *Xenogenesis*, Butler implicitly invites the reader to accept its dual attribution: as aliens and as ontological equals ("The Gothic" 198). Similarly, in "Bloodchild," the term "Tlic people" denotes both their ontological equivalence while also acknowledging their species difference.

21 Bhandari et al. 598–599. They lay their larvae in the wounds left by the flies, mosquitos, and ticks that act as their vector. Their eggs are released at the point when the human host is bitten. It would be ill-advised to attempt removal of the maggots by squeezing or cutting them out because they literally anchor themselves to the host by several ringed, concentric rows of posterior facing spines and a pair of anal hooks. The Tlic in "Bloodchild," like some species of parasitic flies, have both the potential to be a harmful parasite and beneficial symbiont. For instance, a botfly's survival depends on the area not becoming infected, and it rarely does because the larva releases an antibiotic into its burrow while feeding, which guards against infection. There is still some debate about whether the botfly is bacteriostatic or bacteri(o)sidal, or even if such a distinction is necessary if an agent is highly bacteriostatic. See Harrison, *Internal Medicine*, "Ectoparasite"; Kettle, *Medical and Veterinary*; and Passos et al., "Penile Myiasis."

22 The "Red Queen" is a term used in evolutionary biology to account for parallel evolution in linked species, where adaptation by one species threatens the survival of the linked species, triggering a reciprocal evolutionary move (348). Bollinger, "Placental."

23 Conversely, Laurel Bollinger argues that while the Preserve might be an "internment camp," it could also be "a way to keep desperate Tlic from forcing humans into such dangerous pregnancies" ("Placental" 333). Bollinger's reading suggests more mutual symbiosis than parasitic symbiosis. I understand that Bollinger wants to distinguish her reading from those concerning master–slave relations, but I see more power inequity than her reading suggests. She suggests that Butler's depiction of interspecies love, intimacy, emotional closeness, and physical dependence discourages the slavery analogy, but I do not believe that the master–slave relation is incompatible with these "mutualistic ties." See Scheer-Schazler, "Loving" who also makes a similar argument.

24 Florian Bast, in his analysis of *Fledgling*, attempts to correct this common misunderstanding. However, the misunderstanding exists, I would argue, because the idea of symbiosis has been used as a paradigm for understanding human relations. That symbiosis is freighted with evolutionary connotation politicizes its metaphorical uses all the more. Bast, "'I Won't Always Ask.'" See also Peppers, "Dialogic Origins"; Bollinger, "Symiogenesis"; and Haraway, *Primate*; for texts that discuss symbiosis in Butler's work.

25 Immunity has been a prominent metaphor in the metaphysics of modern political philosophy and contemporary theories of the social, at times engaging with scientific studies of the immune system, or more or less ignoring them. I provide an analysis of Octavia Butler's "Bloodchild" that makes a philosophical contribution to this tradition of thought, one that aims to explore how her work rethinks topics central to this tradition—freedom, embodiment, and the sense of the political—and therefore sets her apart. See the following for key works on immunization, but keep in mind that this tradition stretches back to the political philosophies of Hobbes, Rousseau, Locke, and Hegel: Luhmann,

Social Systems; Haraway, "The Biopolitics of Postmodern Bodies"; Martin, *Flexible Bodies*; Derrida, "Autoimmunity"; Cohen, *A Body Worth Defending*; and Esposito, *Immunitas*.

26 Many contemporary symbiosis researchers reinvoke a definition that does not rely on a rigid distinction between parasitism and mutualism, as certain associations may be both parasitic and mutualistic at different stages or under different environmental conditions. Moreover, "benefit" itself may sometimes be difficult to define. Sapp, *Evolution by Association* 203.

27 Gilbert, Sapp, and Tauber provide an extensive list of recent research that suggests "defense" in the face of pathogens and cancer is only a partial view of how the immune system regulates populations.

28 National Institute of Health. "Human Microbiome Project," 2013.

29 "After the Human Genome Project" 2013.

30 Michelle Erica Green has made an argument that "Bloodchild" also indirectly comments on assisted reproductive technology among other reproductive issues such as welfare reform and abortion rights:

Butler published "Bloodchild" during a year when controversies over abortion, in-vitro fertilization, and the prevalence of unnecessary caesarean sections—topics cloaked in the metaphors of the story—reached a peak. 1984 also witnessed a political campaign characterized by the polarization of complex constitutional issues into monolithic positions: school prayer versus religious freedom, welfare abuse versus urban poverty, "pro-life" versus "pro-choice," apartheid versus sanctions. (Green, "There Goes the Neighborhood" 173)

31 In fact, myiasis, or the infestation of a human or other vertebrae's body by parasitic fly larvae, is sometimes intentionally introduced as a medical treatment to clean out necrotic wounds (Greer, "In the Spotlight"). In particular, green bottle fly larvae are most suitable, as they restrict themselves to eating dead tissue. They also help to prevent secondary infection by eating and releasing proteolytic digestive enzymes that dissolve dead tissue, which reduces bacterial activity and stimulates healing. Additionally, as a result of a rise in cases of bacterial resistance to antibiotics, maggot therapy, or "maggot debridement therapy," is increasingly a treatment option (Sherman, "Maggot Therapy"). It was even approved as a therapy by the Food and Drug Administration (FDA) in 2004, making maggots the first FDA-regulated live organism to be marketed in the United States for the treatment of pressure ulcers, venous stasis ulcers, neuropathic foot ulcers, and traumatic and postsurgical wounds that are unresponsive to conventional therapies (Greer 12).

32 This is when slavery analogies are nearly irresistible, despite Butler's protests. Here she seems to illustrate and invite metaphoric considerations of slavery. And some have pursued this interpretation. Such readings are highly generative and convincing. I find it somewhat perplexing that Butler would take such offense to them. Please see Helford, "'Would You Really . . . ?'"; Holloway, "Private Bod-

ies"; and Donawerth, *Frankenstein's Daughter*. However, Orlando Patterson has warned that slavery should not be defined solely through the notion of property. Slavery is commonly a property relation, but it exceeds the property relation: "My objection to these definitions is not that I do not consider slaves to be property objects. The problem, rather, is that to define slavery *only* as the treatment of human beings as property fails as a definition, since it does not really specify any distinct category of persons. Proprietary claims and powers are made with respect to many persons who are clearly not slaves. Indeed, any person, beggar or king, can be the object of a property relations. Slaves are no different in this respect" (Patterson 21–22). Patterson cites a common example: marriage. Both spouses are the property of the other, even if not typically described as such as a matter of social convention but nevertheless are bound by proprietary claims and power. Additionally, I believe it would be possible to write convincingly about how this story resonates with humanitarian forms of "benevolent" tyranny in the forms of refugee camps and foreign aid. I began this chapter looking at how the American narratives of conquest set in motion the cultural politics of colonial affect. However, I would be curious to consider how these narratives shape the story in ways that I leave unaddressed, especially in light of scholarly attention this issue has received as it pertains to *Xenogenesis*, which was produced during the same period and has overlapping themes and symbolism (see for instance, Wallace, "Reading . . . *Xenogenesis*".

33 While anthropologists such as Le Bon, Robertson Smith, and McLennan thought "primitive peoples" lacked the capacity for individuality, others such as Tylor insisted, in a more Hobbesian vein, that "primitive peoples" were excessively individualistic and selfish. The Comaroffs argue, despite the presumptions of anthropological tropes of Euro-individualism versus African communitarianism, "Nowhere in Africa were ideas of individuality ever absent" (Comaroff and Comaroff 17–18). See also Le Bon, *The Crowd*; Stocking, *Victorian Anthropology*; Beidelman, *Robertson Smith*.

34 Here I am extending what Kelly Hurley has classified as "body horror": a "human subject dismantled and demolished: a human body whose integrity is violated, a human identity whose boundaries are breached from all sides" (205). Hurley, "Reading Like an Alien."

35 At one point she states, "I have done what you demanded. I have asked you?" But, she actually never does. She asks, "Would you really rather die than bear my young?" ("Bloodchild" 25). This is an existential question, not a plea for his consent.

36 As Etienne Balibar argues in "'My Self' and 'My Own'": "There is nothing natural in the identification of self and own, which is really a norm rather than a necessity, and reigns by virtue of a postulate" (41). As he argues, "The issues of subjectivity and consciousness are not identical" but tend to be conflated in the discourse of "possessive individualism" (22).

37 See Macpherson, *The Political Theory of Possessive Individualism.*

38 The phrase "Prioprietor of His Own Person" can be found in Locke's *Second Treatise of Government.* See Mitchell's "Can the Mosquito Speak?" for a critique of social science's failure to theorize the way nonhuman agents and nondiscursive forces shape colonial capitalist events. According to Butler's fiction, it is through evolutionary adaptability and relationality that subjectivity unfolds not through autonomous individualism.

39 While some *characters* (like Qui, for instance) in the narrative abject "animals" and "animality," it is crucial to distinguish that from what Butler's narrative(s) performs, which I argue problematizes and ultimately rejects this stance. Critics such as Sherryl Vint and Staci Alaimo offer persuasive arguments that Butler's work characteristically departs from human–animal dualisms.

40 Haraway clarifies that "companion species" is not synonymous with the notion of "companion animals": the latter tends to equate to the notion of pets or domesticated animals whereas "companion species" is "less a category than a pointer to an ongoing "becoming with" (Haraway, "Encounters" 99).

41 Butler's fiction questions definitions of humanity that rely on the abjection of life deemed animal. However, in "Bloodchild," Butler is not directly challenging how humans treat animals. It is not a text on "animal ethics," "rights," or "welfare." And from those perspectives, I am sure her intervention is seen as limited. Having said that, her fiction generally calls for a democratization of force, eating and being eaten, such that humans are not spared from violence. For Butler, violence is an inescapable part of human subjectivity, and humans must confront that our bodies are meat for others. Additionally, her fiction invites the reader to recognize one's own violence and to confront its manifold sources and effects. In *Xenogenesis*, the Oankali's attempts to annul violence only beget more violence. Thus, her writing places emphasis on a practice of interspecies accommodation and compromise rather than invest in top-down notions of human responsibility, pity, and ethics. Moreover, any practice of animal ethics should critically interrogate the status of "the human" as the privileged, even exclusive, agent of ethics. This unidirectional notion of ethics seems to return ethical subjectivity to notions of "stewardship" that underwrote slavery, colonialism, and dominion—albeit a kinder, gentler version.

42 Laurel Bollinger explores "the love story" dimension more than I do. Her argument is persuasive:

> For the story to do the work Butler imagines, Gan cannot be forced to choose the pregnancy, not even to protect his sister, who would otherwise serve as host—the love must be for T'Gatoi, not simply for his own family. Butler makes the point forcefully when Gan realizes that part of what motivates him not to let T'Gatoi, approach his sister is something like jealousy or possessiveness. He finds that he wanted to keep [T'Gatoi] for myself," a recognition he himself struggles to accept: "I didn't understand it, but it was so." Part of his commitment to T'Gatoi means protecting her, even as a private

commitment in his own consciousness: "Take care of her, my mother used to say. Yes" The "yes," a stand-alone sentence, represents a full affirmation of the decision he has made, and affirmation that makes his dynamics with T'Gatoi closer to mutualism than to parasite/host or exploitation. Moreover, T'Gatoi has allowed him the space to affirm his own participation. ("Placental" 334–335)

While I think the "love story" is an important part of the story and advances the argument that "symbiosis" rather than unmitigated "exploitation" characterizes this relationship, I think Bollinger's elevation of the "love story" potentially obscures the very dimensions of their relationship that are so often read as colonialism or slavery. While I do think Butler arrives at mutualism, she does so through a history of interspecies entanglement that suggests parasitism as well. T'Gatoi and Gan's "partnership" is invested in the hope that mutualism could guard against the always present possibility of the recurrence of human violence toward the Tlic and Tlic human "breeding pens." Thus, their relationship is a threshold to mutualism rather than a suggestion that parasitism between the two people is impossible.

43 There's some risk in framing a scene of reproduction—egg implantation by ovipositor—as a scene of sex in that, as Myra Hird notes, "Most of the organisms in four out of five kingdoms do not require sex for reproduction" and "during most of our evolutionary heritage, our ancestors reproduced without sex" (Hird, "Naturally Queer" 86). However, Butler is not simply trying to re-present nature but generate a highly philosophical allegory in order to stimulate interrogation of the politics of species, sex/uality, and gender.

44 The predominate understanding of human impregnation suggests that the female egg is basically passive and unlike sperm, which actively pursues and penetrates the egg. Feminists, such as Linda Birke, among others, have critiqued this idea. See Birke, *Feminism and the Biological*.

45 See Anne Fausto Sterling's *Sexing the Body* for a critique of the idea of binaristic dimorphism in humans. For works that problematize and displace the presumption of dimorphism in nonhuman life see: Hird, "Naturally Queer"; Roughgarden, *Evolution's Rainbow*; Bagemihl, *Biological Exuberance*; Hayward, "Fingeryeyes."

46 Moreover, as Eric White notes regarding *Xenogenesis*, "Undoing the privileging of genital over other erogenous zones, alien sex is polymorphously perverse" ("The Erotics of Becoming" 404).

47 As Myra Hird notes, "Human bodies, like those of other living organisms, are only 'sexed' from a particularly narrow perspective. The vast majority of cells in human bodies are intersex (and this category itself is only possible by maintaining a division between female' and 'male' chromosomes), with only egg and sperm cells counting as sexually dimorphic. Most of the reproduction that we undertake in our lifetimes has nothing to do with 'sex:'" This includes DNA recombination (cutting and patching of DNA strands), cell fertilization via merging, and cell division via meiosis (halving chromosome number, in making sperm and eggs) and mitosis (cell division with maintenance of cell number) (Hird, "Naturally Queer"

85). She states further, "[W]ithin bacterial being, the female/male, sex/gender distinction has no meaning. Since bacteria recognize and avidly embrace diversity, they do not discriminate on the basis of 'sex' or 'gender' differences at all" (87).

48 See Hayward, "Fingeryeyes." See also her "Spider City Sex," where she argues the transsexed body is "emphatically more" in relation to received binaristic categories of sex (245): "I want to proffer that the representational emphasis on *being woman* for mtfs tends to limit other orderings of meaning and materiality at work in transitioning, trans-sexing. These ontological battles over who is a woman or not foreclose—partly because of the pain they cause—discussions about the fullness or moreness of the transitioning body" (235). What undergirds Hayward's thinking here is the processional and improvisational nature of *all* bodies with respect to their entanglement with life history and environment, a matter discussed in these pages: "Sexual differences (not sexual difference) remain unfinished; sexual ontologies stay active, ongoing, differentiating. If sexual difference and sexuality are exuberances, contingencies, then sex is profusive, a superabundant happening" (235).

49 The list of literature here is long, but for work that investigates the function of "the black female body" as icon, specimen, and material metaphor in the bioscientific/medical history of sex/gender, specifically as it pertains to the mutually constitutive development of *intersex, trans,* and *homosexuality* as legible terms, perhaps start with Somerville, "Scientific Racism"; Gilman, "Black Bodies, White Bodies"; Doane, "Dark Continents"; Reis, *Bodies in Doubt*; Schiebinger, *Nature's Body*; Stepan, "Race and Gender."

Objecting to the "acultural" pretense of feminist discourse, one that privileges a biologized conception of (human) being over other(ed) ontological schemas, in "'Genital Mutilation' or 'Symbolic Birth,'" Wynter argues that a *global* conception of "woman" and "patriarchy" can only be brought into view and its accompanying intellectual exchange commence from within these terms alone because these categories are themselves colonial. This is not to say that sexism and patriarchy are not a problem for "other cultures" but that the assessment of the problem must engage the foundational antiblackness and coloniality of the discourse of sex/gender itself.

50 Wilson, "Biologically Inspired Feminism." Relatedly, animal models in experimental science tend to rely on a biologically deterministic conception of sex by bypassing the role of gender in sex difference in humans as well as ignore distinctions of morphological sex and reproduction that demarcate human from nonhuman models: see Richardson, et al., "Opinion."

51 See McClintock, *Imperial Leather* for an analysis of the gendering and sexualization of imperialist discourse in the context of the British Empire. She argues that the "virgin" lands of Africa, Asia, and the Americas were "libidinally eroticized"; imperialism erected a patriarchal narrative on colonized lands thought to be "passively awaiting the thrusting, male insemination of history, language, and reason (McClintock 22, 31). Additionally, Thibodeau reads the story as challenge

to heteronormative notions of "beauty, maternity, partnership, and choice" that are often reproduced in imperialist encounters with extraterrestrials in science fiction. She argues that alien–human relationship is effectively "queer heteronormativity" with respect to "family, birth, eroticism." Amanda Thibodeau states:

The notion that human beings, in their quest to explore the frontier of space and create new possibilities of freedom and proliferation, might end up in such an inverted and subversive sex/gender system queers not only our notions of sex and gender, of family and power, but also queers the very impulse to seek new worlds where anything is possible. ("Alien Bodies" 272–273)

52 Here I am thinking with and borrowing from Eva Hayward's beautiful description of her haptic encounters with coral ("Fingeryeyes").

53 This argument does not discount Arthur Frank's observation that *"experience . . . is the perpetually shifting synthesis of this perpetually spiraling dialectic of flesh, inscription and intention"* (Frank, "Reconciliatory" 58). Neither is it a refutation of "interactive models of causality" and the gendered problem of labeling the body "passive," as articulated by Lynda Birke; rather, it is attentiveness to the limitations of notions of sovereignty, autonomy, and agency attributed to the subject, and it provides a critique of the violence these notions do to subjectivity. It is critical of the *feminization* of the body and does not suggest that women bear the burden of an erroneously gendered vision of corporeality (Birke 22, 29). For another analysis of receptivity, particularly as it pertains to Asian racialization and gay sexuality, see Nguyen, *A View from the Bottom*.

54 Derrida in "The Animal That Therefore I Am" also identifies the physical vulnerability of embodiment.

55 Nahum Chandler provides an important reminder: "As given in the philosophical discourse from John Locke to Immanuel Kant we can name three motifs, dimensions of a contractual horizon: (1) one does not own something, property, if one is not free to do with it as one pleases (one owns something if one can do with it as one pleases); (2) one's negotiation of transfer of property (or participation in a contract) is considered binding only if one is considered autonomous in such transfer or participation; and (3) a slave, as property himself, cannot transfer property, including himself, or enter into contract, in his own name" (160). Mills and Pateman provide indispensable analysis of the history and politics of social contract theory. See Pateman, *Sexual Contract*.

56 As Ferreira da Silva notes, in *Toward a Global Idea of Race*, according to Locke, the "self-possessed" and "self-determined" subject subjects himself to the exterior ruler, "political society" because acknowledging that an "individual" may desire to appropriate another's life, freedom, and possessions—instituting a "state of war" that may lead to a "state of slavery," being under another's absolute power—individuals recognized the need for regulation beyond natural (divine) law: "Freedom from absolute, arbitrary power is so necessary to and closely joined with a man's preservation that he cannot part with it but by what forfeits his preservation and life together" (Ferreira da Silva 52).

57 Haraway, "Encounters" 97–114.

58 However, the more radical argument that symbiogenesis produces speciation is still very controversial.

59 Jan Sapp's history of the theory of symbiosis documents that in 1868 Swiss botanist, Simon Schwendener explained the symbiogenesis of lichen from alga and fungus via an analogy to master–slave relations, and this framework was met with "bitter opposition" because it challenged taxonomical distinctions and troublingly posited master–slave relations as integral to evolution's character (*Evolution* 4). More recently, British biologist Nick Lane in *Power, Sex, Suicide: Mitochondria and the Meaning of Life* refers to the origins of eukaryotic cells by drawing from slavery analogies, including phrases as "shackled" cells and "menial slave cells" (Lane 225). And in 2003, South African British biologist T.B.L. Kirkwood published "Mitochondria and Programed Cell Death: 'Slave Revolt' or Community Homeostasis?" Similarly, the language of the *integrated* organism is gaining traction among historians and advocates of a symbiotic view of life.

60 For a fuller analysis of the complexity of the pamphlet's context and reception see Nyong'o, *The Amalgamation Waltz*.

61 See Coleman, "Race as Technology" for an elaboration of race as a technology.

62 "Cannibalism," a term that emerges from the racial, also surfaces in Margulis and Sagan's *The Origins of Sex* 149–152.

63 For an analysis of the gendering of E. coli, see Spanier 56.

64 Additionally, Margulis commenting on the delayed acceptance of the theory of evolutionary association stated the following: "The healthy, positive, perhaps even feminine connotations of symbiosis and mutualism have suggested that research on these topics is relatively unimportant" ("Words as Battle Cries" 675).

65 While Haraway's early comments on Butler's *Xenogenesis* recapitulate the metaphorical substitution of race for species, her more recent work sharply criticizes such substitutions—yet ironically, via turning intersectionality, a theory about the illegibility of violence against black women and the indifference and/or tepid modes of redress that accompany such illegibility, into a catchall phrase for something like multidimensional analysis: "Loosening the grip of analogies that issue in the collapse of all man's other's into each other, companion species must instead learn to live intersectionally" (Haraway "Encounters" 101). The critique here is not intended to dismiss any of this well-intentioned work; rather, it documents the isohomology and symbiosis of race and species such that even putatively antiracist projects can find their articulations haunted by this enmeshment. Thus, any articulation of the organism that endeavors to "solve" or "correct" the ills of society should be met with as much scrutiny as those that purport objectivity and neutrality. Authors that also create analogies between interspecies hybridity and miscegenation: Luckhurst ("Horror and Beauty") and Green ("There Goes The Neighborhood").

66 Admittedly, the quotes around miscegenation suggest some self-consciousness about this application. However, the use of the term may reveal that "miscegena-

tion" is the primary paradigm through which speciation is understood. "Miscegenation" may in fact be the most readily available language. If so, this is a question for posthumanist criticism to engage alongside investigations of science, technology, and reproduction.

67 I believe that Butler's earlier works are implicated in this very problem. However, it is important to remember that she was the only well-known black woman writer in the science fiction genre—a genre publishers believed black people did not read—for most of her career. *Xenogenesis* is where it is most commonly suggested that aliens were a figure of a racialized "other." And, as Jennifer Wolmark has noted, the first copies of *Xenogenesis* had a white Lilith on the cover despite the character's blackness between the covers (166). It seems to have gone unconsidered that *to some degree* Butler may have refigured "race" as "gender" in her narration of her black female protagonist Lilith: "Do you know understand why they chose you—someone who desperately doesn't want the responsibility, who doesn't want to lead, who is a woman?" (Butler, *Dawn* 157). Some scholars have gone ahead and included the missing racial signifier and proceeded to read the trilogy as a commentary on the specific existential conditions of black women. Additionally, Butler has recounted in interviews that she modified her accounts of race to assuage science fiction's (mostly white) readership. She acknowledged curtailing the violence of slavery in *Kindred* because "there was only so much an audience would take." She also said that *Mind of My Mind* was a commentary on aspects of inner-city black life "that we don't like to talk about, but was only implicitly so, which only some readers got." She recalled in her Charlie Rose interview that an editor told her it wasn't necessary to have any black characters in science fiction because you can say anything you want about race by way of extraterrestrials. This incident inspired Butler to write an article critiquing those kinds of views in the science fiction community. See Francis, *Conversations*; Butler, "Interview with Charlie Rose"; and Wolmark, *Aliens and Others*.

68 Nor would he kill to avoid acceptance of this vulnerability. At the end of the story, he assures T'Gatoi that he would not have shot her, despite the fact that he could (Butler, "Bloodchild" 28).

CHAPTER 4. ORGANS OF WAR

1 Gravlee, "How Race Becomes Biology." See also Duster, "Buried Alive."

2 See Diana Coole for a critique of the Cartesian debates around the concept of the agentic subject and theory of agency as a spectrum of capacities: Coole, "Rethinking Agency."

3 In an interview with Greg Thomas, Wynter puts it yet another way: "I am trying to insist that 'race' is really a code-word for 'genre.' Our issue is not the issue of 'race.' Our issue is the issue of the 'genre' of 'Man.' It is this issue of the 'genre' of 'Man' that causes all the '-isms.'" See Wynter, "ProudFlesh" interview.

4 Wynter, "ProudFlesh" interview.

5 A perturbed system is deviated from its nominal functioning. A perturbation can arise from a source external to a system or the emergence of a variation internal to a system.

6 My understanding of "event" draws directly from the work of Slavoj Žižek and Alain Badiou but also draws influence from thinkers of anticolonial revolution such as David Marriott's reading of the work of Frantz Fanon ("No Lords A-Leaping"). See also Badiou, *Being and Event* and Žižek, *Event*.

7 Art historians and art journalists have typically approached this work via the disciplinary protocols of art history and framed Mutu's work as principally indebted to European artists such as Dadaist Hannah Höch. For instance, A *New Yorker* article on Mutu opens with "The Nairobi-born, Brooklyn-based artist, forty-one, is a modern-day Hannah Hoch, deftly braiding the satirical, the political, and the decorative in her collages" (*New Yorker*, "Wangechi Mutu"). On occasion her work has been put in conversation with African diasporic artists like Romare Bearden but almost never with nonblack women of color artists of color like Frida Kahlo and Ana Mendieta, despite Mutu repeatedly citing their influence. Willis, "Wangechi Mutu."

8 The following provides an excellent analysis of the racialized, gendered, and sexual aesthetics of disrobed African female bodies in the genre of ethnographic photography; perhaps its most iconic case, *National Geographic*, receives systematic attention: Lutz and Collins, *Reading National Geographic*.

9 Rather than call Haeckel's falsification of evidence into question, Haeckel biographer Robert J. Richards invites and performs a reevaluation of the nature of Haeckel's transgressive act—arguing that the Romantic Naturphilosophie of Goethe, which valued the elevation of archetypal forms over realist representation, was the source of Haeckel's inspiration, and thus he did not strive to deceive readers. Richards contends that others have evaluated Haeckel based on present standards of academic honesty and empiricist methodology—standards not embraced by, or unavailable to, Haeckel. As a result of ahistoricist critiques and misrecognitions, Richards argues, a fuller acknowledgement of Haeckel's importance for the history of evolutionary theory has been obscured, making way for a far-too-easy dismissal of Haeckel as anti-Jewish, and even proto-Nazi, in the work of some historians, biologists, and religious critics of evolutionary theory. Richards emphasized two illustrations that undercut the allegation that Haeckel's thought, in particular, provided an unambiguous precursor to Nazism. Unlike some of his contemporaries, Haeckel did not endorse anti-Semitism—placing Ashkenazi Jews at the apex alongside other Europeans in his hierarchical classification of races. Furthermore, the National Socialist Party's Department of Race Politics directly and conclusively rejected an association with Haeckel's monism. That said, while I am persuaded by Richards's reassessment of Haeckel's politics concerning Jewishness, there remains a profound racist legacy imbuing Haeckel's evolutionary theory in general and his recapitulation theory in particular. Assessing the implications of his indisputable antiblack racism, as his artistic legacy surfaces in

the work of Mutu, is the central animating question informing my engagement with Haeckel in this chapter. Richards, *The Tragic Sense of Life*.

10 For instance Agassiz, due to a hardline commitment to polygenesist creationism or Georg Heinrich Otto Volger, based on a uncompromising rejection of transmutation. See Richards's *Tragic* for an analysis of these debates.

11 Darwin is commonly believed to be a monogenesist, a position held to be at least preferable to the polygenesist view. However, I want to caution against drawing too sharp a distinction between these two positions. In the *Descent of Man*, Darwin urged his readers to adopt language that more accurately reflected the common usage of the terms "race" and "species." While Darwin maintained that there was one human species composed of many varieties or races, he also claimed to have long argued that the distinction between "species" and "race" was arbitrary.

12 For a reading of how Medusa was racially marked in nineteenth-century archaeology and in psychoanalysis see: Khanna, *Dark Continents*. My thanks to Eva Hayward for bringing this text to my attention.

13 Rutsky, "Mutation, History, and Fantasy in the Posthuman."

14 See Chelsea Mikael Frazier's "Thinking Red, Wounds, and Fungi in Wangechi Mutu's Eco-Art" for a more sustained reading of this work, particularly as it relates to fungi and the ecological.

15 Rutsky 107.

16 For a sampling of the major players of this transcontinental debate, see Jefferson, *Notes*; Long, *History*; Rush, "Observations"; Imlay, *Topographical*; White and von Soemmering, *An Account*; Buffon et al., *Natural History*; and Burnet, *Of the Origin*.

17 While this story is commonly told, it is often told in a manner that isolates this moment from its historical and epistemological context, resulting in further spectacularization and pathologization of black women's embodiment and sexuality. This is a risk or even an inevitability of the racist misogyny of our times. But my aim, at least, is not to simply re-circulate "shocking" depictions but to contextualize and account for the workings of these fundamental images in the imagination of antiblack racialization and of the logics of sex-gender more generally. I think part of the reason historical and epistemological contexts go unattended is because it draws Europeans and Enlightenment (science and reason) closer to its enabling abjections: passions and mythology.

18 For more historical detail, see Schiebinger, *Nature's Body*.

19 For an expansion of my thoughts on the icon of "the black female body" and measurement, see Jackson, "Theorizing in a Void."

20 Washington, *Medical Apartheid*. See also Owens, *Medical Bondage*.

21 Despite widely documented racial inequities in the severity and impact of a number of persistent pain conditions, researchers have only begun to investigate a link between perceived discrimination and pain-related symptoms. In what is thought to be the first study to examine this question, Edwards found that episodes of "major lifetime discriminatory events were the strongest predictors of back pain

report in African Americans, and perceived day-to-day discrimination was the strongest predictor of back pain report specifically in African American women" (Edwards 379). Additionally, significant relationships also emerged on measures of mental health among African American participants. As a whole, these findings support the biopsychosocial perspective on pain.

22 Frazier, "Thinking Red" 181.

23 Jasbir Puar makes a similar point when she states, in *The Right to Maim*: debility is "a process rather than an identity or attribute, a verb and a doing rather than a happening or happening to or done to" (Puar, *Right* 73).

24 Knopf-Newman, *Beyond Slash, Burn, and Poison*. Stacy Alaimo also discusses the prescience of Lorde's *The Cancer Journals* as well and led me to the Knopf-Newman quote. Alaimo, *Bodily Natures*.

25 Hartman, "Reading the Scar" 159; see also Khalid "Demilitarizing Disease" and Jain, "Cancer Butch" 522.

26 Hartman, "Reading the Scar" 159.

27 See Feagin and McKinney, *Many Costs*, "Significance."; Hayward et al.

28 Michelle Murphy, in a recent article asks "What counts as reproduction? Where does biological reproduction reside?" As an answer to this deceptively simple question, she offers the provocation of "distributed reproduction," which aims to bring into view aspects of reproduction occurring beyond bodies within uneven spatial and temporal structures of environmental injustice and latency. Along the way she reconceptualizes the idea of "assisted reproduction" to include "infrastructures": "state, military, chemical, ecological, agricultural, economic, architectural agencies "that 'assist,' alter, reaarange, foreclose, harm, and participate in the processes of creating, maintaining, averting, and transforming life in the inter-generation time." Further stating, a capacious sense of infrastructures *includes* sedimentations such as colonial legacies, the repetition of gendered norms in material culture, or the persistence of racialization" (emphasis added). My approach here has much in common with Murphy's, but my emphasis is different; with Mutu and Lorde, my aim is to demonstrate that these infrastructures do not "abandon" or harm "unintentionally." They are integral to what Frank Wilderson terms the "gratuitous violence" of antiblackness; in other words I suggest that the spatial and the temporal are arranged by antiblackness. Murphy, "Distributed"; Wilderson, *Red, White, & Black*.

29 S. Lochlain Jain has noted that the marks on the body, commonly associated with cancer, are not a direct result of cancer but rather of cancer treatments born of military technology: "Radiation as a cancer treatment developed post-WWII in an effort to both find peacetime uses of military atomic technologies as well as to study the effects of radiation exposure. . . . Nitrogen mustard was discovered in WWI to destroy quickly dividing cells, and become the first chemotherapeutic. So in terms of the development of treatments, the hundreds of thousands of cancers caused by nuclear testing, and economies of cancer treatment, the multibillion dollar industry of the 'war on cancer' ties in thoroughly with massive infrastructures of the military industrial complex" (524).

On the conditions of possibility for "globality," see Williams, *Capitalism and Slavery*; Ferreira da Silva, *Toward a Global Idea*; Rodney, *How Europe*.

30 Arguably, Lorde's *A Burst of Light*, written during a period when her metastasized cancer spread to her liver, is even more militant in its indictments of the social determinants of disease:

I'm not being paranoid when I say my cancer is as political as if some CIA agent brushed past me in the A train on March 15, 1965 and air-injected me with a long-fused cancer virus. Or even if it is only that I stood in their wind to do my work and the billows flayed me. What possible choices do most of us have in the air we breathe and the water we must drink? . . . When I speak out against the cynical U.S. intervention in Central America, I am working to save my life in every sense. Government research grants to the National Cancer Institute were cut in 1986 by the exact amount illegally turned over to the contras in Nicaragua. One hundred and five million dollars. It gives yet another meaning to the personal as the political. (133)

31 See Quach et al., "Experiences"; Polite and Olufunmilayo, "Breast Cancer". Margaret Whitehead has put forth the term "health inequities" as alternative; the latter better identifies the social rather than biological basis of both race and its unequal health burdens. Whitehead, "Concepts."

32 Taylor et al., "Racial Discrimination" 46, 51. A growing body of literature suggests that mistreatment due to racial discrimination can lead to psychological stress, which likely contributes to somatic disease generally, including breast cancer, especially when black women are under the age of fifty. This leads to higher incidence among young black women and black women's higher breast cancer mortality rates at every age. See Cuevas et al., "Discrimination." See also Lepeak et al., "Persistence."

33 Additionally, Dignam found that doctors are less likely to opt for surgeries that would conserve black women's breasts in cases where less drastic options were medically acceptable: "Black women were much more likely to have received total mastectomy rather than lumpectomy with radiation therapy" (62). Similarly, in Long et al., they found that African American women have lower incidence of uterine cancer but almost twice the mortality rates (Long et al., "Disparities").

34 The decrements imposed by racism have been widely documented in psychological literature, and recent cognitive science studies provide increasing evidence to suggest that racist culture potentially undermines executive functioning: Salvatore and Shelton; Holoien and Shelton; Murphy et al.; Jones et al.; Inzlicht and Kang. See also Krieger; Utsey et al.; Harrell; Blackmore et al.; David and Collins; Dole et al.; Williams, "Race, Socioeconomic Status" and Edwards.

35 See McEwen and Stellar, "Stress and the Individual"; McEwen, "Stress Adoption and Disease".

36 Cole, "Chronic."

37 Here I depart from an argument advanced in a number of recent feminist materialist works, which claim that this moment's "posthumanism" is emblematized by "new" modes of the commodification of life by extending market logics to the

molecular scale. I find this assertion somewhat odd given that it coincides with the public's increased attention, renewed attention even, to "The Tuskegee Experiment" and the HeLa cell—both of which predate "the posthuman." Furthermore, as I have suggested here, the biotechnological encroachment of the market into the sphere of life that they describe is taking place in a manner that is rather uneven and ultimately reinscribes black people's marginalization as consumers in the case of gene-expression profiling for breast cancer, or within the category of the human itself, as in the case of BiDil, a treatment for heart disease marketed in such a way as to suggest a homology between "race" and "species." Rosi Braidotti, *The Posthuman* (John Wiley & Sons, 2013). Melinda Cooper, *Life as Surplus: Biotechnology and Capitalism in the Neoliberal Era* (University of Washington Press, 2008). Hosu Kim and Jamie Bianco, *The Affective Turn: Theorizing the Social.* Eds. Patricia Ticineto Clough, and Jean Halley (Duke University Press, 2007). See Roberts, *Fatal Invention*, for a discussion of BiDil. On BiDil see Anne Pollock, *Medicating Race: Heart Disease and Durable Preoccupations with Difference* (Duke University Press, 2012).

38 A University of Maryland–led study found that racism might accelerate aging at the cellular level. Telomeres are repetitive sequences of DNA capping the ends of chromosomes that protect against DNA degradation. Shorter telomere length is associated with increased risk of premature death and chronic disease such as diabetes, dementia, Alzheimer's disease, arthritis, stroke, and heart disease. The researchers found that the men—irrespective of economic class standing—who had experienced greater racial discrimination and also displayed a stronger implicit (or unconscious) bias against their own racial group had the shortest telomeres. Dr. David H. Chae, assistant professor of epidemiology at UMD's School of Public Health and the study's lead investigator sums up the results in the following way: "African American men who have more positive views of their racial group may be buffered from the negative impact of racial discrimination. In contrast, those who have internalized an antiblack bias may be less able to cope with racist experiences, which may result in greater stress and shorter telomeres . . . Our findings suggest that racism literally makes people old." The results of the University of Maryland–led study are consistent with prior studies (cited in the study) that have found that those with a bias against their own racial group are more vulnerable to the impact of racial stigma and that greater in-group identification and positive racial evaluation may lessen the negative impact of racial discrimination (107–108). See Chae et al., "Discrimination."

CODA

1 Changes in the accessibility of DNA, or the opening and closing of DNA to transcription, relies on molecules labile to environmental influence, including those heritable across mitosis, without involving changes to the underlying DNA sequence (Landecker and Panofsky, "From Social"; 338, 343). Moreover, epigenetically relevant environmental events and agents often establish meaningful changes in gene expression that have the potential to stably persist in mitotic cell

division over many generations of cells, even after the initial agent or event ceases to be present (Landecker and Panofsky 343).

2 Research has particularly traced the variable impact of pollutants, stress, and nutrition on molecular processes and systems. J. Niewohner, "Epigenetics" 279–98.

3 Landecker and Panofsky 349.

4 In addition to the HGP's capitalization on the idea of genetic race, it also had substantial ties to corporate power brokers.

5 While it is not my intention to document all of the social structural and environmental (f)actors said to create epigenetic events, I would add one more point along these lines regarding intergenerational effects. Researchers now claim that nutritional deficiencies and maternal psychosocial stress can change biological settings for children, with effects on such functions as glucose metabolism, blood pressure regulation, fat deposition, and the physiologic response to stress. While they do not rule out completely the theoretical possibility that there may be a genetic cause of these inequities, there is no evidence to support the view that genetic differences between groups explain these inequities (Kuzawa and Sweet, "Epigenetics" 7). Indeed, in light of the Human Genome Project's rejection of genetic racial difference, geneticists were forced to confront the possibility that social (f)actors were essential and not subsidiary to modulations of the body in ways never thought to be imaginable within the reigning biomedical model. Moreover, studies have also shown that the germ cell can be altered through male sperm epigenetically as well. Perhaps, unsurprisingly, relatively few studies examine the male line's contribution of epigenetic outcomes.

6 That being said, the epigenetic impact of past racism would diminish with each successive generation free from exposure to racism. However, even in the hypothetical situation I describe, racism nevertheless would impact generations to come.

7 Metz 111–12. I take note of Julie Guthman's important qualification: stating that something is epigenetically atypical is not to suggest that it is automatically pathological or to imply that pathology is absent from the statistically normal (Guthman, "Doing Justice" 3). Furthermore, if morphological norms are commonly predicated on the assumption that whiteness secures what is "normal," then it is problematic to assume that all deviations from the norm are therefore pathological. As Guthman notes, what is epigenetically "non-normative" may also be a healthy adaptive response: "Epigenetic changes, that is, are not always for the worse. . . . While we need to take biology seriously we must resist efforts to find ethical answers in biological norms" (Guthman 13, 14). The epigenetic production of nonnormativity, on any scale, is not what I am addressing here. Rather, my field of concern is the manner with which socially constructed difference is somatized epigenetically due to differential exposures that produce inequities in impairment, illness, and death.

8 See McLuhan, *Understanding Media* and Stiegler, *Technics and Time* for theorizations of technology as supplemental to the human body and to the development of human culture.

9   Researchers in the United Kingdom and United States decided to test to what
    extent "access" to healthcare could explain black women's significantly poorer out-
    comes from breast cancer treatment, and they found that "equal access" did not
    necessarily lead to improvement in outcomes. Moreover, the inequity in outcome
    appears to be widening even as cancers become easier to detect and treat (Copson
    et al. 231). Similarly, they found not only racially disparate rates of survival despite
    equal "access" but also racially unequal treatment was still coupled with equiva-
    lent rates of access.

10 According to Ron Voorhees, who runs the Allegheny County (PA) Health
    Department and is a professor of epidemiology at the University of Pittsburgh:
    "What we find is that the infants of black mothers who have graduate degrees,
    whether they be doctors, lawyers, professionals, they are people with potential for
    good incomes; they still have much higher rates of infant mortality even com-
    pared with a white woman who dropped out of high school." Beras, "Pittsburgh."
    Other news outlets have reported similar reports: T. Williams, "Infant Mortality."
    Peer-reviewed studies have also documented the devastatingly high rates of infant
    mortality among black women college graduates and professionals: see Schoen-
    dorf et al., "Mortatlity".

11 Similarly, as Pickering has noted, "almost all" of the explanations of racial inequity
    in rates of hypertension have "involved the underlying assumption that there is
    some genetically determined physiological difference" (Pickering 50).

12 Overall, recent studies suggest that the explanatory power of socioeconomic
    variables and the predicative scripts attributed to them have been destabilized
    in the emergent study of racialized patterns of physical health. See Kwate et al.,
    "Experiences." Their study underscores blackness' irreducibility:

    experienced racism did not vary significantly by a variety of demographic
    variables including age, income or education, evidence of the widespread
    nature of racism. . . . Moreover, conscious awareness of racism as a stressor
    may not be necessary to result in physiological stress responses. In our study,
    appraisal of stress due to racism was not related to health outcomes; rather,
    the frequency of racist events alone predicted negative health outcomes.
    (456, 457)

    Additionally, Nancy Krieger, a leading scholar studying racial and gender
    health inequities, has studied the impact of racism on high blood pressure
    and found "the non-significant association" between hypertension and
    socioeconomic variables. Krieger's study, paralleling the findings of others
    cited therein, demonstrated that identified "unfair treatment" and "gender
    discrimination" predicted hypertension status among only black (and not
    white) respondents. "[T] hese data support the view that the experience of
    being black in the United States carries a risk for high blood pressure that
    can be modified by, but not reduced to, gender and class position" (1278,
    1279). Krieger, "Racial and Gender Descrimination." See also Dignam, "Dif-
    ferences," and Quach et al. "Experiences."

13 Researchers have found that medical providers still discriminate against black patients even when blacks have economic class privilege, further suggesting that race is not a metonym for socioeconomic class nor is antiblackness classism in disguise. While poor blacks experience class-associative discrimination rooted in "disgust" and "contempt," professional blacks are viewed as potentially exploitative and untrustworthy:

> They elicit envy and jealousy. In addition, people respond to the misfortunes of these groups with schadenfreude, pleasure at the suffering of others, which also predicts harm. Specifically, when witnessing the misfortunes of members of these groups, people show activation of neural reward centers and display just barely detectable smiles (measured electromyographically from their zygomaticus [smile] muscles). (Dovidio and Fiske, "Under" 946)

According to Dovidio and Fiske both groups experience "active harm" and "attack" responses from healthcare providers. To bring attention to this study is not to reduce racial health inequity to individual physician bias. Surely physician bias is only one among many factors—policies and practices of health care systems, the finance and delivery of services—that produce racial inequality in the healthcare system, but it does challenge the assumption that policies that seek to address "access" are the sine qua non of remedy. See also Smedley, "Lived."

14 See Farmer and Ferraro, "Racial Disparities" for a discussion of earlier work that espoused this view and for their critique of this literature.

15 One notable exception occurs with respect to late-onset breast cancer rates for affluent older white women—that is, breast cancer that presents after the age of fifty-five. However, it has been proposed that the delay of first pregnancy relatively common among white affluent women may help us pinpoint the underlying logic of a correlational link between whiteness and increased rates of breast cancer *in older women*, especially as delayed pregnancy, in the Hall and Rockhill study, has been observed to present similar trends in cancer incidence in black affluent women as well. However, while older white women get late-onset breast cancer at higher rates than black women, for intermediate and higher socioeconomic status (SES) black women inequities in prognosis, treatment, and mortality conform to the racialized pattern found in women diagnosed at an earlier age regardless of SES. To make matters even more complicated, on the one hand, having children at a younger age has been associated with a lower risk of breast cancer over the life course; on the other hand, it is also associated with an increased risk of developing the more pernicious cancers found disproportionately in young black women. See Krieger, "Social Class"; Hall and Rockhill, "Race"; Parise and Caggiano, "Disparities."

Other studies have put forth competing hypotheses (low levels of breast feeding, physical inactivity, poor dietary practices, age at menarche, use of oral contraceptives, etc.); though most have not been satisfactorily studied, they are nevertheless reviewed in Bernstein et. al., "Ethnicity." See also Pathak et al., "Breast Carcinoma."

16 Relatively advantaged black people are found to have poorer physical health along many measures than whites of lower socioeconomic status, and at times, socioeconomic advantage is correlated to decrements in health in the comparative context of blackness, particularly with regard to cardiovascular disease, low birth rate, mortality, and even reported health status. In a broad-based study examining the socioeconomics of racial health inequities, Farmer and Ferraro found a pattern consistent with a "diminishing returns hypothesis" in which as SES levels increase, blacks do not have the same improvements in health as their white counterparts with the racial inequity being largest at the highest levels of SES. See Smedley, "Lived"; Farmer and Ferraro, "Racial"; Calvin et al., "Racism"; Williams and Neighbors, "Racism"; and Dressler, Dressler, "Social." Two studies found that the black–white mortality ratio actually increases with rising socioeconomic status. See Krieger et al., "Racism, Sexism, and Social Class" and David and Collins, "Differing."

Read and Emerson found that more highly educated black immigrants from Europe had worse health than less-educated West Indian immigrants:

We find that black immigrants from Europe look much more like U.S.-born blacks than they do white immigrants from Europe, and white immigrants from Europe look more like U.S.-born whites than they do their black compatriots. What is more, European countries have much higher standards of living than either African or West Indian countries—their incomes and employment rates are higher, better extended vacation time, and better health care. So, on average, European black immigrants should have better health than other black immigrants. We find the opposite. (Read and Emerson, "Racial" 195)

17 D. Williams et al., "Racial Differences" 337. Williams puts it quite plainly: "[S]ES measures are not equivalent across racial groups. That is, there are racial differences in income returns for a given level of education, the quality of education, the level of wealth associated with a given level of income, the purchasing power of income, the stability of employment and the health risks associated with working in particular occupations." See also D. Williams, "Race, Socioeconomic Status, and Health" and Krieger et al., "Racism, Sexism, and Social Class."

18 Dorothy Roberts has also noted that the "snapshot" approach to socioeconomic data collection on the part of biomedical researchers ignores subjects' entire life experience and the economic variability therein, creating false equivalence among subjects. Poverty and deprivation in early life may continue to have consequences later in life (*Fatal* 118).

19 With respect to cardiovascular disease, see Lewis et al., "Chronic." In their study analyzing the link between *perceived* discrimination and cardiovascular disease in black and white women, researchers found that both white and black women reported a history of discriminatory experiences; what made black women's experiences significant is that black women's experiences with discrimination were typified by a generality or "everyday" discrimination. Although the majority of black and white women reported having experienced at least one instance

of racial discrimination, black women ranked higher in measures that tracked chronic discrimination, underscoring the need for studies to disaggregate "racism," "racial discrimination," and "perceived discrimination" and to distinguish acute from chronic experiences of discrimination: "Research suggests that it is the persistence or *chronicity* of stressors over time that contributes to most negative cardiovascular outcomes, rather than the occurrence of an acute event or series of events" (362). See also Troxel et al., "Chronic," which emphasizes the chronicity and pervasiveness of health stressors in the lives of black women and discusses the limitations of using discrete measures to investigate the health burden of gendered racialization.

20 Most studies do not include black people, indigenous people, and people of color in the same study. For the time being, it appears that the antiblack racism correlates to incomparable effects if we look comparatively across nonblack (white and poc) groups. For a study that compares reproductive health inequities among black, indigenous, Asian Pacific Islander, and white women, see Joslyn et al., "Racial."

21 Consider the David and Collins Illinois study ("Birth Weight"), which compared birth outcomes in foreign-born and US-born African Americans but also linked these data with information on birth weights across several generations of children subsequently born in the United States. The first generation of foreign-born black mothers had a birth weight distribution nearly identical to US whites, but among subsequent generations of mothers born in the United States, the birthweight distribution of African immigrants shifted in the direction of a convergence with the lower African American mean.

Similarly, in the first study to disaggregate the health status of black immigrants by their region of birth, comparing the health status of black African, South American, West Indian, and European immigrants to that of US-born blacks and to each other, researchers observed a pattern: while it has been widely reported that black immigrants typically have a better health status than US-born blacks, and *some* health markers even indicate parity with that of US-born whites (like infant mortality mentioned above), this black immigrant health "advantage" appears isolated to those whose reference location is one in which whites are a racial minority (Africa and South America). These immigrants experience better health than those from racially mixed contexts (West Indies), who in turn enjoy better health than those from majority white racial contexts (Europe). Therefore, it is perhaps unsurprising that US-born blacks and black Europeans, both from majority white regions, do not differ significantly on any health status measures and were found to have the most impaired health. Moreover, the study concluded on a sobering note: "If our thesis is correct, the health advantage cannot survive across generations in the United States because black immigrants and their children from all origins will eventually resemble US-born blacks, as their racial contexts shift from abroad to the United States. Irrespective of selective immigration, the health of black immigrants will likely erode as they are exposed to the harmful effects of discrimination and racism," in particular that of "cumulative exposure" to race-related stress (Read and Emerson, "Racial," 195).

22 What must be acknowledged is that few studies actually examine the paternal line. One consequence of this bias is that it gives the problematic impression that the paternal line is either unaffected by the biocultural effects of inheritance and life course or that the impacts of paternal bioculture is inconsequential to intergeneration life. This is a problem that has been acknowledged by a number of feminist science studies scholars. For recent critiques see Sharp et al., "Time to Cut the Cord"; Sharp et al., "It's the Mother!"

Celia Roberts provides a historical analysis of the idea of "sex hormones" that is beneficial for our critical reflection on why the research primarily focuses on female bodies as well as troubles binarized notions of hormonal sex differences ("A Matter of Embodied Fact"). Similarly, Emily Martin has done crucial work on gendered, sexual phantasies of gonads, troubling the construction of female bodies as more passive and receptive ("The Egg and The Sperm"). Sarah S. Richardson has done important work problematizing the reductionism of the movement from a primarily hormonal account of sex to a primarily genetic account of sex: Richardson, *Sex Itself.*

23 Even if it is a given that gender and sex are entangled epigenetic pathways in the distribution of health and debility, epigenetic studies still tend to conflate sex and gender rather than consider how sex and gender (identity, presentation, perfor-mance) may correspond in diffuse and nonlinear ways across a life course. This inattentiveness to gender inhibits these studies' ability to consider how gender mutability and profusion shape the phenomena they study and attempt to account for both among a population and relationally between populations. The follow-ing raise these related questions with respect to the all too common biocentric approach to sex difference in research studies. See Eliot and Richardson, "Sex in Context"; Shattuck-Heidorn and Richardson, "Sex/Gender."

Along these lines, there is some consternation that the epigenetics of endocrine disruption might portend the end of "proper" sexual dimorphism and heteronormative reproduction. A number of recent analyses have offered considered pushback to this kind of sensationalism, underscoring the danger of employing epigenetics to—once again—figure trans and intersex people as a problem. These texts, in their respective efforts, trouble attachments to a sex/gender binarism that is not only fraudulent but hierarchical in its effects. See Guthman and Mansfield, "Plastic People"; Murphy, "Distributed"; Ah-King and Hayward, "Perverting Pollution."

And, finally, Mel Chen reminds us that toxicity is already here, we are all to relatively degrees polluted and yet the distribution of toxicity is of biopolitical concern. See Chen, *Animacies.*

24 Roberts, *Killing the Black Body.*

25 See also Kuzawa and Sweet, "Epgentics" 2; Landecker and Panofsky, "From Social" 335.

26 Dulac, "Brain Function" 728.

27 Citing Krieger, "Stormy Weather."

28 Citing Gluckman et al., "Metabolic"; Vickers et al., "Neonatal."

29 For two perspectives on race as a "variable" in epidemiological research, see Jones, "Invited Commentary" and Kaufman and Cooper, "Commentary."

30 In thinking about what art can do in the way of justice, I have taken inspiration from two conversations: the first is Patricia Saunders in conversation with M. NourbeSe Philip, "Defending the Dead"; the second, Saidiya Hartman and M. NourbeSe Philip: "A Question of Africa." Thanks to Christina Sharpe for bringing these dialogues to my attention.

WORKS CITED

Abdur-Rahman, Aliyyah. *Against the Closet: Black Political Longing and the Erotics of Race*. Duke University Press, 2012.

Acampora, Ralph R. *Corporal Compassion: Animal Ethics and Philosophy of Body*. University of Pittsburgh Press, 2006.

Achebe, Chinua. *Hopes and Impediments: Selected Essays*. Anchor, 2012.

"Aftr the Human Genome Project: The Human Microbiome Project," *Science Daily*, www.sciencedaily.com. Retrieved March 13,2013.

Agamben, Giorgio. *The Open: Man and Animal*, Stanford University Press, 2004.

Ah-King, Malin, and Eva Hayward. "Toxic Sexes: Perverting Pollution and Queering Hormone Disruption." *O-Zone: A Journal of Object-Oriented Studies*, 1: 1–14 (2014).

Ahmed, Sara. "Affective Economies." *Social Text*, 22.2, 2004, pp. 117–139.

Ahuja, Neel. *Bioinsecurities: Disease Interventions, Empire, and the Government of Species*. Duke University Press, 2016.

Alaimo, Stacy. *Bodily Natures: Science, Environment, and the Material Self*. Indiana University Press, 2010.

Alaimo, Stacy. "Displacing Darwin and Descartes: The Bodily Transgressions of Fielding Burke, Octavia Butler, and Linda Hogan 1." *Interdisciplinary Studies in Literature and Environment*, 3.1, 1996, pp. 47–66.

Alpers, Edward A. *East Africa and the Indian Ocean*. Markus Wiener Publishers, 2009.

Ambroise, Jason R. "On Sylvia Wynter's Darwinian Heresy of the '*Third Event*.'" *American Quarterly*, 70.4, 2018, pp. 847–856.

Analog Science Fiction/Science Fact, July 1977.

Anatol, Giselle. "A Feminist Reading of Soucouyants in Nalo Hopkinson's *Brown Girl in the Ring* and *Skin Folk*." *Mosaic*, 37.3, 2004, pp. 33–50.

Andrews, Lindsey. "Black Feminism's Minor Empiricism: Hurston, Combahee, and the Experience of Evidence." *Catalyst: Feminism, Theory, Technoscience*, 1.1, 2015, pp. 1–38.

Andrews, William L. *To Tell a Free Story: The First Century of Afro-American Autobiography, 1760–1865*. University of Illinois Press, 1988.

Archibald, J. David. *Aristotle's Ladder, Darwin's Tree: The Evolution of Visual Metaphors for Biological Order*. Columbia University Press, 2014.

Armstrong, Meg. "'The Effects of Blackness': Gender, Race, and the Sublime in Aesthetic Theories of Burke and Kant." *Journal of Aesthetics and Art Criticism*, 54.3, 1996, pp. 213–236.

Arnoldi, Mary Jo. "Playing the Puppets: Innovation and Rivalry in Bamana Youth Theatre of Mali." *Drama Review*, 32.2, 1988, pp. 65–82.

Badiou, Alain. *Being and Event*. A&C Black, 2007.

Bagemihl, Bruce. *Biological Exuberance: Animal Homosexuality and Natural Diversity*. Macmillan, 1999.

Baker, Neal. "Syncretism: A Federalist Approach to Canadian Science Fiction." *Extrapolation*, 42.3, 2004, pp. 218–231.

Balibar, Etienne. 'My Self' and 'My Own': One in the Same?' *Accelerating Possession: Global Futures of Property and Personhood*, edited by Bill Maurer and Gabriele Schwab, Columbia University Press, 2006, pp. 21–44.

Barad, Karen. *Meeting the Universe Halfway: Quantum Physics and the Entanglement of Matter and Meaning*. Duke University Press, 2007.

Barad, Karen. "Posthumanist Performativity: Toward an Understanding of How Matter Comes to Matter." *Signs*, 28.3, 2003, pp. 801–831.

Barad, Karen Michelle. *What Is the Measure of Nothingness: Infinity, Virtuality, Justice = Was Ist Das Mass Des Nichts?: Unendlichkeit, Virtualität, Gerechtigkeit*. Hatje Cantz, 2012.

Barber, Daniel C. *Deleuze and the Naming of God: Post-Secularism and the Future of Immanence*. Edinburgh University Press, 2013.

Barbieri, Marcello, ed. *Introduction to Biosemiotics: The New Biological Synthesis*. Springer Science & Business Media, 2007.

Barker, David. *Mothers, Babies, Disease in Later Life*. BMJ Publishing, 1994.

Barnes, Barry, and John Dupré. *Genomes and What to Make of Them*. University of Chicago Press, 2008.

Barnett, Kierra, et al. "Infant Mortality in Ohio." Kirwan Institute for the Study of Race and Ethnicity, 2013. www.mih.ohio.gov.

Barthes, Roland. "Mythologies. 1957." *Mythologies*. Translated by Annette Lavers, Hill and Wang, 1972, pp. 302–306.

Bast, Florian. "'I Won't Always Ask': Complicating Agency in Octavia Butler's *Fledgling*." *Current Objectives of Postgraduate American Studies*, 11, 2010. https://copas.uni-regensburg.de.

Beidelman, Thomas O. W. *Robertson Smith and the Sociological Study of Religion*. University of Chicago Press, 1974.

Bekoff, Marc, and Jane Goodall. *The Emotional Lives of Animals: A Leading Scientist Explores Animal Joy, Sorrow, and Empathy—and Why They Matter*. New World Library, 2008.

Bekoff, Marc, and Dale Jamieson. *Interpretation and Explanation in the Study of Animal Behavior*, vol. 1. Westview Press, 1990.

Bekoff, Marc, and Jessica Pierce. *Wild Justice: The Moral Lives of Animals*. University of Chicago Press, 2009.

Beras, Erika. "In Pittsburgh, an Effort to Bring Down the Black Community's Infant Mortality Rate," *WESA*, March 28, 2013. http://wesa.fm. Retrieed March 30, 2013.

Bernstein, Leslie, et al. "Ethnicity-Related Variation in Breast Cancer Risk Factors." *Cancer*, 97.S1, 2003, pp. 222–229.

Bhandari, Ramanath, David P. Janos, and Photini Sinnis. "Furuncular Myiasis Caused by Dermatobia Hominis in a Returning Traveler." *American Journal of Tropical Medicine and Hygiene*, 76.3, 2007, pp. 598–599.

Birke, Lynda. *Feminism and the Biological*. Edinburgh University Press, 1999.

Blackmore, Cheryl A., et al. "Is Race a Risk Factor or a Risk Marker for Preterm Delivery?" *Ethnicity & Disease*, 3.4, 1992, pp. 372–377.

Blake, Kelly. "Racism May Accelerate Aging in African American Men." *UMD Right Now*, January 7, 2014, www.umdrightnow.umd.edu. Retrieved January 8, 2014.

Boas, Franz. *The Mind of Primitive Man*. Macmillan, 1912.

Boas, Franz. *Race, Language, and Culture*. University of Chicago Press, 1982 [1899].

Boggs, Colleen Glenney. *Animalia Americana: Animal Representations and Biopolitical Subjectivity*. Columbia University Press, 2013.

Bogues, Anthony. *Black Heretics, Black Prophets: Radical Political Intellectuals*. Routledge, 2015.

Bollinger, Laurel. "Placental Economy: Octavia Butler, Luce Irigaray, and Speculative Subjectivity." *Literature Interpretation Theory*, 18.4, 2007, pp. 325–352.

Bollinger, Laurel. "Symbiogenesis, Selfhood, and Science Fiction." *Science Fiction Studies*, 37.1, 2010, pp. 34–53.

Borch, Merete. "Rethinking the Origins of Terra Nullius." *Australian Historical Studies*, 32.117, 2001, pp. 222–239.

Bradley, Rizvana. "Reinventing Capacity: Black Femininity's Lyrical Surplus, and the Cinematic Limits of 12 Years a Slave." *Black Camera*, 7.1, 2015, pp. 162–178.

Brand, Dionne. *A Map to the Door of No Return: Notes to Belonging*. Vintage Canada, 2015.

Brickman, Celia. *Aboriginal Populations in the Mind: Race and Primitivity in Psychoanalysis*. Columbia University Press, 2003.

Brinton, Daniel Garrison. *Races and Peoples: Lectures on the Science of Ethnography*. NDC Hodges, 1890.

Brody, Jennifer DeVere. *Punctuation: Art, Politics, and Play*. Duke University Press, 2008.

Brown, Eric C. *Insect Poetics*. University of Minnesota Press, 2006.

Brown, Eric C. "Introduction: Reading the Insect." *Insect Poetics*, edited by Eric Brown, University of Minnesota Press, 2006, ix–xxiii.

Brown, Foxy. "730." *Broken Silence*. Universal Music Publishing Group, 2001.

Brown, Jayna. "Being Cellular: Race, the Inhuman, and the Plasticity of Life." *GLQ: A Journal of Lesbian and Gay Studies*, 21.2–3, 2015, pp. 321–341.

Brown, Kathleen. "Native Americans and Early Modern Concepts of Race." *Empire and Others: British Encounters with Indigenous Peoples, 1600–1850*, edited by Martin Daunton and Rick Halperin, University of Pennsylvania Press, 1999, pp. 79–100.

Brown, Kimberly Juanita. *The Repeating Body: Slavery's Visual Resonance in the Contemporary*. Duke University Press, 2015.

Buffon, Georges Louis Leclerk, William Smellie, and William Wood. *Natural History, General and Particular*. T. Cadell & W. Davies, 1812.

Burnet, Lord James. *Of the Origin and Progress of Language*, vol. 1. T. Cadell, 1774.

Burnham, Margaret A. "An Impossible Marriage: Slave Law and Family Law." *Law and Inequality* 5, 1987, pp. 187–225.

Butler, Judith. *Bodies that Matter: On the Discursive Limits of Sex*. Routledge, 2011.

Butler, Judith. *Gender Trouble: Feminism and the Subversion of Identity*. Routledge, 2002.

Butler, Octavia E. Interview by Charlie Rose. *Charlie Rose*, aired June 1, 2000.

Butler, Octavia. *Bloodchild and Other Stories*. Steven Stories, 1996, pp. 3–29.

Butler, Octavia. *Dawn*. Popular, 1988.

Butler, Octavia. *Fledgling: A Novel*. Seven Stories, 2005.

Butler, Octavia. *Kindred*. Beacon, 1988.

Butler, Octavia. *Mind of My Mind*. Doubleday, 1988.

Butler, Octavia. *Parable of the Sower*. Grand Central, 2000.

Butler, Octavia. *Parable of the Talents*. Grand Central, 2000.

Butler, Octavia. *Xenogenesis*. Grand Central, 1987–1989.

Calarco, Matthew. "The Animal Is Poor in World" and "Heidegger's Zoontolgy." *Animal Philosophy: Essential Readings in Continental Thought*, edited by Matthew Calarco and Peter Atterton, Continuum, 2004, pp. 15–30.

Calvin, Rosie, et al. "Racism and Cardiovascular Disease in African Americans." *American Journal of the Medical Sciences*, 325.6, 2003, pp. 315–331.

Césaire, Aimé. *Discourse on Colonialism*. NYU Press, 2001.

Chae, David H., et al. "Discrimination, Racial Bias, and Telomere Length in African-American Men." *American Journal of Preventive Medicine*, 46.2, 2014, pp. 103–111.

Chandler, Nahum Dimitri. *X-The Problem of the Negro as a Problem for Thought*. Oxford University Press, 2013.

Chen, Mel Y. *Animacies: Biopolitics, Racial Mattering, and Queer Affect*. Duke University Press, 2012.

Chesnutt, Charles Waddell. *The Conjure Woman, and Other Conjure Tales*. Duke University Press, 1993.

Cohen, Ed. *A Body Worth Defending: Immunity, Biopolitics, and the Apotheosis of the Modern Body*. Duke University Press, 2009.

Cole, Steven W. "Chronic Inflammation and Breast Cancer Recurrence." *Journal of Clinical Oncology*, 27.21, 2009, pp. 3418–3419.

Coleman, Beth. "Race as Technology." *Camera Obscura*, 24.1, 2009, pp. 177–207.

Coleman, Monica A. "Serving the Spirits: The Pan-Caribbean African-Derived Religion in Nalo Hopkinson's *Brown Girl in the Ring*." *Journal of Caribbean Literatures*, 6.1, 2009, pp. 1–13.

Comaroff, John L., and Jean Comaroff. "On Personhood: An Anthropological Perspective from Africa." *Social Identities*, 7.2, 2001, pp. 267–283.

Conklin, Beth A. *Consuming Grief: Compassionate Cannibalism in an Amazonian Society*. University of Texas Press, 2001.

Connor, Michael. *The Invention of Terra Nullius*. Macleay Press, 2005.

Cooks, Bridget R. *Exhibiting Blackness: African Americans and the American Art Museum*. University of Massachusetts Press, 2011.

Coole, Diana. "Rethinking Agency: A Phenomenological Approach to Embodiment and Agentic Capacities." *Political Studies*, 53.1, 2005, pp. 124–142.

Cooper, Richard S., et al. "Race and Genomics." *New England Journal of Medicine*, 348, 2003, pp. 1166–1170.

Cope, Edward Drinker. *The Origin of the Fittest: Essays on Evolution*. D. Appleton, 1887.

Copson, Ellen, et al. "Ethnicity and Outcome of Young Breast Cancer Patients in the United Kingdom: The POSH Study." *British Journal of Cancer*, 110.1, 2014, pp. 230–241.

Creed, Barbara. *The Monstrous-Feminine: Film, Feminism, Psychoanalysis*. Routledge Press, 1993.

Cuevas, Adolf G., et al. "Discrimination, Affect, and Cancer Risk Factors Among African Americans." *American Journal of Health Behavior*, 38.1, 2014, pp. 31–41.

Cuvier, Georges. *The Animal Kingdom: Arranged in Conformity with its Organization*. G. & C. & H. Carvill, 1833.

Darwin, Charles. *The Descent of Man, and Selection in Relation to Sex*. John Murray, 1871.

David, Richard J., and James W. Collins, Jr. "Bad Outcomes in Black Babies: Race or Racism?" *Ethnicity & Disease*, 1.3, 1991, pp. 236–244.

David, Richard J., and James W. Collins Jr. "Differing Birth Weight Among Infants of US-Born Blacks, African-Born Blacks, and US-Born Whites." *New England Journal of Medicine*, 337.17, 1997, pp. 1209–1214.

Dawkins, Marian Stamp. *Through Our Eyes Only? The Search for Animal Consciousness*. W. H. Freeman/Spektrum, 1993.

De Castro, Eduardo V. *Cannibal Metaphysics: For a Post-Structural Anthropology*. Translated by Peter Skafish, Univocal Publishing, 2014.

Deleuze, Gilles, and Félix Guattari. *A Thousand Plateaus: Capitalism and Schizophrenia*. Translated Brian Massumi, Bloomsbury Publishing, 1988.

Derrida, Jacques. *The Animal That Therefore I Am*. Translated by David Wills, Fordham University Press, 2008.

Derrida, Jacques. "The Animal That Therefore I Am (More to Follow)." Translated by David Wills, *Critical Inquiry*, 28.2, 2002, pp. 369–418.

Derrida, Jacques. "Autoimmunity: Real and Symbolic Suicides: A Dialogue with Jacques Derrida." *Philosophy in a Time of Terror: Dialogues with Jürgen Habermas and Jacques Derrida*, edited by Giovanna Borradori. University of Chicago Press, 2003, pp. 85–136.

Derrida, Jacques. "'Eating Well,' or the Calculation of the Subject." *Points: Interview, 1974–1994*. Edited by Elizabeth Weber. Translated by Peggy Kamuf and others. Stanford University Press, , pp. 255–287.

Derrida, Jacques. "Geschlecht II: Heidegger's Hand." Translated by John P. Leavey Jr., *Deconstruction and Philosophy*, edited by John Sallis, University of Chicago Press, 1986, pp. 161–196.

Derrida, Jacques. *Margins of Philosophy*. Translated by Alan Bass. University of Chicago Press, 1982.

Derrida, Jacques. *Of Grammatology.* Translated by Gayatri Chakravorty Spivak. Johns Hopkins University Press, 2016.

Derrida, Jacques. *Of Spirit: Heidegger and the Question.* Translated by Geoffry Bennington and Rachel Boulby. University of Chicago Press, 1991.

Descartes, René. *Discourse on Method, Optics, Geometry, and Meteorology.* Translated by Paul J. Olscamp, Hackett, 2001.

Dignam, James J. "Differences in Breast Cancer Prognosis Among African-American and Caucasian Women." *CA: A Cancer Journal for Clinicians,* 50.1, 2000, pp. 50–64.

Doane, Mary Ann. "Dark Continents: Epistemologies of Racial and Sexual Difference in Psychoanalysis and the Cinema." *Visual Culture: The Reader,* edited by Jessica Evans and Stuart Hall. SAGE, 1999, pp. 448–456.

Dole, Nancy, et al. "Psychosocial Factors and Preterm Birth Among African American and White Women in Central North Carolina." *American Journal of Public Health,* 94.8, 2004, pp. 1358–1365.

Donawerth, Donna. *Frankenstein's Daughter: Women Writing Science Fiction.* Syracuse University Press, 1997.

Douglass, Frederick. "Frederick Douglass: He Receives an Ovation at the Hands of the Colored Tennesseans." *Tennessean,* September 19, 1873, p. 4.

Douglass, Frederick. *Narrative of the Life of Frederick Douglass: The Classic Slave Narratives,* edited by Henry Louis Gates Jr., Mentor, 1987.

Douglass, Patrice. "Black Feminist Theory for the Dead and Dying." *Theory & Event,* 21.1, 2018, pp. 106–23.

Dovidio, John F., and Susan T. Fiske. "Under the Radar: How Unexamined Biases in Decision-Making Processes in Clinical Interactions Can Contribute to Health Care Disparities." *American Journal of Public Health,* 102.5, May 2012, pp. 945–952.

Dressler, William W. "Social Class, Skin Color, and Arterial Blood Pressure in Two Societies." *Ethnicity & Disease,* 1.1, 1991, p. 60–77.

Du Bois, William Edward Burghardt. *The Comet.* Grand Central Publishing, 2001.

Dulac, Catherine. "Brain Function and Chromatin Plasticity." *Nature,* 465.7299, 2010, pp. 728–735.

Duster, Troy. "Buried Alive: The Concept of Race in Science." *Genetic Nature/Culture,* edited by Alan H. Goodman, Deborah Heath, and Susan M. Lindee, University of California Press, 2003, pp. 258–277.

Dyer, Richard. *White.* Routledge, 1997.

Edwards, Robert R. "The Association of Perceived Discrimination with Low Back Pain," *Journal of Behavioral Medicine,* 31.5, 2008, pp. 379–389.

Eliot, Lise, and Sarah S. Richardson. "Sex in Context: Limitations of Animal Studies for Addressing Human Sex/Gender Neurobehavioral Health Disparities." *Journal of Neuroscience,* 36.47, 2016, pp. 11823–11830.

Esmeir, Samera. "On Making Dehumanization Possible." *PMLA: The Journal of Modern Languages Association,* 121.5, October 2006, pp. 1544–1551.

Esposito, Roberto. *Immunitas: The Protection and Negation of Life.* Polity, 2011.

Eze, Emmanuel Chukwudi. *On Reason: Rationality in a World of Cultural Conflict and Racism*. Duke University Press, 2008.

Eze, Emmanuel Chukwudi, ed. *Race and Enlightenment: A Reader*. Blackwell, 2008.

Fanon, Franz. *Black Skin, White Masks*. Translated by R. Philcox, Grove Press, 2008.

Fanon, Franz. *The Wretched of the Earth*. Translated by Constance Farrington, Grove Press, 1968.

Fanuzzi, Robert. *Abolition's Public Sphere*. University of Minnesota Press, 2003.

Farmer, Melissa M., and Kenneth F. Ferraro. "Are Racial Disparities in Health Conditional on Socioeconomic Status?" *Social Science & Medicine*, 60.1, 2005, pp. 191–204.

Fausto-Sterling, Anne. *Sex/Gender: Biology in a Social World*. Routledge, 2012.

Fausto-Sterling, Anne. *Sexing the Body: Gender Politics and the Construction of Sexuality*. Basic Books, 2000.

Feagin, Joe R., and Karyn D. McKinney. *The Many Costs of Racism*. Rowman & Littlefield, 2005.

Ferguson, Roderick A. *Aberrations in Black: Toward a Queer of Color Critique*. University of Minnesota Press, 2004.

Ferreira da Silva, Denise. "Toward a Black Feminist Poethics: The Quest(ion) of Blackness Toward the End of the World." *Black Scholar*, 44.2, 2014, pp. 81–97.

Ferreira da Silva, Denise. *Toward a Global Idea of Race*. University of Minnesota Press, 2007.

Fine, Cordelia. *Delusions of Gender: How Our Minds, Society, and Neurosexism Create Difference*. Norton, 2010.

Fitzmaurice, Andrew. "The Genealogy of Terra Nullius." *Australian Historical Studies*, 38.129, 2007, pp. 1–15.

Foreman, Gabrielle P. "Manifest in Signs: The Politics of Sex and Representation in Incidents in the Life of a Slave Girl." *Harriet Jacobs and Incidents in the Life of a Slave Girl: New Critical Essays*, edited by Deborah M. Garfield and Zafar Rafia Cambridge University Press, 1996, pp. 76–99.

Foster, Frances Smith. *Witnessing Slavery: The Development of Ante-bellum Slave Narratives*. Greenwood Press, 1979.

Foucault, Michel. "The Ethics of the Concern for Self as a Practice of Freedom." *Ethics, Subjectivity and Truth Essential Works of Foucault*, edited by Paul Rabinow, vol. 1, New Press, 1997, pp. 281–301.

Foucault, Michel. "The Subject and Power." *Critical Inquiry*, 8.4, Summer 1982, pp. 777–795.

Francis, Consuela. *Conversations with Octavia Butler*. University Press of Mississippi, 2010.

Franck, Didier. "Being and the Living." *Who Comes After the Subject*, edited by Eduardo Cadava, Peter Connor, and Jean-Luc Nancy, Routledge, 2001, pp. 135–147.

Frank, Arthur. "Reconciliatory Alchemy: Bodies, Narratives and Power." *Body and Society*, 2, 2, 1996, pp. 53–71.

Frazier, Chelsea M. "Thinking Red, Wounds, and Fungi in Wangechi Mutu's EcoArt." *Ecologies, Agents, Terrains*, edited by Christopher P. Heuer and Rebecca Zorach. Yale University Press, 2018, 167–194.

Freud, Sigmund. *The Uncanny*. Translated by David McLintock, Penguin Books, 2003.

Frost, Samantha. *Biocultural Creatures: Toward a New Theory of the Human*, Duke University Press, 2016.

Gabriel, Markus. *Why the World Does Not Exist*. Translated by Gregory S. Moss, Polity Press, 2015.

Gaines, Malik, and Alexandro Segade. "Tactical Collage." *A Shady Promise*, edited by Phyllis Fong, Douglas Singleton, and Wangechi Mutu. Damiani, 2008, pp. 145–146.

Gates, Henry Louis, Jr. *The Signifying Monkey: A Theory of African American Literary Criticism*. Oxford University Press, 2014.

Geronimus, Arline T. "The Weathering Hypothesis and the Health of African-American Women and Infants: Evidence and Speculations." *Ethnicity & Disease*, 2.3, 1992, pp. 207–221.

Gibbons, Luke. "Ireland and the Colonization of Theory." *Interventions: International Journal of Postcolonial Studies*, 1.1, 1998, pp. 27.

Giger, Peter. *Conversation and Figuration from the Horizontality of the 2.0 Decade*. Blekinge Institute of Technology, PhD Diss., 2010.

Gikandi, Simon. (2003). "Picasso, Africa, and the Schemata of Difference." *Modernism/Modernity*, 10.3, pp. 455–480.

Gilbert, Scott F., Jan Sapp, and Alfred I. Tauber. "A Symbiotic View of Life: We Have Never Been Individuals." *Quarterly Review of Biology*, 87.4, 2012, pp. 325–341.

Gill-Peterson, Jules. *Histories of the Transgender Child*. University of Minnesota Press, 2018.

Gilman, Sander L. "Black Bodies, White Bodies: Toward an Iconography of Female Sexuality in Late Nineteenth-Century Art, Medicine, and Literature." *Critical Inquiry*, 12.1, 1985, pp. 204–242.

Giscombe, Cheryl L., and Marci Lobel. "Explaining Disproportionately High Rates of Adverse Birth Outcomes Among African Americans: The Impact of Stress, Racism, and Related Factors in Pregnancy." *Psychological Bulletin*, 131, 2005, pp. 662–683.

Glissant, Édouard, and Betsy Wing, *Poetics of Relation*. Translated by Betsy Wing, University of Michigan Press, 1997.

Gluckman, Peter D., et al. "Metabolic Plasticity during Mammalian Development Is Directionally Dependent on Early Nutritional Status." *Proceedings of the National Academy of Sciences*, 104, 2007, pp. 12796–12800.

Goldberg, David Theo. *Racist Culture: Philosophy and the Politics of Meaning*. Blackwell Publishing, 1993.

Gordon, Lewis R. *Existentia Africana: Understanding Africana Existential Thought*. Routledge, 2013.

Gordon, Lewis R. *Fanon and the Crisis of European Man: An Essay on Philosophy and the Human Sciences*. Routledge, 1995.

Goss, Theodora, and John Paul Riquelme. "From Superman to Posthuman: The Gothic Technological Imaginary in *Frankenstein* and *Xenogenesis*." *Gothic and Modernism*:

Essaying Dark Literary Modernity, edited by John Paul Riquelme. Johns Hopkins University Press, 2008, 181–206.

Gotby, Alva. *Body, Geography, Exteriority: Race and Spatiality in the Writings of Denise Ferreira da Silva*. PhD Diss., Institutionen för kultur och lärande, 2016.

Gould, Stephen Jay. *Ontogeny and Phylogeny*. Belknap Press of Harvard University Press, 1977.

Govan, Sandra Y. "Connection, Links, and Extended Networks: Patterns in Octavia Butler's Fiction." *Black American Literature Forum*, 18, 1984, pp. 82–87.

Gramsci, Antonio. *Prison Notebooks*, vol. 2. Translated by Quentin Hoare and Geoffrey Nowell Smith. Columbia University Press, 1992.

Gravlee, Clarence. "How Race Becomes Biology: Embodiment of Social Inequality." *American Journal of Physical Anthropology*, 139, 2009, pp. 47–57.

Gray, Erin. "Necrophagy at the Lynching Block." *GLQ: A Journal of Lesbian and Gay Studies*, 21.1, 2015, pp. 13–15.

Green, Michelle Erica. "There Goes the Neighborhood: Octavia Butler's Demand for Diversity in Utopia." *Utopian and Science Fiction by Women: Worlds of Difference*, edited by Jane L. Donawert and Carol A. Kolmerten. Syracuse University Press, 1994, pp. 166–189.

Greer, Kathleen. "In the Spotlight: Age-Old Therapy Gets New Approval." *Advances in Skin & Wound Care: The Journal for Prevention and Healing*, 18.1, 2005, pp. 12–15.

Grier, Katherine C. *Pets in America: A History*. University of North Carolina Press, 2010.

Griffin, Donald R. *Animal Minds: Beyond Cognition to Consciousness*. University of Chicago Press, 2013.

Guthman, Julie. "Doing Justice to Bodies? Reflections on Food Justice, Race, and Biology." *Antipode*, 2012, pp. 1–19.

Guthman, Julie, and Becky Mansfield. "The Implications of Environmental Epigenetics: A New Direction for Geographic Inquiry on Health, Space, and Nature-Society Relations." *Progress in Human Geography*, 37.4, 2013, pp. 486–504.

Guthman, Julie, and Becky Mansfield. "Plastic People." *Aeon*, February 23, 2015. https://aeon.co.

Hacking, Ian. *Representing and Intervening: Introductory Topics in the Philosophy of Natural Science*. Cambridge University Press, 1983.

Haeckel, Ernst Heinrich Phillip August. *Art Forms in Nature: The Prints of Ernst Haeckel*. Prestel, 1998 [1899].

Haeckel, Ernst. *Freedom in Science and Teaching*. Humboldt Publishing Company, 1888.

Haeckel, Ernst. *Generelle Morphologie der Organismen: Allgemeine Grundzüge der organischen Formen-Wissenschaft, Mechanisch Begrundet Durch die von Charles Darwin Reformirte Descendenz-Theorie: II Allgemeine Entwickelungsgeschichte der Organismen*. G. Reimer, 1866.

Haeckel, Ernst. *The History of Creation or the Development of the Earth and Its Inhabitants by the Action of Natural Causes: A Popular Exposition of the Doctrine of Evolution in General, and of that of Darwin, Goethe, and Lamarck in Particular. From the 8. German Ed. of Ernst Haeckel*, vol. 1. K. Paul, Trench, Trübner & Company, 1892.

Haeckel, Ernst. *Natürliche Schöpfungsgeschichte*. G. Reimer, 1873.

Haeckel, Ernst Heinrich Philipp August. *The Riddle of the Universe at the Close of the Nineteenth Century*. Harper, 1902.

Haeckel, Ernst Heinrich Philipp August. *The Wonders of Life: A Popular Study of Biological Philosophy*. Harper & Brothers, 1904.

Hale, Dorothy J. "Fiction as Restriction: Self-Binding in New Ethical Theories of the Novel." *Narrative*, 15.2, 2007, pp. 187–206.

Hall, Susan A., and Beverly Rockhill. "Race, Poverty, Affluence, and Breast Cancer," *American Journal of Public Health*, 92.10, 2002, p. 1559.

Hammonds, Evelynn. "Black (W)holes and the Geometry of Black Female Sexuality." *The Black Studies Reader*, edited by Jacqueline Bobo, Cynthia Hudley, and Claudine Michel, Routledge, 1994, pp. 301–314.

Hanchard, Michael. "Afro-Modernity: Temporality, Politics, and the African Diaspora." *Public Culture*, 11.1, 1999, pp. 245–268.

Haraway, Donna. "The Biopolitics of Postmodern Bodies: Determinations of Self in Immune System Discourse." *Feminist Theory and the Body: A Reader*, edited by Janet Price and Margrit Shildrick, Routledge, 1999, pp. 203–214.

Haraway, Donna J. *The Companion Species Manifesto: Dogs, People, and Significant Otherness*. Prickly Paradigm Press, 2003.

Haraway, Donna. "Encounters with Companion Species: Entangling Dogs, Baboons, Philosopher, and Biologist." *Configurations*, 14.1–2, 2006, pp. 97–114.

Haraway, Donna. *Primate Visions: Gender, Race, and Nature in the World of Modern Science*. Routledge, 1989.

Haraway, Donna. "Situated Knowledges: The Science Question in Feminism and the Privilege of Partial Perspective." *Feminist Studies*, 14.3, 1988, pp. 575–599.

Haraway, Donna. *When Species Meet*. University of Minnesota Press, 2008.

Haraway, Donna Jeanne, and Thyrza Goodeve. *How Like a Leaf: An Interview with Thyrza Nichols Goodeve*. Psychology Press, 2000.

Harding, Wendy, and Jacky Martin. "Reading at the Cultural Interface: The Corn Symbolism of *Beloved*." *melus*, 19.2, 1994, pp. 85–97.

Harrell, Shelly P. "A Multidimensional Conceptualization of Racism-Related Stress: Implications for the Well-Being of People of Color." *American Journal of Orthopsychiatry*, 70.1, 2000, pp. 42–57.

Harrison Internal Medicine. "Ectoparasite Infestation and Anthropod Bites and Stings, Myiasis." Medical and Veterinary Entomology, edited by Douglas Kettle, 2nd ed. CAB International, 1995, pp. 218–314.

Harman, Graham. *The Quadruple Object*. Zero Books, 2011.

Hartman, Saidiya V. *Scenes of Subjection: Terror, Slavery, and Self-Making in Nineteenth-Century America*. Oxford University Press, 1997.

Hartman, Saidiya. "Seduction and the Ruses of Power." *Callaloo*, 19.2, 1996, pp. 537–560.

Hartman, Saidiya. *Lose Your Mother: A Journey Along the Atlantic Slave Route*. Macmillan, 2008.

Hartman, Saidiya. "Venus in Two Acts." *Small Axe*, 12.2, 2008, pp. 1–14.

Hartman, Saidiya, and M. NourbeSe Philip. "A Question of Africa: Saidiya Hartman and M. NourbeSe Philip." CUNY Center for the Humanities, December 3, 2014. www.centerforthehumanities.org.

Hartman, Stephanie. "Reading the Scar in Breast Cancer Poetry." *Feminist Studies*, 30.1, 2004, pp. 155–177.

Hayward, Eva. "Fingeryeyes: Impressions of Cup Corals." *Cultural Anthropology*, 25.4, 2010, pp. 577–599.

Hayward, Eva. "Spider City Sex." *Women & Performance: A Journal of Feminist Theory*, 20.3, 2010, pp. 225–251.

Hayward, Mark D., et al. "The Significance of Socioeconomic Status in Explaining the Racial Gap in Chronic Health Conditions." *American Sociological Review*, 65.5, 2000, pp. 910–930.

Hearne, Vicki. *Adam's Task: Calling Animals by Name*. Skyhorse, 1986.

Hegel, Georg W. F. *Lectures on the Philosophy of World History*. Edited by Johannes Hoffmeister, translated by H. B. Nisbet, Cambridge University Press, 1975.

Heidegger, Martin. *The Fundamental Concepts of Metaphysics: World, Finitude, Solitude*. Translated by William McNeil and Nicholas Walker, Indiana University Press, 1985.

Heidegger, Martin. *Introduction to Metaphysics*. Translated by Ralph Manheim, Yale University Press, 1959.

Heidegger, Martin. *What Is Called Thinking?* Translated by J. Glenn Gray, Harper & Row, 1968.

Heinlein, Robert. "Science Fiction: Its Nature, Faults and Virtues." *Turning Points: Essays on the Art of Science Fiction*, edited by Damon Knight, Harper and Row, 1977, pp. 3–28.

Heinlein, Robert A. *Starship Troopers*. GP Putnam's Sons, 1959.

Helford, Elyce Rae. "'Would You Really Rather Die than Bear My Young?': The Construction of Gender, Race, and Species in Octavia E. Butler's 'Bloodchild.'" *Black Women's Culture Issue*. Special issue of *African American Review*, 28.2, 1994, pp. 259–271.

Henry, Paget. *Caliban's Reason: Introducing Afro-Caribbean Philosophy*. Routledge, 2002.

Higgins, David. "Postcolonial Science Fiction." *Extrapolation*, 55.1, 2014, pp. 108–112.

Hill, Shannen L. *Biko's Ghost: The Iconography of Black Consciousness*. University of Minnesota Press, 2015.

Hill, Shannen L. "Iconic Autopsy: Postmortem Portraits of Bantu Stephen Biko." *African Arts*, 38.3, September 2005, pp. 1–25.

Hine, Darlene Clark. "Rape and the Inner Lives of Black Women in the Middle West." *Signs: Journal of Women in Culture and Society*, 14.4, 1989, pp. 912–920.

Hird, Myra. "Naturally Queer." *Feminist Theory*, 5.1, 2004, pp. 85–89.

Hird, Myra. *The Origins of Sociable Life: Evolution After Science Studies*. Springer, 2009.

Hoagland, Ericka, and Reema Sarwal, eds. *Science Fiction, Imperialism and the Third World: Essays on Postcolonial Literature and Film.* McFarland, 2010.

Hoffmeyer, Jesper. *Biosemiotics: An Examination Into the Signs of Life and the Life of Signs.* University of Chicago Press, 2008.

Holbraad, Martin. "Definitive Evidence, from Cuban Gods." *Journal of the Royal Anthropological Institute,* 14.s1, 2008, S93–S109.

Hollander, Anne. *Moving Pictures.* Alfred Knopf, 1989.

Holloway, Karla, F. C. *Private Bodies, Public Texts: Race, Gender, and a Cultural Bioethics.* Duke University Press, 2011.

Holoien, Deborah Son, and J. Nicole Shelton. "You Deplete Me: The Cognitive Costs of Colorblindness on Ethnic Minorities." *Journal of Experimental Social Psychology,* 48.2, 2012, pp. 562–565.

hooks, bell. "Eating the Other." *Black Looks: Race and Representation.* South End Press, 1992, pp. 21–41.

Hopkinson, Nalo. *Brown Girl in the Ring.* Warner Books, 1998.

Hopkinson, Nalo, and Uppinder Mehan, eds. *So Long Been Dreaming: Postcolonial Science Fiction and Fantasy.* Arsenal Pulp Press, 2004.

Hulme, Peter. *Colonial Encounters: Europe and the Native Caribbean, 1492–1797.* Routledge, 1992.

Hume, David. "Of National Characters." *Essays, Moral and Political.* A. Millar, 1758.

Hurley, Kelly. "Reading Like an Alien: Posthuman Identity in Ridley's Scott's *Alien* and David Cronenberg's *Rabid.*" *Posthuman Bodies,* edited by Jack Halberstam and Ira Livinstone, Indiana University Press, 1995, pp. 203–224.

Imlay, Gilbert. *A Topographical Description of the Western Territory of North America; Containing a Succinct Account of its Climate, Natural History, Population, Agriculture, Manners and Customs; . . . to Which is Annexed, a Delineation of the Laws and Government of the State of Kentucky . . . In a Series of Letters to a Friend in England.* J. Debrett, 1793.

Inzlicht, Michael, and Sonia K. Kang. "Stereotype Threat Spillover: How Coping with Threats to Social Identity Affects Aggression, Eating, Decision Making, and Attention." *Journal of Personality and Social Psychology,* 99.3, 2010, pp. 467–481.

Jackson, Zakiyyah Iman. *Beyond the Limit: Gender, Sexuality, and the Animal Question in (Afro) Modernity.* PhD Diss., University of California, Berkeley, 2012.

Jackson, Zakiyyah Iman. "Losing Manhood: Animality and Plasticity in the (Neo) Slave Narrative." *Qui Parle: Critical Humanities and Social Sciences,* 25.1–2, 2016, pp. 95–136.

Jackson, Zakiyyah Iman. "Outer Worlds: The Persistence of Race in Movement 'Beyond the Human.'" *GLQ: A Journal of Lesbian and Gay Studies,* 21.2–3, 2015, pp. 215–218.

Jackson, Zakiyyah. "Sense of Things." *Catalyst: Feminism, Theory, Technoscience,* 2.2, 2016, pp. 1–48.

Jackson, Zakiyyah Iman. "'Theorizing in a Void': Sublimity, Matter, and Physics in Black Feminist Poetics." *South Atlantic Quarterly,* 117.3, 2018, pp. 617–648.

Jackson, Zakiyyah Iman. "Waking Nightmares—On David Marriott." *GLQ: A Journal of Lesbian and Gay Studies*, 17.2–3, 2011, pp. 357–363.

Jacobs, Naomi. "Posthuman Bodies and Agency in Octavia Butler's *Xenogenesis.*" *Dark Horizons: Science Fiction and the Dystopian Imagination*, edited by Raffaella Baccolini and Tom Moylan, Routledge, 2003, pp. 91–112.

Jain, S. Lochlann, "Cancer Butch." *Cultural Anthropology*, 22.4, 2007, pp. 501–538.

Jakobson, Roman, et al. "Two Aspects of Language." *On Language*, 1990, pp. 115–133.

James, Ian. *The New French Philosophy*. Polity, 2012.

Jameson, Frederic. *The Political Unconscious: Narrative as a Socially Symbolic Act.* Cornell University Press, 1981.

JanMohamed, Abdul R. *The Death-Bound-Subject: Richard Wright's Archaeology of Death*. Duke University Press, 2005.

Jayasuriya, Shihan D. S. *The African Identity in Asia: Cultural Effects of Forced Migration*. Markus Wiener Publishers, 2008.

Jayasuriya, Shihan D. S., and R. Pankhurst. *The African Diaspora in the Indian Ocean.* Africa World Press, 2003.

Jefferson, Thomas. *Notes on the State of Virginia*. Penguin Books, 1999.

Jennings, Francis. *The Invasion of America: Indians, Colonialism, and the Cant of Conquest*. University of North Carolina Press, 1975.

Jones, Camara Phyllis. "Invited Commentary: 'Race,' Racism, and the Practice of Epidemiology." *American Journal of Epidemiology*, 154.4, 2001, pp. 299–304.

Jones, Kristen P., et al. "Not So Subtle: A Meta-Analytic Investigation of the Correlates of Subtle and Overt Discrimination." *Journal of Management*, 42.6, 2013, pp. 1588–1613.

Jordan, Winthrop. *White Over Black: American Attitudes Toward the Negro, 1550–1812.* Pelican Books, 1968.

Jordan-Young, Rebecca M. *Brain Storm: The Flaws in the Science of Sex Differences.* Harvard University Press, 2011.

Joslyn, Sue A., et al. "Racial and Ethnic Disparities in Breast Cancer Rates by Age: NAACCR Breast Cancer Project." *Breast Cancer Research and Treatment*, 92.2, 2005, pp. 97–105.

Judy, Ronald. "Kant and the Negro." *Surfaces*, 1.8, 1991, pp. 4–70.

Kant, Immanuel. *Critique of Judgment*. Translated by Werner S. Pluhar. Hackett Publishing, 1987.

Kant, Immanuel. "On the Different Races of Man." *This is Race: An Anthology Selected from the International Literature on the Races of Man*, edited by Earl Count. Henry Shuman, 1950, pp. 17–24.

Kaplan, Ga, and Je Keil. "Socioeconomic Factors and Cardiovascular Disease: A Review of the Literature." *American Heart Association*, 88, 1993, pp. 1973–1998.

Kaplan, Sidney. "The Miscegenation Issue in the Election of 1864." *Journal of Negro History*, 34.3, 1949, pp. 274–343.

Kaufman, Jay S., and Richard S. Cooper. "Commentary: Considerations for Use of Racial/Ethnic Classification in Etiologic Research." *American Journal of Epidemiology*, 154.4, 2001, pp. 291–298.

Keeling, Kara. *The Witch's Flight: The Cinematic, the Black Femme, and the Image of Common Sense*. Duke University Press, 2007.

Kerslake, Patricia. *Science Fiction and Empire*. Liverpool University Press, 2007.

Kettle, Douglas S. *Medical and Veterinary Entomology*. 2nd ed. CAB International, 1995, pp. 218–314.

Khalid, Robina Josephine. "Demilitarizing Disease: Ambivalent Warfare and Audre Lorde's 'The Cancer Journals.'" *African American Review*, 42.3-4, 2008, pp. 697–714.

Khanna, Ranjana. *Dark Continents: Psychoanalysis and Colonialism*. Duke University Press, 2003.

Kidd, Benjamin. *The United States and the Control of the Tropics*. Atlantic Media, Inc., 1898.

Kim, Claire Jean. *Dangerous Crossings: Race, Species, and Nature in a Multicultural Age*. Cambridge University Press, 2015.

Kipling, Rudyard. "The White Man's Burden: The United States & The Philippine Islands, 1899." *Rudyard Kipling's Verse: Definitive Edition*. Doubleday, 1929, pp. 323–324.

Kirkwood, Thomas B. L. "Mitochondria and Programed Cell Death: 'Slave Revolt' or Community Homeostasis?" *Genetic and Cultural Evolution of Cooperation*, edited by Peter Hammerstein, MIT Press, 2003, pp. 309–326.

Kitcher, Philip. "Battling the Undead: How (and How Not) to Resist Genetic Determinism." *Thinking About Evolution: Historical, Philosophical, and Political Perspectives*, edited by Rama Singh et al., Cambridge University Press, 2001, pp. 396–414.

Knopf-Newman, Marcy Jane. *Beyond Slash, Burn, and Poison: Transforming Breast Cancer Stories into Action*. Rutgers University Press, 2004.

Krell, David Farrell. *Daimon Life: Heidegger and Life-Philosophy*. Indiana University Press, 1992.

Krieger, Nancy. "Racial and Gender Discrimination: Risk Factors for High Blood Pressure?" *Social Science & Medicine*, 30.12, 1990, pp. 1273–1281.

Krieger, Nancy. "Social Class and the Black/White Crossover in the Age-Specific Incidence of Breast Cancer: A Study Linking Census-Derived Data to Population-Based Registry Records." *American Journal of Epidemiology*, 131.5, 1990, pp. 804–814.

Krieger, Nancy. "Stormy Weather: Race, Gene Expression, and the Science of Health disparities." *American Journal of Public Health*, American Public Health Association, Inc., 95.12, 2005, pp. 2155–2160.

Krieger, Nancy, et al. "Racism, Sexism, and Social Class: Implications for Studies of Health, Disease, and Well-Being." *American Journal of Preventive Medicine*, 9.6, 1993, pp. 82–122.

Kuperus, Gerard. "Attunement, Deprivation, and Drive: Heidegger and Animality." *Phenomenology and the Non-Human Animal*, edited by Corinne Painter and Christian Lotz, Springer, 2007, pp. 13–28.

Kuzawa, Christopher W., and Elizabeth Sweet. "Epigenetics and the Embodiment of Race: Developmental Origins of US Racial Disparities in Cardiovascular Health." *American Journal of Human Biology*, 21.1, 2009, pp. 2–15.

Kwate, Naa Oyo A., Heiddis B. Valdimarsdottir, Josephine S. Guevarra, and Dana H. Bovbjerg. "Experiences of Racist Events Are Associated with Negative Health Consequences for African American Women." *Journal of National Medical Association*, 95.6, June 2003, pp. 450–460.

Lacan, Jacques. *Écrits: A Selection*. Translated by Bruce Fink, Norton, 2002.

Lacan, Jacques. *The Seminar of Jacques Lacan. Book III: The Psychoses*. Edited by Jacques-Alain Miller, translated by Russell Grigg. Norton, 1993.

Landecker, Hannah, and Aaron Panofsky. "From Social Structure to Gene Regulation, and Back: A Critical Introduction to Environmental Epigenetics for Sociology." *Annual Review of Sociology*, 39, 2013, pp. 333–357.

Lane, Nick. *Power, Sex, Suicide: Mitochondria and the Meaning of Life*. Oxford University Press, 2006.

Langer, Jessica. *Postcolonialism and Science Fiction*. Palgrave Macmillan, 2011.

Latour, Bruno. "On the Cult of the Factish Gods." *On the Modern Cult of the Factish Gods*. Duke University Press, 2010, pp. 1–66.

Latour, Bruno. *Politics of Nature*. Translated by Catherine Porter, Harvard University Press, 2004.

Latour, Bruno, and Steve Woolgar. *Laboratory Life: The Construction of Scientific Facts*. Princeton University Press, 2013.

Le Bon, Gustave. *The Crowd: A Study of the Popular Mind*. T. Fischer Unwin, 1910.

Le Guin, Ursula K. *The Left Hand of Darkness*. Hachette, 2012.

Lepeak, Lisa, et al. "Persistence in Breast Cancer Disparities between African Americans and Whites in Wisconsin." *WMJ: Official Publication of the State Medical Society of Wisconsin*, 110.1, 2011, p. 21–25.

Lewis, Tené T., et al. "Chronic Exposure to Everyday Discrimination and Coronary Artery Calcification in African-American Women: The SWAN Heart Study." *Psychosomatic Medicine*, 68.3, 2006, pp. 362–368.

Liebman, Elizabeth. "Unspeakable Passions: The Civil and Savage Lessons of Early Modern Animal Representation." *Representing the Passions: Histories, Bodies, Visions*, edited by Richard Meyer, Getty Publications, 2003, pp. 137–162.

Linnaeus, Carolus. *Systema Naturae per Regna Tria Naturae Secundum Classes, Ordines, Genera, Species*. 12 vols. Impensis Georg Emanuel Beer, 1788.

Linne, Carl von. *The System of Nature*, vol. 1. Lackington, Allen and Co., 1806.

Locke, John. *Second Treatise of Government and a Letter Concerning Toleration*. Oxford University Press, 2016.

Long, Beverly, Liu W. Fong, and Robert E. Bristow. "Disparities in Uterine Cancer Epidemiology, Treatment, and Survival Among African Americans in the United States." *Gynecologic Oncology*, 130.3, 2013, pp. 652–659.

Long, Edward. *The History of Jamaica: Or, General Survey of the Ancient and Modern State of the Island: With Reflections on Its Situation Settlements, Inhabitants, Climate, Products, Commerce, Laws, and Government*. Frank Cass, 1774.

Lorde, Audre. *A Burst of Light: Essays*. Firebrand Books, 1988.

Lorde, Audre. *The Cancer Journals: Special Edition.* Aunt Lute, 1997.

Lowndes, Robert A. W. "In Contrary Motion," *The Proceedings of the Institute for Twenty-First Century Studies.* 141, November 1961. Archived from the original on December 27, 2013. https://web.archive.org.

Lubbock, John (Lord Avebury). *Origin of Civilisation and the Primitive Condition of Man.* Longmans, Green and Company, 1870.

Luckhurst, Roger. "'Horror and Beauty in Rare Combination': The Miscegenate Fictions of Octavia Butler." *Women: A Cultural Review,* 7.1, 1996, pp. 28–38.

Luhmann, Niklas. *Social Systems.* Stanford University Press, 1995.

Lundblad, Michael. *The Birth of a Jungle: Animality in Progressive-Era US Literature and Culture.* Oxford University Press, 2013.

Lutz, Catherine, and Jane Lou Collins. *Reading National Geographic.* University of Chicago Press, 1993.

MacIntyre, Alasdair. *Dependent Rational Animals: Why Human Beings Need the Virtues.* Open Court, 2001.

Macpherson, Crawford Brough. *The Political Theory of Possessive Individualism: Hobbes to Locke.* Oxford University Press, 1962.

Mainor, Kierra Barnett Alexander, and Jason Reece. *Infant Mortality in Ohio.* Kirwan Institute for the Study of Race and Ethnicity, 2013. www.mih.ohio.gov.

Malabou, Catherine. *Plasticity at the Dusk of Writing: Dialectic, Destruction, Deconstruction.* Translated by Carolyn Shread. Columbia University Press, 2010.

Malabou, Catherine. *What Should We Do With Our Brain?* Fordham University Press, 2009.

Maldonado-Torres, Nelson. "On the Coloniality of Being: Contributions to the Development of a Concept" *Cultural Studies,* 21.2–3, 2007, pp. 240–270.

Mannoni, Octave. *Prospero and Caliban: The Psychology of Colonization.* Translated by Pamela Powesland, Praeger, 1964.

Mansfield, Becky. "Race and the New Epigentic Biopolitics of Evironmental Health." *Biosocieties* 7.4 (2012): 352–372.

Margulis, Lynn. "Words as Battle Cries: Symbiogenesis and the New Field of Endocytobiology." *Bioscience,* 40.9, 1990, pp. 673–677.

Margulis, Lynn, and Dorion Sagan. *Acquiring Genomes: A Theory of the Origins of Species.* Basic Books, 2002.

Margulis, Lynn, and Dorion Sagan. *Origins of Sex: Three Billion Years of Genetic Recombination.* Yale University Press, 1990.

Margulis, Lynn, and Dorian Sagan. *Symbiotic Planet: A New Look at Evolution.* Basic Books, 1998.

Marriott, David. "No Lords A-Leaping: Fanon, CLR James, and the Politics of Invention." *Humanities,* 3.4, 2014, pp. 517–545.

Marriott, David. *On Black Men.* Columbia University Press, 2000.

Martin, Courtney J. "Fracture and Action: Wangechi Mutu's Collages 1999–2010." *Wangechi Mutu, Artist of the Year 2010: My Dirty Little Heaven,* edited by Wangechi Mutu, Hatje Cantz, 2010, pp. 47–54.

Martin, Emily. "The Egg and the Sperm: How Science has Constructed a Romance Based on Stereotypical Male-Female Roles." *Signs: Journal of Women in Culture and Society*, 16.3, 1991, pp. 485–501.

Martin, Emily. *Flexible Bodies: Tracking Immunity in American Culture from the Days of Polio to the Age of AIDS*. Beacon Press, 1994.

Mason, Jennifer. *Civilized Creatures: Urban Animals, Sentimental Culture, and American Literature, 1850–1900*. Johns Hopkins University Press, 2005.

Mbembe, Achille. "Necropolitics." Translated by Libby Meintjes. *Public Culture*, 15.1, 2003, pp. 11–40.

Mbembe, Achille. *On the Postcolony*. Translated by Steven Rendell, University of California Press, 2001.

McBride, Dwight A. *Impossible Witnesses: Truth, Abolitionism, and Slave Testimony*. NYU Press, 2001.

McClintock, Anne. *Imperial Leather: Race, Gender, and Sexuality in the Colonial Context*. Routledge, 1995.

McDowell, Deborah. Introduction. *Narrative of the Life of Frederick Douglass, An American Slave*, edited by Deborah McDowell, Oxford University Press, 1999, pp. 101–125.

McEwen, Bruce S. "Stress, Adaptation, and Disease: Allostasis and Allostatic Load." *Annals of the New York Academy of Sciences*, 840.1, 1998, pp. 33–44.

McEwen, Bruce S., and Eliott Stellar. "Stress and the Individual: Mechanisms Leading to Disease." *Archives of Internal Medicine*, 153.18, 1993, p. 2093–2101.

McKittrick, Katherine. "Mathematics Black Life." *Black Scholar*, 44.2, 2014, pp. 16–28.

McKittrick, Katherine, ed. *Sylvia Wynter: On Being Human as Praxis*. Duke University Press, 2014.

McKittrick, Katherine, Frances H. O'Shaughnessy, and Kendall Witaszek. "Rhythm, or On Sylvia Wynter's Science of the Word." *American Quarterly*, 70.4, 2018, pp. 867–874.

McLuhan, Marshall. *Understanding Media: The Extension of Man*. MIT Press, 1994.

McNeill, William. "Life Beyond the Organism: Animal Being in Heidegger's Freiburg Lectures, 1929–30." *Animal Others: On Ethics, Ontology, and Animal Life*, edited by H. Peter Steeves, SUNY Press, 1999, pp. 197–248.

Meaney, Michael J. "Epigenetics and the Biological Definition of Gene x Environment Interactions." *Child Development*, 81.1, 2010, pp. 41–79.

Mehta, Uday Singh. *Liberalism and Empire: A Study in Nineteenth-Century British Liberal Thought*. University of Chicago Press, 1999.

Meillassoux, Quentin. *After Finitude: An Essay on the Necessity of Contingency*. Bloomsbury Publishing, 2010.

Melamed, Jodi. *Represent and Destroy: Rationalizing Violence in the New Racial Capitalism*. University of Minnesota Press, 2011.

Melzer, Patricia. *Alien Constructions: Science Fiction and Feminist Thought*. University of Texas, 2006.

Metz, Christian. *The Imaginary Signifier: Psychoanalysis and the Cinema*. Translated by Celia Britton, Annwyl Williams, Ben Brewster, and Alfred Guzzetti, Indiana University Press, 1982.

Mgbeoji, Iketchi. *Global Biopiracy: Patents, Plants, and Indigenous Knowledge*. University of British Columbia Press, 2014.

Mikkelsen, Jon M., ed. *Kant and the Concept of Race: Late Eighteenth-Century Writings*. SUNY Press, 2013.

Mills, Charles Wade. *The Racial Contract*. Cornell University Press, 1997.

Mitchell, Timothy. "Can the Mosquito Speak?" *Rule of Experts: Egypt, Techno-Politics, Modernity*, edited by Timothy Mitchell. University of California Press, 2002, pp. 19–53.

Moore, Kelli. "Affective Architectures: Photographic Evidence and the Evolution of Courtroom Visuality." *Journal of Visual Culture*, 17.2, 2018, pp. 207–222.

Moran, Shane. *Representing Bushmen: South Africa and the Origin of Language*. University Rochester Press, 2009.

Morgan, Jennifer L. *Laboring Women: Reproduction and Gender in New World Slavery*. University of Pennsylvania Press, 2011.

Morgan, Jennifer L. "'Some Could Suckle over Their Shoulder': Male Travelers, Female Bodies, and the Gendering of Racial Ideology, 1500–1770." *William and Mary Quarterly*, 54, 1997, pp. 167–192.

Morrison, Toni. *Beloved*. Vintage International, 2004.

Morrison, Toni. "Unspeakable Things Unspoken: The Afro-American Presence in American Literature." Presented at the *Tanner Lectures on Human Values*. University of Michigan, 1988.

Morrison, Toni. "Unspeakable Things Unspoken: The Afro-American Presence in American Literature." *Michigan Quarterly Review*, 2, 1988, pp. 1–34.

Moten, Fred. *In the Break: The Aesthetics of the Black Radical Tradition*. University of Minnesota Press, 2003.

Mudimbe, Valentin Y. *The Invention of Africa: Gnosis, Philosophy, and the Order of Knowledge*. Indiana University Press, 1988.

Müller-Wille, Steffan, and Hans Rheinberger. *A Cultural History of Heredity*. University of Chicago Press, 2012.

Murphy, Mary C., et al. "Cognitive Costs of Contemporary Prejudice." *Group Processes & Intergroup Relations*, 16.5, 2012, pp. 560–571.

Murphy, Michelle. "Distributed Reproduction, Chemical Violence, and Latency." *Scholar and Feminist Online*, 11.3 (2013) sfonline.barnard.edu/life-un-ltd-feminism-bioscience-race/distributed-reproduction-chemical-vilonce-nad-latency

Musser, Amber Jamilla. *Sensual Excess: Queer Femininity and Brown Jouissance*. NYU Press, 2018.

Musser, Amber Jamilla. *Sensational Flesh: Race, Power, and Masochism*. NYU Press, 2014.

Mustillo, Sarah, et al. "Self-Reported Experiences of Racial Discrimination and Black–White Differences in Preterm and Low-Birthweight Deliveries: The CARDIA Study." *American Journal of Public Health*, 94.12, 2004, pp. 2125–2131.

Muthu, Sankar. *Enlightenment Against Empire*. Princeton University Press, 2003.

Mutu, Wangechi. *Histology of the Different Classes of Uterine Tumors*. Collage. Saatchi Gallery, 2004.

Mutu, Wangechi. "Interview with Aimée Reed." *Dailyserving: An International Publication for Contemporary Art*, 2010. Retrieved October 22, 2013 http://dailyserving.com.

National Center for Health Statistics. *Health United States 2006 with Chartbook on Trends in the Health of Americans*. U.S. Government Printing Office, 2006.

Nationanl Institute of Health "Human Microbiome Project" http://commonfund.nih.gov. Retrieved March 13, 2013.

New Yorker. "Wangechi Mutu: A Fantastic Journey." *New Yorker*. n.d. www.newyorker.com.

Ngai, Sianne. *Ugly Feelings*. Harvard University Press, 2005.

Nguyen, Tan Hoang. *A View from the Bottom: Asian American Masculinity and Sexual Representation*. Duke University Press, 2014.

Niewohner, J. "Epigenetics: Embedded Bodies and the Molecularisation of Biography and Milieu," *Bio Societies* 693 (2011): 297–298.

Nilges, Mathias. "'We Need the Stars': Change, Community, and the Absent Father in Octavia Butler's *Parable of the Sower* and *Parable of the Talents*." *Callaloo*, 32.4, 2009, pp. 1332–1352.

Nyong'o, Tavia. *The Amalgamation Waltz: Race, Performance, and the Ruses of Memory*. University of Minnesota Press, 2009.

Odierna, Donna H. et al., "Early Developments in Gene-Expression Profiling of Breast Tumors: Potential for Increasing Black-White Patient Disparities in Breast Cancer Outcomes?" *Personalized Medicine*, 8.6, 2011, pp. 669–679.

Oliver, Kelly. *Animal Lessons: How They Teach Us to Be Human*. Columbia University Press, 2009.

Owens, Deirdre Cooper. *Medical Bondage: Race, Gender, and the Origins of American Gynecology*. University of Georgia Press, 2017.

Oyama, Susan. *The Ontogeny of Information: Developmental Systems and Evolution*. Duke University Press, 2005.

Parise, Carol A., and Vincent Caggiano. "Disparities in Race/Ethnicity and Socioeconomic Status: Risk of Mortality of Breast Cancer Patients in the California Cancer Registry, 2000—2010." *BMC Cancer*, 13.1, 2013, p. 449.

Park, Peter K. J. *Africa, Asia, and the History of Philosophy: Racism in the Formation of the Philosophical Canon, 1780–1830*. SUNY Press, 2013.

Parr, Adrian, ed. *Deleuze Dictionary Revised Edition*. Edinburgh University Press, 2010.

Passos, Mauro, et al. "Penile Myiasis: A Case Report." *Sexually Transmitted Infections*, 80, 2004, pp. 183–184.

Pateman, Carole. *The Sexual Contract*. John Wiley & Sons, 2014.

Pathak, Dorothy R., Janet R. Osuch, and Jianping He. "Breast Carcinoma Etiology." *Cancer*, 88.S5, 2000, pp. 1230–1238.

Patterson, Orlando. *Slavery and Social Death*. Harvard University Press, 1982.

Pearson, Susan J. *The Rights of the Defenseless: Protecting Animals and Children in Gilded Age America*. University of Chicago Press, 2011.

Pearson, Wendy Gay, Veronica Hollinger, and Joan Gordon., eds. *Queer Universes: Sexualities in Science Fiction*. Liverpool University Press, 2008.

Peffer, John. *Art and the End of Apartheid*. University of Minnesota Press, 2009.

Peppers, Cathy. "Dialogic Origins and Alien Identities in Butler's Xenogenesis." *Science Fiction Studies*, 22.1, 1996, pp. 47–62.

Peterson, Dale. *The Moral Lives of Animals*. Bloomsbury Press, 2012.

Phelan, James. "Sethe's Choice: *Beloved* and the Ethics of Reading." *Style*, 32.2, 1998, pp. 318–333.

Pickering, Thomas G. "Why Is Hypertension More Common in African Americans?" *Journal of Clinical Hypertension*, 3, 2001, pp. 50–52.

Piercy, Marge. *Woman on the Edge of Time*. Random House, 2016.

Pitts, Jennifer. *A Turn to Empire: The Rise of Imperial Liberalism in Britain and France*. Princeton University Press, 2006.

Pitts-Taylor, Victoria. *The Brain's Body: Neuroscience and Corporeal Politics*. Duke University Press, 2016.

Polite, Blase N., and I. Olopade Olufunmilayo, "Breast Cancer and Race: a Rising Tide Does Not Lift All Boats Equally." *Perspectives in Biology and Medicine*, 48.1, 2005, pp. 166–S175.

Puar, Jasbir K. "Prognonsis Time: Towards a Geopolitics of Affect, Debility, and Capacity." *Women & Performance: A Journal of Feminist Theory*, 19.2, 2009, pp. 161–172.

Puar, Jasbir K. *The Right to Maim: Debility, Capacity, Disability*. Duke University Press, 2017.

Quach, Thu, et al. "Experiences and Perceptions of Medical Discrimination Among a Multiethnic Sample of Breast Cancer Patients in the Greater San Francisco Bay Area, California." *Journal Information*, 102.5, 2012, pp. 1027–1034.

Raengo, Alessandra. *On the Sleeve of the Visual: Race as Face Value*. University Press of New England, 2013.

Raja, Masood A., Jason W. Ellis and Swaralipi Nandi, eds. *The Postnational Fantasy: Essays on Postcolonialism, Cosmopolitics and Science Fiction*. McFarland & Company, 2011.

Ramanath Bhandari, David P. Janos, and Photini Sinnis. "Furuncular Myiasis Caused by Dermatobia Hominis in a Returning Traveler." *American Journal of Tropical Medicine and Hygiene*, 76.3, 2007, pp. 598–599.

Read, Jen'Nan Ghazal, and Michael O. Emerson. "Racial Context, Black Immigration and the US Black/White Health Disparity." *Social Forces*, 84.1, 2005, pp. 181–199.

Rees, Tobias. "So Plastic a Brain: On Philosophy, Fieldwork in Philosophy and the Rise of Adult Cerebral Plasticity." *Biosocieties*, 6.2, 2011, pp. 263–266.

Reis, Elizabeth. *Bodies in Doubt: An American History of Intersex*. Johns Hopkins University Press, 2009.

Reynolds, Henry. *The Law of the Land*. Penguin, 2003.

Richards, Robert J. *The Tragic Sense of Life: Ernst Haeckel and the Struggle over Evolutionary Thought*. University of Chicago Press, 2008.

Richardson, Sarah S. *Sex Itself: The Search for Male and Female in the Human Genome*. University of Chicago Press, 2013.

Richardson, Sarah S., et al. "Opinion: Focus on Preclinical Sex Differences Will Not Address Women's and Men's Health Disparities." *Proceedings of the National Academy of Sciences*, 112.44, 2015, pp. 13419–13420.

Rieder, John. *Colonialism and the Emergence of Science Fiction*. Wesleyan University Press, 2008.

Ring, Betty J. "'Painting by Numbers': Figuring Frederick Douglass." *The Discourse of Slavery: From Aphra Behn to Toni Morrison*, edited by Carla Plasa Nfa, Carl Plasa, and Betty J. Ring, Routledge, 2013, pp. 118–143.

Roberts, Celia. "'A Matter of Embodied Fact' Sex Hormones and the History of Bodies." *Feminist Theory*, 3.1, 2002, pp. 7–26.

Roberts, Dorothy. *Fatal Invention: How Science, Politics, and Big Business Re-create Race in the Twenty-First Century*. The New Press, 2011.

Roberts, Dorothy E. *Killing the Black Body: Race, Reproduction, and the Meaning of Liberty*. Vintage Books, 1999.

Roberts, Dorothy E. "Unshackling Black Motherhood (Symposium: Representing Race)." *Michigan Law Review*, 95.4, 1997, pp. 938–964.

Robinson, Cedric. *Black Marxism: The Making of the Black Radical Tradition*. University of North Carolina Press, 1983.

Rodney, Walter. *How Europe Underdeveloped Africa*. Penguin Random House, 1972.

Roughgarden, Joan. *Evolution's Rainbow: Diversity, Gender, and Sexuality in Nature and People*. University of California Press, 2013.

Rouse, Joseph. *Engaging Science: How to Understand its Practices Philosophically*. Cornell University Press, 1996.

Rowse, Tim. "Terra Nullius." *The Oxford Companion to Australian History*, edited by Graeme Davison, John Hirst, and Stuart Macintyre, Oxford University Press, 2001, p. 320.

Rush, Benjamin R. "Observations Intended to Favour a Supposition that the Black Color (as It Is Called) of the Negroes is Derived From the Leprosy." *Transactions of the American Philosophical Society*, 4, 1799, pp. 289–297.

Rushdy, Ashraf H. A. *Neo-Slave Narratives: Studies in the Social Logic of a Literary Form*. Oxford University Press, 1999.

Rutsky, R. L. "Mutation, History, and Fantasy in the Posthuman." *Subject Matters*, 3.2, 2007, p. 108.

Salisbury, Joyce. *The Beast Within: Animals in the Middle Ages*. Routledge, 2011.

Salvatore, Jessica, and J. Nicole Shelton. "Cognitive Costs of Exposure to Racial Prejudice." *Psychological Science*, 18.9, 2007, pp. 810–815.

Sapp, Jan. *Evolution by Association: A History of Symbiosis*. Oxford University Press, 1994.

Sartre, Jean Paul. *Being and Nothingness: A Phenomenological Essay on Ontology*. Translated by Hazel E. Bames, Philosophical Library, 1993.

Saunders, Patricia. "Defending the Dead, Confronting the Archive: A Conversation with M. NourbeSe Philip." *Small Axe*, 12.2, 2008, pp. 63–79.

Sawyer, Andy. Foreword. *Science Fiction, Imperialism and the Third World: Essays on Postcolonial Literature and Film*, edited by Ericka Hoagland and Reema Sarwal, McFarland & Company, 2010, pp. 1–4.

Scheer-Schazler, Brigitte. "Loving Insects Can Be Dangerous: Assessing the Cost of Life in Octavia Estelle Butler's Novella 'Bloodchild' (1984)." *Biotechnological and Medical Themes in Science Fiction*, edited by Donna Pastourmatzi, University Studio, 2002, pp. 314–322.

Scheper-Hughes, Nancy, and Loïc Wacquant, eds. *Commodifying Bodies*. SAGE, 2002.

Schiebinger, Londa L. *Nature's Body: Gender in the Making of Modern Science*. Rutgers University Press, 1993.

Schoeck, Helmut. *Envy: A Theory of Social Behavior*. Translated by Michael Glenny and Betty Ross, Harcourt Brace, 1966.

Schoendorf, Kenneth C. et al. "Mortality Among Infants of Black as Compared with White College-Educated Parents." *New England Journal of Medicine*. 326.23, 1992, pp. 1522–1526.

Schuller, Kyla. *The Biopolitics of Feeling: Race, Sex, and Science in the Nineteenth Century*. Duke University Press, 2018.

Schuyler, George Samuel. *Black Empire*. UPNE, 1993.

Schwendener, Simon. *Untersuchungenuber den Flechtenthallus*. Beitrage zur Wissenschaftlichen, 1860.

Scott, Darieck. *Extravagant Abjection: Blackness, Power, and Sexuality in the African American Literary Imagination*. NYU Press, 2010.

Scott, David. *Conscripts of Modernity: The Tragedy of Colonial Enlightenment*. Duke University Press, 2004.

Scott, David. *Formations of Ritual: Colonial and Anthropological Discourses on the Sinhala Yaktovil*. University of Minnesota Press, 1994.

Scott, David. *Refashioning Futures: Criticism After Postcoloniality*. Princeton University Press, 1999.

Scott, David. "That Event, This Memory: Notes on the Anthropology of African Diasporas in the New World." *Diaspora: A Journal of Transnational Studies*, 1.3, 1991, pp. 261–284.

Seed, David. "The Course of Empire: A Survey of the Imperial Theme in Early Anglophone Science Fiction." *Science Fiction Studies*, 37.2, 2010, pp. 230–252.

Serres, Michael. *Hermes: Literature, Science, Philosophy*. Johns Hopkins University Press, 1983.

Serres, Michael. *The Parasite*. Translated by Lawrence R. Schehr, University of Minnesota Press, 2007.

Seshadri, Kalpana. *HumAnimal: Race, Law, Language*. University of Minnesota Press, 2012.

Shannon, Laurie. "The Eight Animals in Shakespeare; Or, before the Human." *PMLA*, 124. 2, 2009, pp. 472–479.

Sharp, Gemma C., et al. "It's the Mother! How Assumptions About the Causal Primacy of Maternal Effects Influence Research on the Developmental Origins of Health and Disease." *Social Science & Medicine*, 213, 2018, pp. 20–27.

Sharp, Gemma C., et al. "Time to Cut the Cord: Recognizing and Addressing the Imbalance of DOHaD Research Towards the Study of Maternal Pregnancy Exposures." *Journal of Developmental Origins of Health and Disease*, 10.5, 2019, pp. 509–512.

Sharpe, Christina. *In the Wake: On Blackness and Being*. Duke University Press, 2016.

Shattuck-Heidorn, Heather, and Sarah S. Richardson. "Sex/Gender and the Biosocial Turn." *The Scholar and Feminist Online*, 15.2, 2019. http://sfonline.barnard.edu.

Sherman, Ronald A. "Maggot Therapy Takes Us Back to the Future of Wound Care: New and Improved Maggot Therapy for the 21st Century." *Journal of Diabetes, Science, and Technology*, 3.2, 2009, pp. 336–344.

Shiva, Vandana. *Biopiracy: The Plunder of Nature and Knowledge*. North Atlantic Books, 2016.

Shukin, Nicole. *Animal Capital: Rendering Life in Biopolitical Times*. University of Minnesota Press, 2009.

Simpson, David. *Fetishism and Imagination: Dickens, Melville, Conrad*. Johns Hopkins University Press, 1982.

Singer, Peter. *Animal Liberation: The Definitive Classis of the Animal Movement*. Harper Perennial Modern Classics, 2009.

Smallwood, Stephanie E. *Saltwater Slavery: A Middle Passage from Africa to American Diaspora*. Harvard University Press, 2007.

Smedley, Brian D. "The Lived Experience of Race and its Health Consequences." *Journal Information*, 102.5, 2012, pp. 933–935.

Smith, Justin E. H. *Irrationality: A History of the Dark Side of Reason*. Princeton University Press, 2019.

Somerville, Siobhan B. *Queering the Color Line: Race and the Invention of Homosexuality in American Culture*. Duke University Press, 2000.

Somerville, Siobhan. "Scientific Racism and the Emergence of the Homosexual Body." *Journal of the History of Sexuality*, 5.2, 1994, pp. 243–266.

Spanier, Bonnie B. *Im/partial: Gender Ideology in Molecular Biology*. Indiana University Press, 1995.

Spencer, Herbert. *The Principles of Sociology*, vol. 6. Appleton, 1895.

Spiegel, Marjorie. *The Dreaded Comparison: Human and Animal Slavery*. Mirror Books, 1996.

Spillers, Hortense. *Black, White, and in Color: Essays on American Literature and Culture*. University of Chicago Press, 2003.

Spillers, Hortense J. "Mama's Baby, Papa's Maybe: An American Grammar Book." *Diacritics*, 17.2, 1987, pp. 64–81.

Spivak, Gayatri. *A Critique of Postcolonial Reason*. Harvard University Press, 1999.

Squier, Susan. "Interspecies Reproduction: Xenogenic Desire and the Feminist Implication of Hybrids." *Cultural Studies*, 12.3, 1998, 360–381.

Stanford, Ann Folwell. "Mechanisms of Disease: African-American Women Writers, Social Pathologies, and the Limits of Medicine." *NWSA Journal*, 6.1, 1994, pp. 28–47.

Stearns, Peter. "Gender and Emotion." *Social Perspectives on Emotion*, edited by David D. Franks and Viktor Gecas, JAI Press, 1992, pp. 127–160.

Stein, Rachel. "Bodily Invasions: Gene Trading and Organ Theft in Octavia Butler and Nalo Hopkinson's Speculative Fiction." *New Perspectives on Environment Justice: Gender, Sexuality, and Activism*, edited by Rachel Brown, Rutgers University Press, 2004, pp. 209–224.

Stepan, Nancy Leys. "Race and Gender: The Role of Analogy in Science." *Isis*, 77.2, 1986, pp. 261–277.

Stiegler, Bernard. *Technics and Time, I: The Fault of Epimetheus*. Translated by Richard Beardsworth and George Collins, Stanford University Press, 1998.

Stocking, George. *Victorian Anthropology*. Simon and Schuster, 1991.

Strother, Zoë S. *Inventing Masks: Agency and History in the Art of the Central Pende*. University of Chicago Press, 1998.

Sublette, Ned, and Constance Sublette. *American Slave Coast: A History of the Slave-Breeding Industry*. Chicago Review Press, 2015.

Taylor, Teletia R., et al. "Racial Discrimination and Breast Cancer Incidence in U.S. Black Women." *American Journal of Epidemiology*, 166.1, 2007, pp. 46–54.

Tehranifar, Parisa, et al. "Medical Advances and Racial/Ethnic Disparities in Cancer Survival." *Cancer Epidemiology Biomarkers & Prevention*, 18.10, 2009, pp. 2701–2708.

Thibodeau, Amanda. "Alien Bodies and a Queer Future: Sexual Revision in Octavia Butler's 'Bloodchild' and James Tiptree, Jr.'s 'With Delicate Mad Hands.'" *Science Fiction Studies*, 39.2, July 2012, pp. 262–282.

Thompson, Robert F. *Flash of the Spirit: African and Afro-American Art & Philosophy*. Vintage, 1984.

Tinsley, Omise'eke Natasha. "Black Atlantic, Queer Atlantic: Queer Imaginings of the Middle Passage." *GLQ: A Journal of Lesbian and Gay Studies*, 14.2–3, 2008, pp. 191–215.

Tiptree, James, Jr. "The Screwfly Solution." *Analog Science Fiction/Science Fact*, July 1977. http://lexal.net.

Tompkins, Kyla Wazana. "'Everything 'Cept Eat Us': The Antebellum Black Body Portrayed as Edible Body." *Callaloo*, 30.1, 2007, pp. 201–224.

Tompkins, Kyla Wazana. *Racial Indigestion: Eating Bodies in the 19th Century*. NYU Press, 2012.

TRAFFIC. "What's Driving the Wildlife Trade?: A Review of Expert Opinion on Economic and Social Drivers of the Wildlife Trade and Trade Control Efforts in Cambodia, Indonesia, Lao PDR and Vietnam." *East Asia and Pacific Region Sustainable Development Discussion Papers*. East Asia and Pacific Region Sustainable Development Department, World Bank, 2008.

Travis, Molly Abel. "Beyond Empathy: Narrative Distancing and Ethics in Toni Morrison's *Beloved* and J. M. Coetzee's *Disgrace*." *Journal of Narrative Theory*, 40.2, 2010, pp. 231–520.

Troxel, Wendy M., et al. "Chronic Stress Burden, Discrimination, and Subclinical Carotid Artery Disease in African American and Caucasian Women." *Health Psychology*, 22.3, 2003, p. 300.

Turk, Dennis C., and Elena S. Monarch. "Biopsychosocial Perspective on Chronic Pain." *Psychological Approaches to Pain Management: A Practitioner's Handbook*, edited by Dennis C. Turk and Elena S. Monarch, Guilford Press, 1996, pp. 3–32.

Tylor, Edward B. *Primitive Culture: Researches into the Development of Mythology, Philosophy, Religion, Art, and Custom*, vol. 2. Murray, 1871.

Utsey, Shawn O., et al., "Cultural, Sociofamilial, and Psychological Resources That Inhibit Psychological Distress in African Americans Exposed to Stressful Life Events and Race-Related Stress." *Journal of Counseling Psychology*, 55.1, 2008, pp. 49–62.

Valls, Andrew, ed. *Race and Racism in Modern Philosophy*. Cornell University Press, 2005.

Vickers, Mark H., et al. "Neonatal Leptin Treatment Reverses Developmental Programming." *Endocrinology*, 146, 2005, pp. 4211–4216.

Vince, Gaia. "Organised Ganges Target Wildlife Trade." *New Scientist*, June 17, 2002. https://www.newscientist.com/article/dn2413-organised-gangs-target-wildlife-trade/

Vint, Sherryl. *Bodies of Tomorrow: Technology, Subjectivity, and Science Fiction*. University of Toronto Press, 2007.

Von Uexküll, Jakob. *A Foray Into the Worlds of Animals and Humans: With a Theory of Meaning*. Translated by Joseph D. O'Neil. University of Minnesota Press, 2010.

Vycinas, Vincent. *Earth and Gods: An Introduction to the Philosophy of Martin Heidegger*. Springer Science & Business Media, 2012.

Waddington, Conrad. "The Epigenotype." *International Journal of Epidemiology*, 41.1, 1942, pp. 10–13.

Wadiwel, Dinesh. "Chicken Harvesting Machine: Animal Labor, Resistance, and the Time of Production." *South Atlantic Quarterly*, 117.3, 2018, pp. 527–549.

Walcott, Derek. *Ti-Jean and His Brothers*. Alexander Street Press, 2003.

Wallace, Michelle. "The Prison House of Culture: Why African Art? Why the Guggenheim? Why Now?" *Dark Designs and Visual Culture*, edited by Michelle Wallace, Duke University Press, 2004, pp. 460–473.

Wallace, Molly. "Reading Octavia Butler's *Xenogenesis* after Seattle." *Contemporary Literature*, 50.1, 2009, pp. 94–128.

Washington, Harriet A. *Medical Apartheid: The Dark History of Medical Experimentation on Black Americans from Colonial Times to the Present*. Doubleday, 2006.

Weheliye, Alexander G. *Habeas Viscus: Racializing Assemblages, Biopolitics, and Black Feminist Theories of the Human*. Duke University Press, 2014.

Wheeler, Wendy. *The Whole Creature: Complexity, Biosemiotics and the Evolution of Culture*. Lawrence & Wishart, 2006.

White, Charles, and Samuel Thomas von Soemmerring. *An Account of the Regular Gradation in Man, and in Different Animals and Vegetables, and from the Former to the Latter*. C. Dilly, 1799.

White, Eric. "The Erotics of Becoming: *Xenogenesis* and *The Thing*." *Science Fiction Studies*, 20, 1993, pp. 395–408.

Whitehead, Margaret. "The Concepts and Principles of Equity and Health." *Health Promotion International*, 6.3, 1991, pp. 217–228.

Wilderson, Frank B., III. *Red, White and Black: Cinema and the Structure of US Antagonisms.* Duke University Press, 2010.

Wilderson, Frank B., III. "The Vengeance of Vertigo: Aphasia and Abjection in the Political Trials of Black Insurgents." *InTension Journal,* 5, 2011, pp. 1–14.

Williams, David R. "Race, Socio-economic Status, and Health: The Added Effects of Racism and Discrimination." *Annals of the New York Academy of Sciences,* 896.1, 1999, pp. 173–188.

Williams, David R., et al. "Racial Differences in Physical and Mental Health: Socio-Economic Status, Stress and Discrimination." *Journal of Health Psychology,* 2.3, 1997, pp. 335–351.

Williams, David R., and Harold Neighbors. "Racism, Discrimination and Hypertension: Evidence and Needed Research." *Ethnicity and Disease,* 11.4, 2001, pp. 800–816.

Williams, Eric. *Capitalism and Slavery.* University of North Carolina Press, 1944.

Williams, Patricia J. *The Alchemy of Race and Rights.* Harvard University Press, 1991.

Williams, Timothy. "Tackling Infant Mortality Rates Among Blacks," *New York Times,* October 14, 2011. nytimes.com/2011/10/15/US/efforts-to-combat-high-infant-mortality-among-blacks

Willis, Deborah. "Wangechi Mutu," *Bomb,* February 28, 2014, https://bombmagazine.org.

Wilson, Elizabeth. "Biologically Inspired Feminism: Response to Helen Keane and Marsha Rosengarten, 'On the Biology of Sexed Subjects.'" *Australian Feminist Studies,* 17.39, 2002, pp. 283–285.

Wolfe, Cary. *Animal Rites: American Culture, the Discourse of Species, and Posthumanist Theory.* University of Chicago Press, 2003.

Wolfe, Cary. *What is Posthumanism?* University of Minnesota Press, 2010.

Wolmark, Jenny. *Aliens and Others: Science Fiction, Feminism and Postmodernism.* University of Iowa Press, 1994.

Wood, Sarah. 'Serving the Spirits': Emergent Identities in Nalo Hopkinson's *Brown Girl in the Ring. Extrapolation,* 46.3, 2005, pp. 315–326.

Wright, Richard, and Marcosarruda. "Blueprint for Negro Writing." *Race & Class,* 21.4, 1980, pp. 403–419.

Wu, Yung-Hsing. "Doing Things With Ethics: *Beloved, Sula,* and the Reading of Judgment." *Modern Fiction Studies,* 49.4, 2003, pp. 780–805.

Wynter, Sylvia. "1492: A New World View." *Race, Discourse, and the Origin of the Americas: A New World View,* edited by Vera L. Hyatt and Rex Nettleford, Smithsonian Institution Press, 1995, pp. 5–57.

Wynter, Sylvia. "Beyond Miranda's Meanings: Un/silencing the 'Demonic Ground' of Caliban's Women." *Out of the Kumbla: Caribbean Women and Literature,* edited by Carole B. Davies and Elaine S. Fido, Africa World Press, 1990, pp. 355–372.

Wynter, Sylvia. "The Ceremony Must Be Found: After Humanism." *Boundary,* 2, 1984, pp. 19–70.

Wynter, Sylvia. "'Genital Mutilation' or 'Symbolic Birth?'—Female Circumcision, Lost Origins, and the Aculturalism of Feminist/Western Thought." *Case Western Reserve Law Review,* 47.2, 1996, pp. 501–552.

Wynter, Sylvia. "Is 'Development' a Purely Empirical Concept or also Teleological? A Perspective from 'We the Underdeveloped.'" Edited by Aguibou Y. Yansani. *Contributions in Afro-American and African Studies*, 1996, pp. 299–311.

Wynter, Sylvia. "Novel and History, Plot and Plantation." *Savacou*, 5, 1971, pp. 95–102.

Wynter, Sylvia. "On Disenchanting Discourse: 'Minority' Literary Criticism and Beyond." *Cultural Critique*, 7, 1987, pp. 207–44.

Wynter, Sylvia. "Race and Our Biocentric Belief System: An Interview with Sylvia Wynter." *Black Education: a Transformative Research and Action Agenda for the New Century*, edited by Joyce E. King, American Educational Research Association/Lawrence Erlbaum Associates, 2005, pp. 361–366.

Wynter, Sylvia. "Towards the Sociogenic Principle: Fanon, Identity, the Puzzle of Conscious Experience, and What it is Like to Be 'Black.'" *National Identities and Sociopolitical Changes in Latin America*, edited by Mercedes F. Durán-Cogan and Antonio Gómez-Moriana, Routledge, 2001, pp. 30–66.

Wynter, Sylvia. "Unsettling the Coloniality of Being/Power/Truth/Freedom: Towards the Human, After Man, its Overrepresentation—An Argument." *CR: The New Centennial Review*, 3.3, 2003, pp. 257–337.

Wynter, Sylvia, and David Scott. "The Re-Enchantment of Humanism: An Interview with Sylvia Wynter." *Small Axe*, 8, September 2000, pp. 183–197.

Wynter, Sylvia, and Greg Thomas. "*ProudFlesh* Inter/Views: Sylvia Wynter." *ProudFlesh: A New Afrikan Journal of Culture, Politics and Consciousness*, 4, 2006. https://www.proudfleshjournal.com/issue4/winter.html

Žižek, Slavoj. *Event: A Philosophical Journey Through a Concept*. Melville House, 2014.

INDEX

Italic page numbers refer to figures in insert.

Abdur-Rahman, Aliyyah, 187–88
abjection, 33–34, 85, 103, 126, 131; animal, 1–4, 12–15, 18–20, 37; in *Beloved*, 38, 47, 62, 68–69, 73, 82; black maternity and, 210; in "Bloodchild," 142, 145, 157, 247n39, 247n41; in *Brown Girl in the Ring*, 90, 108; in *The Cancer Journals*, 192; Hartman on, 46; in *Histology of the Different Classes of Uterine Tumors*, 189; racially gendered, 5, 8, 23, 27–29
abolitionism, 26, 49–52, 56–57, 222n6, 223n18
Acampora, Ralph, 96–97
African masks, 110–11, 114
Agamben, Giorgio, 21, 160, 224n27
Age of Discovery, 25
Ahuja, Neel, 104, 239n2
Alaimo, Staci, 42, 247n39, 255n24
American Indians, 25, 172, 239n2
Anatol, Giselle Liza, 234n37
Andrews, Lindsey, 231n15
animal studies, 12, 14, 16–17, 85, 223n19
animism, 238n58
Anthropocene, 150
anthropocentrism, 130, 147, 148, 149, 223n19, 224n20; critiques of, 15; Eurocentric, 77–78, 123, 156; humanism and, 81
anthropology, 8, 100, 117, 238n58; fetishization of African masks, 111; human/animal relationship in, 160; primitiveness in, 139, 246n33; race in, 117–18, 183, 237n55
anti-Semitism, 253n9
apartheid, 31, 33, 234n33, 245n30
Aristotle, 24, 26, 221n25

Armstrong, Meg, 231n19
Autenrieth, Johann Heinrich Ferdinand von, 173
autopoiesis, 5, 122, 163, 179, 212, 243n17
Avebury, Lord (John Lubbock), 173

Baartman, Sara ("Hottentot Venus"), 8
Balibar, Etienne, 142–43, 246n36
Bantu peoples, 31
Barad, Karen, 42, 150, 184, 228n2, 232n22, 239n59
Barthes, Roland, 231n18, 241n10
Bast, Florian, 244n24
Bernal, Martin, 234n33
bestialization, 23, 27, 190; of blackness, 1, 4, 13, 18, 37, 48, 59, 67, 183
big like us ideology, 137–38
Biko, Steve, 31
biocentrism, 159–65, 169, 171, 199, 201, 263n23; definition, 42
biology, 87, 95–96, 127–31, 152–53, 161–71, 181, 193–94, 197–214; in *Beloved*, 81; biosemiotics and, 242n14; in "Bloodchild," 40–41, 122, 125, 136–38, 143–44, 148–51, 157, 241n11; in *The Cancer Journals*, 43, 191–92; Darwin and, 18; evolutionary, 244n22; Hegel and, 30; in *Histology of the Different Classes of Uterine Tumors*, 42–43; plasticity and, 3, 226n42; in "The Screwfly Solution," 239n6; sex and, 9, 159, 249n50, 255n28; slavery and, 47; species discourse and, 37, 156

ABOUT THE AUTHOR

Zakiyyah Iman Jackson is Assistant Professor in the Department of English at the University of Southern California.

Printed and bound by CPI Group (UK) Ltd, Croydon, CR0 4YY

11/05/2023

03217980-0002